Sustainability and Management

In the wake of the 1987 Brundtland Report, sustainable development has become key to the management systems within businesses, and a means by which companies can increase their long-term value. Being a 'sustainable company' increasingly means 'staying alive in business' and has become a necessity for all kinds of enterprises, from the micro-sized to global corporations. In more recent years, many companies, and indeed governments, have looked at sustainability as a means to combat the multiple challenges of environmental accidents, global warming, resource depletion, energy, poverty and pollution.

However, being sustainable or maintaining sustainability is not an easy task for a company's management function. It needs continuous support and engagement from the board, the executive management, staff and other stakeholders alike. Additionally, it brings extra costs to the company in terms of hiring trained staff, organising continuous training in the company, publishing sustainability reports and subscribing to a rating system. Sustainability must be nourished by a company's board as well as by all of its departments, such as accounting, marketing and human resources. By the same token, it is not enough for a company simply to declare itself a 'sustainable business' or rely on past measures and reputation; sustainability is an ongoing activity and one which has to be proved by periodically disclosing sustainability reports, according to international rating systems.

In *Sustainability and Management: An International Perspective*, Kıymet Çalıyurt and Ülkü Yüksel bring together international authors from a variety of specialisations to discuss the development, aspects, problems, roadmap, trends and disclosure systems for sustainability in management. The result is a lively, insightful exposition of the field.

Kıymet Çalıyurt is the founder of the International Group on Governance, Fraud, Ethics and Social Responsibility (IGonGFE&SR) and the president of the National-International-Students' Conference Series on Governance, Fraud, Ethics and Social Responsibility (IConGFE&SR). She also founded the International Women and Business Group, which organises a global annual conference. Kıymet has published papers and book chapters both nationally and internationally on fraud, social responsibility, ethics in accounting/finance/aviation disciplines and NGOs.

Ülkü Yüksel is a Senior Lecturer of Marketing at the University of Sydney Business School in Australia. Ülkü is an active member of the International Centre for Anti-consumption Research (ICAR), representing the University of Sydney Business School, Australia. Her research revolves around the application of consumer marketing concepts in various contexts, including services marketing, international business and cross-cultural consumer behaviour. Specifically, she investigates the effects of culture and psychological pressure on decision-making by managers and consumers, as they confront the risk and cost of their decisions.

Sustainability and Management

An International Perspective

**Edited by Kıymet Çalıyurt
and Ülkü Yüksel**

Routledge
Taylor & Francis Group

LONDON AND NEW YORK

First published 2017
by Routledge

2 Park Square, Milton Park, Abingdon, Oxfordshire OX14 4RN
52 Vanderbilt Avenue, New York, NY 10017

Routledge is an imprint of the Taylor & Francis Group, an informa business

First issued in paperback 2020

British Library Cataloguing in Publication Data
A catalogue record for this book is available from the British Library

Library of Congress Cataloging in Publication Data
Names: Çalıyurt, Kıymet Tunca, editor. | Yüksel, Ülkü, editor.
Title: Sustainability and management : an international perspective /
    edited by Kıymet Tunca Çalıyurt and Ülkü Yüksel.
Description: New York : Routledge, 2017. | Includes index.
Identifiers: LCCN 2016030484 | ISBN 9781472455055 (hardback) |
    ISBN 9781315611440 (ebook)
Subjects: LCSH: Sustainable development. | Industrial management.
Classification: LCC HC79.E5 S86162 2017 | DDC 658.4/083—dc23
LC record available at https://lccn.loc.gov/2016030484

ISBN: 978-1-4724-5505-5 (hbk)
ISBN: 978-0-367-60596-4 (pbk)

Typeset in Bembo
by Apex CoVantage, LLC

Contents

Figures

Tables

Contributors

Rasim Abutalibov earned his Bachelor's and Master's degrees in Business Administration at the Azerbaijan State Economic University. His PhD dissertation was titled "Socio-economic Development of the Regions of Azerbaijan Republic." He has been working as a head lecturer in the Business Administration Department at Qafqaz University since 2007. His research interests are in leadership, entrepreneurship, management, marketing, psychological management, business ethics, business plan development, strategic management, technoparks and clusters. Associate Professor Abutalibov has participated in different local and international conferences and he is the author of more than 20 scientific and methodological articles, as well as a co-author of the book *Management*, published in 2009 and 2014. He is the founder of AzMarketing Limited Liability Company, the Vice President of the Azerbaijan Advertising Association, Chief Editor of the journal *Marketing & Management* and an editor and reviewer for the *Journal of China–USA Business Review* and *Chinese Business Review*. He has been a member of the International Management Research Academy (IMRA) since 2012. Currently, he is doing postdoctoral work in the Erasmus Mundus Program in Poland.

Çağatay Akarçay, Assistant Professor, received his Bachelor's degree in Business Administration, Master's in Accounting and Finance and PhD in Accounting and Finance from Marmara University, Turkey. He is currently a faculty member in the Department of Business Administration at Yeditepe University, Turkey. He teaches courses on financial, cost, managerial and tax accounting at both the undergraduate and graduate levels. His research interests include international financial accounting standards, sustainability reporting and taxation.

Maria Aluchna is an Associate Professor in the Department of Management Theory, Warsaw School of Economics, Poland. She specialises in corporate governance, strategic management and corporate social responsibility. She teaches corporate governance, transition in central and eastern Europe and strategic management. She was awarded the Deutscher Akademischer Austauchdienst (DAAD, 2001/2002) scholarship for research at Universität Passau, Germany, and the Polish-American Fulbright Commission Scholarship for research at Columbia University, New York City (2002/2003). Maria Aluchna is a member of the European Corporate Governance Institute (ECGI), European Academy of Management (EURAM), the editorial teams of the *Journal of Knowledge Globalization* and of the Polish journals *Przegląd Organizacji* [Organization Review] and *e-Mentor*. She is also the Academic Director of the Community of European Management Schools (CEMS) program at the Warsaw School of Economics. She is a team member at the law firm Głuchowski, Siemiątkowski i Zwara, Warsaw.

Yasar Bayraktar graduated from the Faculty of Economics and Administrative Sciences, Mugla Sıtkı Kocman University, Mugla, Turkey. His Master's degree is ongoing in accounting and finance from the Social Science Institute, Karadeniz Technical University. His research interests are in financial accounting, social and environmental accounting, ethics education in accounting and railway transportation accounting.

Jing Bian teaches in the Faculty of Law and Social Sciences, SOAS, University of London, UK. Formerly, she was a civil servant in the justice department in China. Dr. Jing Bian's research interests focus on comparative and international financial regulation, corporate governance, merger and acquisition, Chinese law, and the legal and regulatory aspects of financial management. She has consulted for international institutions as well as international transactions.

Kıymet Çalıyurt graduated from the Faculty of Business Administration and Economics, Marmara University, Istanbul, Turkey. Her Master's and PhD degrees are in Accounting and Finance from the Social Graduate School, Marmara University. She holds Certified Public Accountant (since 2000) and Certified Fraud Examiner (since 2005) titles. She studied with Professor David Crowther as a postgraduate at London Metropolitan University, focusing on corporate social responsibility in accounting in 2004. Her research interests are in accounting, auditing, fraud, social responsibility, corporate governance, finance and business ethics, with special interest in NGOs, aviation management and agricultural companies. She is the founder of the International Group on Governance, Fraud, Ethics and Social Responsibility (IGonGFE&SR) and the president of the National-International-Students' Conference Series on Governance, Fraud, Ethics and Social Responsibility (IConGFE&SR). She has published papers and book chapters both nationally and internationally on fraud, social responsibility, ethics in accounting/finance/aviation disciplines and NGOs. She is a founding partner of Herme Consulting.

Martha J.B. Cook, professor emerita at Malone University, Canton, Ohio, USA, is a nationally accredited counsellor and has taught for more than 60 years at nearly every formal grade level. She has done research on bibliotherapy, which emphasises using comparative ideas to enhance basic power and decision-making. Her book *Grammar toward Professionalism* was published in 2006. Recently she completed a total program on teaching English as a second language which is based on using the computer and its thesaurus plus her grammar book as tools for vocabulary building and grammar assistance. Another book is in progress using bibliotherapy in a humorous genre called *Funny Things Happened to Me on the Way to Retirement*. Dr Cook also has been published in peer-reviewed journals, the most recent being the *Journal of the North American Management Society*. She is noted (sometimes notoriously) for her precise editing of books and papers which has been meant as 'a labor of learning and love.' Dr Cook may be a one-person army on the side of using correct grammar even in email.

David Crowther (BA, MBA, MEd, PhD, DSocSc, DSc, PGCE, FCMA, CGMA, CPFA, MCMI), is Professor of Corporate Social Responsibility at De Montfort University, UK. David Crowther is an expert in various fields: he is a specialist in business administration, a games theoretician and a psychologist, and has worked as an accountant, systems specialist and general manager in local government, industry and commerce for 20 years. After a number of years in the financial services sector, including a period as a divisional managing director during which he set up and ran a credit card scheme, he decided to leave the business world and become an academic. In 1994 he joined Aston University and there obtained a PhD in 1999 for research into corporate social performance. He is now Professor of Corporate Social Responsibility at De Montfort University. David has published more than 40 books and has also contributed several hundred articles to academic, business and professional journals and to edited books. He has also spoken at conferences and seminars worldwide and acted as a consultant to a wide range of government, professional and commercial organisations. In 2002 he established the Social Responsibility Research Network, an international body which in 2016 has 1,000 members, together with associated international conference series, journals and book series. In 2010 he established the Organization Governance Network and conference series. He is listed in Who's Who in the World and various other directories. His research centers on governance and corporate social responsibility with a particular emphasis on the relationship between social, environmental and financial performance.

Teresa Davis is an Associate Professor of Marketing at the University of Sydney Business School, Australia. Her main research interest lies in culture and consumption – specifically in examining 'cultures of transition' such as consumption of/in childhood and migrant groups. She studies aspects of food and consumption consciousness amongst young consumers. Teresa has published articles in *Sociology, Consumption Markets and Culture* and other journals. She has presented papers at many international conferences and invited seminars. Her teaching focuses on consumer behaviour and marketing communications. Teresa is co-convenor of the Australian Food, Culture and Society Network and co-leader of the University of Sydney Business School's Business of Health Research Network (http://sydney.edu.au/business/health).

Ayse Ergül was born in 1976 in Antalya. She finished her undergraduate education in Business Administration of Tourism at Ege University, Turkey, in 2009. She completed her Master's degree in the Accounting-Finance Discipline at Dokuz Eylül University, Turkey, in 2011. She is currently writing her doctoral thesis.

Mehmet Erkan, Prof. Dr. in Accounting and Finance at Istanbul University. He was born and grew up in Afyon, Turkey. He earned his Bachelor's degree in Accounting at Eskisehir Anadolu University, Turkey, and his PhD in Financial Accounting at the same university. He has held many different roles as academician and manager at Eskisehir Anadolu University, Afyon Kocatepe University, and Istanbul University for more than 34 years. He is also a member of and contributor to such prestigious global accounting associations in Turkey as AARCF (Accounting Academician's Research and Collaboration Foundation) and AAFA (Association of Accounting and Finance Academicians).

Rosane Beatriz Juliano de Aguiar Figueiredo earned her Master of Science degree in Social Responsibility and Sustainability Management Systems from the Fluminense Federal University, Brazil, her MBA in Marketing from PUC-Rio, Brazil, her postgraduate diploma in Business Communication from the Getúlio Vargas Foundation in Rio de Janeiro, her Bachelor of Science degree in Communications with an emphasis in Public Relations from Gama Filho University, Brazil and her Bachelor of Arts degree in Literature with emphasis in English Literature from Rio de Janeiro State University, Brazil. She currently works as a Social Investment Manager in the Social Responsibility Department at energy company Petrobras.

Sergio Luiz Braga França holds a DSc degree and a PhD in Civil Engineering with emphasis in Management, Production, Quality and Sustainable Development. He is a graduate in Civil Engineering and a Specialist in Engineering Work Safety and holds numerous other academic positions and distinctions.

Julie E. Francis is a Lecturer in the School of Management, Operations, and Marketing at the University of Wollongong, Australia. She holds a PhD from the Macquarie Graduate School of Management (MGSM). Her main teaching areas are consumer behaviour, services and relationship marketing and marketing research. Julie's research interests include sustainability as well as online consumer behaviour, service quality, volunteering behaviour and the consumer socialisation of children.

Seymur M. Guliyev graduated with distinction from the Faculty of Economic and Administrative Sciences, Department of Business Administration, Qafqaz University, Baku, Azerbaijan. He then received his Master's degree in Marketing at the Stirling Management School, University of Stirling, Scotland. Presently, he is working toward his PhD in Business Administration at Qafqaz University. His dissertation is about "Brand Equity and Its Effects on Consumer Purchasing Behaviours in the Food and Beverage Industry of Azerbaijan." He lectures on marketing for undergraduate and graduate students in the Business Administration program at Qafqaz University. His research interests are in marketing, branding, sales, consumer behaviour, consumer perception and marketing communications. He is a co-author of the book *Fundamentals of Management,* published in 2009 and 2014. In addition, he is an editor and reviewer for the *Journal of China–USA Business Review* and *Chinese Business Review* and Chief Editor of *Marketing & Management.* He has been a member of the International Management Research Academy (IMRA) since 2012. Mr Guliyev has been working as an export marketing professional in the Crude Oil and Oil Products Export Operations Division, part of the Marketing and Operation Department of the State Oil Company of the Azerbaijan Republic, since 2012.

Carmela Gulluscio graduated from the Faculty of Business Administration, Roma Tre University, Rome, Italy. Her Master's and PhD degrees are in Business Economics from the Roma Tre University. Her research interests are in accounting, accounting history, social responsibility and public sector accounting. She has been an Assistant Professor in Business Economics at the Unitelma Sapienza University in Rome since 2008, and teaches courses on Business Economics and Auditing. She has published papers, monographs and book chapters, both nationally and internationally, on accounting, accounting history, corporate social responsibility and public sector accounting.

Ali Haydar Güngörmüş is currently pursuing a PhD in Accounting while teaching financial accounting and other accounting courses at the Vocational School of Fatih University, Turkey. He is a CPA and has private sector experience in the accounting field. His research interests are related to financial accounting, corporate reporting and the Turkish Uniform Chart of Accounts. His research papers have been published in various national and international journals.

Razana Juhaida Johari, PhD, is Senior Lecturer in the Faculty of Accountancy, Universiti Teknologi MARA (UiTM), Malaysia. Currently, she is the Coordinator of the Research Interest Group and Research Innovation Business Unit, UiTM Kelantan Campus. Her main research interests are auditing, accounting ethics, corporate governance, fraud and accounting education. She has won several research awards at national and international conferences and published her works in a number of refereed journals. Razana Juhaida Johari is a member of Chartered Accountants, registered with Malaysian Institute of Accountants, part of the editorial team of UiTM Kelantan's *Journal of Academic Minds* and a fellow of the World Business Institute (WBI), Australia. She teaches auditing, business ethics and corporate governance, management accounting and control, and strategic management.

Uğur Kaya is a professor who graduated from the Faculty of Political Sciences, Ankara University, Turkey. His Master's and PhD degrees are in accounting and finance from the Social Science Institute at Ankara University, and Karadeniz Technical University, respectively. His research interests are in financial accounting, social and environmental accounting and human resource accounting. He has published papers on ethics, derivatives and accounting standards and books on environmental accounting and human resource accounting.

Steven Kooy, the Global Sustainability Manager at Haworth, Inc., graduated from the School of Engineering, University of Michigan, USA. He also has completed a few courses in the Master of Business Administration Program at Grand Valley State University, Grand Rapids, Michigan. He has worked in the field of sustainability for 15 years, holding a variety of positions aimed at pollution reduction, continuous improvement and environmental compliance. His work interests include sustainability strategic planning at the corporate level, interacting with clients and nongovernmental organisations to align sustainability initiatives and driving cultural changes within the workplace. He has contributed to many articles associated with the sustainability industry and spoken at conferences around the world to promote responsible business practices. He serves on the board of Foresight Design and is a core member of the Manufacturing Advisory Panel – Health Product Declaration Collaborative, a core member of Architectural Institute of America Materials Working Group, and is an LEED Accredited Professional.

Susan Kuzee is currently Account Executive/Project Manager at ddm marketing & communications in Grand Rapids, Michigan, USA. Immediately prior to this position, she was Senior Marketing Communications Project Manager at Haworth, Inc. She has more than 18 years of marketing and communications experience, mostly in the furniture industry, developing and implementing plans for new product launches and corporate initiatives such as sustainability. This experience gives her a thorough understanding of the process that is necessary to build and maintain a successful brand.

Maria Lai-ling Lam is Professor of Business Administration at Malone University, Canton, Ohio, USA. She holds the degrees of Bachelor of Business Administration, Master of Business Administration and Master of Art in Religion Studies from the Chinese University of Hong Kong, as well as a PhD in Business Administration from George Washington University, Washington, DC, USA. She has published one book, seven peer-reviewed book chapters and more than 30 peer-reviewed articles. Her articles are in the *Journal of Business Ethics, Management Research Review, Journal of International Business Research and Practice, Journal of Biblical Integration in Business, International Journal of Sustainable Development, Journal of the North American Management Society, Journal of Social Ecology and Sustainable Development* and the *International Journal of Humanities.*

Walter Leal is a Professor of Environment and Technology at Hamburg University of Applied Sciences, Germany. His professional qualifications include Chartered Biologist, Registered European Biologist, Fellow of the Institute of Biology, Fellow of the Linnean Society, Fellow of the Royal Society of Geography and Fellow of the Royal Society of Arts. Professor Leal directs the International Climate Change Information Programme, a leading programme on climate change education, information and communication. He is an honorary professor at the University of Blagoevgrad, Bulgaria; the University of Rezekne, Latvia; the University of Applied Sciences Zittau-Görlitz, Germany; and a visiting professor at various other universities. His research interests are on sustainable development, climate change and renewable energy. He has authored or co-authored over 300 publications among authored/edited books, book chapters and papers published in refereed journals and/or presented at international conferences. His field experience involves missions undertaken on behalf of various international organisations (e.g. European Union, World Bank, OECD, UNESCO, UNEP).

Rufat Mammadov received his Master's degree in Tourism from Dokuz Eylül University in Ismir, Turkey. Currently he is pursuing his PhD degree in tourism at the Economic Reforms Institute, part of the Economic Development Ministry in Azerbaijan. He is the author of several scientific articles on tourism and its effects on the economy. In addition to tourism, he is interested in ethics, business ethics and corporate social responsibility in enterprises. Mr Mammadov has been Senior Lecturer of Business at Qafqaz University since 2008, where he is Assistant Head of the Business Administration Department.

Marcelo Jasmim Meiriño has a PhD in Civil Engineering and an MSc in Civil Engineering. He is Vice Coordinator of the Innovation and Technology Center for Sustainability and Commissioner of Social Responsibility of the Brazilian Petroleum Institute and Gas, and holds other academic and professional positions.

Ayça Akarçay Öğüz received her Bachelor's degree in Economics, Master's degree in Accounting and Finance, and PhD in Accounting and Finance from Marmara University, Turkey. She is currently an Assistant Professor in the Faculty of Business Administration at Marmara University. She teaches courses on financial, corporate, bank and public accounting at both the undergraduate and graduate levels. Her research interests include international financial accounting standards, sustainability reporting, auditing and fraud. She is an active member of the Institute of Internal Auditing – Turkey and the Supervisory Board of Nihad Sayar Education Foundation.

Ercüment Okutmuş is an Assistant Professor in Accounting and Finance and a consultant in the tourism sector. Born in 1968 in Istanbul, he finished his undergraduate education in the Business Department of Eskisehir Anadolu University, Turkey, in 1991. He worked as an administrator under the Financial Coordinatorship of Toprak Holding Company from 1991 to 1995. In 2004 he finished his Master's degree and PhD at Afyon Kocatepe University. He started working as an academician at Akdeniz University in 1995 and continues there. Ercüment has published numerous scientific studies and articles in the field of accounting and finance.

Noorain Omar is a graduate of Huddersfield University, UK, with a BA in Accountancy Studies. Her Master's degree is in International Accounting from the Business School at Universiti Utara, Malaysia. Her research interests are in accounting, finance, financial reporting, financial market and social responsibility. She is still new in writing and publication but has recently published a paper in the *Social Responsibility Journal*.

Normah Omar is the Director of the Accounting Research Institute (ARI), a Higher Institution Centre of Excellence (HICoE) which is recognised and funded by the Ministry of Education, Malaysia. Prof. Dr. Normah Omar's research interest is in the area of forensic accounting and financial criminology. As a proponent of applied research, she has collaborated on research works with government agencies, professional bodies, regulators, non-government organisations and the corporate sectors in Malaysia. To mention just two, she has successfully completed the research projects Corporate Governance Rating; The Development of Financial Fraud Red Flags and the Governance of Non Profit Organizations (NPO) within the AML–CFT Regime. Currently Professor Normah is heading one of the Malaysian Institute of Integrity's (MII) collaborative research projects on the Corporate Integrity System. To date, Professor Normah is an editor for seven international refereed journals. She is also the vice president and founding committee member of the Asia-Pacific Management Accounting Association (APMAA).

Krishna Parameswaran is currently President of tfgMM Strategic Consulting in Scottsdale, Arizona, USA. He received a Bachelor of Technology degree in Metallurgical Engineering from the Indian Institute of Technology, Bombay, in 1968, a Master of Science degree in Metallurgical Engineering from the University of Missouri–Rolla in 1971 and a Doctor of Philosophy in Metallurgy from Pennsylvania State University in 1974. He is a licensed professional engineer in Pennsylvania. He recently retired from ASARCO LLC (Asarco), an integrated primary copper producer, after 34 years of service. His most recent position at Asarco was Director of Environmental Services and Compliance Assurance in Asarco's Environmental Affairs Department in Tucson, Arizona. His responsibilities included oversight of environmental permitting and compliance activities at Asarco's operating facilities, coordination of environmental activities among the facilities, providing technical support to environmental programs within the operations, developing environmental policy, goals and objectives for the company and operations and ensuring internal consistency within Asarco on environmental issues. In addition he coordinated the company's sustainable development activities and managed its Environmental Management System (EMS) and compliance auditing programs. In June 2005 he coedited a book entitled *Sustainable Mining Practices: A Global Perspective.* He has published a number of papers and made numerous presentations on sustainability, innovative reclamation techniques, utilisation of copper slags and tailings to produce geopolymers as an effective cement substitute, water management in mining industry and fostering renewable energy projects on disturbed mine lands. In September 2014 he was appointed by the US Secretary of Interior to the Bureau of Land Management Arizona Resource Advisory Council for a three-year term representing mineral and energy interests. Dr. Parameswaran until recently served on the Board of Directors of the Arizona Mining Association and is a member of the Minerals, Metals & Materials Society, Society of Mining Engineers and ASM International – The Materials Information Society.

Ravi Parameswaran is a tenured Professor of Marketing in the Management and Marketing Department at the School of Business Administration, Oakland University, Rochester, Michigan, USA. He holds a Bachelor of Science degree with a major in Physics and minor in Mathematics, a Master's degree in International Management, a Master's degree in Business Information Systems and a PhD in Marketing. He has done extensive academic research in international business and international marketing (specialising in country of origin studies), in marketing measurements and research and buyer-supplier relationships. He is widely published in journals such as the *Journal of Marketing Research, Journal of the Academy of Marketing Science, Journal of Advertising, Journal of International Business Studies, International Marketing Review, Journal of Business and Industrial Marketing, International Journal of Quality and Reliability Management, Allied Journal of Business Research, Global Finance Journal, Journal of International Information Management* and the *Journal of Marketing Education.* His current research interests (in addition to the ones mentioned above) include sustainability issues, emerging markets and global interdisciplinary synergies. Prior to his academic career at Oakland University, Dr. Parameswaran also gained wide industry experience. He has served at Ford Motor Company on its marketing research staff; Carson Roberts (a subsidiary of Ogilvy & Mather); Focus Advertising, India; and Richardson Merrell (now a part of Procter &

Gamble), India. Dr. Parameswaran has also taught at University of Michigan–Dearborn; Indiana University, Bloomington (on a sabbatical); Wayne State University, Detroit; and Georgia State University, Atlanta (as a PhD student).

Osvaldo Luiz Gonçalves Quelhas holds a DSc degree and is an Associate Professor at Fluminense Federal University (UFF), Brazil, where since 1992 he has been in the Civil and Production Engineering Departments. From 2006 to 2009 he was President of the Brazilian Association of Production Engineering (ABEPRO). He is a member of the Social Responsibility Commission of the Brazilian Oil Institute (Instituto Brasileiro de Petróleo-IBP). He is Coordinator of the Technology, Business Management and Environmental Laboratory (Latec) in Brazil; Coordinator of the Professional Master Course in the Management Systems (Strictu Sensu) and Professor of the Civil Engineering Master's and Doctorate Programs in Civil and Production Management: Management System with emphasis in Sustainability (environmental, social responsibility and work safety). He worked as an Engineer and Process Manager in several national and international organisations such as the Brazilian Naval Arsenal in Rio de Janeiro, Mills Cover Letter Equipamentos Ltda and Shell Brasil S.A. Professor Gonçalves Quelhas graduated in Civil Engineering in 1978 and earned his Master's Degree in Civil Engineering in 1984. He received his PhD in Production Engineering from the Federal University of Rio de Janeiro in 1994.

Rashidah Abdul Rahman, PhD, is a professor in Corporate Governance and Islamic Finance. She is currently a Research Fellow of the Accounting Research Institute (ARI), Universiti Teknologi MARA, Shah Alam, Malaysia. She is also a Visiting Professor at Aston University, Birmingham, UK. With research interests in corporate governance, Islamic finance, Islamic microfinance, intellectual capital, financial reporting, corporate ethics, corporate social responsibility and mergers and acquisitions, she has presented and published more than 100 articles in refereed journals. She sits on the Editorial Board of *Malaysian Accounting Review*, is the Chief Editor of the *Journal of Financial Reporting and Accounting,* and has reviewed articles for local and international journals. She has been an external examiner for postgraduate students at local universities and abroad. Among her publications are *Effective Corporate Governance, and Corporate Governance in Malaysia: Theory, Law and Context, Self-Regulating Corporate Governance* and *CSR-Based Corporate Governance.* Her books and research work have won several national and international accolades.

Arpit Raswant is a sessional academic at the University of Sydney Business School, Australia. Mr Raswant holds a Bachelor of Commerce degree from the University of Sydney Business School and an MA in International Commerce with thesis from the Korea University. He teaches global business at the postgraduate level and is currently working on several academic papers while preparing for doctoral research. In 2010 he was awarded the POSCO Asia Fellowship to pursue his postgraduate degree, and has since worked for LG and Korean Air. He has consulted for companies in the areas of internationalisation, innovation and cross-cultural management.

Roshima Said, PhD is an Associate Professor at Universiti Teknologi MARA, Malaysia. She acts as an Accounting Research Institute (ARI) Associate Fellow of Universiti Teknologi MARA, Malaysia. Her research interest is in the area of corporate governance, corporate social responsibility, corporate reporting, ethics and financial criminology.

She has conducted a number of studies that were presented at international and local seminars and published in proceedings and journals. In addition, she has published papers, books and book chapters both nationally and internationally. Dr Said is on the Editorial Advisory Board for the *Social Responsibility Journal* and is a member of the board of *Issues in Social and Environmental Accounting (Issues in SEA)*.

Zuraidah Mohd Sanusi is an Associate Professor in the Faculty of Accountancy, Universiti Teknologi MARA (UiTM), Malaysia, and a Deputy Director (Postgraduate and Innovation) at the Accounting Research Institute, UiTM. She holds a PhD in Business Administration (Accounting) from Universiti Kebangsaan Malaysia, and has a Master of Science degree and a Bachelor of Science degree in Accounting from Syracuse University, New York, USA. Her main research interests are auditing, forensic accounting, corporate reporting, corporate governance, management accounting and management. She has received several awards at conferences and product innovation exhibitions. She has published in a number of national and international journals. She has been appointed as a journal administrator and reviewer for several international journals. She also collaborated with research group members from various universities to conduct joint conferences and seminars, research workshops, publications and academic visits. In addition to teaching, she supervises and advises Master's and doctoral students and reviews articles for several academic journals. She also has presented a series of talks on governance, data analysis and research methodology.

Shahla Seifi (www.shahlaseifi.com) is an industrial engineer who has been employed by ISIRI (the Institute of Standards and Industrial Research of Iran) for 20 years. In this capacity she has been a member of the Iranian Shadow ISO 26000 working group. Her main concerns are with aspects of sustainability and quality and the development of appropriate consumer information to assist socially responsible choices. She has been the secretary of many national standards (more than 200). Recently she has authored two books on topics related to governance as well as a number of articles and chapters in books, all related to sustainability or social responsibility. She has previously translated the 11 ISO development manuals for developing countries which were the basis for teaching standardisation in Iran. She is currently finalising a PhD at Universiti Putra Malaysia. She has a BSc in Applied Physics from Azad University of Iran and an MSc in Industrial Engineering from Iran University of Science and Technology. She is currently based in the UK.

Hesam Shabaniverki, Professor of Engineering, was born in Qazvin, Iran, in 1985. He received his Master of Science degree in Highway and Transportation Planning and Engineering from Islamic Azad University of Tehran Science and Research Branch in 2013. He received his BS in Civil Engineering from Imam Khomeini International University, Qazvin, Iran, in 2009. He currently works as a traffic consultant in Asia and Europe. Additionally, he teaches at the University of Applied Science and Technology, Qazvin Branch and is the Research Associate Professor at Tarahan Parseh Transportation Research Institute in Tehran. His fields of interest are airport planning and management, transportation facilities, traffic safety and Importance of Traffic System (ITS). His recent papers are "Stochastic Approach in Airport Passenger Terminals," *Journal of Traffic and Logistics Engineering,* March 2013; "Planning under Uncertainty in Airport Passenger Terminals," "Bicycle Use and Attitude Survey of Qazvin City" and "Positive and Negative Consequences of the Law Requiring the Use of Bicycle Helmets," all at the 7th

National Congress on Civil Engineering, 2013, Iran; and "Airport Passenger Terminal Capacity Planning" at the Air Transport Research Society, June 2013, Italy. He is the consultant on design and construction of the first "Zero Energy City" in Tehran, Iran.

Alexander Stich studied Psychology (specialised in Industrial and Organizational Psychology, subsidiary subject Business Administration, extended subject Marketing and Consumer Psychology) at the University of Mannheim, Germany. Currently he is working as a doctoral assistant and PhD student for Professor Tillmann Wagner, Chair of Services Marketing, at WHU – Otto Beisheim School of Management, Germany. His research focus is in the area of sustainability and corporate social responsibility. He has published in *Advances in Consumer Research* as well as presented his research at international academic conferences.

Catherine Sutton-Brady is an Associate Professor of Marketing at the University of Sydney Business School, Australia. Dr Sutton-Brady holds an Honours Bachelor of Commerce Degree and a Master's in Business Studies from University College Cork, National University of Ireland, and a PhD in International Marketing from the University of Western Sydney. Her research concentrates on international marketing and relationships and networks in business markets. She has published extensively in the area of marketing education. She is a member of the editorial board for *Industrial Marketing Management.*

John Taskinsoy has been Senior Lecturer in the Faculty of Economics and Business at the University Malaysia Sarawak (Unimas) since 2011, where he is also pursuing his PhD in Finance. After graduating from San Francisco State University in 1997, he was offered a management position at Nortel Networks where he had worked for several years. During 20 years of professional life, he has held director positions in various companies and managed projects in diverse places. He teaches courses related to finance, marketing and business communication. He has published academic articles and papers in various national and international journals.

Huriye Toker is an Assistant Professor in the Faculty of Communication at Yasar University, Turkey. She has administrative and research experience on many national and international projects. Her research interests include communication, media, gender studies, European politics, political elections and corporate social responsibility.

Patrizia Torrecchia qualified with a Master's degree in Business Studies magna cum laude at the Università degli Studi di Palermo in 2004 and earned a PhD in Business Studies at Università di Messina in 2007. She was Visiting Researcher at Bocconi University, Milan, in 2006, Visiting Researcher at Saïd Business School, Oxford, in 2007 and Assegnista di Ricerca at Università degli Studi di Palermo in 2010. Patrizia's field of research is accounting for public administration, international accounting and accounting history, and corporate social responsibility.

Duygu Türker is an Assistant Professor in the Department of Business Administration at Yasar University, Izmir, Turkey. She has earned numerous degrees from universities in Turkey, including a Bachelor's degree in Business Administration, an MBA and a PhD in Public Administration from Dokuz Eylül University and a Master of Science in Environmental Sciences from Ankara University. She is involved in various projects as researcher or administrator. Her research interests include corporate social responsibility (CSR), business ethics, interorganisational relations and entrepreneurship.

Ali Uyar is a member of the College of Business Administration, American University of the Middle East, Egaila, Kuwait. He received his PhD in Accounting and Finance from Marmara University, Turkey. He teaches cost accounting, managerial accounting and financial accounting. His research interests are related to cost and management accounting practices, corporate reporting and voluntary disclosure. His research papers have been published in various national and international journals.

Tillmann Wagner is a Professor of Marketing and holds the Chair of Services Marketing at WHU – Otto Beisheim School of Management, Germany. He was previously on the faculty of Texas Tech University where he received the New Faculty Award. Professor Wagner holds a doctoral degree in marketing from the University of St. Gallen in Switzerland and has been a visiting doctoral scholar at the University of Florida's marketing department. His research interests lie in the areas of customer relationships and loyalty in services as well as corporate social responsibility. Professor Wagner has published in the *Journal of Marketing*. His work on the concept of corporate hypocrisy received the Best Published Paper Award from the Oxford University Centre for Corporate Reputation, Saïd Business School, University of Oxford.

Ülkü Yüksel has made the move from industry to an academic career after a 13-year-long professional business career in the international services sector. Her substantial industrial experience and positions as Director of Sales and Marketing in the hospitality, advertising, and financial services industries, with two giant corporations of these sectors, Citibank corporate HQs and Kempinski-Lufthansa, provided the context for her research interests. Ülkü's research revolves around the application of consumer marketing concepts in various contexts, including services marketing, international business and cross-cultural consumer behaviour. She investigates the effects of culture and psychological pressure on decision-making by managers and consumers, as they confront the risk and cost of their decisions. Consumption and managerial decision-making under various risk perceptions, such as various types and degrees of stress and uncertainty, anti-consumption and political marketing (e.g., boycott behaviour), are the specific areas she investigates within this concept. Her recent research explores consumers' evaluations as the consequences of their decisions affect their multifaceted selves, such as the personal self, collective self (in-group), impersonal self (anonymity), and others (out-group). Her research focuses on answering the following questions: (1) How do consumers/managers perceive stimulus and stress and react to information for their decisions on action versus inaction? (2) How do consumers evaluate the fairness of and react to marketing strategy and manufacturing tactics (e.g., boycotts)? (3) When and how does culture affect these constructs? Ülkü uses experiments to collect data, although she also makes use of mixed methodologies when the research question necessitates.

Ülkü's research is useful for marketers, managers and social policy makers as they try to understand the effects of culture, environmental uncertainty and turbulence and perceived stress on consumer or managerial decision-making.

Foreword

There have been many changes in the business world during the past decade. Some of these have been prompted by the recent global financial crisis, but much also has arisen because of an increasing concern amongst business managers and all stakeholders concerning the sustainability of business models and the need to ensure that all affected by business are taken into consideration. Thus it is now accepted that a business cannot operate in isolation and has some responsibility for its effects regardless of its place in the supply chain. The organisation is no longer constrained by its boundaries. For example, customers are concerned with the supply chain of a business and the human rights of employees, even if they are employees of a supplying chain. Similarly, environmental issues have risen in importance. At the same time, there has been increasing concern worldwide about governance and ethical behaviour. These can all be considered to be part of the effects of globalisation. Much has been written about globalisation, some of it positive and much of it negative. It is a subject which arouses definite opinions. It is something which is central to all debates about business ethics and corporate social responsibility – and of course to any consideration of sustainability.

One recent development, therefore, has been an increasing concern with stakeholders – a recognition that they are affected by the behaviour of business and the decisions made by managers – and a recognition of the rights of all stakeholders and the duty of a business to be accountable in this wider context has been a recent phenomenon. Only recently, however, has the economic view of accountability only to owners been subject to any considerable debate. Nevertheless, there have always been some business owners who recognise a responsibility to other stakeholders, and this is evident from the early days of the Industrial Revolution. Thus, for example, in the nineteenth century Robert Owen (1816, 1991) demonstrated dissatisfaction with the assumption that cost minimisation and the consequent profit maximisation were the only things of concern to a business. Furthermore, he put his beliefs into practice through the inclusion within his sphere of industrial operations the provision of model housing for his workers at New Lanark, Scotland. Further examples of socially responsible behaviour have continued to exist since these days. Thus there is evidence throughout the history of modernity that the self-centred approach of accounting for organisational activity only to shareholders was not universally acceptable. These stakeholders have not just an interest in the activities of the firm but also a degree of influence over the shaping of those activities. This influence is so significant that it can be argued that the power and influence of the stakeholders is such that it amounts to quasi-ownership of the organisation.

In considering why this situation has arisen, we must acknowledge that basically there are problems with accounting, with auditing and with people's expectations. We must remember that the myth of the free market is grounded in classical liberal economic theory – subsequently developed into Utilitarianism and the foundation of the capitalist economic system, and as propounded by people such as John Stuart Mill in the nineteenth century, which, briefly summarised, states that anything is OK as long as the consequences are acceptable. The regulatory regime of accounting has been increasingly changed over time to serve the interests of businesses rather than their owners or society. Thus no longer is it expected that the accounting of a business should be undertaken conservatively by recognising potential future liabilities while at the same time not recognising future profit. Instead profit can be brought forward into the accounts before it has been earned while liabilities (such as the replacement of an aging electricity distribution network) can be ignored if they reduce current profitability. A study of the changes made in accounting standards over the years shows a gradual relaxation of this requirement for conservatism in accounting as these standards have been changed to allow firms to show increased profits in the present. This of course makes the need for strong governance procedures even more paramount.

It was as long ago as 1967 that Marshall McLuhan first stated that we now live in a global village and that technology was connecting everyone. Much has changed in terms of technology since then and now. With Internet access available to virtually everyone, we truly do now live in a global village in which anyone can interact with anyone else wherever they are living and whatever time zone they are residing in. The Internet has changed the world as never before, resulting in profound consequences for people everywhere. McLuhan was prophetic in some respects. When he was talking about this global village, he also said that war would continue to be a feature of the world but there would be an increasing emphasis upon economic war rather than physical war. Physical war has not gone away, but it might be argued that the reasons for wars in the present are to do with economic reasons at least as much as they are to do with imperialistic or ideological reasons – at least as far as governments and countries are concerned. But governments, as the epitome of the nation-state, are becoming less important. What is becoming more important than governments and nation-states is the multinational company, operating in a global environment. Some of these multinationals are very large indeed – larger than many nation-states and a good deal more powerful. Arguably it is here that the economic war for the global village is taking place. The internet, however, has opened up business for public scrutiny and given more power to individuals as customers and as concerned citizens. This is where the power redistribution has occurred, and it has resulted in increasing concern with ethics and with such things as human rights and environmental issues. This can be expected to change to an even greater extent in the near future.

One of the consequences of the acquisition of governmental influence by these corporations is the myth of the free market as being beneficial to all. It is widely accepted – almost unquestioningly – that free markets will lead to greater economic growth and that we will all benefit from this economic growth. Around the world people are arguing – and winning the argument – that restrictions upon world economic activity caused by the regulation of markets is bad for our well-being. And in one country after another, for one market after another, governments are capitulating and relaxing their regulations to allow complete freedom of economic activity. So the world might not yet be a global village but it is rapidly becoming a global marketplace for these global corporations. At the same time, of course, there has been an increasing concern with many of the topics in this book and with the sustainable performance of organisations and their managers.

A concern for sustainability naturally brings to the forefront the triple bottom line – Brundtland's three pillars of the economic, environmental and social – and the equality of those pillars. One of the tasks of managers concerned with sustainability must therefore be a concern with these factors. Very often we see that these pillars are not treated as equal and one is neglected. Significantly, managers never neglect the economic (financial) pillar, as this would lead to disaster. Neglecting the others will also lead to disaster but perhaps not so quickly, and therefore one task of sustainability proponents must be to raise an understanding of the need for equal treatment of all three parts of the triple bottom line.

The contributions to this book represent the range of concern for this relationship and the range of topics which fall within the subject of business and sustainability. Many topics are addressed in this book and a range of current issues and debates are investigated. The purpose of the book is not so much to provide the answers (as there are no simple answers) but rather to inform the reader about current debates. These debates are relevant to all of us – as consumers and customers, as citizens and social individuals and also, probably, as employees, managers, investors and progenitors of future generations. We are all global citizens, and what happens affects us all to some extent. This book is therefore important in giving such perspectives on current issues and debates.

David Crowther

Acknowledgements

We express our deepest appreciation to the contributors, the members of the International Group on Governance Fraud Ethics and CSR and Prof. Dr. David Crowther, the father of corporate social responsibility.

Additionally, if Kristina Abbots of Taylor & Francis did not help us, this book would not be finished. We thank her very much.

We dedicate this book to Kemal Ataturk, founder of the Turkish Republic, who was very sensitive to environmental protection and sustainability in business.

Kıymet Çalıyurt and Ülkü Yüksel

Introduction

The need of sustainability in management

Kıymet Çalıyurt and Ülkü Yüksel

"Sustainability" has been defined as that which 'meets the needs of the present without compromising the ability of future generations to meet their own needs' (Brundtland et al., 1987, 16) When this definition appeared in 1987, nobody predicted that it would change management systems completely in the twenty-first century. After the Brundtland Report, sustainability became one of the top issues in the business world – or, put another way, a 'revolutionary approach to management systems'. Since then, many in the business community have tried to understand, learn and implement sustainability in their business process. However, becoming a sustainable company is not easy: it requires study, continuous training, staff, time, budget and a new point of view.

"Sustainability economics" is a new type of economics that is different from "economic sustainability". "Sustainability economics" connotes resources and their value, and the costs of being sustainable. Nongovernmental organisations and governments now urge companies to be sustainable, which helps "sustainability economics" become bigger and bigger every day. Much research states that sustainability helps to protect the environment and can also improve a company's financial performance. Unfortunately, though, recent scandals have shown us that "sustainability economics" can also be a way to make money dishonestly and cheat stakeholders. Scandals in sustainability forced us to think that there is another face to sustainability economics. This is called "fraud in sustainability".[1] At present there is no well-known, worldwide "external sustainability auditing system"[2] except for attempts made by a few auditing companies, so most probably we will hear about many sustainability fraud cases in the near future. Clearly, an "external sustainability auditing system" should be included in the "sustainability economics" system.

External auditors in some countries have to report on companies' greenhouse gas emissions. The International Federation of Accountants has developed a new International Standard on Assurance Engagements (ISAE) addressing professional accountants' responsibilities with respect to assurance engagements on a Greenhouse Gas (GHG) Statement. (IFAC, Assurance on a Greenhouse Gas Statement). According to the International Standard on Assurance Engagements, ISAE 3410, 'Assurance Engagements on Greenhouse Gas Statements', published by the International Auditing and Assurance Standards Board (IAASB), the objectives of the practitioner are:

1   To obtain reasonable or limited assurance, as appropriate, about whether the GHG statement is free from material misstatement, whether due to fraud or error, thereby enabling the practitioner to express a conclusion conveying that level of assurance;

2   To report, in accordance with the practitioner's findings, about whether:

  a   In the case of a reasonable assurance engagement, the GHG statement is prepared, in all material respects, in accordance with the applicable criteria; or

  b   In the case of a limited assurance engagement, anything has come to the practitioner's attention that causes the practitioner to believe, on the basis of the procedures performed and evidence obtained, that the GHG statement is not prepared, in all material respects, in accordance with the applicable criteria; and

3   To communicate as otherwise required by this ISAE, in accordance with the practitioner's findings.[3]

Transforming into a sustainable company requires *budget, human resources, time* and, of course, *intention. Sustainability costs* consist of the following elements:

- *Absorbing sustainability into the company:* Company management should absorb sustainability into the management environment. Prerequisites for implementing sustainability include surveys and discussions to understand the points of view of the board, top management and lower echelon executives. A sustainability expert may consult on this research and discussion.
- *Continuous training on sustainability:* This element also needs additional effort, such as attending conferences and certificate programmes on sustainability. The need for management to read books, reports and papers on sustainability means allocating budget, time and staff.
- *Working with a consultant on sustainability:* Ideally, a company will design a separate sustainability department staffed by experienced professionals who have certification and training on sustainability, such as the global reporting initiative (GRI) system. If a company does not want to create a sustainability department, it can work with a consulting company. This element also needs budget, time and staff.
- *Joining in a ranking system on sustainability:* If a company attests that it should be called "sustainable" and discloses sustainability reports, it is recommended to join a well-known ranking system on sustainability. However, like the points mentioned above, joining a ranking system also requires budget, time and staff.

Academia has a big responsibility to train future managers as warriors for a sustainable business world. As such, master's and doctorate programmes on sustainability management or similar have been created. Many institutions have developed sustainability reporting models with different contents, and of course, there are now many sustainability rating systems.

Sustainability is a large umbrella which consists of regulations, systems, ratings and continuous development trends, and it also includes business ethics, corruption, corporate social responsibility, reputation management, accountability, gender issues and, of course, plans for the future.

At the beginning, sustainability was considered a fad. However, economic crises and corruption showed that "being sustainable" means "staying alive". Many studies have proved and continue to prove that sustainability helps companies to increase their long-term firm value. Recently, some companies and governments have viewed sustainability as a way to protect against problems like economic crises, environmental disasters and pollution, global warming, resource depletion and energy shortage, as well as staff loyalty and higher share value. Another positive aspect is that some governments help companies to practice sustainability by making their sustainability expenses tax-exempt. If a company follows certain governmental regulations relating to sustainability, it will pay less tax than others. Furthermore, being a sustainable company may help a company to have credit with less interest.

Sustainability in management affects many disciplines from marketing to accounting, from production to human resources, from waste management to finance, from training to supply chain operation. In addition, certified public accountants, lawyers, external auditors, medical doctors and engineers cannot say that sustainability is not their business. For example, according to the International Auditing Standards IAPS 1010 (International Auditing Practice Standards), an external auditor should report on a company's environmental issues while auditing its financial statement. Another example is International Auditing Standards 570. This standard helps the auditor to evaluate a company's financial sustainability.

To create a sustainable business world, we must train business people from different disciplines and urge them to learn more about sustainability issues in their own areas. This will help companies to discuss and absorb sustainability in their company quickly. Recently, many companies have created the position of "sustainability director". This shows us how sustainability is an emerging issue in the business world.

It is equally important for people and institutions in business and academia to learn, follow, publish and implement various sustainability issues. All of us need to:

- have training on sustainability
- subscribe to publications about sustainability
- report and disclose sustainability
- have an audit system on sustainability
- create a sustainability department and hire staff
- provide data for stakeholders on sustainability.

That's why, for this book, we asked distinguished academicians around the world who study different aspects of sustainability to write a chapter about their specialisation in sustainability.

Although there are many positive results of being sustainable in business, there are negatives as well. We rarely discuss sustainability auditing and fraud in sustainability. Most companies claim that they follow international sustainability regulations while trading and publish sustainability (corporate social responsibility) reporting. They claim that invoices have been paid for developing sustainability in the company or maintaining social responsibility projects so that they can declare less tax to financial regulators.

In this book, authors from different countries with varying specialisations discuss development, aspects, problems, road maps, trends and disclosure systems on sustainability in management and recommend solutions for creating a sustainable business.

David and Shahla in their chapter assert that resources of the world are overused and usage is not sustainable at this level. They demonstrate that there is starting to be a general understanding of the meaning of resource depletion. BRIC (Brazil, Russia, India, China) have access to a large proportion of the remaining natural resources of the world while also having large populations and therefore great scope for rapid economic growth. They claim that resource depletion will negatively affect the economic environment. However, it is not yet fully recognised that development in other parts of the world will exacerbate this pressure and lead to greater competition for the available resources. This competition will be economic but could also become physical as the world adjusts to a new geopolitical environment.

Carmela and Patrizia propose socially responsible reporting for health care organizations in Italy. They claim that in the context of social accounting reports, the past decades saw a shift of attention on results and measurement. Evaluation was not limited to the domain of quantitative-monetary variables but went to more general dimensions: non-monetary and qualitative-quantitative. The process has taken as a central tenet the production of information as the condition upon which build rational choices, trying to overcome the vagueness that has largely characterised the non-economic and financial objectives. Carmela and Patrizia propose a new health value table which includes evaluation of economic results, health protection activities effectiveness, ability to provide services in a short time and in comfortable conditions, compliance with regional/national planned objectives, efficiency, organizational climate and leadership style, and contribution to medical and health knowledge creation and/or improvement.

Maria presents the results of the analysis of sustainability principles adopted in strategies formulated by Polish companies included in the WIG20 Index. The WIG20 index covers the largest and the most liquid companies of the Warsaw Stock Exchange, which are viewed as role models for the rest of the listed companies. The goal of Maria's chapter is to provide answers to research questions on the role and place of sustainability in the strategic management framework as formulated in strategies and pursued in activities of sample companies, as well as its relations to CSR.

Tillmann and Alexander addresss the consumer's point of view on sustainability, noting that it is interesting to understand how consumers classify the concept. Building on in-depth interviews as well as existing theory, their research develops a conceptual framework for consumer sustainability. In general, their results show that consumer sustainability consists of ecological, social and personal facets. The subjective importance of these facets differs depending on relative closeness and distance.

Merve and Ali searched for a positive association between firm size (as measured by sales revenues) and corporate social and environmental disclosure level, or a positive association between the performance (as measured by return on equity [ROE]) and corporate social and environmental disclosure level. According to the findings of their study, firm size, presence of independent directors and auditor firm size has a positive and significant relationship to the corporate social and environmental reporting disclosure level. As the firm size increases, the corporate and social environmental reporting disclosure level of the firm increases.

Uğur and Yaşar shed light on some basic concepts and terms related to environmental reporting. The purpose of their study is to analyse environmental disclosures of corporations and disclose how corporations report environmental information. Samples of the study comprise 26 Turkish companies from various industries listed on the Borsa İstanbul Corporate Governance Index (XKURY) in the financial year 2012.

John and Ali explore sustainability reporting in the airline industry. The magnitude of global financial and economic crises in recent years has increased significantly and become almost unbearable, causing investors to lose confidence in the whole financial system. A wide range of internal and external factors can certainly influence the intensity of a financial crisis. Their research papers, however, indicate that the recent crises since 1996 have been more damaging, in large part, due to the lack of corporate economic sustainability predominantly caused by lack of transparency about economic, environmental and social impacts. They present research about the sustainability reporting of Turkish Airlines, which happens to be the largest airline in Turkey as well as an important global player in the airline industry. Their paper is organized around the results of this research and provides some implications for Turkish Airlines and also for the industry.

Mehmet, Ercüment and Ayşe studied internal control systems in the prevention of mistakes and fraud in hospitality management. One of the most important factors in terms of development and growth of organizations is the existence of an internal control system (besides the audit) designed to prevent the mistakes and fraud. The internal control system enables the processes within the organizations to run regularly. These authors state that the designation and establishment of the internal control system will protect against fraud in hospitality management related to departments of food and beverages.

Jing has studied banking and sustainable development in China, observing that with the growth of the Chinese economy, sustainable development has become a significant concern. Her chapter explores the role of the banking industry in supporting sustainable development. Beginning with a historical review of the evolution of sustainable development, she then gives a brief introduction to the Chinese banking industry. She analyses the policy and legal framework in this regard. Moreover, she looks at the approaches adopted by the Chinese banking industry to achieve and facilitate sustainable development. The promotion of "Green Credit" is examined as a case study. Last but not least, after identifying the key obstacles and shortages in this area, she makes suggestions on the future development of sustainable banking.

Rasim, Rufat and Seymur discuss in their chapter ethical issues in business administration and their effects on social and economic development. They state that to ensure sustainable development, management must be efficient and effective. Every day we hear a lot about poor business ethics: poisoning, deaths and dangerous working conditions, pollution of the environment such as the emission of harmful substances, corruption scandals, abuse of office, ill-gotten gains and use of child labor in heavy industry – all are very important to the future of humanity. Notwithstanding the existence of health and safety laws and regulations on preventing such cases, there is a need for business ethics.

Duygu and Senem in their chapter review integrated sustainability and social responsibility communication. They state that in parallel to the growing number of social and environmental problems, business organizations must start to adopt more sustainable and socially responsible ways of doing business. Corporate sustainability and social responsibility communication (SSRC) is a long-term process that requires an organisational awareness for the changing needs, expectations and interests of all stakeholders, and their participation in the decision-making process must be increased to achieve more balanced organizational decisions and actions. Duygu and Senem's study provides an overview of SSRC.

Hesam, in his chapter, explores sustainability in airlines. He has stated that airlines, as a system for scheduled air transport of passengers and freight, cooperate in a wide range of circumstances that influence environmental, business, economic and other concerns. Airlines are huge public relations endeavors with large numbers of customers per year. The combination of private and public management creates successful airlines. Balancing demands, instruments, regulation and social responsibility is not always sufficient to integrate different priorities and conflicting sustainability needs of countries and airlines. He notes that airline sustainability depends heavily on the preferences and values of the various players involved. In addition, the methods that managers use differ from airline to airline.

Çağatay and Ayça discuss sustainability reporting. Although sustainability is not a new concept, developments in the business world and increased competition have caused business entities to refocus on this concept in order to ensure success. Sustainability requires reporting a company's performance related to environmental, social and economic dimensions. These reports may take the form of social responsibility reports, environmental reports, triple bottom line reports, corporate sustainability reports, and non-financial reports. Sustainability practices and reports should not be limited to a number of enterprises, but they should be applied by the entirety of the business world. Although these reports are mainly prepared by multinational and large industrial enterprises, it would be beneficial to generalise the use of sustainability reports even to small and medium-sized enterprises. The academic community can take the lead, and with the full support of the business world, this can be achieved through conducting seminars, meetings and workshops to emphasize the importance of sustainability reports.

Razana, Zuraidah, Rashidah and Omar in their chapter consider ethical issues and its relevance to auditors' ethical decision-making in Malaysia. "Ethical issues" – or "moral intensity construct" in Jones' (1991) model – refers to 'the extent or degree of issue-related moral imperative in a situation'. Their current study extends the previous work on moral intensity by examining the influence of moral intensity components on the first three stages of the auditors' ethical decision-making process (i.e. ethical sensitivity, ethical judgment and ethical intentions) in developing countries.

Roshima and Noorain delve into the fact that many companies have experienced bankruptcy, been de-listed from the Bursa Malaysia and are in financial distress. This phenomenon has created a new area for research. There is little research on the relationship between human capital, corporate governance and firm performance in Malaysia, so the researchers have taken steps to investigate this matter especially in the context of Malaysia. Their study found that the most significant variables that influence the firm's performance are the knowledge background of the chairman and the age of the chairman. The authors also noticed that corporate governance characteristics are no longer significant in influencing a firm's performance compared to a decade ago. In Malaysia the Code of Corporate Governance was introduced in 2000. Since then it has been well developed in most companies.

Maria and Martha, two professional educators from two generations and from eastern and western cultures respectively, shared their insights into sustainability that are built on more than eighty years total management education experience, extensive literature review and previous research on sustainability, ethics and moral character development. They share their insights to develop students' knowledge, skills and practices to become responsible consumers and decision makers building on the best of the past, adapting it with the present and sustaining it for the future.

Julie and Teresa have stated that consumers have a vital role in driving the change to more sustainable consumption practices. Thus, marketers must develop a better understanding of the consumer's perspective on sustainability – to understand the nature of their concerns, to effectively segment and target sustainability-concerned consumers and to help mitigate the gap between sustainable attitudes and unsustainable behaviour (Kotler, 2011; Prothero et al., 2011). As such, their chapter develops a framework for understanding and measuring the sustainability concerns of consumers.

Ravi and Krishna examine how sustainability concepts can be applied to marketing through a case study of sustainable practices employed by Haworth, Inc., a Michigan-based global leader in the design and manufacture of office furniture and organic workspaces. Based on the Brundtland Commission's definition of sustainable development as '(d)evelopment that meets the needs of the present without compromising the ability of future generations to meet their own needs,' the authors discuss how sustainability concepts that have been applied to diverse activities such as mining, manufacturing, agriculture and forestry can be adapted to marketing. The application of these concepts is illustrated through practices currently being employed by Haworth, and the authors explore how they should be applied in the future.

Rosane, Osvaldo, Sergio, Marcelo and Walter have written a chapter on Agenda 21 as a tool for managing the relationship between companies and communities. They have mentioned that the concepts of sustainability and corporate social responsibility have begun to permeate the debate on the postures as well as entrepreneurial attitudes. When it comes to managing relationships with their stakeholders, companies must adopt new management standards. This research aims at analyzing the contribution of Local Agenda 21 to promoting cooperative relations and mutual trust between companies and communities by privileging autonomy, empowerment and interaction among social actors.

Arpit and Catherine argue that sustainability is no longer just a new business buzzword; it is something that various companies and industries have begun to take very seriously. Their chapter begins by explaining the role of sustainability in supply chains and showing the benefits companies can achieve through sustainable practices. The authors then present real-life examples showing how some companies approach sustainability effectively, to their advantage in their industry, while others fail to see the advantages and suffer the consequences.

Notes

1 Christoph Rauwald, Alan Katz and Kartikay Mehrotra, (2016), "VW Reported Close to $10 Billion Deal with U.S. for Diesel Fraud", http://www.insurancejournal.com/news/national/2016/04/21/406021.htm
2 "Adding Credibility to the Published Information in Your Sustainability or Corporate Responsibility Report", http://www.pwc.co.uk/services/audit-assurance/assurance-regulatory-reporting-sustainability.html
3 International Federation of Accountants, International Standard on Assurance Engagements (ISAE 3402) Assurance Reports on Controls at a Service Organization. https://www.aicpa.org/Research/Standards/AuditAttest/ASB/Documents/Mtg/1207/ISAE%203410-Final%206–6–12.pdf

References

Brundtland, G.H., Khalid, M., Agnelli, S., Al-Athol, S.A. and Chidzero, B. (1987). Report of the world commission on environment and development: Our common future, UN General Assembly, www.un-documents.net/our-common-future.pdf (Retrieved October 8, 2014).

International Federation of Accountants (IFAC). Statement, https://www.ifac.org/auditing-assurance/projects/assurance-greenhouse-gas-statement (Retrieved March 14, 2015).

Jones, T.M. (1991). "Ethical decision-making by individuals in organizations". *An issue of Academy of Management: The Academy of Management Review*, 16(2), 366–95.

Kotler, P. (2011). "Reinventing marketing to manage the environmental imperative". *Journal of Marketing*, 75(July), 132–5.

Pricewaterhouse, Adding credibility to the published information in your sustainability or corporate responsibility report, http://www.pwc.co.uk/services/audit-assurance/assurance-regulatory reporting-sustainability.html (Retrieved October 8, 2014).

Prothero, A., Dobscha, S., Freund, J., Kilnourne, W.E., Luchs, M.G., Ozanne, L.K. and Thogersen, J. (2011). "Sustainable consumption: Opportunities for consumer research and public policy". *Journal of Public Policy and Marketing*, 30(1), 31–8.

Rauwald, Christoph, Katz, Alan and Mehrotra, Kartikay. VW reported close to $10 Billion deal with U.S. for diesel fraud, http://www.insurancejournal.com/news/national/2016/04/21/406021.htm (Retrieved April 10, 2016).

Part I

Sustainability and management in Europe

Part 2

Sustainability and management in Europe

1 The flawed logic of sustainable development

David Crowther and Shahla Seifi

1 Introduction

The logic of the economic system under which the world operates is predicated on an assumption that development is possible and that the pricing system mediates the acquisition of the additional resources required for that development. This is perfectly in accordance with the assumptions made by Brundtland and accepted ever since. Consequently governmental attention has been focused upon the operation of the pricing system with a desire to reduce transaction costs and the various rounds of GATT[1]/WTO[2] as a mechanism for reducing the transaction costs of international trading. Meanwhile environmentalists have been showing that the resources of the world are overused and usage is not sustainable at this level, and there is starting to be a general understanding of the meaning of resource depletion.

While this has been occupying the minds of people in the developed Western world, a number of countries have adopted a strategy of rapid growth and economic development. Principal among these have been the BRIC countries. These countries have access to a large proportion of the remaining natural resources of the world while also having large populations and therefore great scope for rapid economic growth. This development therefore puts a lot of pressure upon the world economic system and has the effect of bidding up the cost of resources and placing a limitation upon the possibility of development by increasing the cost of economic activity and diverting resources into the bidding process instead of into production. This has the effect of reducing the pace of development and placing tension on the world economic system.

Now let's have a review of the details of remaining resources available in these countries. China is the largest country in the world as well as the fastest growing in terms of GDP – with a consequent demand for resources in terms of energy and raw materials. It has deposits of every one of the 150 minerals found so far in the natural world. The amount of proven deposits in the country has been made clear for 135 of them. Of these, more than 20 rank in the forefront of the world. Ranking first in the world, in proven deposits, are 12 minerals: tungsten, antimony, titanium, vanadium, zinc, rare earth, magnesite, pyrite, fluorite, barite, plaster stone, and graphite. Ranking second and third are six: tin, mercury, asbestos, talcum, coal, and molybdenum; and ranking fourth are five: nickel, lead, iron, manganese, and the platinum family. China ranks third in the world in the deposit of 45 important minerals. It is one of a few countries where mineral deposits are rich and varieties are fairly complete.

Brazil is also a rapidly developing country. It contains the Amazon jungle with therefore considerable access to both timber and to mineral resources such as quartz, diamonds, chromium, iron ore, phosphates, petroleum, mica, graphite, titanium, copper, gold, oil, bauxite, zinc, tin, and mercury.

The main natural resources of India are iron ore, bauxite, and copper ore. India is one of the major producers of iron in the world. Gold, silver, and diamonds make up a small part of other natural resources available in India. A major portion of the energy in India is generated from coal. It is estimated that India has around 120 billion tons of coal in reserve, enough to last for around 120 years. Huge reserves of petroleum have been found off the coast of Maharashtra and Gujarat. Additionally, electrical energy is generated by hydroelectric power, coal, and nuclear energy. Half of the hydroelectric power is generated by snowfield reservoirs high up in the Himalayas. Huge dams have also been built across many major rivers to produce electricity and water for irrigation.

Russia is the world's largest mineral and energy supply and is known as an "energy superpower", containing 22 per cent of the world's oil, 16 per cent of the world's coal, and 40 per cent of the world's natural gas. It is also very well known for its trees, and has 20 per cent of the world's timber and wood. The most common natural resources are iron ore, nickel, coal, gold, diamonds, furs, petroleum, zinc, aluminium, tin, lead, platinum, titanium, copper, tungsten phosphates, and mercury. It also has the world's largest oil reserves, the second largest coal reserves, largest lead reserves, largest reserves of water in lakes, the largest diamond deposits, the second largest potassium reserves, and enormous fish reserves.

Not only do these four countries contain a significant proportion of the world's reserves of raw materials but they are also rapidly developing countries with development fuelled by their raw materials. One effect of this is that the resources available to other countries in the developed world are constrained by this rising demand, with a number of possible consequences.

2   Sustainability in the present

The world is moving into a different era, an era in which it is recovering from a severe economic crisis while also grappling with the consequences of climate change, and therefore there are a number of issues which become more important for manufacturing companies. One of these is that of managing in a post–Hubbert's Peak world (Kerr 1998), which requires ever more efficient use of energy. Efficient operations make for least cost of manufacture and this in itself is a factor in the development of sustainability (Waeyenbergh and Pintelon 2002). To address this problem requires a holistic approach which integrates corporate social responsibility (CSR) into all the operations of the company, including its production and maintenance activities. It also requires a different approach to risk management. It has implications not only for the products which are manufactured but also for how those products are produced, both at the level of the individual firm and at the levels of the national and global economies.

The question of sustainability has risen to prominence in recent times – not just in the business world or in the academic world but in popular consciousness. It seems that everyone is concerned with sustainability and that this has been brought about by a general acceptance of the existence of climate change and by a general recognition of the problems stemming from resources depletion. Indeed, many people can talk knowledgeably about their carbon footprint (Wiedman and Minx 2007) and about Hubbert's Peak, and many businesses are making statements about their aim for carbon neutrality (Weidema et al. 2008).

An important component of production and of sustainability is that of risk management. This too provides an intersection with operational requirements, as minimizing exposure to risk makes a company both more socially responsible and more sustainable but also reduces cost in the longer term (Aras and Crowther 2008). Often, however, the methodologies for the evaluation of risk are deficient in their effectiveness of evaluating – particularly of environmental risk. In order to fully recognize and incorporate environmental costs and benefits into the investment analysis process, the starting point needs to be the identification of the types of costs and revenues which need to be incorporated into the evaluation process. Once these types of costs have been identified, then it becomes possible to quantify such costs and to incorporate qualitative data concerning those less tangible benefits which are not easily subject to quantification. The completion of an environmental audit will enhance the understanding of the processes involved and will make this easier. In considering environmental benefits, as distinct from financial benefits, it is important that an appropriate time horizon is selected which will enable those benefits to be recognized and accrued. This may imply a very different time horizon from one which is determined purely by the needs of financial analysis.

It will be apparent therefore that there is considerable synergetic relationship between operational procedures and CSR as many of the issues are shared. It should also be apparent that the minimization of the use of resources is central to this concern – both environmental resources and financial resources. Indeed, the way to minimize the use of financial resources is through the minimization of the use of environmental resources, and this is particularly apposite to any consideration of energy utilization. This will become more important in the future as energy costs continue to rise because of the increasing scarcity.

This scarcity increases the costs of operation, and a manufacturing plant tends to be energy-intensive, which concomitantly increases the cost of production. So an efficiently operating plant makes for an efficient and low-cost company. This makes sound financial sense but it also makes the company socially responsible because it is minimizing the use of environmental resources. Additionally, it is socially responsible because efficient operations also mean a minimization of pollution and waste.

3 The Brundtland Report

In 1983 the United Nations established the World Commission on Environment and Development (WCED) under the chairmanship of Gro Harlem Brundtland. It subsequently became known as the Brundtland Commission, and its report, "Our Common Future", is typically known as the Brundtland Report. The commission was created to address a growing concern 'about the accelerating deterioration of the human environment and natural resources and the consequences of that deterioration for economic and social development'. In establishing the commission, the UN General Assembly recognized that environmental problems were global in nature and determined that it was in the common interest of all nations to establish policies for sustainable development. The report highlighted the urgency of making progress toward economic development that could be sustained without depleting natural resources or harming the environment and thereby raised the profile of a concern for sustainability which had previously only been expressed by some NGOs. It was primarily concerned with securing global equity, and with redistributing resources towards poorer nations whilst encouraging their economic growth. The report suggested that equity, growth, and environmental maintenance – the Triple Bottom Line – are simultaneously possible and that each country is capable of achieving its full economic potential whilst at the same time enhancing its resource base. The report also recognized that achieving this equity and sustainable growth would require technological and social change. *Our Common Future* was published by Oxford University Press in 1987. The report deals primarily with sustainable development and the change of politics needed for achieving that. The definition of this term in the report is very well known and often cited:

> Sustainable development is development that meets the needs of the present without compromising the ability of future generations to meet their own needs.

A direct outcome of the Brundtland Report was a conference which was held five years later, in 1992, in Rio de Janeiro.[3] This was the United Nations Conference on Environment and Development, better known as the Earth Summit. Representatives of 172 governments participated, with 108 considering it important enough to send their heads of state or government. In addition, over 2,000 representatives of NGOs attended, with around 15,000 other people at the parallel NGO Forum; these people had what was known as consultative status. The issues addressed in the conference included:

- A scrutiny of patterns of production – particularly production with hazardous components or waste, such as lead in petrol, or poisonous waste from other products
- Alternative sources of energy to replace fossil fuels which had already been linked to global climate change
- A reliance on public transport systems in order to reduce vehicle emissions, congestion in cities and the health problems caused by polluted air and smog
- The growing scarcity of water as a resource in various parts of the world.

An important achievement of the conference was an agreement on the Climate Change Convention which in turn led to the Kyoto Protocol.[4]

4   Global warming

The changes to the weather systems around the world are apparent to most people and are being manifested in such extreme weather as excessive rain or snow, floods, droughts, heat waves, and hurricanes which have been affecting many parts of the world. Indeed, most people remember, for example, Hurricane Katrina, which devastated New Orleans. Global warming and climate change, its most noticeable effect, is a subject of discussion all over the world and it is generally, although by no means universally, accepted that global warming is taking place and therefore that climate change will continue to happen. Opinion is divided, however, as to whether the climate change which has taken place can be reversed or not. Some think that it cannot be reversed. According to Lovelock (2006), climate change is inevitable with its consequences upon the environment and therefore upon human life and economic activity. Nevertheless, he remains certain that it is possible to adapt and is thereby more positive than some other commentators.[5] Although many factors contribute to global warming, it is clear that commercial and economic activity plays a significant part. Many people talk about "greenhouse gases", with carbon dioxide being the main one, as a direct consequence of economic activity. Consequently many people see the reduction in the emission of such gases as being fundamental to any attempt to combat climate change. This of course requires a change in behaviour – of people and of organizations. Such a perceived need for change is one of the factors which has caused the current concern with sustainability.

Another factor which is occupying the minds of people in general is that of their ecological footprint – the amount of physical area of the earth needed to provide for each person. Ecological footprint analysis compares human demand on nature with the biosphere's ability to regenerate resources and provide services. It does this by assessing the biologically productive land and marine area required to produce the resources a population consumes and absorb the corresponding waste, using prevailing technology. This approach can also be applied to an activity such as the manufacturing of a product or driving of a car. A possibly more fashionable term at the moment, however, is that of carbon footprinting (Wiedman and Minx 2007).

A carbon footprint can be considered to be the total amount of carbon dioxide (CO_2) and other greenhouse gases emitted over the full life cycle of a product or service. Normally a carbon footprint is expressed as a CO_2 equivalent (usually in kilogrammes or tonnes), which accounts for the same global warming effects of different greenhouse gases (UK Parliamentary Office of Science and Technology POST, 2006).[6] There are a number of ways of calculating this footprint and a number of online resources to assist, at least as far as individuals are concerned.

For an individual the definition of "carbon footprint" is the total amount of carbon dioxide attributable to the actions of that individual (mainly through their energy use) over a period of one year. This definition underlies the personal carbon calculators that are widely used. The term owes its origins to the idea that a footprint is what has been left behind as a result of the individual's activities. Carbon footprints can either consider only direct emissions (typically from energy used in the home and in transport, including travel by cars, aeroplanes, rail, and other transport), or can also include indirect emissions (including carbon dioxide emissions as a result of goods and services consumed) (Weidema et al. 2008). Bottom-up calculations sum such emissions from individual actions; top-down calculations take total emissions from a country (or other high-level entity) and divide these emissions among the residents (or other participants in that entity). A number of studies have calculated the carbon footprint of organizations and nations. In one such study the UN (2007) examined age-related carbon emissions based on expenditure and consumption. The study found that, on average, people aged 50–65 years old have a higher carbon footprint than any other age group: these individuals have a carbon footprint of approximately 13.5 tonnes/person per annum, compared to the UK average of 12 tonnes.

Although scientific opinion has more or less reached a consensus that global warming is taking place and therefore that climate change is happening, there are still a considerable number of sceptics and other people who deny that it is happening.[7] There are others who argue that the human contribution to global warming is negligible: they argue therefore that it is useless or even harmful to concentrate on individual contributions.

5   Resource depletion

There can be no argument that the resources of the planet are finite and that this is a limiting factor to growth and development, which is relevant to this paper. The depletion of the resources of the planet, however, is one of the factors which has helped create the current interest in sustainability. Of particular concern are extractive industries and the fact that such things as aluminium and tin are becoming in short supply. So too are many of the minerals required for the electronics industry. In Malaysia the tin upon which Kuala Lumpur was founded has been fully extracted and recycling has become an important aspect of the industry. Kuala Lumpur was founded for this tin[8] because the tin in the UK had been fully extracted long ago and the thriving industries based around them are long gone. Thus the British in their drive for development moved to exploiting the resources of other parts of the world. As other resources – such as coal – are extracted in total, then the companies based upon them disappear, and with them the jobs in those industries. This is an obvious source of concern for people.

Of particular concern is the extinguishing of supplies of oil, because much economic activity is fuelled by the energy created by the use of oil. Many would argue that the wars in the Middle East,[9] particularly the problems in Iraq and Iran, are caused by oil short-ages, actual or impending, and the problems thereby caused, rather than by any concern for political issues. Most people have now heard of Hubbert's Peak[10] (Deffeyes 2004) and engaged with the debate as to whether or not it has been reached. Certainly it has in such parts of the world as the USA and the North Sea, but it is less certain if it has been reached for the world as a whole. Nevertheless the whole crux of sustainability – and sustainable development – is based upon the need for energy and there are insufficient alternative sources of energy to compensate for the elimination of oil as a source of fuel. Consequently, resource depletion, real or imagined, and particularly energy resources, is one of the most significant causes of the current interest in sustainability.

6   Sustainability and sustainable development

Although it is now more than 25 years since the Brundtland Report was produced, it still continues to dominate the sustainability debate. Indeed, almost all current definitions of sustainability refer back, at least implicitly, to Brundtland and the importance of not reducing the choices available to future generations. The same wording for sustainable development is exactly used in ISO 26000 (2010), "Guidance on Social Responsibility".

It is generally accepted that sustainable development is a process which aims to fulfil human needs while also maintaining the quality of the natural environment indefinitely. It is often thought that such development was first recognized by Brundtland, but actually the link between environment and development was globally recognized in 1980, when the International Union for the Conservation of Nature published its report "World Conservation Strategy", in which it made use of the term "sustainable development". Admittedly, however, the term came into general usage following the publication of the Brundtland Report. Despite the three pillars defined by Brundtland, it has been argued (ISO Central Secretariat, 2006) that standardization is one of the three pillars of sustainable development, the other two being metrology and conformity assessment. On the other hand, it is claimed (Lindsey 2007) that there are numerous examples where legislation is supported by standards already, but standards can play a far bigger role and in much wider areas than before. Examples include:

- The greater use of management systems in areas such as environmental management, food safety, and health safety
- Legislative areas that have not traditionally used standardization such as health care, education, and security
- Standards to support the implementation of the Services Directive
- Standards to support sustainable development.

Sustainability implies the acceptance of any costs involved in the present as an invest-ment for the future (Crowther 2012). Sustainable development is concerned with the effect which action taken in the present has upon the options available in the future. A sustainable society is the society which provides for its needs without impairing the needs of the future generations. Therefore, sustainability implies that society must use no more of a resource than can be regenerated. Considering current levels of consumption, the way people live is not sustainable at all. Hence, sustainability is a matter of international concern which requires the emergence of international standards. This requirement is exacerbated by the recent movement towards globalization. Indeed, globalization requires a worldwide integration; therefore, countries should adopt international standards and avoid regional or national standards as barriers to trade.

With the increasing globalization of markets, international standards (as opposed to regional or national standards) have become critical to the trading process, ensuring a level playing field for exports, and ensuring imports meet internationally recognized levels of performance and safety. International standards and their use in technical regulations on products, production methods, and services play a vital role in sustainable development and trade facilitation – through the promotion of safety, quality, and compatibility. The benefits derived are significant. Standardization contributes not only to international trade but also to the basic infrastructure that underpins society, including health and environment, while promoting sustainability and good regulatory practice (ISO Central Secretariat, 2006).

7   Renewable energy

Concern for the effect of traditional energy sources upon climate, through the production of greenhouse gases, has combined with an awareness of the finiteness of the sources of energy production[11] to cause an increased interest in renewable energy supply. Renewable energy is energy which comes from natural resources such as sunlight, wind, rain, tides, and geothermal heat, which are renewable (naturally replenished). About 16 per cent of global final energy consumption comes from renewables, with 10 per cent coming from traditional biomass, which is mainly used for heating, and 3.4 per cent from hydroelectricity. New renewables (small scale hydroelectricity generation, modern biomass, wind, solar, geothermal, and biofuels) accounted for another 3 per cent and are growing very rapidly. The share of renewables in electricity generation is around 19 per cent, with 16 per cent of global electricity coming from hydroelectricity and 3 per cent from new renewables.[12]

Wind power is growing at over 20 per cent annually, with a worldwide installed capacity of 238,000 megawatts (MW) at the end of 2011,[13] and is widely used in Europe, Asia, and the United States. Since 2004, photovoltaics have surpassed wind as the fastest-growing energy source, and since 2007 their use has more than doubled every two years. At the end of 2011 the photovoltaic (PV) capacity[14] worldwide was 67,000 MW, and PV power stations are popular in Germany and Italy (Renewable Energy 2012). Solar thermal power stations operate in the USA and Spain, and the largest of these is the 354 MW Solar Energy Generating Systems (SEGS) power plant in the Mojave Desert. The Moroccan government in late 2012 established a $1 billion project to produce solar power.[15] The world's largest geothermal power installation is the Geysers in California, with a rated capacity of 750 MW. Brazil has one of the largest renewable energy programs in the world, involving production of ethanol fuel from sugarcane, and ethanol now provides 18 per cent of the country's automotive fuel.[16] Ethanol fuel is also widely available in the USA.

Many renewable energy projects are large-scale, and renewable technologies are suited to rural and remote areas, where energy is often crucial in human development. As of 2011, small solar PV systems provide electricity to a few million households, and micro-hydro configured into mini-grids serves many more. Globally, over 44 million households use biogas made in household-scale digesters for lighting and/or cooking, and more than 166 million households rely on a new generation of more efficient biomass cooking stoves.[17] The United Nations Secretary-General, Ban Ki-moon, has said that renewable energy has the ability to lift the poorest nations to new levels of prosperity.[18]

Climate change concerns, coupled with high oil prices, peak oil, and increasing government support, are driving increasing renewable energy legislation, incentives, and commercialization (United Nations 2007). The existence of government spending, regulation, and policies in many countries has helped develop these industries and helped them to survive the global financial crisis better than many other sectors. According to a 2011 projection by the International Energy Agency, solar power generators may produce most of the world's electricity within 50 years, dramatically reducing the emissions of greenhouse gases that harm the environment.

There are many kinds of renewable energy sources. These include sunlight, wind, rain, tides, geothermal, and biomass. Among these, solar has gained more attention thus far, maybe due to its generous accessibility to all. A proof to this claim is standards developed by countries with unfavourable weather conditions and low irradiance. Scientists have devised storage devices to harness solar energy in daylight and use later at nights. Another noble idea is to use renewable energy as a hybrid system or as a backup system. This will lead to a higher efficiency even in worse climatic conditions (Lynas 2008).

8   Energy efficiency

Today everyone is being bombarded with messages to become environmentally conscious and reduce the impact of climate change. As weather systems become unpredictable, with longer, hotter summers, extended droughts, and shorter and milder winters, most people everywhere are experiencing the wrath of nature, arguably resulting from human activities. Humans have exploited the depths of the Earth to extract precious metals and generated a seemingly insatiable need for oil in order to develop economically and technologically (see, for example, the Stern Report 2006). Fertile land has been claimed and deforestation has been undertaken to create more space for dwellings and make factories for newer, smaller products for the expanding human population. The life cycle of products has considerably decreased and there is now a common practice, for example, of buying newer models rather than fixing or retaining the older version of televisions or cars. The human race is nevertheless awakening and realizing the detrimental and in many instances irreversible damage that past actions have done to the planet.

A number of initiatives can and are being adopted by individuals at home and within many industrial sectors to curb the application of equipment and practices that produce greenhouse gas emissions. Most people are attempting to behave better towards the ecological environment so that future generations are, at least, not worse off than the current generations and enjoy the same if not better access to natural landscapes, a clean environment, and resources.

9   Critiquing sustainability

Various factors have brought to prominence a concern for sustainability, and this is integrated with a concern for raw material and energy consumption and conservation. In this context, sustainability implies that society must use no more of a resource than can be regenerated. This can be defined in terms of the carrying capacity of the ecosystem (Hawken 1993) and described with input–output models of resource consumption. Viewing an organization as part of a wider social and economic system implies that these effects must be taken into account, not just for the measurement of costs and value created in the present, but also for the future of the business itself. This approach to sustainability is based upon the Gaia hypothesis (Lovelock 1979) – a model in which the whole of the ecosphere, and all living matter therein, is co-dependent upon its various facets and forms a complete system. According to this hypothesis, this complete system and all components of the system are interdependent and equally necessary for maintaining the earth as a planet capable of sustaining life.

Such concerns are pertinent at a macro level of society as a whole, or at the level of the nation-state, but are equally relevant at the micro level of the corporation or individual. At this level, measures of sustainability would consider the rate at which resources are consumed by the organization in relation to the rate at which resources can be regenerated. Unsustainable operations can be accommodated either by developing sustainable operations or by planning for a future lacking in resources that are currently required. In practice, organizations mostly tend to aim towards less unsustainability by increasing the efficient use of resources. An example would be an energy efficiency programme.

Sustainability is a controversial topic because it means different things to different people. Nevertheless, there is a growing awareness that there is a debate about what sustainability means and the extent to which it can be delivered by corporations in the easy manner they promise and as assumed by the Brundtland Commission – or even at all (United Nations Commission on Environment and Development (Schmidheiny 1992). It has become part of a policy landscape being explicitly contested by the United Nations, nation-states and big business through the vehicles of the World Business Council for Sustainable Development (WBCSD) and ICC International Chamber of Commerce (ICC) (see, for example, Beder 1997; Mayhew 1997; Gray and Bebbington 2001).

There is further confusion surrounding the concept of sustainability: to the purist, sustainability implies nothing more than stasis – the ability to continue in an unchanged manner – but often it is taken to imply development in a sustainable manner (Marsden 2000; Hart and Milstein 2003) and the terms "sustainability" and "sustainable development" are for many viewed as synonymous. As far as corporate sustainability is concerned, then, the confusion is exacerbated by the fact that the term "sustainable" has been used in the management literature over the last 30 years (see, for example, Reed and DeFillippi 1990) to merely imply continuity. Thus Zwetsloot (2003) is able to conflate corporate social responsibility with the techniques of continuous improvement and innovation to imply that sustainability is thereby ensured.[19]

An almost unquestioned assumption is that growth remains possible (Elliott 2005) and therefore sustainability and sustainable development are synonymous. Indeed, the economic perspective of post-Cartesian market-driven ontologies predominates and growth is considered to be not just possible but also desirable (see, for example, Spangenberg 2004). So it is possible therefore for Daly (1992) to argue that the economics of development is all that needs to be addressed and that this can be dealt with through the market by the clear separation of the three basic economic goals of efficient allocation, equitable distribution, and sustainable scale. Hart (1997) goes further and regards the concept of sustainable development merely as a business opportunity, arguing that once a company identifies its environmental strategy, then opportunities for new products and services become apparent.

There seem therefore to be two commonly held assumptions which permeate the discourse of corporate sustainability. The first is that sustainability is synonymous with sustainable development. The second is that a sustainable company will exist merely by recognizing environmental and social issues and incorporating them into its strategic planning. Both of these assumptions are rejected as they are based upon an unquestioning acceptance of market economics predicated in the need for growth. While such market economics is not necessarily rejected, it is argued that the acceptance of market economics has led to the assumptions about sustainability which have confused the debate. Thus it is considered imperative at this point to reiterate the basic tenet of sustainability, that sustainable activity is activity in which decisions made in the present do not restrict the choices available in the future. If this tenet of sustainability is accepted, then it follows that development is neither a necessary nor desirable aspect of sustainability. Sustainable development (Daly 1996) may well be possible, and even desirable in some circumstances, but it is not an integral aspect of sustainability.

Most analysis of sustainability[20] (e.g. Dyllick and Hockerts 2002) recognizes only a two-dimensional approach of the environmental and the social. A few (e.g. Spangenberg 2004) recognize a third dimension, which is related to organization behaviour. Aras and Crowther (2007a) argue that restricting analysis to such dimensions is deficient. One problem is the fact that the dominant assumption by researchers is based upon the incompatibility of optimizing, for a corporation, both financial performance and social/environmental performance. In other words, financial performance and social/environmental performance are seen as being in conflict with each other (see Crowther 2002; 2012). Consequently, most work in the area of corporate sustainability does not recognize the need for acknowledging the importance of financial performance as an essential aspect of sustainability and therefore fails to undertake financial analysis alongside – and integrated with – other forms of analysis for this research.[21] Aras and Crowther (2007b) argue that this is an essential aspect of corporate sustainability and therefore adds a further dimension to the analysis of sustainability. Furthermore, they argue that the third dimension sometimes recognized as organizational behaviour needs to actually comprise a much broader concept of corporate culture. They therefore argue that there are four aspects of sustainability which need to be recognized and analyzed, namely:

- **Societal influence**, which is defined as a measure of the impact that society makes upon the corporation in terms of the social contract and stakeholder influence
- **Environmental impact**, which is defined as the effect of the actions of the corporation upon its geophysical environment
- **Organizational culture**, which is defined as the relationship between the corporation and its internal stakeholders, particularly employees, and all aspects of that relationship
- **Finance**, which is defined as providing an adequate return for the level of risk undertaken.

These four must be considered as the key dimensions of sustainability, all of which are equally important. This analysis is therefore considerably broader – and more complete – than that of others.

Often sustainability and sustainable development are conflated, but they are actually different. Sustainable development is development that attempts to bridge the divide between *economic growth* and *environmental protection*, while taking into account other issues traditionally associated with development. It seeks to develop means of supporting economic growth while supporting biodiversity, relieving poverty, and without using up natural capital in the short term (Daly 1999) at the expense of long-term development. There is a growing consensus that firms and governments in partnership should accept moral responsibility for social welfare and for promoting individuals' interest in economic transactions (Amba-Rao 1993).

As already stated, there is a considerable degree of confusion surrounding the concept of sustainability: to the purist, sustainability implies nothing more than stasis – the ability to continue in an unchanged manner – but often it is taken to imply development in a sustainable manner (Marsden 2000; Hart and Milstein 2003) and the terms "sustainability" and "sustainable development" are for many viewed as synonymous. In this chapter the definition has been taken as being concerned with stasis (Aras and Crowther 2008); at the corporate level, if development is possible without jeopardizing that stasis, then this is a bonus rather than a constituent part of that sustainability. Moreover, sustainable development is often misinterpreted as focusing solely on environmental issues. In reality, it is a much broader concept as sustainable development policies encompass three general policy areas: economic, environmental, and social. In support of this, several United Nations texts, most recently the 2005 World Summit Outcome Document, refer to the 'interdependent and mutually reinforcing pillars' of sustainable development as economic development, social development, and environmental protection.

10   Reacting to sustainability: energy efficiency

Energy use in the residential sector is defined as the energy consumed by households, excluding transportation uses. In 2007 about 14 per cent of the world's delivered energy was consumed in the residential sector, and an average growth rate of 1.1 per cent per year is expected from 2007 to 2035.[22] World energy consumption in the residential sector doesn't seem even, and countries use energy according to factors such as their income levels, natural resources, climate, and available energy infrastructure. Therefore, due to a higher income level, typical households in OECD nations generally use more energy than those in non-OECD nations. This is partly because higher income levels allow OECD households to have larger homes and purchase more energy-using equipment. Larger homes generally require more energy to provide heating, air conditioning, and lighting, and they tend to include more energy-using appliances, such as televisions and laundry equipment. Smaller structures usually require less energy, because they contain less space to be heated or cooled, produce less heat transfer with the outdoor environment, and typically have fewer occupants.

A comparison of the United States and China as an example proves this claim. The average residence in China currently has an estimated 300 square feet of living space or less per person than in the United States, where the average residence has an estimated 680 square feet of living space per person.[23] The US GDP per capita and its estimated residential energy use per capita in 2007 were $43,076 and 37.2 million Btu respectively,[24] whereas the same data for China amounted to only $5,162 and 4.0 million Btu, which means only about one-eighth and one-ninth the US level, respectively.[25]

Energy usage is of course dependent upon the cost of that energy – and primarily therefore the price of oil. Over the last decade the price of crude oil has varied between $16 per barrel and $150, although currently around $100.[26] It is expected, however, that the price will continue to follow a rising trend as demand continues to increase at a faster rate than supply. This has implications for sustainable development which need to be considered.

In an environment in which the shortage of oil has an effect upon energy, then consumption is an important issue for economic reasons as well as for environmental reasons. In the current environment of economic crisis coupled with a concern for the environment brought about by the general acceptance that climate change is taking place, there is a greater concern for sustainability and for sustainable consumption. Such consumption is based upon making decisions on criteria other than price, or at least purchase price. This is particularly true of consumer durables, which comprise significant items of household expenditure. Running costs become more important – not just to survive in the recession but also as a proxy for energy consumption, which is concerned with effects upon climate change. Basically, the lower the energy consumption, the more sustainable and the greater the effect upon the climate. In general, therefore, there are twin motives for the purchasing of energy efficient consumer durables.

Both reasons have an effect upon purchasing decisions as far as consumer durables are concerned. Ellis et al. (2007) have indicated that a decrease in average energy consumption of appliances has been witnessed, together with their becoming cheaper. This means energy efficiency would lead to reduced running costs together with capital costs.

'Upgrading your appliances to new, more efficient models can make a great impact in how much water and energy you use each day. Manufacturers have made great progress in reducing the environmental impact of appliances'. This is the exact wording used on the website of the Association of Home Appliance Makers (AHAM)[27]and it can be considered as a clever way to motivate consumerism. The scientific research, however, verifies such a claim. According to the Atomic Energy Authority (AEO), residential delivered energy consumption in the AEO 2011 Reference case grows from 11.1 quadrillion Btu in 2009 to 11.7 quadrillion Btu in 2035, 0.4 quadrillion Btu less than in the AEO 2010 Reference case.

In its report AEO has claimed, 'The recent consensus agreement among efficiency advocates and manufacturers leads to lower projected energy use for residential refrigerators and freezers, clothes washers, clothes dryers, dishwashers, and room air conditioners'. This is an emphasis on the major role of manufacturers in the world of energy-saving.

11   Standardization and manufacturing

A high production volume along with reduced variety was the major characteristic of mass production introduced by Henry Ford. The approach of his peer auto manufacturers is that the customer can have a car painted any colour that he wants so long as it is black (Ford 1922). In order to simplify the production process, auto manufacturers standardized their products. Such an attitude towards production allowed manufacturers to make use of specialized machinery without requiring highly proficient workers. Manufacturers could make standardized cars in mass volumes and appropriate costs, which is referred to as "economy of scale".

Today, standards are a vital part of everyone's life. They grow in number or modify in context along with the growth in scientific and economical life. When products and services meet people's expectations, they tend to take this for granted and be unaware of the role of standards. However, when standards are absent, it is soon noticed. People soon care when products turn out to be of poor quality, do not fit, are incompatible with equipment that they already have, or are unreliable or dangerous.

Dependence on standardization is directly related to the development level of industry and knowledge. Endless innovations and new ideas necessitate more standards or modified ones. Sustainability is indicated as the fashionable concept of the moment (Aras and Crowther 2008). Some people may believe that this almost modern and fashionable concept demands new standardization activities, as the International Organization for Standardization (ISO) strategic plan 2005–2010 is titled "Standards for a Sustainable World". It means that ISO aims at providing new standards which would contribute effectively to sustainability. Still, others may believe in the necessity of drastic changes in the standardization process to accommodate sustainability. For instance, although about 75 per cent of ISO membership comprises developing countries, their actual participation in drafting and voting process is limited. Therefore, international standards, aimed at establishing the acceptable minimum quality levels, are normally prepared based on comments received from the active 25 per cent. The developing countries, i.e. the majority of ISO members, usually find it difficult to conform to international standards. Hence, as the international standardization process does not encompass all the stakeholders' needs, at least for the time being, it is not a process that conforms to sustainability requirements. This is a fact opposing to the ISO strategy mentioned above. Among issues of concern, it should be noted that the many studies carried out by the Food and Agriculture Organization (FAO) of the United Nations, the United Nations Industrial Development Organization (UNIDO), and others, relating to evaluation of current standardization policies and strategies in developing countries, reveal that their implementation is hindered by a number of constraints. Of these, the most significant are:

- Inadequacy of the regulatory and institutional framework set to govern standardization activities
- Weakness of the actors from public agencies, the private sector, and civil society alike
- Insufficient funding allocated to standards development and distribution activities
- Lack of metrology and quality control infrastructure and tools.

As a result, the developing countries may need to modify international standards to make them appropriate for use in their countries, which is contrary to the ISO's global relevance policy according to which 'the required characteristic of an international standard is that it can be used and implemented as broadly as possible by affected industries and other stakeholders in markets around the world'.

As an example, ISO 15502 recently adopted as IEC 62552 specifies a storage temperature test with such loose limitations. The problem arises that if it is necessary for the appliance to cycle when testing the storage temperatures, it is required that a limit be set for the number of cycles. At the this time, there is no difference between an appliance working at 98 per cent and another working at just 40 per cent of its capacity, if they meet the temperatures specified. Nor is the standard sustainability friendly. Due to environmental concerns, it is incumbent on a modern standard for refrigerating appliances to specify the range of permitted refrigerants and foaming (insulating) materials. The existing standard lacks this specification.

However, this is not the case with most IEC standards, which limit the quality level and let the operator specify what a good or bad product is. Standards for safety of household appliances are a good example in this regard, although some standards, such as those of TVs, lack the clarity and transparency necessary to be a socially responsible standard.

Implementation of standards is another matter of concern. Some people believe in the necessity of mandatory application of standards. They believe that society has not yet attained a high enough ethical awareness to let it act as it wishes. They believe that such an expectation is achieved only in a utopia. Besides, it would be devastating to take the risk of relying on voluntary social responsibility solely to lead people to a heavenly world of integrity and high quality products and services. Other people may believe society should avoid implementing standards as just so many more rules and regulations. Such people agree on the need to enhance social responsibility, which would then act automatically to control people's performance. Therefore, it would be wise, they believe, to raise one's ethical culture rather than to set rules and standards to control people. According to such a philosophy, EU Commission [(2002) 347 final: 5] has defined corporate social responsibility as: '. . . a concept whereby companies integrate social and environmental concerns in their business operations and in their interaction with their stakeholders on a voluntary basis'.

However a standard is going to be applied, it needs tools and substrates, known as conformity assessment. Conformity assessment is 'the process of determining that a product, process or service complies with specified requirements' (ISO Development Manual: 2). Testing, inspection, and certification are among tools of conformity assessment. The process of conformity assessment is a matter needing greater concern. Conformity assessment, if applied through the right aspects, results in a harmonized control over products, which supports equity in marketing. These aspects are as important as or even more important than the standard itself. The existence of notified bodies to authorize conformity assessment bodies, if different from the national standards body, is a matter of great concern, especially in developing countries that lack enough resources. There are instances of authorized testing laboratories lacking needed competencies as being unbiased. In some developing countries, manufacturers have instituted laboratories for testing products of the same type as their own. Surprisingly, they are authorized as independent bodies to test products manufactured inside or outside the country. It is clear that such authorized bodies are not 100 per cent socially responsible enterprises that issue test results that might even work against their own interests.

12 Conclusions

The discourse in the developed world is towards the conservation of resources and towards energy efficiency. This is reflected in both manufacturing resources and consumer purchasing decisions. It is generally accepted that resource depletion will affect the economic environment. It is not yet fully recognized, however, that development in other parts of the world will exacerbate this pressure and lead to greater competition for the available resources. This competition will be economic but could also become physical as the world adjusts to a new geopolitical environment. This is not yet recognised.

Notes

1 General Agreement on Trade and Tariffs.
2 World Trade Organization – the successor to GATT.
3 And repeated, although in a much less pronounced manner, in 2012.
4 The Kyoto Protocol is an agreement made under the United Nations Framework Convention on Climate Change. Countries that ratify this protocol have committed themselves to reducing their emissions of carbon dioxide and five other greenhouse gases, or to engage in emissions trading if they maintain their emissions of these gases or do not reduce them to the extent agreed upon. At present the USA and Kazakhstan are the only signatory countries which have not ratified the protocol.

5 See, for example, Reay (2005).
6 http://www.parliament.uk/documents/post/postpn268.pdf/.
7 Thus this is generally accepted in Europe and much of Asia, but the consensus is by no means worldwide.
8 Ampang was the principal area for tin mining. The Suria KLCC shopping mall has always been at the centre of Kuala Lumpur life, and the Petronas twin towers stand in this area. The extinct tin has been replaced by oil and gas as the fuel for Kuala Lumpur development but this too is ending as it becomes fully extracted.
9 And most probably any other parts of the world also – it would be instructive to correlate the presence of oil with conflicts.
10 In 1956 Dr King Hubbert, a geologist working for Shell Oil, developed his theory about the depletion of finite resources like fossil fuels. Now commonly known as Hubbert's Peak, his theory explains that production rates of oil and gas will increase to a peak and then rapidly taper off as reserves are depleted. He developed his theory to explain the coming reduction in production of oil in the United States, and it is generally accepted that his theory was correct about this.
11 Principally this means oil and gas, which are extracted from underground or, more recently, from the surface, such as from the oil shales of Canada. As these sources become scarcer, the climate effects of extracting the oil and gas become more profound. Indeed, the latest technique of fracking is considered by many to be environmentally disastrous.
12 'Renewables 2011: Global Status Report', p. 17, 1. http://www.ren21.net/Portals/97/documents/GSR/GSR2011_Master18.pdf/.
13 'Renewables 2011: Global Status Report', p. 15. http://www.ren21.net/Portals/97/documents/GSR/GSR2011_Master18.pdf/.
14 Photovoltaic systems (PV system) use solar panels to convert sunlight into electricity.
15 http://www.ventures-africa.com/2012/09/morocco-awards-1bn-solar-power-contract-to-saudis/.
16 'America and Brazil Intersect on Ethanol'. Renewableenergyaccess.com. http://www.renewableenergyaccess.com/rea/news/story?id=44896. Retrieved 21 November 2011.
17 'Renewables 2011: Global Status Report', p. 14. http://www.ren21.net/Portals/97/documents/GSR/GSR2011_Master18.pdf/.
18 'U.N. Secretary-General: Renewables Can End Energy Poverty'. Renewable Energy World. http://www.renewableenergyworld.com/rea/news/article/2011/08/u-n-secretary-general-renewables-can-end-energy-poverty?cmpid=WNL-Friday-August26–2011.
19 Still, in some parts of the world there are industrial engineers who don't know the exact meaning of social responsibility and think of it as something related to social sciences, rather than an integral aspect of sustainability. Sustainability requires research and development and technological development – which is what industrial engineering is concerned with.
20 Some people consider sustainability and sustainable development as synonymous, while others do not. Still others conflate it with social responsibility. For the purposes of this chapter, these differences do not matter.
21 Of course, the fact that many researchers do not have the skills to undertake such detailed financial analysis even if they considered it to be important might be a significant reason for this.
22 http://webcache.googleusercontent.com/search?q=cache:KuKQPH4yOGQJ:www.scribd.com/doc/52469321/Energy-and-Resources+Energy+use+in+the+residential+sector,+which+accounted+for+about+14+percent&cd=8&hl=en&ct=clnk&gl=my&client=firefox-a&source=www.google.com.my, Energy and Resources – Uganda Energy Production and Consumption Uganda SubSaharan Africa World/.
23 World Energy and Economic Outlook, International Energy Outlook 2008, Report #:DOE/EIA-0484(2008) Release Date: June 2008 http://www.xof1.com/energyConsumption.php/.
24 For example, Al Gore, a committed and visible environmental campaigner and Nobel Peace Prize winner for his work on climate change, has been extensively criticized because his Tennessee mansion is said to consume 20 times as much power as the average US home and 400 times as much as an average African home.
25 US Department of Energy, US Energy Information Administration, state energy information, detailed and overviews, http://www.eia.doe.gov/state – accessed 20 February 2011.
26 As at June and January 2012.
27 http://aham.typepad.com/ahams_blog/energy_efficiency/.

References

Amba-Rao, S.C. (1993). Multinational corporate social responsibility, ethics, interactions and third world governments: An agenda for the 1990s. *Journal of Business Ethics*, 12, 553–72.

Aras, G. and Crowther, D. (2007a). Sustainable corporate social responsibility and the value chain, in D. Crowther and M.M. Zain (eds.), *New Perspectives on Corporate Social Responsibility*. Aldershot: Gower, 109–28.

Aras, G. and Crowther, D. (2007b). Is the global economy sustainable?, in S. Barber (ed.), *The Geopolitics of the City*. London: Forum Press, 165–94.

Aras, G. and Crowther, D. (2008). Governance and sustainability: An investigation into the relationship between corporate governance and corporate sustainability. *Management Decision*, 46(3), 433–48.

Beder, S. (1997). *Global Spin: The Corporate Assault on Environmentalism*. London: Green Books.

Conformity Assessment tools to support public policy, http://www.iso.org/sites/cascoregulators/03_considerations.html (Retrieved on October 20, 2015).

Crowther, D. (2002). *A Social Critique of Corporate Reporting*. Aldershot: Ashgate.

Crowther, D. (2012). *A Social Critique of Corporate Reporting: Semiotics and Web-Based Integrated Reporting*. Farnham: Gower.

Daly, H.E. (1992). Allocation, distribution, and scale: Towards an economics that is efficient, just, and sustainable. *Ecological Economics*, 6(3), 185–93.

Daly, H.E. (1996). *Beyond Growth*. Boston, MA: Beacon Press.

Daly, H.E. (1999). *Ecological Economics and the Ecology of Economics*. Cheltenham: Edward Elgar.

Deffeyes, K.S. (2004). Hubbert's Peak: The impending world oil shortage. *American Journal of Physics*, 72(1), 126–7.

Dyllick, T., and Hockerts, K. (2002). "Beyond the business case for corporate sustainability". *Business Strategy and the Environment*, 11, 130–141.

Elliott, S.R. (2005). Sustainability: An economic perspective. *Resources Conservations and Recycling*, 44, 263–77.

Ellis, M., Jollands, N., Harrington, L. and Meier, A. (2007). Do energy efficient appliances cost more? Proceedings of the ECEEE 2007 Conference. http://www.eceee.org/library/conference_proceedings/eceee_Summer_Studies/2007/Panel_6/6.025/paper (Retrieved on Mar 12, 2014).

Ford, H. (1922). *My Life and Work*. New York: Doubleday.

Gray, R.H. and Bebbington, K.J. (2001). *Accounting for the Environment*. London: Sage.

Hart, S.L. (1997). Beyond greening: Strategies for a sustainable world. *Harvard Business Review*, 75(1), 66–76.

Hart, S.L. and Milstein, M.B. (2003). Creating sustainable value. *Academy of Management Executive*, 17(2), 56–67.

Hawken, P. (1993). *The Ecology of Commerce*. London: Weidenfeld & Nicolson.

International Organization for Standardization, Social Responsibility IAO 26000, http://www.iso.org/iso/home/standards/iso26000.htm (Retrieved on October 10, 2015).

ISO central secretariat (2006); Metrology, standardization and conformity assessment: Building an infrastructure for sustainable development www.iso.org/iso/devt_3pillars_2006.pdf (Retrieved on October 20, 2015).

Kerr, R.A. (1998). The next oil crisis looms large – and perhaps close. *Science*, 281, 1128–31.

Lindsay (2007). International standards and public policies; ISO General Assembly 2007 www.iso.org/iso/livelinkgetfile?llNodeId=110665&llVolId=-2000 (Retrieved on September 14, 2015).

Lovelock, J. (1979). *Gaia*. Oxford: Oxford University Press.

Lovelock, J. (2006). *The Revenge of Gaia*. Harmondsworth: Penguin.

Lynas, M. (2008). *Six Degrees: Our Future on a Hotter Planet*. London: HarperCollins.

Marsden, C. (2000). The new corporate citizenship of big business: Part of the solution to sustainability. *Business & Society Review*, 105(1), 9–25.

Mayhew, N. (1997). Fading to Grey: The use and abuse of corporate executives' 'representational power', in R. Welford (ed.), *Hijacking Environmentalism: Corporate Response to Sustainable Development*. London: Earthscan, 63–95.

Reay, D. (2005). *Climate Change Begins at Home*. Basingstoke: Macmillan.

Reed, R. and DeFillippi, R. J. (1990). Causal ambiguity, barriers to imitation, and sustainable competitive advantage. *Academy of Management Review*, 15(1), 88–102.

Renewable Energy, http://www.liquisearch.com/renewable_energy (Retrieved on June 9, 2015)

Schmidheiny, S. (1992). *Changing Course*. New York: MIT Press.

Spangenberg, J.H. (2004). Reconciling sustainability and growth: Criteria, indicators, policy. *Sustainable Development*, 12, 76–84.

Stern, Nicholas. Stern Review on the Economics of Climate Change, 30 October 2006. http://mudancasclimaticas.cptec.inpe.br/~rmclima/pdfs/destaques/sternreview_report_complete.pdf (Retrieved on October 20, 2015).

The Commission of the European Communities, Corporate Social Responsibility: A business contribution to Sustainable Development, Brussels, 2nd July 2002 COM(2002) 347 final http://trade.ec.europa.eu/doclib/docs/2006/february/tradoc_127374.pdf (Retrieved on October 20, 2015).

United Nations Environment Prog Analysis of Trends and Issues in Developing Countries. http pdf (Retrieved on Sept 23, 2016)

United Nations Environment Programme. (2007). Global Trends in Sustainable Energy Investment 2007: Analysis of Trends and Issues in the Financing of Renewable Energy and Energy Efficiency in OECD and Developing Countries. http://www.unep.org/pdf/72_Glob_Sust_Energy_Inv_Report_(2007).pdf (Retrieved on Sept 23, 2016).

Waeyenbergh, G. and Pintelon, L. (2002). A framework for maintenance concept development. *International Journal of Production Economics*, 77(3), 299–313.

Weidema, B.P., Thrane, M., Christensen, P., Schmidt, J. and Lokke, S. (2008). Carbon footprint: A catalyst for life cycle assessment? *Journal of Industrial Ecology*, 12(1), 3–6.

Wiedman, T. and Minx, J. (2007). A definition of 'carbon footprint'. ISAUK Research report 07–01. ISAUK Research & Consulting. http://citeseerx.ist.psu.edu/viewdoc/download?doi=10.1.1.467.6821&rep=rep1&type=pdf (Retrieved on Sept 23, 2016).

Zwetsloot, G.I.J.M. (2003). From management systems to corporate social responsibility. *Journal of Business Ethics*, 44(2/3), 201–7.

2 The representation of produced value for health care organizations

A proposal for "socially responsible reporting" through "non-social" reporting tools in the Italian health care sector[1]

Carmela Gulluscio and Patrizia Torrecchia

1 Introduction

In the context of social accounting reports, the last decades saw a shift of attention to the results. Its measurement and evaluation was not limited to the domain of quantitative-monetary variables, but it expanded toward more general dimensions: non-monetary and qualitative-quantitative. For this reason, information is now considered the base upon which to build rational choices, trying to overcome the vagueness that has largely characterized the non-economic and financial objectives. In this context, even in the health care sector, a strong focus has emerged on the definition of "produced value" and towards the identification of suitable instruments to measure it.

In public administration and, in this case, health care facilities, the assessment of performance was mainly based on economic indicators found in the financial statements. In fact, the capacity of public health agencies to "create value" cannot be confined simply to achieve conditions of economic equilibrium, financial and capital. Their achievement is a minimum condition, necessary but not sufficient, to ensure their survival in time. In this view, is not sufficient that the external reporting of public health agencies focuses solely on their ability to operate in conditions of economic and financial equilibrium. The ability to be effective (matching all the different health needs) and efficient must also be taken into account.

The traditional documents (i.e. financial statements) provide only some information on the ability of health care to create a higher value than the value of the utilities consumed in the production process and payment of benefits. They do not provide information on a number of factors that are crucial in the ability to create value. As an example, they give no information on the facility's ability to meet the health needs of the community, which is the basic objective that guides the establishment and maintenance of these organizations.

After highlighting the current reporting system and its main characteristics, this chapter proposes the adoption of a system of accountability which is broader than traditional economic and financial communications, taking into account the multidimensionality of the health value and also the conspicuous presence of determinants that cannot be measured with traditional accounting tools. This concept is extended from financial statements to the largest organizational information system, with specific reference to public health sector. Thus, we affirm the existence of a relationship among: a) the selection of the stakeholders to whom the information is reported; b) the purposes attributable to the information system of an organization; c) the main types of information that the corporate information system is called upon to provide.

To this end, we identify some tools to communicate to various stakeholders the most relevant aspects of the value produced. Thus, we propose to use an information tool as part of the traditional patterns accompanying the financial statements to provide information normally contained in the tools used to support (corporate) social responsibility. In essence, we suggest using a "non-social" reporting tool to comply with the requirements of "social accountability".

2   Some critical notes and a first proposal for the income statement

In consideration of the financial statement, as required by Italian law and according to the ministerial structure for public health organizations, legislators thought to adapt this model according to the peculiarities of the sector.

Over the past years, several rules have changed the content of public health organizations' financial statements – in particular, the Ministerial Decree 20 October (1994), the Ministerial Decree 11 February (2002), the Ministerial Decree 13 November (2007), Ministerial Decree 31 December (2007) and, ultimately, the Legislative Decree N. 118/2011.

By reference to Article 2423-ter of the Civil Code made by D. Lgs. (Legislative Decree) No 502/92 amended by D. Lgs. No 517/93, the regions had the opportunity to make ministerial changes to the outline of the statement, and Lgs. N. 118/2011 tried to solve the problem in an attempt to standardize financial statements, providing a model of good budgeting for all health care organizations.

Before Legislative Decree N. 118/2011, the financial statements of public health organizations appeared as the balance sheet, income statement and notes (although only the first two documents were the subject of specific rules in terms of structure and content). Now, however, these documents are accompanied by the financial report and the management report.

We will focus on the content of the balance sheet and the income statement.

Paragraph 5, Article VI, of the D. Lgs. N. 502/92 shows the demand for specific schemes for financial reports summarizing the public health agencies. This task, assigned to the Ministries of Health and the Treasury, was accomplished by the Ministerial Decree 20 October (1994).

The drafters of the decree have seen fit to borrow from civil law, defining a financial statement structure that follows the kind required for limited companies. They made changes only as needed, for formal entries specifically related to the special requirements of the health care field. As regards the balance sheet, the section is divided into four macro classes of assets:

1   Fixed assets
2   Current assets

3   Accrued income and prepaid expenses
4   Memorandum accounts, divided into six liabilities:

    a   Equity
    b   Provisions for risks and charges
    c   Indemnities
    d   Payables
    e   Accruals and deferred
    f   Memorandum accounts.

As can be seen already, there are strong similarities and few differences with the statutory balance sheet (art. 2424 c.c.). The similarities relate to its structure in macro classes, classes and items, respectively, preceded by capital letters, Roman numerals and Arabic numerals.

If we look at the differences, we see that there is no letter *A* at the macro level. This would obviously be meaningless, as it provides the statutory accounts for "Loans from shareholders for capital contributions". In the section on liabilities, the Equity macro class has a different composition. With regard to the scheme indicated by the Ministerial Decree 20 October (1994) for the income statement, this takes a scalar form, again in line with the statutory model (art. 2425 c.c.).

This scheme is divided into macro classes:

1   Value of production
2   Cost of production
3   Financial income and expense
4   Impairment of financial assets
5   Extraordinary income and expenses.

The form chosen should allow for "intermediate outcomes". However, there is a clear representation of the results arising from operations, which could lead to useful considerations in relation to the overall economic performance in a given year. Even for the income statement, you see the full overlap between the macro classes provided by the scheme and those of the ministerial statutory scheme. The few differences emerge at the level of individual items, and in the macro class the "production value" is the "capitalized cost" instead of "capitalization of internal construction".

It should be noted, in fact, that we are talking about public companies whose major revenues are represented in the first item of the income statement or by the operating grants, and not from the proceeds arising from production and, therefore, directly linked to related costs.

For everything mentioned above, one wonders at this point whether accounting earnings, capital, held for more according to the system of income, are really best suited to represent the trends of public health agencies. The accounting system, in fact, is commonly used in Italy by the industry to investigate the main return on capital invested, with particular attention to ownership interests. For all the things above mentioned, it is perhaps simplistic to transpose this approach uncritically from the field of private firms to that of public health agencies in consideration to their significant social value. It would be more correct to consider a more strictly economic social account, held in the second example, the system of value-added, which also looks at the remuneration of the other factors of production. In a hypothetical balance sheet, a criterion of an accounting nature for classification as a function would be used, in opposition to the civil law that classifies the entries according to the progressive cash criterion.

Then, our proposal arises from the intersection between the tradition in public accountancy (Cassandro, D'Ippolito) and the accounting system of value-added (Ardemani), all adapted to a specific class of companies.

Through an analysis of the different stakeholders' expectations, it is reasonable to claim that the objective that should guide public health management is the "health value", a particular configuration of the public value. This is defined as 'the satisfaction of (expressed or latent) health needs of single individuals or the community, respecting the objectives established by the public planning (national, regional, etc.), timely, in comfort [sic] conditions, without waste of resources, maintaining the conditions of economic, financial and capital balance, with the parallel social balance, enhancing the intellectual capital and guaranteeing the knowledge development and improvement in the medical and health sector' (Torrechia P. and Gulluscio C., 2014, 198–199).

The accounting dimension (economic and financial) is only a part of the overall value that the public health administrations have to produce and distribute to the stakeholders.

Despite the fact that Italian health administrations are among the first public organizations in the country that abandoned traditional public sector accounting in favour of full accrual (commercial) accounting, adopting a financial statement model used in private companies (according to the Fourth Council Directive 78/660/EC of 25 July 1978), the results obtained were unexciting.

Health value is a mixed concept, made of different dimensions. Some of these dimensions relate to quantitative analysis (for instance, economic and financial data, number of cases treated, etc.), but other dimensions can be expressed only with qualitative aspects (for example, patients' satisfaction, the courtesy, kindness and availability of personnel, treatment, facility security, etc.).

Wanting to make one of the most significant examples of socio-economic survey in accounting, you can take into account the wages to employees, and, as is known, the system of income represents a change in economic and income received in the accounts of income derived in the series.

In the shift from income to value-added system, the nature of the account changes. The option in favour of economic and social accounts would be received, internal lines to the accounting system, that is, without carrying the so-called reclassification, to a configuration of value-added income. In a sort of comparison between the income statement of costs, revenues and inventories and the value-added income, the cost for staff, although always in the back section of the "give", assumes a very different meaning. In fact it is no longer a cost of production to be contrasted with the same value to determine "the" operating profit, but a provision of value-added, that "one" of the production income. Figure 2.1 is a sketch of the financial accounts.

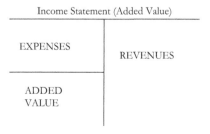

Figure 2.1 Accounting

But there is more. The configuration of value-added, in fact, is still used in the business world. It could be generalized effectively by resorting to the typical economic flows, however, making some adjustments as indicated above. Recall, in particular, that these flows had on the positive side the name of "active transfers"; on the negative side the name of "fuel supply". The configuration adopted, therefore, will highlight the institutional management or, more correctly, the final management, separately from the others and, perhaps more important, with a terminology that is attributable to each of the configurations as the budget comes from a tradition of journalism specifically.

So it is called the "entrance", "shopping", "surplus or deficit" without, however, that the words can be confused with the nearly homonym "cash flows". With respect to this proposed configuration, which could be called "added value and delivery of services" for purposes of determining the economic viability of the companies in question, the balance sheet is to have a secondary importance and therefore will be ignored at this time. Suffice to mention that it will provide a summary in which are recorded the quality and quantity of the assets of operating in an economic instrument aimed to the prospectus, however, the determination of the value-added and the results of different management, first and foremost that final. So in a hypothetical balance sheet a criterion will be used for classification as a function of an accounting nature, unlike the civil law that classifies the entries according to the progressive cash.

In summary, then, our proposal stems from the intersection of a tradition in the strict sense of public accountancy (Cassandro, D'Ippolito) with the accounting system of value-added (Ardemani), all adapted to a specific class of companies. At the conclusion of our analysis, we would like to gather all the critical remarks that were previously undertaken in a unique pattern of purposeful character. Evidently the latter was unable to take any definitive but it may be useful to check the consistency of all that has been said so far. As was anticipated, the income statement shows a pattern in it set up to 'added value and delivery of services'. The positive economic flow management is the final representation in A) of the prospectus, and negative in B) and C).

The difference between A) and B) is that you get the added value of managing the final phase of training. Subtracting C), this gives the so-called surplus/deficit of the final management. Again, with reference to the economic results, it is preferred to use a terminology typical of public companies when the net flow results from a non-productive management. Considering, again, the fact that under physiological conditions the above "surplus/deficit" is basically zero, the value-added of the final management turns out to be equal to the sum of C), or to pay for the production factor labour, analogous to what happens in the national accounts.

3 Capacity and limits of financial statements to represent the value

Business economics theory (Onida, 1951; Capaldo, 1998; Zanda, 2007) identified a link among:

1 choice of privileged financial disclosure stakeholder
2 financial statement purpose
3 revenue and capital configuration.

The theory affirms that the purpose of a financial statement is strictly connected to the knowledge requirements of the main stakeholders. For public health administrations, the privileged recipients of the current financial statement model are the state and regional public authorities responsible for their control. To guarantee this control, the financial statement focuses on elements linked to the achievement of balances that are traditionally measured by accounting instruments (economic and financial). This financial statement model seems therefore oriented to determine minimal conditions to guarantee the survival of the health administration.

Actually, these public administrations are not the only ones interested in the management of public health organizations. Additional stakeholders[2] should be added and, among them, relevant roles are that of citizens, constituting the administered collectivity,[3] and human resources.[4] These subjects, together with superior public administrations, can be considered as leading stakeholders of public health organizations, not only because their interests deserve a dedicated protection, but also because these coincide with the interests of other stakeholders. Through an analysis of the different stakeholders' expectations, it is reasonable to claim that the objective that should guide public health management is the "health value", a particular configuration of the public value. This is defined as 'the satisfaction of (expressed or latent) health needs of single individuals or the community, respecting the objectives established by the public planning (national, regional, etc.), timely, in comfort conditions, without waste of resources, maintaining the conditions of economic, financial and capital balance, with the parallel social balance, enhancing the intellectual capital and guaranteeing the knowledge development and improvement in the medical and health sector' (Gulluscio, 2011).

As shown in the proposed definition, the accounting dimension (economic and financial) is only a part of the overall value that the public health administrations have to produce and distribute to the stakeholders. Therefore, it is fair to extend the prior remarks on the financial statement (forecasting and actual amounts) to the broader administration's disclosure system. A link should be made among:

1   Choice of the privileged stakeholder for the information of administration
2   Goals of the information system of administration
3   Main information types that the information system of administration should provide.

With reference to the health value definition, the current financial statements used by public health administrations provide for only some of these aspects. In particular, it focuses almost exclusively on economic and financial management, disregarding other aspects that would enable an assessment of creation or destruction of value. There is a lack of information related to the effectiveness of actions taken for health protection, with particular reference to the spin-off effect of prevention, diagnosis, care and rehabilitation activities on individuals and on community (outcome). It is therefore necessary to widen the information of public health administrations, including the aspects of health value that are "disregarded" by the traditional accounting information instruments.

4   Public sector social responsibility instruments and their ability to highlight the health value

The Italian business economics literature broadly debated the financial statement's inability to answer several knowledge needs of companies' stakeholders. As a result, several proposals, belonging to the context of social responsibility, were formulated. In particular, in the public administrations sector, social responsibility led to the adoption of several instruments, among them social, environmental and mandate balance. These instruments are combined with the traditional financial statement documents in an attempt to enhance the financial disclosure with additional content to satisfy the knowledge requirements of numerous stakeholders.

Several types of socially responsible reporting are added, on a voluntary basis, to official accounting documents. These do not follow rigid and predefined drafting schemes (as in the case of financial statements), but have a free structure acquiring different characteristics according to the organization and to stakeholders' knowledge requirements. Frequently, these instruments are based on drafting standards that gained credibility through use. For instance, several social accountability standards were formulated, including the Global Reporting Initiative (GRI), Accountability 1000 (AA1000), Gruppo di Studio per il Bilancio Sociale (GBS). Nonetheless, these documents are drafted differently from entity to entity and sometimes these reports are different within the same entity over time.

The lack of rigid and established schemes in social accounting constituted at the same time a quality and a fault:

- A quality, because, in the context of social responsibility, the possibility of testing new models enabled the developers to create interesting instruments that can continuously adapt to organizations and to their stakeholders' requirements in the attempt to balance the information with the actual users' needs.
- A fault, because, in the lack of established schemes, the risk exists that organizations create self-referenced instruments where only positive elements are highlighted and critical points are neglected.

Due to the many contributions offered by the theory and practice of social accounting, this chapter focuses on an instrument that normally describes only economic and financial aspects of the performance: the financial statement. This chapter investigates whether the financial statement is effectively unable to provide information on "social" aspects of company performance or, if appropriately structured, it can fulfil wider knowledge requirements.

Despite the fact that Italian health administrations are among the first public organizations in the country that abandoned traditional public sector accounting in favour of full accrual (commercial) accounting, adopting a financial statement model used in private companies (according to Fourth Council Directive 78/660/EEC of 25th July 1978), the results obtained were unexciting. Many health administrations follow a financial logic whereby they transformed financial accounting data into full accrual accounting data, adopting mechanisms that were not always effective. Furthermore, until recently, Italian laws on public health administration accounting just regulated the balance sheet and the income statement, disregarding the notes to the financial statement, the cash flow statement and the supplements (including the director's report on operations). The director's report on operations seems to be suitable for reporting some information related to the health value.

It is interesting to consider the contribution of Legislative Decree N. 118/2011, which provided 'regulations to harmonize accounting systems and financial statement schemes of regions, local authorities and their organizations, according to art. 1 and art. 2 of Law n. 42 5 May 2009'. As a consequence of this decree, a more detailed discipline was provided for public health administration financial reporting. It was not limited to the balance sheet and the income statement but also included the notes, the cash flow statement, the statement of changes in equity in the period and the report on operations.

We will analyse the director's report on operations, evaluating the possibility for it to contain some information on health value, as an alternative to the social report or other instruments that are typically used in the context of social responsibility. We do not intend to diminish the importance of reporting instruments in social responsibility, but to evaluate the possibility of using a "mandatory" reporting instrument to provide information that is currently communicated on a "voluntary" basis. We will also analyse the possibility of producing socially responsible reporting through "non-social" reporting tools.

5   Describing health value through the director's report on operations

Health value is a mixed concept, made of different dimensions. Some of these dimensions relate to quantitative analysis (for instance, economic and financial data, number of cases treated, etc.), but other dimensions can be expressed only with qualitative aspects (for example, patients' satisfaction, the courtesy, kindness and availability of personnel, treatment, facility security, etc.).

Considering that the health value is composed of verified, estimated and abstract quantities (Onida, 1971), but mainly by qualities that are not measurable, any attempt at quantification is questionable. Rather than looking for a quantitative identification, it is reasonable to seek a qualitative-quantitative description, combining numeric data with information on determined "qualities". To show this information, we propose to employ the report on operations, that is, an annex to the financial statement of public health administrations. According to the Legislative Decree N. 118/2011, the report must provide all the necessary information, whether prescribed by law or not,[5] regarding financial and economic activities. For each area comprising the health value (which will be briefly examined later on), we detected some information instruments that could provide descriptions to answer the stakeholders' needs. In particular, we propose to use:

1   Financial statement data (including classified data) to analyse economic and financial activities
2   Performance indicators and parameters to deepen the economic and financial management aspects, but also to highlight the satisfaction of health need, the performance of services in time and comfortable conditions, the achievement of goals set through national and regional planning and the efficient use of resources
3   Investigation of leadership style and degree of employee satisfaction, primarily through anonymous questionnaires, to analyse the organization climate
4   Parameters on research and personnel retraining, to analyse knowledge improvement in the health and medical sector.[6]

The use of performance parameters and indicators is not new in the health sector, as some administrations use these instruments to provide required information or to draft social accounting documents. These parameters and indicators are an instrument to provide some brief information on the creation of health value by a given administration. The report on operations will include some concise data as it will not be possible to include all these parameters and indicators. Therefore they will not appear in full but only as a synthesis.

In this chapter we propose to divide the operations report into two parts: a first part, with information required by law (in Italy Legislative Decree No 118/2011), and a second part, with information on the health value.

In the second part, whose contents are analysed below, a split into two subparts is proposed:

1   A first subpart, composed of seven sections, corresponding to the areas of the health value and containing qualitative and quantitative information. The quantitative information briefly presents the main indicators/parameters used to evaluate each specific value area, whereas the qualitative information provides a short assessment by the financial statement drafters on the contribution provided by the health administration for the production of value in that specific area.
2   A second subpart contains a brief table on the health value and provides a summary picture of value creation/destruction by the administration during a set period of time.

To summarize, in this chapter we focus exclusively on this second part, where the information is exclusively qualitative. Two quality typologies are assigned to each area of the health value: a positive quality (briefly indicating that the administration created a value), represented by the plus sign (+); and a negative quality (simply indicating that the administration did not manage to create value), represented by the minus sign (−).

The determination of positive and negative qualities should be carried out based on a subjective evaluation of the parameters and indicators chosen for the specific value area analysed (for instance, the evaluation could focus on financial and economic indicators, indicators related to patient satisfaction, the outcome of surveys on leadership and personnel satisfaction, the results contained in the research and personnel retraining accounts, etc.). These assessments, which are necessarily subjective, should be expressed by:

•   Health administration managers (general director, administrative director, health activities director)
•   A representative for each category of stakeholders, including:

   a   a representative from a patients' rights association
   b   a representative from a superior public administration of reference (for example the region)
   c   a human resources representative
   d   a representative from a research assessment centre or an expert on personnel training.

In order for the procedure to be rigorous, the assessments should be measured against standards set at regional and national levels.

It is important to provide information on the health value following a precise sequence, corresponding to a logical order here described. This sequence (Figure 2.2) divides the health value in the following areas:

1   Economic and financial equilibrium
2   Community health need satisfaction (expressed or implied)
3   Performance of services promptly and in comfortable conditions
4   Compliance with regional/national planned objectives set during the regional and national planning
5   Efficiency evaluation
6   Evaluation of an organizational climate favorable to the satisfaction of medical and health personnel
7   Contribution to medical and health knowledge creation or improvement.

HEALTH VALUE AREAS AND INSTRUMENTS USED FOR THE EVALUATION	Positive (+) or negative value (-)
1) ECONOMIC RESULTS EVALUATION	
1.A) DATA DERIVED FROM THE CLASSIFIED INCOME STATEMENT	
Data derived from the classified income statement related to the area of operational (health) management:	
1.A.1) value of health production	+/-
1.A.2) operational expenditures for consumption of external production factors	+/-
1.A.3) health added value	+/-
1.A.4) expenditures for consumption of internal production factors	+/-
1.A.5) health surplus/deficit	+/-
1.B) DATA DERIVED FROM THE ECONOMIC PERFORMANCE INDICATORS	
1.B.1) Economic performance indicators	+/-
2) HEALTH PROTECTION ACTIVITIES EFFECTIVENESS EVALUATION	
Data on external effectiveness (evaluation on the health need satisfaction – expressed or implied – by health services consumers) obtained through:	
2.A) external effectiveness indicators	+/-
2.B) customers' satisfaction survey results	+/-
3) EVALUATION OF ABILITY TO PROVIDE SERVICES IN SHORT TIME AND IN COMFORTABLE CONDITIONS	
Data on the external effectiveness (assessment of the perceived quality on services) gathered through:	
3.A) customer satisfaction survey results	+/-
4) EVALUATION ON COMPLIANCE WITH REGIONAL/NATIONAL PLANNED OBJECTIVES	
Data on internal effectiveness (achievement goals set by national/regional planning) gathered through:	
4.A) internal effectiveness indicators	+/-
5) EFFICIENCY EVALUATION	
Efficiency data gathered through:	
5.A) efficiency indicators	+/-
6) EVALUATION OF THE ORGANIZATIONAL CLIMATE AND LEADERSHIP STYLE	
Data on the presence/absence of an organizational climate favorable to the satisfaction of medical and health personnel:	
6.A) leadership style parameters and indicators	+/-
6.B) organizational climate parameters and indicators	+/-
6.C) parameters and indicators on performances connected to the leadership style	+/-
7) EVALUATION OF THE CONTRIBUTION TO MEDICAL AND HEALTH KNOWLEDGE CREATION AND/OR IMPROVEMENT	
Data on:	
7.A) contribution to the research activity	+/-
7.B) personnel retraining	+/-
1) FINANCIAL RESULTS EVALUATION	
1.C) DATA DRAWN FROM THE BALANCE SHEET	
Data drawn from the balance sheet related to the financial balances	
1.C.1) data related to the financial situation	+/-
1.D) DATA OBTAINED BY FINANCIAL PERFORMANCE INDICATORS	
1.D.1) financial performance indicators	+/-

Figure 2.2 Health value table

Number 1 is about compliance with the conditions of financial and economic balance. This area is divided into two subparts relating to the economic situation and the financial situation.

Although the first objective of public health organizations is to satisfy the health needs of the community, we decided to place the accounting balance compliance in first position because:

1   It is assumed that financial statement data should constitute a starting point to analyse the health value
2   This dimension represents an important aspect for value creation. In particular, within the economic situation, an important position is that of operating activities. The ability of the administration to cover the operating costs of the financial year with typical health income is an extremely significant indicator in the process of value creation.

Therefore, we decided to create a table on health value, putting first the information relating to economic activities (with specific attention to the area of operating activities). Only subsequently, at the end of the table, are the values on the financial situation provided as a closing element of the document. Thus particular relevance is given to the financial statement data, representing the opening and closing element of the analysis. In the first section of the table, which contains data on the economic situation, the data coming from the classification of the income statement in paragraph 5 were used.

Number 2 is about the effectiveness evaluation of the health protection activities. This immediately follows economic and financial management, as it represents the most important aspect of the health value. It is not possible to assess the value produced by the health administration without taking into account the institutional goal, which is the satisfaction of community health needs.

Having decided to represent the health value starting from financial statement data, we placed the information related to effectiveness in the second position,[7] referring to external effectiveness. The main instruments for its evaluation are external effectiveness indicators and other external parameters deriving from customer satisfaction surveys.

Number 3 is about evaluation of the ability to provide services promptly and in comfortable conditions. This aspect is connected to external effectiveness. As in Number 2, this evaluation is mainly based on customer satisfaction surveys.

Number 4 is about evaluation of compliance with regional/national planned objectives. This assesses internal effectiveness and is based on specific indicators and parameters (they can include, for instance, information on compliance with the maximum spending amount set via national or regional planning, presence of contributions by superior public administrations to cover the losses, compliance with the waiting times expected for specialized check-ups, etc.).

Number 5 is about the efficiency evaluation, with particular attention to operating efficiency. The specific indicators include those relating to the physical-technical outcome of production factors.

Number 6 is dedicated to evaluation of the presence or absence of an organizational climate that satisfies the expectations of medical and health personnel. More precisely, this area includes the following aspects:

•   Leadership type/quality and ability to motivate the employees
•   Leadership style consequences of the organizational climate

- Analysis of some performance indicators connected to the leadership style and organizational climate.

Number 7 is about assessment of the health administration's contribution to medical and health knowledge creation and/or improvement. This information is obtained through parameters and indicators relating to:

- Research activity performed (showing a direct contribution to knowledge, competencies and ability development)
- Personnel training and retraining (showing an indirect contribution).

For the sake of concision, it is not possible to provide an analysis of the parameters and indicators that are here proposed.

Figure 2.2 shows the health value creation/destruction path. The left column indicates, for each of the seven value areas, the data (parameters, indicators, etc.) used to assess the value created or destroyed by the administration. The right column can display either the positive sign (+), indicating a creation of value in a specific area, or a negative sign (–), indicating a destruction of value.

Thus the health value is expressed as a set of qualities (positive and negative) highlighting whether or not the health administration was able to achieve the goals that were considered as positive by the stakeholders of reference.

Notes

1 The idea of the chapter and bibliography is due to the common work of the two authors; points 1, 2 and 3 are to be attributed to Patrizia Torrecchia; points 4, 5 and 6 are to be attributed to Carmela Gulluscio.
2 Health administration stakeholders include citizens, health and non-health personnel, subjects operating according to agreements with the health administration, other public administrations, suppliers, universities and other research centres, trade unions, professional associations, voluntary associations and media.
3 These subjects are interested in health services that meet their needs and in fair consistency between the costs related to the funding of the health services (taxes, etc.) and the related benefits.
4 Human resources are principally interested in proportional remuneration to the quality and quantity of work provided, occupational health and safety, the possibility of career improvement and a stimulating, gratifying and involving work atmosphere.
5 For concision, the content of this report will not be described. Nonetheless, it is worth pointing out that, according to Legislative Decree N. 118/2011, the report on operations must include the following information: details on the territory, population assisted and entity's organization; details on services structure and organization; reports on production data for the time period analysed, split by assistance level; and economic-financial situation. This report could be the appropriate document to include information on the health value.
6 It is important to point out that Legislative Decree N. 118/2011 provided, for the scientific hospitalization and care institutes (Istituti di Ricovero e Cura a Carattere Scientifico), the introduction of the "research section budget". This is a specific economic account where research contribution, direct research costs, indirect management costs and net results are indicated. The net result is the difference between the research contributions (positive income elements) and the cost connected to the research (negative income elements). It is important to take into account the scientific research also for local health authorities and hospitals. Although research is not their main activity, they nonetheless contribute to knowledge, competencies and skills development in the health and medical field. It is furthermore significant to consider, not only costs and income produced by the research, but also the social consequences of these activities.
7 Although effectiveness is most relevant among public health administrations, it was placed in positions 2, 3 and 4 of the table to link the health value analysis to the financial statement data that are enriched by additional information (accounting or not).

References

Capaldo, P. (1998). *Reddito, capitale e bilancio di esercizio. Una introduzione.* Milan: Giuffrè.

Gulluscio, C. (2011). Le aziende sanitarie pubbliche: riflessioni in tema di bilancio e di valore. Rome: RIREA.

Onida, P. (1951). *Il bilancio d'esercizio nelle imprese. Significato economico del bilancio, problemi di valutazione.* Milan: Giuffrè.

Onida, P. (1971). *Economia d'azienda.* Turin: Utet.

Torrecchia, P., and Gulluscio, C. (2014). Social Responsibility and Healtcare Public Sector: Some Notes on the Concept of "Value" Corporate Social Responsibility in the Global Business World. eds. Asli Yuksel Mermod and Samuel O. Idowu, Springer, Heidelberg.

Zanda, G. (2007). *Il bilancio delle società. Lineamenti teorici e modelli di redazione.* Turin: Giappichelli.

3 The notion of sustainability in strategies of Polish companies

The perspective of WIG20 firms

Maria Aluchna

1 Introduction

Sustainability, also referred to as sustainable development, is a concept which aims at providing balanced strategies for economic and social growth while also assuring global, international, interregional and intergenerational equilibrium as well as fairness with respect to the use of natural resources and income distribution. Sustainability places the aspects of social and environmental performance in the centre of the discussion (Malone et al., 2009). The social performance is understood as 'the organization's capacity to meet demand and expectations of constituencies beyond those linked directly to its products and markets' (Marcus, 1996: 89). "Environmental performance" refers to changes in corporate policy and operation in order to lower the negative impact upon the environment (Crane et al., 2008). The economic development observed in western Europe, North America and Japan was initially believed to be driven by human intelligence, innovation and implementation of efficient production systems and techniques. In the second part of the twentieth century, however, it became obvious that the intensive improvement of living standards in developed countries is rooted also in the excessive demand for natural resources and taking advantage of politically and economically weak developing regions. Hence, the prosperity of the developed countries was realized at the cost of the poor societies (Dowbor, 2011) and at the cost of the environment (Singer, 2002). Moreover, it became clear that the increasing power of large global corporations led to their significant impact upon the global society and economy. The negative influence of business operation and of the process of globalization proved to be highly problematic for less-developed economies, which suffer from the corporations' reallocations and the volatility of the global financial system (Singer, 2002; Dowbor, 2011). In the natural environment, fauna and flora became the silent victim as no organizations or political leaders represented their interests and needs. These problems and challenges gave rise to the concept of sustainable development and its implementation in companies. Sustainable business is viewed as a strategic framework for integrating the principles of sustainability by creating innovative solutions to complex needs of business requirements and thinking strategically about leading change (Rainey, 2006). Therefore, companies which intend to meet the demands and expectations of stakeholders are required to incorporate the dimensions of social and environmental performance and adopt these criteria for the evaluation of their strategies.

This chapter presents the results of the analysis on sustainability principles adopted in strategies formulated by Polish companies that are included in the WIG20 Index. The WIG20 Index covers the largest and the most liquid companies of the Warsaw Stock Exchange, which by definition are viewed as the role models for the rest of the listed companies. The goal of the chapter is to provide answers to research questions on the role and place of sustainability in the strategic management framework as formulated in strategies and pursued in undertaken activities of sample companies as well as its relations to CSR.

The chapter is organized as follows. Section 2 delivers the theoretical framework outlining the origin and areas of sustainability. It also discusses the concept of sustainability within strategic management and the related approaches of corporate social responsibility, triple bottom line, stakeholder theory and Carroll's pyramid. Section 3 discusses the so-called business case for sustainability, placing its requirements and recommendations for social and environmental performance within the strategic management context. Section 4 focuses on research into WIG20 companies' policies of sustainability presenting the methodology and the research findings. The discussion of the research results, its limitations and directions for further analysis are presented in section 5. The final remarks are included in the conclusion section.

2   The theoretical framework of sustainability

2.1   *The origin of the concept*

As defined by the World Commission on Environment and Development, "sustainable development" is 'meeting the needs of the present without compromising the ability of future generations to meet their own needs' (UN, 1987). It is a process in which development can be sustained for generations and affords to future generations the same capacity to prosper as the present generation has – or more (Ratnesh, 2006). Sustainability emphasizes the problem of intergenerational equity and demands that the current generation pass on to the following generations a world of natural resources not worse than the current generation's. It also becomes a crucial framework for business operations which sets new directions for future development (as the traditional rules will no longer apply), as well as changes in societal expectations and regulatory constraints. The rise in importance of sustainability and companies' interest in the concept are driven by significant challenges rooted in environmental, social and economic dimensions. The list of the reasons behind the development of the sustainability concept is presented in Table 3.1.

Table 3.1 The reasons behind the development of the sustainability concept

The reason category	The detailed problems/challenges
Environmental aspects	Ecological footprint
	GHG emission
	Water consumption
	Natural resources depletion
	Damage to fauna and flora
	Waste generation and management
	Climate change
Social aspects	Swelling population
	Income inequality
	Poverty and poor living conditions
Economic aspects	The change in conditions for business operation
	Hindered access to customers in emerging markets
	Pressure upon developed economies

Source: the authors.

As shown in Table 3.1, the environmental aspects driving the development of sustainability address the issues of ecological footprint, CO_2 and other greenhouse gas emissions, excessive water consumption, natural resource depletion (air pollution, land degradation, mineral resources, deforestation, biodiversity under threat), the so-called ethics of what we eat, waste generation and climate change, which constitute significant limitations for business operation and further growth. The second group of reasons encompasses social problems relating to the swelling population and income inequality, leading to inadequate living standards in poor countries (measured by the scope of malnutrition and starvation, infant mortality, access to health care and education systems). The third category refers to economic issues, pointing at the role and importance of developing countries and the dramatic change in the conditions for business operation and sustainable development that some believe will help to mitigate these problems. The concept of sustainability evolved in response to the above listed challenges (Mebratu, 1998) and was driven by following forces:

- Social pressure by societies, stakeholders and communities towards corporations and governments addressing the growing social and environmental challenges (Benn, 2010)
- The regulatory reaction of governments and international organizations to provide standards and action in order to decrease the negative human impact upon the environment (IISD, 2010)
- The corporate response viewed as the voluntary actions undertaken by business to accept the regulatory standards and fulfil the stakeholders' expectations (Kuhndt and Tuncer, 2007)
- The plentiful research which can be divided into four theories: classical economic (Malthusian) theory, neoclassical economic theory, human capital theory and neo-Malthusian theory. These theories draw attention to the problem of limited resources facing increasing consumption and production due to population growth (Aguirre, 2002).

The concept of sustainability is linked to two publications. The first, *Blueprint for Survival* by Edward Goldsmith and Robert Allen, with additional help from Michael Allaby, John Davoll and Sam Lawrence, was published in 1972 and occupied the entire issue of *The Ecologist* (Goldsmith and Allen, 1972). The second seminal document was "Limits to Growth," prepared and published in 1972 by the Club of Rome (Meadows et al., 1972). Additionally, the United Nations Conference on the Human Environment, held in Stockholm the same year, drew public attention to the limits of the environment for further economic development. In 1987 the concept received worldwide recognition as a result of a report by the World Commission on Environment and Development (known as the Brundtland Commission) called "Our Common Future". The commission, chaired by Norway's Prime Minister Gro Harlem Brundtland, developed today's generally accepted definition of sustainability, stating that sustainable development is 'development that meets the needs of the present without compromising the ability of future generations to meet their own needs'.[1] The first United Nations Conference on Environment and Development (UNCED) was held in Rio de Janeiro in 1992 (Goethe Institute). The conference focused on the relationship between environmental and developmental goals. The delegates adopted the Rio Declaration and Agenda 21, which was an action plan for global sustainable development making the concept of sustainability a formal political principle.[2] It was recognized that global environmental protection is only possible if economic and social aspects are also taken into consideration. In 1992 the Australian government expressed sustainability as 'using, conserving and enhancing the community's resources so that ecological processes, on which life depends, are maintained, and the total quality of life, now and in the future, can be increased' (Council of Australian Governments, 1992).

The concept of sustainability has been evolving in line with the development of such related themes as:

- Carroll's pyramid, which suggests that, besides the legal and economic responsibilities, companies need to consider ethical and (discretionary) philanthropic obligations to the communities and environment they are operating in (Carroll, 1979).
- The stakeholder theory recommends considering the interests of different groups of stakeholders and incorporating their expectations into corporate strategy (Freeman, 1984).
- Triple bottom line, which requires a company to incorporate the expectations of stakeholders in its strategy and operations. The triple bottom line embraces the 'social, economic and environmental' dimensions of corporate activity, which targets fulfilling the requirements and considering the limitations of people, planet and profit (Elkington, 1997).
- Natural resource economics (Tietenberg and Lewis, 2008), which is a field of study adopting a microeconomic approach to the problem of scarcity of natural resources. It conducts an empirical calculation of constraints, negative effects and losses to economic activities. It also explains the optimal structuring of taxes and regulations.

The development of the sustainability concept supported by the regulatory framework and active stakeholders' and NGOs' engagement translates into significant changes in the role business is expected to play in the economy and society. The changing dynamics of the leading paradigms represent the pattern and structure of governance in both the economic system and the company and reveal the relationship between business, government and community. Consequently, 'the traditional decision making of the powerful bureaucracy and corporations of the industrial era is no longer either appropriate or acceptable' (Benn and Dunphy, 2007). The discussion illustrates the changing dynamics in the hierarchy of key success factors in company's operation and the importance of different management approaches. It also contributes to the key themes and decision support tools for risk management.

2.2   *The dimensions of sustainability*

The concept of sustainable development assumes a balance between three dimensions of a company's activity with respect to its performance and impact on the society and environment addressing economic, environmental and social dimensions as shown in Figure 3.1.

As shown in Figure 3.1, economic and environmental requirements lead to viable activities, and combining social and economic requirements results in equitable activity, whereas encompassing environmental and social requirements provides for bearable activity (Pesqueux, 2009). Thus it is crucial to emphasize that sustainable development requires fulfilling all three requirements at the same time. The general description of the three dimensions of sustainability is presented in Table 3.2.

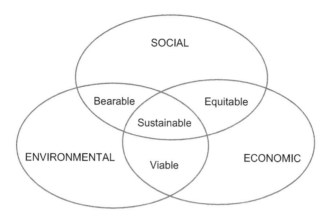

Figure 3.1 The notion of sustainable development

Source: Adams W. (2006). "The future sustainability: re-thinking environment and development in the twenty-first century", Report of the IUCN Renowned Thinkers Meeting, http://cmsdata.iucn.org/downloads/iucn_future_of_ sustainability.pdf.

Table 3.2 Dimensions of sustainability

Dimension	Representative stakeholders	Core aspects	Key examples
Economic growth	Shareholders, investors	Creating value in a way that enables a company to remain economically viable for an indefinite time	Sufficient cash flow to ensure liquidity, persistent returns to capital providers, R&D investment, an assets base that the market evaluates as having future value creation potential
Environmental integrity	Natural environment and ecosystems, customers, communities, suppliers	Limiting impact of firm activities on the natural environment while minimizing the use of natural capital	Various emission reduction actions in company facilities and processes, various resource-saving actions in company facilities and processes, energy efficiency in operations, risk assessment of impacts on natural environment, reduced impact on environment
Social responsiveness	Employees, customers, communities	Continually contributing to the social well-being of society and individuals	Job evaluation systems, fair trade, work-life balance, human rights, gender mainstreaming, codes of ethics, employee training, health and safety precautions, sponsorships and donations

Source: Galbreath J. (2006) "Sustainable development in business: A strategic view", in Schaltegger S., Wagner M. (eds). *Managing the Business Case for Sustainability: The Integration of Social, Environmental and Economic Performance*, Greenleaf Publishing, pp. 97–98.

As shown in Table 3.2, the economic dimension is the prime goal of every business entity as sound economic performance remains the essential incentive for executives and entrepreneurs. Corporate profitability is the requirement for company survival in the competitive market. Moreover, it cannot be stated that economic growth by definition has a negative impact on the environment, as the direction of the influence may be different

(Strandberg and Brandt, 2001). As noted by Pearce, sustainable economic development 'involves maximizing the net benefits of economic development, subject to maintaining the services and quality of natural resources over time' (Pearce et al., 1987). The economic goals include the action towards growth, equity and efficiency. The concept of sustainable business assumes that a company operating within social and environmental requirements assures sound economic performance since social and environmental aspects are heavily considered in customers' choices. Green production, acceptable conditions for animal breeding, limitation of packaging or adoption of efficient technologies are expected to be part of customers' purchasing criteria. Sustainable companies will not only be able to achieve market share and keep loyal customers but also will be able to demand a higher premium for their products or services. Additionally, the use of natural resources should assure rationality and accountability as uncontrolled and irresponsible consumption ultimately leads to severe constraints on business activity in the longer run (depletion of resources, environmental damage, pollution, etc.). Efficient use of natural resources, lower energy and materials consumption, waste management and plans for rebuilding natural resources should create global wealth. The economic dimension also covers several problems related to the desire of developing countries to reach the consumption standard of well-developed economies.

The environmental dimension of sustainability is viewed as the most crucial issue due to current environmental damage, degree of pollution and depletion of resources (Singer, 2002). At the same time, however, environmental dimensions seem to be the most neglected aspect, since fauna and flora as well as clean water and clean air have no lobbyists in international organizations or representatives on corporate boards. As a result, though many regulations or recommendations are formulated, enforcement is marginal. The environmental priorities have changed over the years along with the main problems and technology limitations humanity is facing at any given time (Ehrlich and Holden, 1974; Edwards, 2010). Attempts at environmental protection suggest a need for implementation of advanced and highly efficient technologies as well as change in consumption patterns according to the well-known greening hierarchy[3] (Mohan Das Gandhi et al., 2006).

The social dimension of sustainability refers to the social responsibility of companies covering such topics as human rights, working conditions, social justice, individual ethics and lifestyles and ethical consumerism. Social system goals include empowerment, social cohesion and cultural diversity (Elliott, 2009). Fulfilling the social dimension is intended to improve the company's social performance with respect to criteria accompanied by stakeholder dialogue, community consultation, cooperation with NGOs and customer communication (Spirig, 2006).

3 Corporate response to sustainability

The corporate perspective on introducing the principles of sustainable development into business and operating according to environmental limitations and social expectations leads to the formulation of sustainable business and sustainable enterprises. Five principles of sustainable development as formulated by the UK government are presented in Table 3.3.

The sustainable business should therefore be understood as economic activity which is based on the three elements of financial (profitability) viability, environmental protection and social responsibility. The strategies of sustainable business include formulating plans whereby corporate goals are tied to sustainable development and actions taken are in line with the requirements of sound economic performance, environmental protection and

Table 3.3 Five principles of sustainable development (UK government, 2005)

Living within environmental limits	Ensuring a strong, healthy and just society
Respecting the limits of the planet's environment, resources and biodiversity – to improve our environment and ensure that the natural resources needed for life are unimpaired and remain so for future generations	Meeting the diverse needs of all people in existing and future communities, promoting personal wellbeing, social cohesion and inclusion, and creating equal opportunity for all

Achieving a sustainable economy	Promoting good governance	Using sound science responsibly
Building a strong, stable economy which provides prosperity and opportunities for all and in which environmental and social costs fall on those who impose them (polluter pays) and efficient resource use is incentivized	Actively promoting effective participative systems of governance in all levels of society – engaging people's creativity, energy and diversity	Ensuring policy is developed and implemented on the basis of strong scientific evidence while taking into account scientific uncertainty (through the precautionary principles) as well as public attitudes and values

Source: Porritt J. (2006). *Capitalism As If the World Matters.* London: Earthscan, p. 29.

social responsibility. Another similar approach perceives sustainable business as 'the CSR in the ecological environment' and suggests the following actions (Crane et al., 2008):

- Using natural resources efficiently and minimizing waste due to the Earth's limited resources and finite capacity for absorbing waste
- Preventing pollution via implementation of clean technologies in production
- Establishing product stewardship that addresses the ecological impact of products and services
- Making innovations in products, processes and services
- Managing climate change with reference to greenhouse gas emissions from industrial processes
- Ensuring resource security and resource justice – addressing the rights of resource owners and those who are able to access them.

The concept of sustainable business requires analysis of corporate practice and case study illustrations. Some elements of sustainable business may be perceived as an additional burden resulting from increased regulation, the temptation of governments and NGOs to influence companies and limit their freedom of operation or simply as an additional cost of doing business. However, many companies are aware of the impending consequences to businesses and societies that are rooted mostly in environmental damage and depletion of resources (Singer, 2002). Some companies note a significant shift in their policies (Epstein and Roy) as they adopt measures of social and environmental sustainability. Companies may perceive their involvement in sustainability as an emerging competitive advantage. Combining environmental, economic and social challenges may help companies intro-duce groundbreaking innovations which would increase efficiency of used resources and lower (or at least not increase) the costs of offered products and services. Studies show precisely that effective adoption of the sustainable business concept and compliance with standards and guidelines requires a company to integrate sustainability as a part of overall corporate strategy (Wheeler and Sillanpää, 1997) and corporate governance (Crane and

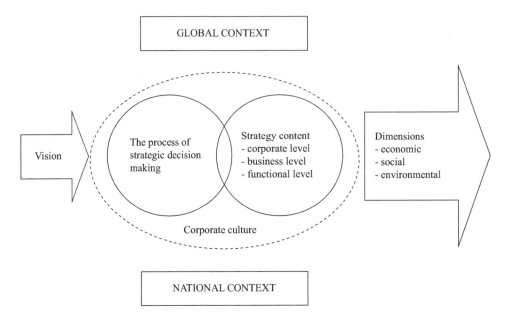

Figure 3.2 Sustainable business as an element of strategy

Matten, 2007). In other words, the prime requirement for the effective adoption of the sustainable business model depends upon whether its principles are adopted at all levels of organizational structure and areas of operation. The model of sustainable business as an element of strategy is presented in Figure 3.2.

As shown in Figure 3.2, the ideas of sustainable business should first be implemented at the top, represented by the board of directors. This requirement means that the recommendations of sustainable business in terms of need for social responsibility and environmental protection have to be incorporated in the board of directors' work (e.g. nomination of directors, meetings agenda, executive evaluation) as well as in the overall process of monitoring and control (e.g. executive compensation, reporting and disclosure, balancing interests of shareholders and stakeholders). Secondly, the principles of sustainability should be applied at the corporate, business and functional levels, which cover the strategic management process, including strategic planning, strategy implementation and strategic control. The corporate level strategy refers to the portfolio management undertaken by business/corporate groups or large conglomerates (decision of purchase/sale of subsidiaries or associated companies) or by companies managing a wide range of products/services (decision on purchase/sale of a given product/service or related to entering or withdrawal from market segments). At this level the company adopting the sustainable business concept should use the sustainability criteria (social, economic and environmental) in the decision-making process of reconstructing its product or services portfolio. The business level strategy refers to the process of strategic analysis, strategy formulation (core values, vision and mission statements, strategic goals, strategic competitive advantage). The company adopting the sustainable business concept should apply the sustainability aspects to its core values, vision and mission statements, should include sustainability criteria (social, economic and environmental) for the formulation of the strategic goals and should refer to these criteria in the process of formulating its competitive advantage and the core of its business strategy. Studies show that the concept of sustainable development and the green revolution provide substantial opportunities for business (Wos, 2010) as new technologies, certifications (Vorbrodt, 2011) and green marketing (Kaczmarczyk, 2011) will play more and more important roles. And finally, the functional level strategy refers to marketing, human resources, production or finance strategies. The company adopting the sustainable business concept should use the sustainability criteria in the decision-making process of formulating any of the functional strategies.

Additionally, as shown in Figure 3.2, the operations on four listed levels should lead to performance in economic, social and environmental dimensions. The main assumptions of sustainable business should be supported by a corporate culture which allows for translating the goals into practice and provides for strong leadership, effective communication and employee motivation and contribution. From the operational and practical point of view, the requirements for sustainability implementation require a set of actions and integration of a company's core areas. The requirements for adopting sustainability include the following (Epstein, 2008):

- Sustainability must be an integral part of corporate strategy
- Leadership must be committed to sustainability
- Sustainability strategies should be supported with management control, performance measurement and reward systems
- Sustainability strategies should be supported with mission, culture and people
- Managers must integrate sustainability in all strategic and operational decisions
- Managing sustainability performance should be viewed not as risk avoidance and compliance but as an opportunity for innovation and competitive advantage.

In sum, adopting a sustainable business strategy in a company requires nine principles addressing actions in ethics, governance, transparency, business relationships, financial return, community development/economic development, value for products and services, employee practices and environmental protection (Epstein, 2008).

4 Research on the sustainability policies of WIG20 companies

4.1 Methodology

This section focuses on the research on the policies of sustainability practices adopted in strategies formulated by Polish companies included in the WIG20 Index. The WIG20 Index covers the largest and the most liquid companies of the Warsaw Stock Exchange, which by definition are viewed as the role models for the rest of the listed companies. The goal of the research is to provide answers to the formulated research questions on the policy of sustainability in the strategic management framework and its relation to CSR. The research questions referred to the problem of the place and importance assigned to the concept of sustainability by sample companies and included the following:

- Do sample companies have a dedicated sustainability section of their website?
- Do sample companies integrate the concept of sustainability into their mission?
- Do sample companies integrate the concept of sustainability into their strategic goals and strategy?

Table 3.4 Sample companies and their general characteristics (as of 3 October 2013)

No.	Company	Code ISIN	Sector of operation	Market capitalization (PLN)	Share in the index (%)
1	PKOBP	PLPKO0000016	Banking	26 171 720 640	14.528
2	PZU	PLPZU0000011	Insurance	23 953 876 000	13.297
3	PEKAO	PLPEKAO00016	Banking	23 574 960 000	13.086
4	KGHM	PLKGHM000017	Copper mining	16 300 995 000	9.049
5	PKNORLEN	PLPKN0000018	Petroleum	13 739 111 360	7.627
6	PGE	PLPGER000010	Energy generation	12 257 339 200	6.804
7	BZWBK	PLBZ00000044	Banking	9 989 024 850	5.545
8	PGNIG	PLPGNIG00014	Gas and oil extraction	9 883 149 720	5.486
9	BRE	PLBRE0000012	Banking	6 316 217 600	3.506
10	TPSA	PLTLKPL00017	Telecommunication	5 567 270 200	3.090
11	TAURONPE	PLTAURN00011	Energy generation	4 977 924 300	2.763
12	JSW	PLJSW0000015	Coal mining	3 939 804 600	2.187
13	BOGDANKA	PLLWBGD00016	Coal mining	3 741 430 000	2.077
14	HANDLOWY	PLBH00000012	Banking	3 691 032 000	2.049
15	ASSECOPOL	PLSOFTB00016	IT	3 658 197 110	2.031
16	EUROCASH	PLEURCH00011	Retail	3 574 925 640	1.984
17	KERNEL	LU0327357389	Agriculture	2 456 177 800	1.363
18	SYNTHOS	PLDWORY00019	Chemical fertilizers	2 408 946 500	1.337
19	LOTOS	PLLOTOS00025	Petroleum	2 225 133 600	1.235
20	GTC	PLGTC0000037	Construction	1 721 298 020	0.955
		Total	–	180 148 534 140	100

Source: the author, based on http://www.gpw.pl/portfele_indeksow#WIG20.

The research methodology included the identification of companies in the WIG20 with the reference to the market capitalization and sector of operation as presented in Table 3.4.

The research included analysis of the content of the sample companies' websites, with particular interest given to:

*   Identification of the dedicated sustainability/CSR section of sustainability
*   Identification of the sustainability report published by sample companies
*   Analysis of the mission of sample companies with reference to sustainability
*   Analysis of strategic goals and strategies formulated by sample companies with reference to sustainability.

5   Findings

The research included analysis of the content of the sample companies' corporate websites with respect to selected aspects of the incorporation of the sustainability concept into the strategies and programs. All data was hand collected. The findings are presented in Table 3.5.

Table 3.5 Incorporation of the sustainability concept into strategies of sample companies

Company	Sustainability section on the website	Sustainability report	Sustainability incorporated into mission	Sustainability incorporated into strategy and goals
PKOBP	Yes, as CSR with reference to 'obligation towards natural environment'	No	Partially, referring to stakeholders' expectations	No, reference to financial and market goals
PZU	Yes, as CSR with reference also to 'environmental friendliness'	Yes, known as CSR report, including environmental issues	No	No, reference to financial and market goals
PEKAO	Yes, as CSR with reference to environmental protection and sustainable development	No, but detailed description on the website	Yes, reference to CSR, sustainability, stakeholders' expectations	No, reference to financial and market goals
KGHM	Yes, with reference to CSR and sustainability	Yes, known as CSR report, including environmental issues	Yes, CSR and sustainability (ecology)	Yes, reference to sustainable investment and operation
PKNORLEN	Yes, with reference to CSR, sustainable development, complete and elaborate section of 'responsibilities'	Yes, integrated reporting according to GRI standards	No, reference to the use of natural resources	No, reference to financial and market goals
PGE	Yes, with reference to CSR and 'environment'	Yes, environmental and CSR report	No, reference to set of responsibilities toward customers, shareholders and employees	No, reference to financial and operational performance and market goals
BZWBK	Yes, with reference to CSR and set of responsibilities toward 'environment' and stakeholders	Yes, corporate foundation report, code of conduct, policy	No, reference to set of responsibilities toward customers	No, reference to financial and operational performance and market goals
PGNIG	Yes, with reference to CSR and sustainable development	Yes, CSR report with environmental section	Yes, CSR, sustainable development, environmental protection	Yes, CSR, sustainable development, environmental protection
BRE	Yes, with reference to CSR	Yes, CSR report	No, reference to performance and employees	No, reference to financial and market goals
TPSA	Yes, with reference to CSR	Yes, CSR report	Yes, CSR and reducing the negative impact upon environment	Yes, CSR and reducing the negative impact upon environment

(Continued)

Table 3.5 (Continued)

Company	Sustainability section on the website	Sustainability report	Sustainability incorporated into mission	Sustainability incorporated into strategy and goals
TAURONPE	Yes, with reference to 'responsible business'	Yes, sustainable development report	Yes, best practice in CSR, sustainable development, environmental protection	Yes, best practice in CSR, sustainable development, environmental protection
JSW	Yes, with reference to 'responsible business'	Yes, environmental and CSR report	Yes, CSR, sustainable development, environmental protection	Yes, CSR, sustainable development, environmental protection
BOGDANKA	Yes, with the reference to sustainable development	Yes, integrated reporting according to ISO 9001:2008; PN-N 18001:2004; ISO 14001:2004.	Yes, CSR, sustainable development, environmental protection	Yes, CSR, sustainable development, environmental protection
HANDLOWY	Yes, with reference to CSR but no reference to environmental issues	Yes, corporate foundation report	Yes, CSR	Yes, CSR
ASSECOPOL	No	No	No, reference to sector of operation	No, reference to financial and market goals
EUROCASH	No, with reference to set of responsibilities toward customers, shareholders and employees	No	No, reference to sector of operation	No, reference to financial and market goals
KERNEL	Yes, with reference to sustainable development	No	No, reference to sector of operation	No, reference to financial and market goals
SYNTHOS	Yes, with reference to 'environmental protection'	No	No, reference to sector of operation	No, reference to financial and market goals
LOTOS	Yes, with reference to CSR, sustainable development, complete and elaborate section of 'responsibilities'	Yes, integrated reporting according to GRI standards	Yes, reference to sustainable development	Yes, reference to sustainable development
GTC	Yes, with reference to CSR and 'green idea'	No	No, reference to shareholder value and market position	No, reference to financial performance and market goals

Source: the author, based on the corporate websites.

As shown in Table 3.5, the WIG20 companies differ significantly in terms of incorporation of the sustainability concept into their strategies, communicating and reporting policies. First of all, the sample companies are more familiar with the term "corporate social responsibility" than "sustainability". Of 20 companies, 13 have a section devoted to CSR although the issues of environmental protection and stakeholder dialogue are also addressed in these sections. Only three of the analyzed companies refer to sustainable development directly with a dedicated section on their websites. Interestingly, 3 of 20 companies do not refer in their online communications to either CSR or sustainable development, addressing only the expectations of customers and the challenges of market conditions. As many as seven of the analysed companies do not publish a separate report on CSR/sustainability, which may seem disappointing as these are the largest and the most liquid companies listed on the Warsaw Stock Exchange. Thirteen companies do publish CSR reports on their website, discussing the expectations of and responsibilities towards customers, suppliers, communities, the general public and so on. As depicted in the analysis, Polish companies do engage in various CSR activities ranging from education for customers and training for employees to local and nationwide initiatives for helping the victims of natural disasters and serious accidents; sick and poor people and orphans; and developing programs that support culture, restore national heritage and protect the environment. Companies do inform the public about their policies and initiatives, develop the employee volunteering programs and indicate the number of hours and the sum of funds dedicated to CSR/sustainability actions. Three of the WIG20 companies make their reports according to integrated frameworks following the Global Reporting Initiative (GRI) and International Organization for Standardization (ISO) principles. Further analysis targeted the mission and vision of the analysed companies as well as the way they formulate their strategic goals and strategies. Interestingly, only 10 of the sample companies have a direct reference to sustainability in their mission. The other half of the WIG20 firms prefer to address the issues of the sector of operation, performance, delivering value to customers and creating shareholder value. They adopt financial and market indices for setting goals and formulating strategy. Only eight companies use the terms "sustainability" or "sustainable development" in their mission statements and use this framework for setting corporate goals. In the case of 12 companies, "strategic goals" refers to market performance, creating shareholder or customer value, and product and service quality. The principles of sustainability are not integrated into the strategies of these companies.

Discussion

The analysis reveals that the companies included in the WIG20 index differ significantly in how or if they incorporate the sustainability concept into their strategies, communications and reporting policies. The sample companies are much more familiar with the term "corporate social responsibility" than "sustainability", which most likely can be explained by the greater popularity of the CSR concept related to its earlier emergence in publications and introduction into corporate practice. While the issues of environmental protection are addressed in the CSR sections, sustainability seems to be viewed as a part of CSR responsibilities and not the reverse. As shown in Table 3.5, it is generally easier for companies to address the CSR and sustainability issues on their corporate website by creating a separate section than to incorporate these principles into mission and strategy. Therefore, this brief analysis shows that the CSR and sustainability initiatives may be viewed as additional separate actions that are not fully integrated in the company strategy and operation. Still, half of the sample companies do not address either CSR or sustainability principles in their missions and strategies; rather, they focus mostly on market and financial performance and the relations between customers and employees. The poor showing at the top organizational levels casts serious doubts about transferring sustainability to the operational levels, into a motivation system as well as leadership and corporate culture values.

If we refer the obtained results to the general characteristics of the sample companies, two observations can be noted. First, the companies which operate in the socially and environmentally controversial sectors of energy generation, coal mining or oil and gas extraction do incorporate the notions of sustainability into their mission, strategies and reporting more often than companies operating in environmentally neutral industries. This is most likely driven by the expectations of stakeholders and pressure from NGOs and regulators, as it is, for instance, in the case of PGE, which controls the brown–coal miners, belongs to the biggest emitters of CO in the EU and is constantly targeted by Greenpeace actions and protests. Companies operating in environmentally unfriendly sectors also engage in social dialogue and develop communications for the local communities. The petroleum giant PKN Orlen as well as gas-extracting PGNiG constitute the perfect illustration for such activities. On the other hand, companies which operate in neutral sectors do not show dedication to sustainability and environmental protection. Instead, they focus on the market and financial performance, relations to customers and employees as well as building trust amongst the company and the public. Second, companies operating in neutral sectors yet controlled by the foreign strategic (industry) investor do reveal higher awareness of CSR and sustainability principles following the internationally recognized standards. Handlowy Bank (controlled by Citigroup) and TPSA (controlled by Orange) illustrate this phenomenon.

This research delivers some insights on the popularity of sustainability amongst WIG20 companies as well as how sustainability principles are incorporated into reporting practices and formulation of missions and strategies. However, the analysis reveals some limitations, mostly the small sample of studied companies. Moreover, the studies of corporate website content reveal the companies' public declarations and do not depict the real incorporation and realization of the formulated goals. Nor does the research explain the motivation behind the companies' policies and choices. Therefore, further analysis on the incorporation and practical dimensions of corporate sustainability adoption is needed as it will help us understand how companies put the concept into their operation.

7   Conclusion

In light of social challenges and environmental limitations, sustainability aiming at balanced strategies for economic and social growth and assuring for global equilibrium and fairness with respect to the use of natural resources and income distribution is viewed as the only possible direction for further growth and development. Therefore, companies as well as societies and communities truly need to transform their traditional business models to incorporate the environmental constraints and the expectations of global stakeholders. The new approach needs to consider the dimensions of social and environmental performance and not focus solely on financial measures and creating shareholder value.

As shown in the research, companies included in WIG20 Index differ significantly in how they incorporate sustainability concepts into their reporting practices and strategies. Companies which operate in the socially and environmentally controversial sectors of energy generation, coal mining or oil and gas extraction do incorporate the notions of sustainability into their mission, strategies and reporting. Also, companies operating in neutral sectors yet controlled by the foreign strategic (industry) investor do reveal higher awareness of CSR and sustainability principles following the internationally recognized standards. However, the issue of the real understanding of the sustainability principles behind the declaration still remains an open question requiring further research and studies.

Notes

1   The major proposals of the Brundtland report include: (1) reviving growth, (2) changing the quality of growth, (3) meeting essential needs for jobs, food, energy, water and sanitation, (4) ensuring a sustainable level of population, (5) conserving and enhancing the resource base, (6) reorienting technology and managing risks, (7) merging environment and economics decision-making (Kirkby et al., 1995).
2   The Agenda 21 statements included: (1) Agenda 21 predicated on economic growth as within WCED, (2) emphasis on the familiar environmental issues and management of earlier reports such as the World Conservation Strategy, (3) heavily techno-centrist including the means through which sustainable development will be achieved, building on science, information and sound technologies, (4) assumes change will arise through mutual interests of northern and southern hemispheres and of current and future generations, (5) calls for participation on behalf of a 'rainbow coalition' of women, children, young people, indigenous people, trade unionists, business professionals, industry farmers, local authorities, and scientists (Adams, 2002).
3   The hierarchy includes, from bottom to top, the following directions: disposal without energy recovery, disposal with energy recovery, recycle, reuse, reduce (Mohan Das Gandhi et al., 2006).

References

Adams, W. (2002). Sustainable development?, in R. Johnston, P. Taylor and M. Watts (eds.), *Geographies of Global Change: Remapping the World*. New York: Wiley, 412–26.

Aguirre, M. (2002). Sustainable development: Why the focus on population? *International Journal of Social Economics*, 29(12), 923–45.

Benn, S. (2010). Social partnerships for governance and learning towards sustainability. ARIES Working Paper 01/2010, University of Technology, Sydney, http://aries.mq.edu.au/publications/aries/Working_Papers/Social_Partnerships_for_Gov_&_Learning.pdf/.

Benn, S. and Dunphy, D. (2007). New forms of governance, in S. Benn and D. Dunphy (eds.), *Corporate Governance and Sustainability: Challenges for Theory and Practice*. London: Routledge, 9–35.

Bonn, I. and Fisher, J. (2011). Sustainability: The missing ingredient in strategy. *Journal of Business Strategy*, 32(1), 5–15.

Carroll, A. (1979). A three-dimensional conceptual model of corporate performance. *The Academy of Management Review*, 4(4), 497.

Council of Australian Governments. (1992). National Strategy for Ecologically Sustainable Development, prepared by the Ecologically Sustainable Development Steering Committee, December, http://www.environment.gov.au/about/esd/publications/strategy/intro.html#WIESD.

Crane, A. and Matten, D. (2007). *Business Ethics: Managing Corporate Citizenship and Sustainability in the Age of Globalization*. New York: Oxford University Press.

Crane, A., Matten, D. and Spence, L. (2008). *Corporate Social Responsibility*. London: Routledge.

Dowbor, L. (2011). Economic democracy. Strolling through theories, http://dowbor.org/09economicdemocracykd.doc/.

Edwards, B. (2010). *Rough Guide to Sustainability*. London: RIBA Publishing Earthscan.

Ehrlich, P. and Holden, J. (1974). Human population and the global environment. *American Scientist*, 62(3), 282–92.

Elkington, J. (1997). *Cannibals with Forks: The Triple Bottom Line of 21st Century Business*. Oxford: Capstone.

Elliott, J. (2009). Sustainable development, in R. Kitchin et al. (eds.), *International Encyclopedia of Human Geography*. Oxford: Elsevier, 117–31.

Epstein, M. (2008). *Making Sustainability Work*. San Francisco, CA: Greenleaf Publishing.

Freeman, R. (1984). *Strategic Management: A Stakeholder Approach*. Boston, MA: Pitman.

Galbreath, J. (2006). Sustainable development in business: A strategic view, in S. Schaltegger and M. Wagner (eds.), *Managing the Business Case for Sustainability: The Integration of Social, Environmental and Economic Performance*. San Francisco, CA: Greenleaf Publishing, 97–8.

Goldsmith, E. and Allen, R. (1972). Blueprint for survival. *The Ecologist*, 2(1), January. IISD reporting services, http://www.iisd.ca/.

IISD reporting services, http://www.iisd.ca/.

Kaczmarczyk, M. (2011). Zielony marketing. *Forbes*, November, p. 17.

Kirkby, J., O'Keefe, P. and Timberlake, L. (1995). *The Earthscan Leader in Sustainable Development*. London: Earthscan.

Kuhndt, M. and Tuncer, B. (2007). Sustainability as a business challenge: The concept of responsible corporate governance, in R. Bleischwitz (ed.), *Corporate Governance of Sustainability*. Northampton: Edward Elgar, 8–25.

Malone, E., Bradbury, J. and Dooley, J. (2009). Keeping CCS stakeholder involvement in perspective. *Energy Procedia*, 1, 4789–94.

Marcus, A. (1996). *Business and Society: Strategy, Ethics and the Global Economy*. Chicago, IL: Irwin.

Meadows, D., Randers, J. and Meadows, D. (1972). *Limits to Growth*. New York: Universe Books.

Mebratu, D. (1998). Sustainability and sustainable development: Historical and conceptual review. *Environmental Impact Assessment Review*, 18(6), 493–520.

Mohan Das Gandhi, N., Selladurai, V. and Santhi, P. (2006). Unsustainable development to sustainable development: A conceptual model. *Management of Environmental Quality: An International Journal*, 17(6), 654–72.

Pearce, D. and Barbier, E. and Markandy, A. (1987). Sustainable development and cost-benefit analysis. London Environmental Economics Centre Paper (88–01) as quoted in Redclift, M. (1992). The meaning of sustainable development, *Geoforum*, 23(5), 395–403.

Pesqueux, Y. (2009). Sustainable development: A vague and ambiguous 'theory'. *Society and Business Review*, 4(3), 231–45.

Porritt, J. (2006). *Capitalism as if the World Matters*. London: Earthscan.

Rainey, D. (2006). *Sustainable Business Development*. Cambridge: Cambridge University Press.

Ratnesh, K. (2006). *Environmental Economics: Theory and Practices*. New Delhi: Deep & Deep Publications.

Singer, P. (2002). *One World: The Ethics of Globalization*. Melbourne: Test Publishing.

Spirig, K. (2006). Social performance and competitiveness, in S. Schaltegger and M. Wagner (eds.), *Managing the Business Case for Sustainability: The Integration of Social, Environmental and Economic Performance*. San Francisco, CA: Greenleaf Publishing, 82–105.

Strandberg, L. and Brandt, N. (2001). Sustainable development in theory and practice: An inter-Nordic Internet course for regional and local officials and practitioners. *International Journal of Sustainability in Higher Education*, 2(3), 220–5.

Tietenberg, T. and Lewis, L. (2008). *Environmental and Natural Resource Economics*. New York: Irwin/McGraw-Hill.

UK Government. (2005). Guiding principles for sustainable development, https://www.gov.uk/government/uploads/system/uploads/attachment_data/file/323193/Guiding_principles_for_SD.pdf (accessed October 25, 2016).

UN. (1987). Report of the World Commission on Environment and Development, no. 42, http://www.un.org/documents/ga/res/42/ares42-187.htm.

Vorbrodt, A. (2011). Zrownowazony rozwoj, rosnacy zysk, *Forbes*, November, p. 11.

Wheeler, D. and Sillanpää, M. (1997). *The Stakeholder Corporation*. London: Pitman Publishing.

Wos, R. (2010). Biznes nie zamierza przespac zielonej rewolucji. *Dziennik Gazeta Prawna Magazyn*, November 26–28, pp. M 8–9.

4 Towards a classification of consumer sustainability

Tillmann Wagner and Alexander Stich

1 Introduction

Sustainability is highly relevant for companies (e.g. Chabowski, Mena, and Gonzalez-Padron, 2011). They sometimes regard sustainability as one strategic business goal among others, which reflects their view that sustainability is a new trend. Companies build on this trend, for example by using the term "sustainability" in their advertising and communication. Furthermore, they increasingly invest in corporate social responsibility initiatives. This development clearly indicates that companies have realized that sustainability and economic profits can be mutually supportive. Nevertheless, sustainability seems to be more than an additional strategic business goal, because famous researchers describe sustainability not only as trend but as an 'emerging megatrend' (Lubin and Esty, 2010, p. 44) and as the most important challenge for marketing (Kotler, 2011; Sheth, 2011). Sustainability can also be the key driver for innovation, that is, sustainability might determine if a company will survive or not (Nidumolu, Prahalad, and Rangaswami, 2009).

Sustainability is also relevant for consumers (e.g. Nidumolu et al., 2009). Notably, companies which use sustainability claims in their corporate marketing can increase consumers' support of the company in terms of purchase rates, word of mouth, or loyalty. Therefore, it seems useful to understand how consumers classify sustainability for themselves and which aspects they consider to be most important (Sheth, Sethia, and Srinivas, 2011). In other words, companies which advertise and talk about matters of sustainability should know about consumers' understanding of the term. However, as current sustainability research in business focuses on a corporate perspective, an axiomatic sustainability classification from a consumer's perspective seems useful.

This chapter is structured as follows: First, a brief theoretical background about sustainability in business is given. Second, the applied methodology and the key findings of the conducted in-depth interviews are presented, thereby developing a conceptual framework. Finally, implications, limitations, and future research directions are discussed.

2 Sustainability in business

From a company's point of view, sustainability is often described to consist of three main goals, that is, economic, social, and environmental sustainability (e.g. Dyllick and Hockerts, 2002). Many authors refer to the so-called triple bottom line when talking about these three goals (Elkington, 1998). In general, economy, society, and the environment can be illustrated as three concentric circles (e.g. Gibson, Hassan, Holtz, Tansey, and Whitelaw, 2005, p. 57), three pillars (e.g. Hutchins and Sutherland, 2008), or three integrated circles (e.g. Schumann, Saili, Taylor, and Abdel-Malek, 2010). Economic sustainability describes the company's ability to create value as well as to improve its own financial performance in the long term (Chabowski et al., 2011). "Social sustainability" refers to the consideration of societal issues such as employees' rights, and environmental or ecological sustainability characterizes the "maintenance of natural capital" (Goodland, 1995, p. 10).

From an individual's perspective, "sustainability" can have many different meanings (Schumann et al., 2010), thus it appears quite difficult to grasp the term. This might be a reason why, to the best of our knowledge, a profound classification of consumer sustainability has not yet been developed. Notably, Sheth et al. (2011) emphasize that there is a clear lack of sustainability research focusing on the consumer's perspective. However, when looking at the literature about sustainability and sustainable consumption, one can gain first insights on which aspects might belong to a consumer's perspective of sustainability.

Recently, Sheth et al. (2011) conceptualized the idea of the mindful mindset, which consists of caring for nature, for the community, and for oneself. In other words, people show consumption lifestyles focusing on ecological, social, and personal well-being. To begin, the motivation to care for nature can be rather instrumental but also stem from more intrinsic desires (Kilbourne, 2006; Wapner and Matthew, 2009), thereby encompassing a wide range of environmental issues such as biodiversity, water, and the carbon footprint. Moreover, people care for the community they belong to (Sheth et al., 2011), especially for their family members and friends (e.g. Batson, 2002). On the whole, the authors suspect that caring for nature and caring for the community should be strongly related with common issues from environmental sustainability, respectively social sustainability. The third dimension (i.e. caring about the self) describes personal well-being, including both eudemonic and economic aspects (Sheth et al., 2011). Actually, people who disregard their own economic health through overconsumption are said to have a reduced life-satisfaction in the long term (e.g. Csikszentmihalyi, 2000). This overconsumption might also result in overwork and stress (Schor, 1999) and thus seriously harm people's physical health. Therefore, individual overconsumption can be seen as closely connected to unsustainable consumption (Sheth et al., 2011). Last but not least, there are some other researchers who connect either the whole individual organism (Costanza and Patten, 1995) or specific individual aspects such as human health and well-being (Dovers and Handmer, 1992; McMichael et al., 1999) to the concept of sustainability. Nevertheless, it seems still hard to find research which comes up with a complete classification of sustainability issues from a consumer's point of view.

In addition to that, Ray and Anderson (2000) developed a detailed framework about consumers who tend to care about a wide range of sustainability issues (i.e. cultural creatives). Interestingly, the descriptions of cultural creatives show a certain similarity to the mindful mindset concept insofar as they indicate that this class of people is defined by shared values which point in the direction of environmental, social, and individual sustainability. In particular, cultural creatives care about the environment (e.g. show interest in nature, are concerned about the planet), other humans (e.g. engage with society, help each other), and their own quality of life (e.g. believe in holistic health, are not very materialistic).

To sum up, the authors speculate that sustainability is constituted of three main facets: ecological, social, and individual sustainability. These three facets can be surmised by the cultural creatives descriptions provided by Ray and Anderson (2000), and they show a certain similarity to the mindful mindset concept by Sheth et al. (2011). However, despite these theoretical indicators, there is still need to empirically investigate in detail how consumers classify sustainability and which facets it consists of. The goal of this research approach is to take a first step towards an understanding of consumer sustainability. First, the aforementioned idea of the mindful mindset represents the point of departure for a classification of consumer sustainability. Second, as the underlying research question is still highly explorative, in-depth interviews are used in order to build a new conceptual framework (see, e.g., Bengtsson and Ostberg, 2006). Third, the derived structure might help marketers to detect consumer-relevant aspects of sustainability.

3 Methodology

The authors conducted a series of 20 in-depth interviews (face to face, video, and phone) with German consumers. Participants differed in gender, age, level of education, and occupation. For the reason of representativeness and also to have a more moderate sample, very "green" consumers were excluded from sampling. The underlying research question was part of a broader investigation about consumers' unsustainable consumption behaviour (Stich and Wagner, 2012). (Interviews took between 46 and 146 minutes. They were audiotaped and transcribed verbatim. Table 4.1 summarizes participants' profiles as well as the basic facts of the interviews.)

According to the usual practice, in-depth interviews were mainly unstructured, that is, the term "sustainability" was discussed in general and in rather broad aspects. Nevertheless, a short interview guide was used to explore consumer-relevant sustainability issues

Table 4.1 Profiles of interview participants and basic interview facts

Gender	Age	Occupation	Type of interview	Length of interview
Female	20	Hairdresser	Face to face	50 minutes
Female	27	Unemployed	Phone	81 minutes
Female	27	Teacher (academic high school)	Phone	46 minutes
Female	34	Occupational health and safety practitioner	Video	68 minutes
Female	38	Administrative assistant	Face to face	49 minutes
Female	43	Electrician	Phone	60 minutes
Female	48	General practitioner & housewife	Phone	54 minutes
Female	58	Teacher (junior high school)	Phone	122 minutes
Female	58	Child care worker	Phone	75 minutes
Female	77	Housewife	Phone	85 minutes
Male	25	Research assistant (marketing)	Face to face	146 minutes
Male	27	Research assistant (sociology)	Phone	87 minutes
Male	27	Plasterer	Phone	52 minutes
Male	29	Glassblower	Phone	54 minutes
Male	30	Fundraiser	Video	106 minutes
Male	44	Kitchen worker	Face to face	60 minutes
Male	48	Sales manager	Phone	66 minutes
Male	50	Marketing assistant	Phone	87 minutes
Male	53	Administration secretary	Phone	50 minutes
Male	82	Retiree	Phone	120 minutes

and their subjective importance ratings. After a brief introduction, participants commented on the following questions:[1]

1   What do you think when you hear the word "sustainability"?
2   In your opinion, which issues belong to sustainability?
3   What role does sustainability play for you?
4   Which sustainability aspects are most important for you? Why?
5   Which sustainability aspects are less important for you? Why?
6   What do you think when you hear "sustainability" and "consumption" at the same time?

The interviews were analysed via coding and clustering the codes into higher-order categories (e.g., Creswell, 2009). The analysis combined qualitative data and theoretical background knowledge (e.g., Workman, Homburg, and Gruner, 1998). Comments stated below were double-back translated.

4   Findings

As expected from theory, participants described a wide range of different sustainability issues. However, these issues share two general characteristics. First, sustainability issues refer to the long-term perspective (i.e., doing or not doing something in the long term). And second, sustainability issues are closely connected to the preservation of something positive (as opposed to something negative). Moreover, participants mentioned similar aspects across interviews when asked which issues they associate with sustainability. These 35 main issues can be clustered into eight objectives and three higher-order categories (Stich and Wagner, 2012), as illustrated in Figure 4.1.

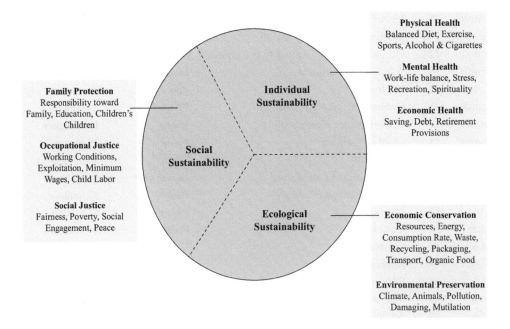

Figure 4.1 Sustainability objectives of consumers and connected issues

To begin with, interviewees emphasized the significance of ecological sustainability (which is equivalent to environmental sustainability) for the whole construct. Analyses revealed that ecological sustainability constitutes the most prominent sustainability facet and can be seen as the basis for further sustainability aspects. The environmental movement, which is one of the most famous historical developments in ecology, is said to have contributed to the rise of the term "sustainability":

> Actually, sustainability is always ecological sustainability for me. Because this term, sustainability, pretty much comes from the environmental movement. Although it could for sure belong to many other areas, but as I said 'vague term', for me actually this is all ecological sustainability . . . relating to the environment and to protecting it.
>
> (Female, 34 years)

> Ecological sustainability, okay, in my opinion this is an automatism that sustainability also has to be related to ecological sustainability, sure.
>
> (Male, 50 years)

Participants discussed several issues under the umbrella of *ecological sustainability*. Notably, issues of *economic conservation* were repeatedly mentioned. Economic conservation includes issues focusing on the consumption of natural resources in a way which enables future generations to live with at least this amount of resources. Therefore, natural resources like water, oil, or lumber have to be consumed in an efficient and economical way. As worldwide oil reserves dwindle, interviewees especially stressed the importance of saving energy in order to face the energy crisis. For example, they talked about taking public transportation instead of going by car and buying primarily local goods to avoid long transport routes. Furthermore, participants emphasized that overconsumption is a problem which should be replaced by a lower consumption rate. Finally, several participants discussed recycling issues, including waste separation and the general necessity to reduce waste.

Whilst economic conservation issues indicate that natural resources have to be conserved in order to ensure certain living standards, interviewees also came up with more selfless motivations to preserve the natural environment. This intrinsic desire to care about nature can lead to the protection of plants and especially animals. Moreover, participants blamed human behaviour for climate change (i.e. temperature on earth is rising). In particular, they thought that humanity does not have the right to pollute, damage, or mutilate the planet:

> Yes, indeed, this is a perfect example, ecological sustainability. Ecology, that is the ecosystem, and here I am thinking about the conservation of the resources, so let's say for the most part about the conservation of resources, that means that we do not consume more resources than can grow back, than one can replace once again . . . I for one put what is on my way, an earthworm, I throw it into the next meadow so that it won't get trodden upon the sidewalk. And snails, I search for locations for them where they are safe so that they do not get trampled on the road, that is my inner need, which means to save life in every form, to protect it.
>
> (Male, 81 years)

> Well, when it comes to ecological sustainability, I particularly think about the environment . . . not to absolutely thoughtlessly exploit and consume away things. And

also not to damage something during the exploitation of another thing. Well, for example, that I, if I want to grow soya plants, that I don't clear the rainforest for this.

(Male, 30 years)

Next, *social sustainability* is characterized by a wide range of societal issues, which can be categorized into three main objectives. First, interviewees regarded the protection of people in their proximity, especially their own family (*family protection*), as very important. This perceived responsibility for one's own family comes with a very strong focus on children, that is, caring about a decent education as well as giving priority to children's needs. Participants also emphasized the obligation to bear in mind the needs of future generations. Notably, the future of their children's children was repeatedly mentioned to be very important.

As a second objective of social sustainability, several labour issues were discussed again and again (*occupational justice*). In general, these issues include unfair, unhealthy, and inse-cure working conditions at home and abroad. The exploitation of workers, mainly in developing countries, was highly criticized, but low wages in the developed world were also considered to be a big problem, which is why some interviewees spoke up for binding minimum wages. In addition, child labour practices in the developing world were said to constitute a very important issue in the field of social sustainability.

Participants also commented on broader aspects of long-term *social justice*. For example, they stressed matters of fairness in the sense of giving everybody the chance to get a good job or trying not to shift problems of the present to the future. Widespread poverty (not only in foreign countries but also in Germany) as well as the strong need for fundamental peace are very abstract aspects which resulted from participants' ethical considerations. Last but not least, concrete social engagement seems to constitute an important issue of social justice. In particular, interviewees reported the necessity of helping other people in various ways (e.g., foreign aid, neighbourly help, community services):

Well, okay, social sustainability. So, I think that in general the most important resource for the future, that means our future, is our children. And this is why it is in my opin-ion very important to give children a decent education, that means healthy and hearty as well and not letting them munch this bunch of trash and junk and chips.

(Female, 58 years)

Such a salary gap between lower and upper tiers in a firm, I don't think this is socially sustainable because I think that because of this the lower tier in a firm, let's say 'the simple worker', has, relatively speaking, only bad, worse opportunities. . . . [W]e are actually living at the expense of the developing countries, that is, for example, that some poor worker is sitting in an Apple factory in China and becomes in fact lastingly etched or inhales some toxic dust the whole time, so that I can use my computer . . . and buy it as cheap as possible. This would be another example for social non-sustainability.

(Male, 30 years)

Finally, as reflected by the theoretical concept of a mindful mindset, personal issues should constitute a part of consumer sustainability. Participants showed a strong need to care for their own long-term well-being, which is different from pure selfishness as selfish motives are mainly connected with a short-term view. Altogether, the authors identified three objectives encompassing several issues of *individual sustainability*.[2] First of all, there was a strong emphasis on harmful or useful actions with regard to the human body (i.e. physical health). In particular, the interviewees mentioned the consumption of healthy food, a balanced diet, as well as watching one's weight. Furthermore, they assert that alcohol and cigarettes should only be consumed in small quantities. The principle behind these points is to exercise temperance instead of overindulging. Additionally, regular physical exercise was said to be essential for physical health.

Next, participants described general lifestyles serving the emotional well-being which can be subsumed under the term "mental health". For example, it was indicated that a proper work-life balance (i.e. a reasonable relation between working hours and leisure time) is very important for a person's individual sustainability. This includes avoiding high stress levels and planning regular recovery phases. Mental health can also be connected with a specific philosophy of life, which might help the individual experiencing positive emotions.

In addition to that, participants talked about issues of *economic health*, which is based on the individual's goal to operate economically in order to be well prepared for the future. Interviewees stated that, to ensure their own financial sustainability, debts should not go sky high. People should also save some money for bad times or for their own retirement:

> Hygiene of life in the sense of somehow eating right, be good to yourself, somehow ensure a healthy lifestyle, both mentally and physically, 'mens sana in corpore sano'; absolutely, and as I said in relation with others. That is how I define individual sustainability. . . . Exactly, so individual sustainability is very important to me, amongst them hygiene of life . . . that means also to be frugal with semiluxury foods and use them actually only as semiluxury foods.
>
> (Female, 27 years)

> Yes, yes, yes, that definitely belongs to individual sustainability, definitely. Well, I think it is very important that everyone decides for himself, you know that differs for everyone . . . how much he likes to work and . . . how many goods in terms of wealth and consumer goods are important for himself; and what he is willing to accept for it. Well, for example, if I like to buy a Porsche, then I simply have to work hard-core . . . I think that something like a work-life balance is most important to me, that means a personal . . . sustainability of time, so to say . . . Well, one thing that also belongs there when I think about it, is also a sustainable dealing with my own resources, so to say, that is, that I have really a look at it. Well, that I am self-supporting and for example do not run up more and more debts to buy something or to make a living; so that I have a look at my personal financial sustainability, that it is ensured, basically.
>
> (Male, 30 years)

After the objectives and the most important issues of consumer sustainability had been discussed, the three sustainability dimensions were systematically classified according to the perceived subjective importance of each one. Interviewees elaborated on how important they rank the different sustainability facets. Interviews revealed that most participants rank sustainability facets alongside a dimension of closeness and distance:

> I think the motivation behind this is really when it affects you personally, that means everything that happens around you. The closer it is, this is kind of a question of

closeness and distance, so the closer it is to you, the more important it is. That means also things you are wearing or consuming. Then people who are in your personal surroundings . . . [w]ell, and then things which are further away of course, so you can consider this as concentric, so to say. Everything of it, the individual in the middle of the centre, then in circular shape the issues, which are always, which are further away from me. These don't affect me directly.

(Female, 27 years)

First, first, first I am totally egoistic. I have to [see] that my family is doing well. Of course I cannot take this out of context and say '[W]hat's the sense if my family is okay but at the same time I do not care about the surroundings; and my daughter or my grandchildren will not be able to play in a forest in 30 years?' I realize the big picture, of course, this is the ecological sustainability, the most important one by far.

(Male, 48 years)

Comments led the authors to arrange consumer sustainability facets in eight systemic concentric circles (see Figure 4.2). Individual sustainability (i.e. the ego) constitutes the basis of the conceptualization. When asked about the subjective importance of sustainability issues, participants expressed a strong tendency to give priority to individual aspects. However, they also emphasized the importance of the family, first of all their own children and grandchildren, which constitutes the innermost circle of social sustainability. Furthermore, broader aspects of social sustainability (i.e. issues regarding other humans) surround these two circles, thereby ranging from close friends to distal unknown people. Emotions

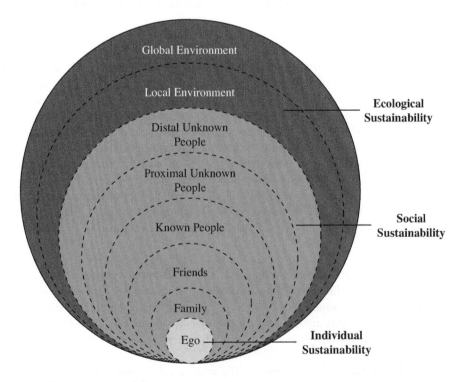

Figure 4.2 Consumer sustainability as a concentric construct

such as having a bad conscience are stronger for proximal than for distal persons. Many participants also share a general tendency to care more for humans than for the environment. In other words, even though interviewees realize ecological sustainability is the essential basis for further sustainability facets, social sustainability appears to be of higher personal relevance than ecological sustainability. Therefore, areas of local and global environment complete the system of circles.

5   Discussion

Companies focusing on the "right" sustainability issues "in the right way" are said to improve their financial performance (e.g. Chabowski et al., 2011). Therefore, the development of corporate strategies that build on a consumer's perspective of sustainability might be useful (Sheth et al., 2011). The developed circle approach shows similarity to the classification by Gibson et al. (2005, p. 57); however, the latter approach is based on a corporate perspective of sustainability (i.e. economy, society, and ecology). In particular, the sustainability circles can be associated with specific consumer-relevant issues.

The authors give three examples: improving the child's education (i.e. a social sustainability case), watching weight (i.e. an individual sustainability case), and saving the rain forest (i.e. an ecological sustainability case). First, the need to improve children's education seems to be most important to one's own family, but is also relevant to the ego and to other members of the society, with relevance declining from friends to distal unknown individuals. Second, watching one's weight shows highest priority to the ego and lower relevance for the society, with relevance declining from family to distal unknown people. And third, saving the rain forest is most important for the global environment and becomes less relevant when it comes to more inner circles of the sustainability system.

To sum up, this framework can help revealing the respective systems affected by a particular sustainability case. Whilst this seems accurate for average consumers, individual characteristics and preferences as well as cultural differences certainly influence the subjective importance ratings of a specific sustainability issue. For example, there are people who show a stronger orientation towards the environment than towards societal issues (e.g. eco-activists). Other consumers might give priority to close friends and not to family life. Moreover, people differ in their degree of long-term orientation (e.g. de Mooij and Hofstede, 2002) or egocentrism (e.g. Stagner, 1977). Finally, the different sustainability objectives and issues are not completely independent from each other but share several links (Goodland and Daly, 1996).

Despite the limitations mentioned above, this research approach might outline marketing-relevant sustainability objectives and issues. The concentric circles could be used as a starting point to develop marketing strategies which focus on the consumer. The conceptual framework can be seen as an initial attempt to classify and systematize consumers' sustainability objectives and issues. Notably, being in line with the concept of a mindful mindset (Sheth et al., 2011), aspects of individual sustainability could be integrated into the sustainability construct. Interestingly, there is an analogy between companies and consumers insofar as companies try to ensure their long-term existence by economic sustainability whilst individuals ensure their own long-term well-being through individual sustainability. Moreover, economic aspects also play an important role for consumers, thereby being objectives of both ecological (i.e., economic conservation) and individual sustainability (i.e., economic health).

Finally, as this approach takes a first step towards a conceptual framework of consumer sustainability, future research is certainly needed in this area. To begin with, developing a scale for the measurement of consumer-relevant aspects of sustainability would be promising. This scale could then be used for asking consumers to evaluate companies, brands, or products which deal (or do not deal) with these sustainability issues, thereby using (or not using) the word "sustainability" in their communication. To further investigate the practical utility of the consumer sustainability construct, empirical evidence about the interrelatedness of the numerous sustainability issues seems necessary.

Notes

1 The complete interview guide contained additional questions concerning consumers' consumption behaviour. These are not stated here because only the listed questions were relevant to the underlying research topic.
2 In addition to the three identified facets of individual sustainability, there was also some evidence for a fourth component, that is, social health. Social health includes the motive to have long-term relationships as well as long-lasting friendships. Nevertheless, further evidence seems necessary to strengthen this facet before it can be incorporated into a classification of consumer sustainability.

References

Batson, C. (2002). Addressing the altruism question experimentally. In S. Post, L. Underwood, J. Schloss and W. Hurlbut (eds.), *Altruism and Altruistic Love: Science, Philosophy, and Religion in Dialogue*. Oxford: Oxford University Press, 89–105.

Bengtsson, A. and Ostberg, J. (2006). Researching the cultures of brands. In R.W. Belk (ed.), *Handbook of Qualitative Research Methods in Marketing*. Aldershot: Edward Elgar, 83–93.

Chabowski, B.R., Mena, J.A. and Gonzalez-Padron, T.L. (2011). The structure of sustainability research in marketing, 1958–2008: A basis for future research opportunities. *Journal of the Academy of Marketing Science*, 39(1), 55–70.

Costanza, R. and Patten, B.C. (1995). Defining and predicting sustainability. *Ecological Economics*, 15(3), 193–6.

Creswell, J.W. (2009). *Research Design: Qualitative, Quantitative, and Mixed Method Approaches*, 3rd edn. Thousand Oaks, CA: Sage.

Csikszentmihalyi, M. (2000). The costs and benefits of consuming. *Journal of Consumer Research*, 27(2), 267–72.

De Mooij, M. and Hofstede, G. (2002). Convergence and divergence in consumer behavior: Implications for international retailing. *Journal of Retailing*, 78(1), 61–70.

Dovers, S.R. and Handmer, J.W. (1992). Uncertainty, sustainability and change. *Global Environmental Change*, 2(4), 262–76.

Dyllick, T. and Hockerts, K. (2002). Beyond the business case for corporate sustainability. *Business Strategy and the Environment*, 11(2), 130–41.

Elkington, J. (1998). *Cannibals with Forks: The Triple Bottom Line for 21st Century Business*. Oxford: Capstone.

Gibson, R.B., Hassan, S., Holtz, S., Tansey, J. and Whitelaw, G. (2005). *Sustainability Assessment: Criteria, Processes and Applications*. London: Earthscan.

Goodland, R. (1995). The concept of environmental sustainability. *Annual Review of Ecology and Systematics*, 26, 1–24.

Goodland, R. and Daly, H. (1996). Environmental sustainability: Universal and non-negotiable. *Ecological Applications*, 6(4), 1002–17.

Hutchins, M.J. and Sutherland, J.W. (2008). An exploration of measures of social sustainability and their application to supply chain decisions. *Journal of Cleaner Production*, 16(15), 1688–98.

Kilbourne, W.E. (2006). The role of the dominant social paradigm in the quality of life/environmental interface. *Applied Research in Quality of Life*, 1(1), 39–61.

Kotler, P. (2011). Re-inventing marketing to manage the environmental imperative. *Journal of Marketing*, 75(4), 131–5.

Lubin, D.A. and Esty, D.C. (2010). The sustainability imperative. *Harvard Business Review*, 88(5), 42–50.

McMichael, A. J., Bolin, B., Costanza, R., Daily, G.C., Folke, C., Lindahl-Kiessling, K., Lindgren, E., and Niklasson, B. (1999). Globalization and the sustainability of human health. *Bioscience*, 49(3), 205–10.

Nidumolu, R., Prahalad, C.K. and Rangaswami, M.R. (2009). Why sustainability is now the key driver of innovation. *Harvard Business Review*, 87(9), 56–64.

Ray, P., and Anderson, S.R. (2000). *The Cultural Creative*. New York: Harmony.

Schor, J.B. (1999). *The Overspent American: Why We Want What We Don't Need*. New York: Harper Perennial.

Schumann, K., Saili, L., Taylor, R. and Abdel-Malek, R. (2010). Hydropower and sustainable development: A journey. Retrieved 24 February 2012, fromhttp://89.206.150.89/documents/congresspapers/392.pdf/.

Sheth, J.N. (2011). Impact of emerging markets on marketing: Rethinking existing perspectives and practices. *Journal of Marketing*, 75(4), 166–82.

Sheth, J.N., Sethia, N.K. and Srinivas, S. (2011). Mindful consumption: A customer-centric approach to sustainability. *Journal of the Academy of Marketing Science*, 39(1), 21–39.

Stagner, R. (1977). Egocentrism, ethnocentrism and altrocentrism: Factors in individual and intergroup violence. *International Journal of Intercultural Relations*, 1(3), 9–30.

Stich, A., and Wagner, T. (2012). Fooling yourself: The role of internal defense mechanisms in unsustainable consumption behavior. *Advances in Consumer Research*, 40, 408–16.

Wapner, P. and Matthew, R.A. (2009). The humanity of global environmental ethics. *Journal of Environment and Development*, 18(2), 203–22.

Workman, J.P., Jr., Homburg, C. and Gruner, K. (1998). Marketing organization: An integrative framework of dimensions and determinants. *Journal of Marketing*, 63(3), 21–41.

Part II

Sustainability and management in Asia

5 Investigation of internal and external factors causing unethical behavior of accounting professionals

Ali Uyar and Ali Haydar Güngörmüş

1 Introduction

Ethical awareness is very important in the accounting profession as in some other ethics-sensitive fields, such as law and medicine. The ethics concept touches every part of life indeed: people, firms, states, laws and regulations, and so on. Thus, instilling ethical values in people is possible only with the collaboration of all these parties. While an employee is trying to behave ethically, employers or the regulatory environment should not motivate him or her to behave otherwise. All of these parties have to agree on a peaceful and ethical working environment. Otherwise, environmental conditions and people having moral weaknesses will give rise to a corrupt society and corporate scandals, as evidenced in recent years. Low et al. (2008) state that while some of the ethical dilemmas may not be particularly harmful, others may influence the organization's existence and subsequently affect society with destructive consequences. For example, the reliability of financial and other information provided by accountants is a necessary condition for the efficient operation of capital markets (Geiger & O'Connell, 1999). Shareholders, retirees, and others have lost billions of dollars due to fraudulent financial statements that were certified as materially correct by public accounting firms (Misiewicz, 2007).

Recent business scandals worldwide have indicated the importance of business ethics once again. These scandals have made ethical issues a prevailing research topic in the field of accounting (Su, 2006; Rashid & Ibrahim, 2008).In most of these scandals, unethical behavior of accounting professionals and executives played a key role. Stanga and Turpen (1991), Clement (2006), and Low et al. (2008) document the examples of both past and recent infamous accounting scandals and unethical attitudes from a variety of firms. Professional knowledge alone is not sufficient and is unable to fill the gap emerging from the absence of ethical attributes. A code of ethics is a crucial element in forming a profession, and professional organizations in various countries maintain codes of ethics in the accounting profession (Smith et al., 2005). An increasing number of scholarly publications on ethics supports this argument. Academicians try to find out the reasons behind unethical behavior, and search for solutions to the problem. In addition, they try to incorporate accounting ethics education into undergraduate and graduate curricula, either as a stand-alone course or as part of existing courses in the curriculum. How ethics should be taught is another question which still remains unanswered.

Based on the previous work of Cottone and Claus (2000), Sheng and Chen (2010) state that people's ethical attitudes are affected by external and internal factors. They say that the attitudes of decision makers, in different situations, are shaped by related events or the opinions of others, such as national laws, social expectations or consensus, stakeholders' demands, individual or group gains and losses, and the like. However, past studies have seldom explored which of the two influences on personal attitudes toward ethical decision making is more significant (Sheng & Chen, 2010). Hence, this study aims to examine internal and external factors that cause accounting professionals in Turkey to behave unethically. For this purpose, we administered an online questionnaire to professional accountants in various geographical areas of the country.

In Turkey, just as in other countries, accountants, academicians, and regulatory bodies are concerned with ethical issues. Thus, some research studies have been conducted by academicians in Turkey and the results have been documented in various national journals. Most of these studies were local studies, conducted in a single city or neighboring cities (Aymankuy & Sarıoğlan, 2005; İşgüden & Çabuk, 2006; Kutlu, 2008; Kısakürek & Alpan, 2010; Angay Kutluk & Ersoy, 2011). These studies dealt with various aspects of ethical issues, such as ethics education, ethical dilemmas accountants face, perceptions of accountants and students on ethical issues, and so on. This research study has been conducted on accountants from almost all geographical areas of Turkey. Thus, it is a countrywide investigation of the matter focused particularly on motivations for unethical behavior.

In the next section, the accounting profession in Turkey and development of ethical values is summarized. The literature review regarding unethical behavior of accounting professionals is provided in the third section. In the fourth section, scope and methodology are presented. In the fifth section, results are analyzed. In the last section, concluding comments are provided.

2   The accounting profession in Turkey and development of ethical values

In Turkey, accounting practices were tied to some rules with the promulgation of a law, namely the Commercial Code, adopted from the French Commercial Code in 1850. Later on, the first Turkish Commercial Code was enacted in 1926. This law brought some regulations regarding bookkeeping, profit calculation, balance sheets, and profit and loss accounts. Further regulations regarding accounting were expanded with the Turkish Tax Procedural Law in 1950 and the revised Turkish Commercial Code in 1956. Subsequently, the Turkish Capital Markets Law was enacted in 1981, parallel to developments in the private sector. This law affected the accounting practices of publicly traded companies. One of the giant steps in the development of accounting practices was taken by the Ministry of Finance, which published "Communiqué on the Application of Accounting System" in 1992. It included the Turkish Uniform Chart of Accounts, basic accounting concepts, and principles of financial statement preparation. Firms have been required to conduct accounting practices according to this communiqué since then. Meanwhile, the Capital Markets Board has required publicly traded companies to adopt the International Accounting Standards since 2005 by promulgation of a law. The Turkish Commercial Code was revised comprehensively once again in 2011. This revision refers to implementation of accounting standards which were adopted from International Accounting Standards.

In Turkey, accounting began to be considered as a profession in 1989 by promulgation of Law No. 3568. This law delineated three titles for the accounting profession: Independent Accountant (IA), Certified Public Accountant (CPA), and Sworn-in Certified Public Accountant (SCPA). However, the latest law, enacted in 2008, no longer permits the Independent Accountant title; only two titles remain today.

According to a U.S. study, public accountants perceive their own professional body (the American Institute of Certified Public Accountants) and the use of peer review as the most effective mechanisms for establishing ethical standards, while government regulation is ranked the least effective one (Cohen & Pant, 1991). In Turkey, there are several regulations which guide and set ethical principles in the accounting profession directly or indirectly. These are (Selimoğlu, 2006; Sakarya & Kara, 2010):

*   "Communiqué on the Application of Accounting System", which includes 12 basic accounting concepts, including some regarding ethical principles such as social responsibility.
*   Law No. 3568 on Independent Accountancy, Certified Public Accountancy, and Sworn-in Certified Public Accountancy provides some points of professional ethics.
*   Communiqué on functioning principles of TURMOB (the Union of Chambers of Certified Public Accountants and Sworn-in Certified Public Accountants of Turkey), which includes some points regarding professional ethics.
*   Communiqué No. 2499, enacted by the Capital Markets Board, covers some principles in relation to professional ethics.
*   "The Mandatory Professional Decision on Code of Ethics for IA, CPA, and SCPA Professionals", issued by TURMOB in 2001.
*   "Communiqué No. 26675 on Ethical Principles That IA, CPA and SCPA Will Implement in Professional Activities", issued by TURMOB in 2007.

3   Unethical behavior of accounting professionals

Not practicing according to ethical values has negative impacts on corporations, national economy, investors, the accounting profession itself, accountants, and accounting students. Such unethical behavior instigated many corporate scandals that led to the bankruptcy of many investors and to a loss of confidence in the marketplace. Regaining such trust may take years. The image of the profession is smeared due to unethical conduct. Accountants have to live under suspicion. Therefore, professional bodies and accountants themselves have to try to preserve ethical standards within the profession zealously and voluntarily. The results of a survey indicate that accounting majors are influenced by corporate scandals in such a way that even if they become more interested in the profession itself, they express less interest in working for a Big 4 accounting firm (Comunale et al., 2006).

Oseni (2011) states that a professional accountant's responsibility is not merely to satisfy the needs of an individual client or employer but to act in the public interest, complying with the code of ethics for this profession. Disregard for this view is exemplified in most worldwide scandals. The collapse of companies such as Enron, WorldCom and Global Crossing in the USA, HIH Insurance and OneTel in Australia, and Parmalat in Italy, and subsequently the demise of one of the then "Big 5" accounting firms, Arthur Andersen, have caused investors to lose their confidence in the financial reporting system (Jackling et al., 2007).

Unfortunately, empirical evidence indicates that accountants are increasingly concerned with the ethical conduct of those in the profession, and they believe that unethical behavior is on the increase among practicing accountants (Finn et al., 1994). There are several factors in this worsening situation. Competition is cited as one of the reasons for unethical behavior (Finn et al., 1994). It is argued that the pressures of the marketplace may lead to even more unethical behavior to secure or retain clients (Finn et al., 1994).

Several studies have been conducted on the reasons for unethical behavior in the accounting profession. In a Turkish study, Aymankuy and Sarıoğlan (2005) found that 55% of the respondents agreed with the statement that "accounting professionals attach importance to ethics as monthly earnings increase". However, 42.5% disagreed with the statement. (The remainder had no opinion.) Thus, the statement did not receive widespread support even though the majority seemed to agree with it. Accounting professionals state that they face ethical dilemmas in their professional life, and that the primary reason for such dilemmas is the fear of losing clients (Kutlu, 2008) who put pressure on accountants to lower the prices of services they offer (İşgüden & Çabuk, 2006). Another reason for ethical dilemmas is the clients who try to avoid tax burdens, and accountants believe that lowering tax rates can reduce such attempts (Kutlu, 2008). Insufficient financial auditing and legal gaps result in increasing client pressure and conflict among accountants (İşgüden & Çanuk, 2006). Furthermore, accountants use such legal gaps to benefit their clients (Aymankuy & Sarıoğlan, 2005). Kutluk and Ersoy (2011) found that desire to earn more, insufficient auditing, inadequate education, market conditions, and clients are the main reasons for unethical behavior; moreover, the present laws are not fully effective in preventing unethical behavior. It is imperative for governmental bodies and laws/regulations to stipulate more effective applications.

Previous studies on ethical issues provide inconsistent results with respect to their incidence vis-à-vis respondent characteristics. The frequency of facing ethical dilemmas differs based on income level, age, education level, gender, and number of clients (Kutlu, 2008). Keller et al. (2007) also found differences in individual ethical standards based on gender, educational level, work experience, and religiosity. However, Kutluk and Ersoy (2011) found significant difference in terms of ethical decision-making for gender only, but not for age, education level, and job title.

4   Methodology

In recent years, there has been a growing tendency to utilize online questionnaires rather than mailed ones. We opted for the former because it has some advantages over traditional mail questionnaires such as being less costly, faster, and more reliable than the traditional questionnaire survey (Uyar & Gungormuş, 2011).

Although many previous studies have focused on ethics in accounting, there is a need to investigate the antecedents of unethical behavior in professional accountants. For this purpose, we prepared an online questionnaire adopted from earlier studies and sent it to professional accountants in Turkey. Data was collected during November and December 2011. A total of 219 accountants responded to the survey. The questionnaire we prepared consisted of thirteen sections. This chapter covers the analyses of only four questions, which were adapted from (Aymankuy & Sarıoğlan, 2005; Kısakürek & Alpan, 2010; Kutluk & Ersoy, 2011; Uyar and Gungormuş, 2011). Section 1 includes demographic questions; Section 2 includes evaluations of skills required in job applicants; Section 3 and Section 4 question external and internal factors of unethical behavior respectively. Hence, four sections of the questionnaire were structured to answer the following research questions:

RQ1: What skills do professional accountants expect from job applicants who are interested in the accounting profession?

RQ2: What external factors cause accountants to behave unethically?

RQ3: What internal factors cause accountants to behave unethically?

RQ4: Are there any significant differences among various sub-groups (e.g. gender, income level, education level, experience) of the respondents in terms of external and internal factors of unethical behavior of accountants?

5   Analyses and results

Demographic background

In the first section of the questionnaire, we asked about demographic properties of the respondents for the purpose of investigating whether or not there are significant differences among respondents' views in relation to demographic factors. In this section, we asked questions to determine respondents' gender, job title, income level, education, and experience. The answers given to this section's questions indicated that 179 respondents are male and 40 are female. Additionally, 124 respondents have working experience of less than or equal to 10 years, while the remaining 95 have more than 10 years. Most of the respondents are university graduates, while some hold a master's degree or PhD. Other demographic properties are in relation to "title of the accountant", and "income level". The majority of the respondents are from Istanbul, and the remainder are from various other cities. The detailed statistics for all demographic properties are given in Table 5.1.

Table 5.1 Demographic background

	Frequency	Percent
I. Gender		
Female	40	18.3
Male	179	81.7
Total	219	100.0
II. Experience		
1–5 years	62	28.3
6–10 years	62	28.3
11–15 years	41	18.7
16–20 years	23	10.5
Over 20 years	31	14.2
Total	219	100.0
III. Education		
High school	9	4.1
2-year college	13	5.9
University	144	65.8
Master's degree/PhD	*53*	*24.2*
Total	219	100.0
IV. Title		
Intern	66	30.1
Independent Accountant (IA)	14	6.4

(*Continued*)

Table 5.1 (Continued)

	Frequency	Percent
Certified Public Accountant (CPA)	106	48.4
Sworn-in Certified Public Accountant (SCPA)	6	2.7
No title	27	12.3
Total	219	100.0
V. Income level		
Less than 1.000 TL*	11	5.0
1.000–3000 TL	134	61.2
3001–5000 TL	48	21.9
5001–10.000 TL	24	11.0
Over 10.000 TL	2	0.9
Total	219	100.0
VI. City of residence		
İstanbul	128	58.4
Bursa	26	11.9
Ankara	15	6.8
Kayseri	13	5.9
Kütahya	5	2.3
Others (less than 5)	32	14.6
Total	219	100.0

* Turkish liras

Skills expected from job applicants

As is the case in almost every field, accounting requires mastery of certain skills in those who are interested in and want to enter the field. Based on the literature review (Uyar & Gungormuş, 2011), we compiled eight different types of skills and asked the respondents to evaluate their relative importance. Including "ethical values" among these skills, we wanted to see how ethics is rated compared to the others. The respondents were required to rate the importance of these skills based on a Likert scale ranging from 1 to 5 (1 = not important and 5 = extremely important). The purpose of this section was to determine the most important skills that job applicants should have for the accounting field.

Table 5.2 indicates the importance of eight skills required in applicants for accounting jobs. As shown in the table, means of all skills except that of "leadership skills" (mean = 3.79) are above 4.00. This means that all skills, other than "leadership skills", are perceived to be important or very important by professional accountants. Furthermore, when the skills are ranked according to their means to compare their relative importance, the rankings indicate that "ethical values" is considered to be the most important, followed closely by "technical accounting knowledge". Uyar and Gungormuş (2011) also found, in an earlier study, that auditors regard work ethics and ethical awareness among the most important skills for the auditing profession. Thus, the results corroborate the importance of ethics for the accounting profession along with technical knowledge. This finding

Table 5.2 Skills expected from job applicants

	Mean	Std. Dev.	Rank
Ethical values	4.51	0.638	1
Technical accounting knowledge	4.50	0.726	2
Communication skills	4.35	0.729	3
Interpersonal communication skills	4.34	0.708	4
Critical & analytic thinking	4.28	0.807	5
Strategic thinking	4.17	0.875	6
Professionalism	4.09	0.897	7
Leadership skills	3.79	1.031	8

Table 5.3 External factors causing unethical behavior

	Mean	Std. Dev.	Rank
Clients	4.26	0.882	1
Colleagues	3.56	1.212	2
Credit providers	3.41	1.143	3
Insufficiency of laws	3.32	1.249	4
Governmental bodies	3.32	1.179	5
Professional bodies	3.01	1.290	6

supports Selimoğlu (2006), who states that professional ethics and professional knowledge are two inseparable parts of a whole in the accounting field.

External factors causing unethical behavior

In the relevant literature, there are some external factors which are assumed to cause accountants to behave unethically. We compiled six factors based on the work of Aymankuy and Sarıoğlan (2005) and asked the respondents to rate their importance based on a Likert scale ranging from 1 to 5 (1 = not important and 5 = extremely important). Means of all six items in Table 5.3 indicate that external factors do not play much of a role in unethical behavior of professional accountants, except for the factor of "clients" (mean = 4.26). Thus, the clients are pointed at as putting pressure on accountants and causing them to deviate from laws, rules, and ethical principles and values. Generally, the motivation is assumed to be paying less tax by requiring accountants to pump up expenses and lower revenues. "Colleagues" seem to play a secondary role in unethical behavior (mean = 3.56) since those who break the rules and engage in unfair competition set examples for the others. Other external factors do not significantly affect unethical behavior. Aymankuy and Sarıoğlan (2005) found that the most effective factor in unethical behavior is the client; other factors, such as insufficiency of laws, colleagues, governmental bodies, credit institutions, and so on, play only a small role.

Table 5.4 Internal factors causing unethical behavior

	Mean	Std. Dev.	Rank
Desire to earn more	4.42	0.817	1
Fear of losing the client	4.39	0.785	2
Moral weakness	4.23	0.973	3
Not knowing ethical rules well	3.37	1.251	4
Political tendency	3.13	1.183	5
Insufficient experience	3.05	1.282	6

Internal factors causing unethical behavior

In the relevant literature, in addition to external factors, there are some frequently mentioned internal factors that cause unethical behavior. We compiled six factors, based on the work of Kısakürek and Alpan (2010), and asked the respondents to rate their importance based on a Likert scale ranging from 1 to 5 (1 = not important and 5 = extremely important). The results revealed that "desire to earn more" (mean = 4.42), "fear of losing the client" (mean = 4.39) and "moral weakness" (mean = 4.23) are the three most important internal factors causing unethical behavior in the accounting profession (see Table 5.4). The remaining three factors, namely, "political tendency" (mean = 3.13), "not knowing ethical rules well" (mean = 3.37) and "insufficient experience" (mean = 3.05) are not significantly influential in unethical behavior. Furthermore, we conducted Pearson correlation analysis and saw that there is a strong correlation between "clients" in external factors and "fear of losing the client" in internal factors. This might mean that these two factors affect each other. Thus, clients' pressure causes fear of losing the client, and those who fear losing the client may feel the pressure of clients more. This countrywide study corroborates the finding of another study which found that "desire to earn more" and "moral weakness" are the primary motivations of unethical behavior (Kısakürek & Alpan, 2010). Therefore, an individual's personal values play a more prominent role than any code of ethics in resolving ethical dilemmas (Low et al., 2008).

Sub-group analysis

The answers of sub-groups regarding the reasons for unethical behavior were compared on the basis of job title, income level, gender, education level, and experience. When the results of one-way ANOVA analysis and independent samples t-test are evaluated, we see that there is little significant difference among sub-groups (see Tables 5.5 and 5.6). Thus, sub-groups seem to concur on acceptance or rejection of external and internal reasons for unethical behavior.

One-way ANOVA analysis was used to compare answers of respondents having different job titles (Table 5.5). According to the results, there is a significant difference among respondents in terms of only a single item, namely "insufficiency of laws". The means of this item indicate that SCPAs, who have the highest ranking in job title, are against the statement "insufficiency of laws cause unethical behavior" more firmly than other accountants. There are no significant differences in terms of other items.

Table 5.5 Comparison of means of sub-groups based on titles regarding factors of unethical behavior

	No title	Intern	Independent Accountant	CPA	SCPA	F-value
	(N = 27)	(N = 66)	(N = 14)	(N = 106)	(N = 6)	
External factors						
Insufficiency of laws	3.37	3.36	2.79	3.42	2.17	2.183*
Governmental bodies	3.11	3.36	3.21	3.41	2.33	1.463
Credit providers	3.26	3.56	2.86	3.46	2.83	1.679
Professional bodies	3.00	3.00	3.00	3.01	3.33	0.094
Clients	4.07	4.32	4.07	4.30	4.00	0.716
Colleagues	3.63	3.52	3.07	3.65	3.17	0.920
Internal factors						
Desire to earn more	4.44	4.39	4.21	4.48	4.00	0.787
Fear of losing the client	4.26	4.39	4.00	4.49	4.17	1.627
Moral weakness	4.04	4.17	3.93	4.39	3.67	1.891
Political inclinations	2.70	3.35	2.79	3.17	2.83	1.890
Not knowing ethical rules well	3.48	3.44	3.29	3.32	3.33	0.159
Insufficient experience	2.78	3.05	3.36	3.08	3.17	0.523

*Significant at 0.10 level; **Significant at 0.05 level; ***Significant at 0.01 level

For the other sub-groups, independent samples t-test was conducted (Table 5.6). Accountants, classified according to income level, have no significant differences in terms of any of the twelve factors. There is a significant difference between female and male accountants for only one factor: fear of losing the client. Comparison of means of this item reveals that male accountants feel more pressure from clients than do their female counterparts. Alternatively, clients may tend to put more pressure on male accountants than on female ones. Furthermore, education level makes a significant difference for only a single factor too; namely, insufficient experience. Master's degree or PhD holders feel that insufficient experience does not contribute much to unethical behavior. However, it should be kept in mind that, although there is a significant difference for this item between these two groups, the means (3.16 for non–Master's degree/PhD holders, 2.70 for Master's degree/PhD holders) are already quite low compared to "4 = agree and 5 = strongly agree" level. Finally, experience is said to have a little impact, since it has significant difference for two items: colleagues and insufficient experience. Based on the means of items, we can say that the less experienced accountants think that colleagues cause them to behave unethically, possibly due to their unjust competitive behaviors. For example, if some colleagues in the sector yield to the improper demands of clients, this might cause other accountants to manipulate the regulations in a similarly unethical manner as well. On the contrary, more experienced accountants think more strongly than less experienced ones that insufficient experience contributes to unethical behavior. However, the means of this item for two sub-groups are also much lower than "4 = agree and 5 = strongly agree" level. Moreover, if the means of all twelve items are compared, one will realize that the means of external factors are lower for more experienced accountants than those for less experienced ones, whereas the means of internal factors display just the opposite.

Table 5.6 Comparison of means of sub-groups regarding factors of unethical behavior by independent samples t-test

	Income level		t-test	Gender		t-test	Education level		t-test	Experience		t-test
	<3.000TL (N = 145)	>3.000TL (N = 74)		Male (N = 179)	Female (N = 40)		Non-MD/PhD (N = 166)	MD/PhD (N = 53)		<=10 years (N = 124)	>10 years (N = 95)	
External factors												
Insufficiency of laws	3.36	3.26	-0.570	3.33	3.30	0.135	3.36	3.21	-0.780	3.40	3.22	-1.070
Governmental bodies	3.30	3.35	0.325	3.35	3.18	0.830	3.37	3.15	-1.165	3.34	3.28	-.338
Credit providers	3.51	3.22	-1.810	3.40	3.48	-0.391	3.38	3.51	0.719	3.50	3.29	-1.319
Professional bodies	3.03	2.99	-0.222	3.03	2.93	0.480	3.02	2.98	-0.211	3.03	2.99	-.243
Clients	4.32	4.14	-1.448	4.28	4.13	1.037	4.25	4.26	0.080	4.34	4.15	-1.596
Colleagues	3.61	3.45	-0.970	3.56	3.53	0.185	3.61	3.40	-1.111	3.72	3.35	-2.263**
Internal factors												
Desire to earn more	4.45	4.36	-0.714	4.42	4.40	0.172	4.42	4.42	-0.051	4.40	4.44	.349
Fear of losing the client	4.38	4.42	0.353	4.45	4.13	2.413**	4.37	4.45	0.640	4.37	4.42	.467
Moral weakness	4.20	4.28	0.602	4.18	4.43	-1.417	4.19	4.36	1.119	4.20	4.26	.463
Political inclinations	3.12	3.15	0.145	3.16	3.00	0.782	3.17	3.02	-0.802	3.09	3.19	.624
Not knowing ethical rules well	3.39	3.35	-0.195	3.31	3.65	-1.546	3.41	3.26	-0.736	3.29	3.48	1.137
Insufficient experience	3.01	3.14	0.699	3.07	2.95	0.546	3.16	2.70	-2.319**	2.84	3.33	2.834***

*Significant at 0.10 level; **significant at 0.05 level; ***significant at 0.01 level.

6 Conclusion

This study provides evidence that internal factors rather than external ones play an important role in accountants' engagement in unethical behavior. In particular, we have seen that clients force accountants to behave unethically, and accountants' fear of losing clients fuels unethical behavior. According to the findings, moral weakness also contributes to unethical professional practices. Above all, making more money appears to be the primary reason for unethical behavior. A person often acts immorally or unethically for personal benefit. This finding is based on the individual level; however, corporate-level scandals also occur due to the same reason. Every individual, as well as every corporation, tries to make more money. Greed leads people to manipulate laws, regulations, and principles; in short, to unlawful and ethical practices.

The findings have some implications for the education system, corporations, families, and individuals. In order to prevent immoral or unethical behavior, an early foundation must be set at the very beginning, namely, by the family and the educational system. Formal or informal education given to individuals in the early years is especially important since it will shape the personality, and in turn, the behavior of people who may face ethical dilemmas in later years. Environment is also an important factor in controlling unethical behaviors. Corporations should take precautions and guide their employees in how to behave under certain dichotomous situations. They may adopt an ethics policy and make employees aware of their institutional ethics. Besides, a robust corporate governance structure will ensure the achievement of corporate targets without resorting to unethical applications. Professional bodies are also a cornerstone of establishing and maintaining codes of professional conduct. They should take on an active role in policing and reprimanding accountants who do not comply with ethical standards.

References

Angay Kutluk, F., & Ersoy, A. (2011). Muhasebe meslek üyelerinin etik yargı düzeyleri üzerine bir araştırma. *Ege Akademik Bakış Dergisi, 11*(3), 425–438.

Aymankuy, Y., & Sarioğlan, M. (2005). Muhasebe meslek mensuplarının meslek etiğine yaklaşımları ve Balıkesir il merkezinde bir uygulama. *Balıkesir Üniversitesi Sosyal Bilimler Enstitüsü Dergisi, 8*(14), 23–45.

Clement, R.W. (2006). Just how unethical is American business? *Business Horizons, 49*, 313–327.

Cohen, J.R., & Pant, L.W. (1991). Beyond bean counting: Establishing high ethical standards in the public accounting profession. *Journal of Business Ethics, 10*, 45–56.

Comunale, C.L., Sexton, T.R., & Gara, S.C. (2006). Professional ethical crises: A case study of accounting majors. *Managerial Auditing Journal, 21*(6), 636–656.

Cottone, R.R., & Claus, R.E. (2000). Ethical decision-making models: A review of the literature. *Journal of Counseling and Development, 78*(3), 275–283.

Finn, D.W., Munter, P., & McCaslin, T.E. (1994). Ethical perceptions of CPAs. *Managerial Auditing Journal, 9*(1), 23–28.

Geiger, M.A., & O'Connell, B.T. (1999). Accounting student ethical perceptions: An analysis of training and gender effects. *Teaching Business Ethics, 2*, 371–388.

İşgüden, B., & Çabuk, A. (2006). Meslek etiği ve meslek etiğinin meslek yaşamı üzerindeki etkileri. *Balıkesir Üniversitesi Sosyal Bilimler Enstitüsü Dergisi, 9*(16), 59–86.

Jackling, B., Cooper, B.J., Leung, P., & Dellaportas, S. (2007). Professional accounting bodies' perceptions of ethical issues, causes of ethical failure and ethics education. *Managerial Auditing Journal, 22*(9), 928–944.

Keller, A.C., Smith, K.T., & Smith, L.M. (2007). Do gender, educational level, religiosity, and work experience affect the ethical decision-making of U.S. accountants? *Critical Perspectives on Accounting, 18*, 299–314.

Kısakürek, M.M., & Alpan, N. (2010). Muhasebe meslek etiği ve Sivas ilinde bir uygulama. *Muhasebe ve Finansman Dergisi, 47*, 213–228.

Kutlu, H.A. (2008). Muhasebe meslek mensupları ve çalışanlarının etik ikilemleri. *Ankara Üniversitesi SBF Dergisi, 63*(2), 143–170.

Low, M., Davey, H., & Hooper, K. (2008). Accounting scandals, ethical dilemmas and educational challenges. *Critical Perspectives on Accounting, 19*, 222–254.

Misiewicz, K.M. (2007). The normative impact of CPA firms, professional organizations, and state boards on accounting ethics education. *Journal of Business Ethics, 70*, 15–21.

Oseni, A.I. (2011). Unethical behavior by professional accountant in an organization. *Research Journal of Finance and Accounting, 2*(2), 106–111.

Rashid, M.Z., & Ibrahim, S. (2008). The effect of culture and religiosity on business ethics: A cross-cultural comparison. *Journal of Business Ethics, 82*, 907–917.

Sakarya, Ş., & Kara, S. (2010). Türkiye'de muhasebe meslek etiğine yönelik düzenlemeler ve meslek mensupları tarafından algılanması üzerine bir alan araştırması. *KMÜ Sosyal ve Ekonomik Araştırmalar Dergisi, 12*(18), 57–72.

Selimoğlu, S.K. (2006). Türk muhasebe uygulamalarında etik. *Mali Çözüm, Sayı 76*, 437–456.

Sheng, C.-W., & Chen, M.C. (2010). The influence of environmental practices on ethical attitudes: Internal principles vs external factors. *Social Responsibility Journal, 6*(4), 510–521.

Smith, L.M., Smith, K.T., & Mulig, E.V. (2005). Application and assessment of an ethics presentation for accounting and business classes. *Journal of Business Ethics, 61*, 153–164.

Stanga, K.G., & Turpen, R.A. (1991). Ethical judgments on selected accounting issues: An empirical study. *Journal of Business Ethics, 10*, 739–747.

Su, S. (2006). Cultural differences in determining the ethical perception and decision-making of future accounting professionals: A comparison between accounting students from Taiwan and the United States. *The Journal of American Academy of Business, Cambridge, 9*(1), 147–158.

Uyar, A., & Gungormuş, A.H. (2011). Professional knowledge and skills required for accounting majors who intend to become auditors: Perceptions of external auditors. *Business and Economics Research Journal, 2*(3), 33–49.

6 Corporate environmental reporting in Turkey

Status and challenges

Uğur Kaya and Yaşar Bayraktar

1 Introduction

The environment is humans' and other living beings' life support system. It includes what they depend on during their life span, such as natural resources (air, water, soil and so on).

When making decisions about environmental values, different approaches are available. The first of them is to exclude environmental values and suppose that environmental values are worthless for corporations. The second approach is to pay more attention to environmental values and suppose that the environment and the corporation are interrelated. The third approach is about environmental impact analysis. After comparing environmental and financial circumstances, a decision about environmental values is made. The fourth approach is related to benefit and cost analysis and the purpose is to see all benefits and costs before evaluating the circumstance (Milne, 1991: 81). The various approaches show that perspectives on the environment are changeable. It is inarguable that corporations' operations do have positive or negative effects on the environment. Economic growth, industrialization, overpopulation, and irresponsible consumption cause environmental crises. Day by day, air pollution, water pollution, soil pollution and global warming threaten life on Earth. Because of the negative effects, many corporations are under external pressures to improve their environmental performance.

During the past few decades, because of serious environmental crises, there has been a significant increase in the public awareness of our natural environment. With this increase, stakeholders began to question corporations' information about their environmental activities. Many corporations were thus obliged to adopt environmental policies and disclose their environmental performance in an annual reports or stand-alone environment reports.

All activities related to environmental accounting and reporting started with the developed countries because those countries largely caused the environmental problems. In addition, those corporations have implemented environmental reporting practices as a result of pressures from various stakeholders. From the perspective of developing countries, accounting issues (including environmental accounting and reporting) might seem trivial when compared with the basic needs of large majorities of the population.

As a result, environmental accounting and reporting practices in developing countries lag behind those of the more developed countries. It is believed that lack of adequate resources and qualified personnel has led to patchy environmental accounting and reporting practices in these countries.

From the perspective of Turkey, there has been a steady increase in awareness of environmental issues since the 1980s. In spite of this attention to environmental issues, due to lack of legal requirements, shortage of staff and cost of reporting, environmental accounting and reporting terminology are quite new for Turkish companies.

The purpose of this study is to examine environmental reporting practices in developing countries within the context of Turkey and determine the implementation problems of environmental reporting in Turkey.

The remainder of the study is organized as follows: the second section discusses both the key concept and the terms related to environmental reporting and concentrates on environmental reporting practices in Turkey as a developing country. The third section concerns the challenges of environmental reporting.

2   Environmental reporting

In this section, for shedding light on subjects of this chapter, we will first discuss some basic concepts and terms related to environmental reporting.

Definition and scope of environmental reporting

Environmental reporting is a sub-concept of environmental accounting. Therefore, it is useful to define environmental accounting. Environmental accounting has various meanings. In other words, its definition changes according to different purposes. For instance, on the one hand, it supports national income accounting; on the other hand, it deals with financial accounting. Thus, environmental accounting should be defined from different perspectives to make a conceptual analysis of all aspects of environmental accounting.

According to the Environmental Protection Agency's (EPA) approach, environmental accounting arises from three different contexts: national income accounting, financial accounting and managerial accounting.

In *national income accounting*, environmental accounting can help to measure gross domestic product correctly, because the consumption of a nation's natural resources (both renewable and non-renewable) can be determined as a physical and monetary unit. In *financial accounting*, "environmental accounting" refers to the estimating and reporting of environmental liabilities and environmental costs and how financial transactions related to the environment are recorded. Lastly, in *managerial accounting*, "environmental accounting" refers to controlling environmental costs and integrating these costs into managerial decisions (EPA, 1995).

Sefcik et al. (1997) define environmental accounting as a new concept which investigates how environmental issues affect traditional accounting sub-disciplines. Steele and Powell (2002) describe environmental accounting as the identification, allocation, and analysis of material streams and their related money flows by using environmental accounting systems to provide insight into environmental impacts and associated financial effects.

Considering the above definitions and other explanations, environmental accounting can be defined as a process of measuring and recording the environmental impacts of business on society and reporting these impacts for stakeholders in special reports or traditional financial statements.

Traditional financial statements are important for stakeholders in decision-making because they provide the knowledge on how a business runs its operations. Thus the external users can evaluate the use of the scarce resources so that internal users can utilize them for operational planning and monitoring the results of operations. Traditional accounting tries to provide partial information by excluding non-priced transaction and crucial natural resources which are crucial to the assessment of human welfare and deals with resources that have clearly defined property rights and market prices (Herath, 2005: 1038). But environmental accounting focuses on the monetary implications of the environmental impact and aspects of a company, including implications for cash outlays, revenue and so on. It translates environmental impact and concern into monetary values. Companies that wish to demonstrate those environmental activities should prepare effective environmental reports.

Environmental reporting is prepared to present corporations' financial and non-financial information related to interaction with the physical and social environment, in their annual reports or stand-alone reports to stakeholders (Kavut, 2010).

An effective environmental report plainly explains the environmental impacts of a corporation and shows how a corporation tries to lessen the effects of its operations by disclosing its environment policies, strategies and achievements.

The major users of environmental data are internal managers, non-governmental organizations, lenders, unions, suppliers, investors, customers, employees and regulatory agencies. Transparency and disclosures of corporations' environmental status are a way of getting into touch with these stakeholders. An environmental report includes organization profile, environmental policy statement, goals and achievement, performance and compliance, management system and procedures and an independent verification statement (ACCA, 2001).

Within this definition, it can be concluded that "environmental accounting" is an umbrella term which encompasses environmental reporting, environmental performance evaluation and environmentally related financial reporting.

Benefits of environmental reporting

Environmental reporting can lead to crucial benefits for corporations as well as benefits for the environment. These benefits maximize corporations' profit and provide a better environment to live in for the community and corporations alike. Benefits include (DEFRA, 2006):

- Cost-saving and productivity gains
- Improved sales and profitability
- Improved reputation of corporations
- "Preferred supplier" status
- Improved environmental situation
- Increased attractiveness to the investors
- Minimized risk of regulatory intervention with effective self-regulation
- Product and service innovation
- Enhanced employee motivation and performance
- Strengthened stakeholder relations
- Providing other companies with a benchmark for environmental improvement
- Major role in risk management
- General public approval and increasing competitive advantage.

Taking the environment into account provides an increase in the numbers of stakeholders who consider, respect or share the same values.

Environmental reporting theories and methods

The main purpose of corporations is to profit and to be sustainable, but corporations are social structures and they should care about the environment to exist and survive. Besides financial and social performance, environmental performance is required to be sustainable and to be supported by stakeholders. Social and environmental reporting is affected by theories which are crucial for corporate governance. These are described by Kavut (2010):

- **Stakeholder Theory:** "Stakeholder" can be defined as any human agency that can be influenced by, or can influence, the activities and performances of reaching a corporation's goals. The theory's main approach is to treat all stakeholders equally and honestly. Corporations that adopt stakeholder theory must report environmental issues in annual reports or stand-alone environmental reports because they owe accountability and transparency to all stakeholders.
- **Legitimacy Theory:** Corporations can survive only if their operations are commensurate with their society's values and belief system. Thus operations can be legitimized through environmental reporting.
- **Accountability Theory:** For legal and moral reasons, a corporation has to give information about its operations to its shareholders. When obtaining environment-related permits and licenses, corporations are responsible for compliance with rules and laws. This is accountability for corporations to its shareholders.

Kaya and Durgut (2008) define three methods for communicating information about a corporation's environmental activities and performance to the stakeholders. These are:

- **The expansion of annual reports:** The environmental information is shown as a balance sheet or income statement items in fundamental financial statements, or it is presented in the corporation's annual report.
- **Stand-alone reporting:** The environmental information is shown in a report which is separate from the annual reports.
- **Combined reporting:** This method includes both the expansion of an annual report and a stand-alone report. It is mostly used by corporations with a high sensitivity to the environment.

3   Environmental reporting in Turkey as a developing country: Status and challenges

An overview on environmental reporting in developing countries

In general, most accounting techniques are adopted and implemented by developed countries. Environmental accounting as a new development in the field has been mainly a phenomenon of developed countries. Developed countries have achieved a lot of progress in this field while developing countries are still in early stages (Jahamani, 2003: 37).

In developing countries, environmental reporting is more acute because the current world economic system – characterized by increasing globalization, international trade and international capital flows, portfolio investments and debt – puts these countries in an unfavourable position vis-à-vis developed countries (Nuhoglu, 2003: 1). Therefore, environmental reporting in these countries is limited.

Gray and Kouhy (1996) stated that the main reason for this situation is that global environmental degradation created by the developing countries, as opposed to that created by the developed countries, is relatively unimportant. They put forward two main reasons for starting advances in environmental accounting with developed countries. They can be summarized as follows:

- Developed countries will have greatest impact
- Developed countries largely caused the problems in the first place
- Sustainability for the world can't be achieved by the developing countries alone.

The second reason is that environmental accounting issues are not so important when compared to more pressing matters for developing countries. In developing countries, most of the population's basic needs are so far from being met that, under conventional current thinking, some economic development is required to provide the people with a level of basic sustenance commensurate with human dignity before they can be expected to consider the importance of environmental accounting.

In spite of the above difficulties, governmental agencies and communities in these countries have recently given greater attention to environmental issues (Jahamani, 2003: 37–8). As a consequence of this attention, a few companies have begun to report their environmental activities in their annual reports.

Savage (1994) examined corporate social disclosure practices in South Africa. He concluded that environmental accounting needs much more attention in South Africa and descriptive and assertive reporting reigns supreme compared to quantitative and audited form disclosures.

Imam (1999) studied environmental reporting in Bangladesh. He found that environmental disclosures remain minimal and companies tend to disclose relatively minor things when compared with large corporate financial disclosures. In the final section, he stated that in all cases disclosures were descriptive and positive and there was no attempt to quantify the disclosures.

Lodhia (2000) in his study on environmental reporting in Fiji reports that practices in Fiji were far from satisfactory, with limited disclosures in corporate annual reports that focused primarily on "good news".

Rajapakse (2002: 3–4) carried out a study on environmental reporting practices in Sri Lanka. He summarized the results of his study as follows: 'Environmental reporting is not of a standard to satisfy the information needs of various groups of report users. Despite the increasing demand from stakeholders for information on the impact of business organizations there is no sign of any significant improvement in social and environmental reporting. Thus there is a gap between stakeholders' interest on information and the extent of providing information by business organizations in the country'.

Ahmad and Gao (2005) examined corporate environmental reporting in Libya. They concluded it is obvious that expectations for Libya to develop environmental disclosure practices are misplaced. Other than that, the exceptionally low levels of disclosure make any conclusions impossible.

Sumiani et al. (2007) studied environmental reporting in Malaysia. They pointed out that the level of environmental information reported in Malaysian corporate annual reports is rather low and only qualitative terms are included in annual reports. The research shows us that ISO certification is related to voluntary environmental reporting.

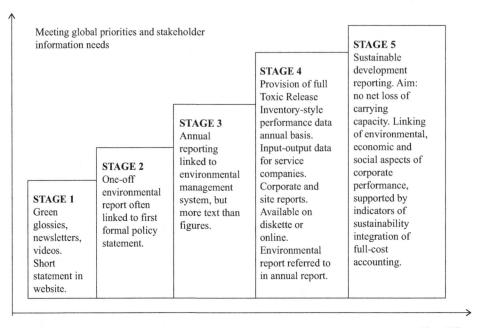

Time, Effort

Figure 6.1 Stages in corporate environmental reporting
Source: UNEP IE (1994).

Pramanik et al. (2008) suggested that instead of voluntary reporting, rigid guidelines in the forms of standards, rules or acts should be implemented, and long-term environmental sustainability ensures that corporations can thrive in the future. Also, corporate accountants must compile and present environmental information.

Because of limited empirical studies about developing countries in terms of environmental accounting and reporting (most of the studies related to environmental reporting) only a few countries were examined. Based on these limited studies, we can conclude that far more serious environmental reporting is needed for developing nations to counteract some of the prevalent social and environmental problems that exist in their countries. It seems unlikely that companies' environmental reports would qualify as having advanced beyond Stage 1 of the Sustainability 5 Stage Reporting Model which is used by the United Nations Environment Programme (UNEP) to assess the accountability of 100 pioneering corporate reporters. Figure 6.1 shows a five-stage reporting model, characterizing various styles of environmental reporting and mapping out the possible elements of sustainability.

When considering this diagram and environmental practices in these countries, it became obvious that companies' reports can be evaluated within Stage 1 or 2.

Status of environmental reporting in Turkey

Turkey has a unique geographic position at the crossroads between Europe and Asia. The country covers an area of 779,452 square kilometers. Turkey's 8,333-kilometer coastline extends along the Black Sea, the Sea of Marmara, the Aegean Sea and the Mediterranean

Sea (Okumus, 2002: 7). Turkey's population reached an estimated 75.6 million in 2012 and its annual growth is 2.27 per cent.

Turkey has characteristics of both developed and developing countries. In 1996 it entered the EU Customs Union. The European Council confirmed in 1999 that Turkey was a candidate to join the EU based on common criteria. During the December 2004 negotiations between Turkey and the EU, a number of commentators noted that Turkish companies worked more constructively with other organizations such as government, civil society groups and even other business actors such as labour unions and their own suppliers.

The EU has also some regulations about environmental reporting. Those regulations began in the early 1990s with the development of an environmental policy for Europe as part of the Agreement on the European Economic Area. This required nations to protect and improve the quality of natural environment and ensure rational utilization of resources. Based on these regulations, the EU began to address environmental reporting issues. The European Commission's Fifth Action Programme on the Environment, named "Towards Sustainability", called for companies (Gray et al., 1996: 168) to:

- disclose in their annual reports details of their environmental policy and activities, and the effects thereof
- detail in their accounts the expenses of environmental programming
- make provision in their accounts for environmental risks and future environmental expenses.

This programme is also called "full cost accounting", which has been described as a tool to identify, quantify and allocate the direct and indirect environmental costs of ongoing company operations (Skillius and Wennberg, 1998: 5). This tool requires companies to take into account the use and consumption of environmental resources to determine production cost, so that this cost can be calculated more accurately.

Turkey, as a candidate to join the EU, should make some regulations about environmental accounting and reporting parallel with EU regulations. Although there has been an increase in attention given to environmental issues (legislation such as environment law, environmental impact assessments, environmental auditing and the formation of the Ministry of the Environment), regulatory enforcement and institutional difficulties are severely reducing the effectiveness of environmental legislation (Nuhoglu, 2003: 2).

The framework of environmental legislation in Turkey can be summarized as follows (İnce et al., 2007: 5–6):

- Regulation on Prevention and Control of Industrial Air Pollution (22 July 2006, No. 26230)
- Regulation on Assessment and Management of Environmental Noise Pollution (1 July 2005, No. 25682)
- Water Pollution Control Regulation (31 December 2004, No. 25687)
- Regulation on Water for Human Consumption (17 February 2005, No. 22730)
- Solid Waste Control Regulation (14 March 1991, No. 20814)
- Environmental Impact Assessment Regulation (16 December 2003, No. 25318)
- Regulation on Control of Hazardous Wastes (14 March 2005, No. 25755)
- Regulation and Guidelines on Occupational Health and Safety (Work Law, 22 May 2003, No. 4857)

- Regulation on Control of Waste Oils (21 January 2004, No. 25353)
- Groundwater Law (23 December 1960, No. 10688)
- Electricity Market Law (20 February 2001, No. 4628)
- Natural Gas Market Law (18 April 2001, No. 4646)
- Environment Law (9 August 1983, No. 2872)
- Regulation on Control of Excavation Soil, Construction and Debris Waste (18 March 2004, No. 25406)
- Related EU Directives and International Conventions
- Borsa Istanbul Sustainability Index and Corporate Governance Index

The Borsa Istanbul Sustainability Index[1] project is crucial for corporations to manage corporate risks and opportunities. It was initiated by Borsa Istanbul and the Turkish Business Council for Sustainable Development (TBCSD) with the aim of launching a Turkish sustainability benchmark for Borsa Istanbul–listed companies. It provided competitive advantages for corporations and it offers an opportunity to compare corporations' sustainability performance on local and global levels. The index provides corporations to access global clients, capital and lower-cost finance more easily and it also allows stakeholders to easily see corporations' approach to global warming, draining of natural resources, health, security and employment.

The Capital Markets Board of Turkey (CMB)[2] is the regulatory and supervisory authority in charge of the securities markets in Turkey. The Corporate Governance Index (XKURY) is related to the Corporate Governance Principles published by CMB. Principles have been regulated by law and CMB has the authority to establish rules regarding principles. A rating institution authorized by CMB evaluates listed companies on Borsa Istanbul (BIST) in terms of compliance with corporate governance principles, which comprise shareholders, public disclosure and transparency, stakeholders and board of directors.

The Corporate Governance Principles Compliance Report is required of listed companies. According to the report's 17th article, companies are required to provide information on environment and public activities. If companies are sued for reasons related to environmental damage, companies are required to provide information to stakeholders on lawsuits and their results. Corporations listed in the index should be transparent and report complete information to stakeholders (Kaya and Karakaya, 2008: 157).

4   Research

Literature review

Most of the environmental reporting practices and literature have focused on developed countries. Only a handful of studies are available on developing countries. Because of this lack of empirical studies on developing countries, there is only scant knowledge about their environmental reporting practices. Turkey, as a developing country, is no exception.

The following studies on environmental accounting and reporting practices in Turkey provide examples of Turkish companies and environmental issues.

Sürmen and Kaya (2003) studied 28 companies which have ISO 14001 certificates. They found that, like many other developing countries, Turkey has not seen environmental issues as a priority. In Turkey environmental accounting and reporting are still a relatively new phenomenon and unlikely to advance as much as necessary.

The study, which examined environmental reporting practices in 16 companies (10 of 16 were ISE-30 companies, others multinational companies operating in Turkey), was carried out by Nuhoglu (2003). She reported in her conclusion that Turkish companies' reports were lower quality and prepared much less seriously compared to multinational companies' reports and environmental reporting was not yet seen as important in Turkey.

Nemli (2004) studied two companies' environmental performance and corporate sustainability. She stated that for a corporation to be sustainable, it must change its viewpoint about the environment.

Kaya and Varıcı (2008) studied environmental reporting practices in 100 companies (according to Istanbul Chamber of Industry data). They found that 55 of 100 companies reported environmental information in regular reports and 41 of 100 companies reported information in stand-alone reports. They mentioned that lack of standardization is a crucial problem for Turkish companies to report effectively.

Kavut (2010) examined the nature and extent of the environmental disclosures in Corporate Governance Principles Compliance Reports (CGPR) and annual reports of Istanbul Stock Exchange 100 (ISE 100) companies for 2003 and 2004. She stated that when comparing environmental disclosures of ISE 100 companies with the international environmental reporting practices, the companies' reporting came up short.

Based on the results of these studies, it can be stated that environmental accounting and reporting practices are too weak in Turkey. However, the positive effects of joining the EU and competition in the world markets may help to end the inertia in Turkish environmental accounting and reporting.

Purpose and methodology

The purpose of the study is to analyse the environmental disclosures of corporations and disclose how corporations report environmental information. Samples of the study comprise 26 Turkish companies from various industries listed on the Borsa İstanbul Corporate Governance Index (XKURY) in the financial year 2012.

The annual report is the primary source of corporate environmental reporting, and annual reports were obtained via the Internet because in Turkey annual reports of listed companies on the Borsa İstanbul Corporate Governance Index are the most accessible source of information.

In Turkey, corporations report environmental information on a voluntary basis. Whether to release information about environmental performance in a regular annual report or a stand-alone report is up to the corporations. Corporations that we examined in this study report environmental information in annual reports, not in stand-alone reports. Therefore, in annual reports little information about environmental performance is available, and the necessary data for analysis were obtained via the content analysis method. Content analysis was employed on the corporate annual reports to examine the types and nature of environmental information and performance being disclosed.

A disclosure checklist in this study was built based on a study by Sumiani et al. (2007). The checklist contains 37 items of environmental information, which have been grouped into seven categories, namely environment management system, environmental planning and policy, environmental preservation and prevention activities, environmental expenditures and financial factors, litigations, audit works and other environmentally related information. Levels of extensiveness for each of the environmental parameters are measured according to two categories: non-disclosure (NONE) and available information.

"NONE" means corporations don't report any environmental information in their annual reports. "Available information" means corporations report their environmental activities and performances in qualitative and quantitative forms in annual reports. Data obtained from content analysis were analysed by the SPSS 20.0 Windows Program. Availability of environmental information was determined numerically and the Chi-Square test was applied to find the relationship between ISO 14001 certification and environmental information disclosure. In the study we tried to analyse the extent of environmental information reported by these companies and analyse the relationship between ISO certification and environmental items.

5   Results and discussion

In this study we found that 26 companies listed on the Borsa İstanbul Corporate Governance Index reported some kind of environmental information in their annual reports. All of these companies report their environmental information in their annual reports, not in a stand-alone report.

ISO 14001 is related to an environmental management system and it constitutes a framework for corporations to follow and run effective environmental management systems in their business. The purpose of this standard is to improve resource efficiency and reduce waste. Corporations use this standard voluntarily to improve their environmental performance and minimize costs. In this study we tried to explore the relation between the voluntary reporting behaviour of ISO 14001 and how ISO-accredited and non-accredited corporations disclose their environmental information. Table 6.1 shows that out of 26 environmental reporting companies, only 77 per cent (20) companies were ISO 14001 certified. Nonetheless, 6 non-ISI-certified companies made environmental disclosures in their annual reports. This means that ISO 14001 certification is an influencing factor for corporations to make some form of environmental reporting.

In this study, using statistical analyses at the 95 per cent significance level, we tried to find the relationships between ISO 14001 and environmental disclosure practices. Most of the 37 environmental items shown in Table 6.2 were found to have some relationship with the ISO 14001 certification factor.

Table 6.2 demonstrates the environmental information which is reported in corporations' annual reports. The environmental information was classified in two forms, either "none" or "available". ISO-certified and non-ISO-certified corporations reported environmental information mostly in qualitative form. The nine environmental items were mostly reported by more than 75 per cent ISO-certified and non-ISO-certified corporations. Only future estimates of expenditures and costs for environmental activities were

Table 6.1 Environmental reports and ISO 14001 certification

ISO 14001	Disclose		Total
	Yes	*No*	
ISO	20% 77	–	20
Non-ISO	6% 23	–	6
Total	26% 100	–	26

Table 6.2 Relationship between ISO certification and environmental items

Environmental information	Level of extensiveness/ extent		Chi-square tests		
	None	Available	Value	sig*	contingency
1. Environment management system					
Environmental analysis	16	10	4.875	**0.027**	0.397
Top management commitments, responsibility	5	21	4.754	**0.029**	0.393
Continuous improvement	3	23	11.304	**0.001**	0.550
Sustainable development	6	20	3.185	0.074	0.330
Capture interest of stakeholders	9	17	0.816	0.366	0.174
Development of environmental standards	19	7	0.163	0.686	0.079
Participation in projects related to environmental management	16	10	1.565	0.211	0.238
Environmental activities and programs	7	19	2.111	0.146	0.274
Training of employees	8	18	4.719	**0.030**	0.392
Environmental unit	24	2	0,650	0.420	0.156
2. Environmental planning and policy					
Environmental goals and targets	4	22	7.180	**0.007**	0.465
Existence of environmental policy	4	22	7.180	**0.007**	0.465
Environmental research and development	13	13	3.467	0.063	0.343
Planned, proactive and precautionary approach	19	7	0.417	0.518	0.126
3. Environmental preservation and prevention activities					
Waste management	4	22	7.180	**0.007**	0.465
Strategies for environmental protection	5	21	0.999	0.318	0.192
Conservation of natural resources	4	22	7.180	**0.007**	0.465
Emission to air, water and solid waste pollution data	5	21	0.999	0.318	0.192
Environmental end product and services	9	17	3.540	0.060	0.346
Reconversion and recycling	7	19	2.111	0.146	0.274
4. Environmental expenditures and financial factors					
Past and current expenditures	22	4	0.010	0.921	0.019
Environmental equipment and technology	19	7	0.163	0.686	0.079
Future estimates of expenditures and costs	26	–	–	–	–
Environmental liabilities	19	7	0.417	0.518	0.126
5. Litigations					
Past and current litigations	24	2	0.650	0.420	0.156
Potential litigations	24	2	0.885	0.347	0.181
Compliance with environmental standard	7	19	12.616	**0.000**	0.572
Environmental penalties	17	9	1.110	0.292	0.202
6. Audit works					
Environmental auditing (internal and external)	21	5	1.857	0.173	0.258
Compliance with prior targets	20	6	0.181	0.671	0.083

(Continued)

Table 6.2 (Continued)

Environmental information	Level of extensiveness/extent		Chi-square tests		
	None	Available	Value sig* contingency		
7. Other Environmentally related information					
Afforestation	12	14	4.338	**0.037**	0.378
Establishment of protected areas for wildlife	23	3	1.017	0.313	0.194
Awards	13	13	3.467	0.063	0.343
Environmental achievements	11	15	1.896	0.169	0.261
Pioneering environmental activities	15	11	0.189	0.664	0.085
Positive effects of environmental awareness	18	8	3.467	0.063	0.343
Efforts to increase interest and awareness of stakeholders	11	15	1.896	0.169	0.261

* 95% Significant Level

not reported at all by any ISO-certified or non–ISO-certified corporations. When evaluating the extent, we found that the most reported environmental item in qualitative information is continuous improvement (23 cases). With regard to whole environmental items, the categories of audit works and environmental expenditures and financial factors were reported by less than 30 per cent ISO-certified and non–ISO-certified corporations. In the study, we found less quantitative environmental information in annual reports, and continuous improvement was reported by almost all corporations in different ways. The least-reported environmental information item was the environmental unit, the establishment of natural areas for wildlife environmental auditing and litigations. In this category less than 25 per cent of 26 corporations make such disclosure in their annual reports.

Of 37 environmental items studied, 10 were found to have some relationship between the ISO certification factors, especially environmental analysis, top management commitments, continuous improvement, environmental goals and targets, the existence of environmental policies, waste management, conservation of natural resources, compliance with environmental standards and afforestation are the most related-to certification of ISO 14001. We found that ISO 14001 certification influences voluntary reporting. In particular, it plays a significant role on reporting information about environment management systems. In the statistical test, contingency values also showed that ISO 14001 certification is an effective factor for corporations to voluntarily report some environmental information, and the values that are under the significance level showed the reported information related to ISO 14001.

The study shows that 26 Turkish companies listed on Borsa İstanbul Corporate Governance Index report some environmental activities in their annual report, and that ISO 14001 certification cannot be ignored as an effective factor for corporations to improve their environmental performance.

In the next section of this study, the challenges of environmental reporting in Turkey are discussed. In other words, we try to find the answer for the question of why Turkish companies are not interested in environmental reporting and what kinds of problems they are facing in implementing environmental reporting.

6 Challenges of environmental reporting

As stated previously, in Turkey, environmental accounting and reporting applications are at a low level that seems unlikely to advance as necessary. Although this situation resulted from many challenges, we will discuss here only the most important challenges. The sections below present an analysis of some of the major challenges that need to be addressed before any significant reporting procedures are developed. However, it should be stated that those challenges are not limited to Turkey. In other words, many developing countries share these challenges.

Acceptance of responsibility for the natural environment

Although a broad definition of social responsibility for businesses seems to be accepted by a large segment of society, a significant minority believe the role of business is solely to make an economic profit and that it should devote all resources to this end (Hurley, 1982: 8). Based on this belief, businesses do not accept that they disturb the natural environment. Therefore, they do not allocate anything for environmental accounting and reporting.

Measurement problems

The problem that has received the most attention in the literature is the problem of measurement. Within context, both the social cost of companies' operations and the valuation of environmental liabilities are discussed. The term "social cost" (also called "external cost") represents the cost of companies' impacts on the environment and society for which company is not legally liable. These costs include environmental degradation for which companies are not legally liable and adverse impacts on human beings, their property and their welfare (EPA, 1995: 16).

At present, social costs cannot be measured objectively in traditional monetary units. Due to this lack of objectivity, environmental reports cannot be subjected to an audit in the traditional accounting sense. In spite of these difficulties, a major North American power utility, Ontario Hydro, has made a commitment to determine external impacts and suggests four different approaches to damage costing. Those approaches can be summarized as follows (Epstein and Roy, 1998: 109–10):

1   The *market price method* uses information on market prices of products which have been damaged or lost due to toxic emissions.
2   The *hedonic pricing method* uses geographical differences in real estate values or wage rates, supposing that those differences are attributable to relative environmental quality.
3   The *travel cost method* uses information on travel cost from polluted areas to other areas not affected by environment damage.
4   The *contingent valuation method* uses survey responses on perpetrators' willingness to pay and victims' willingness to accept physical manifestations of environmental impact in monetary units.

Besides these approaches, there is another called *cost of control*. This approach uses the cost of reducing or avoiding environmental damage before it occurs to approximate the damage cost itself (Epstein and Roy, 1998: 109).

Although none of these methods is a perfect proxy for determining the cost of environmental damage, each approach makes it possible to get information about non–market values which decision-makers otherwise would not have.

The second aspect of measurement problem is valuing environmental liabilities. To overcome this problem, some valuation approaches were improved. Those approaches are actuarial techniques, professional judgements, engineering cost estimation, decision analysis techniques modelling and scenario techniques and valuations methods (EPA, 1995: 121–2).

Lack of regulations

There is a growing demand for regulation of environmental reporting. The debate is about the nature of the regulation. Who should guide environmental disclosures in the accounting process? The controversy is whether the government (command and control), the market (taxes and other incentives) or self-regulation is best (Herath, 2005: 1040). Recent studies show that government involvement is imperative as the regulator. The problem arises as to whether governments can act as credible regulators after their disastrous failures as regulators in privatized industries in many of the developing countries. Some argue that voluntary forms of regulation are preferred to traditional "command and control" approaches.

Shortage of staff

There are few companies with accountants who have expertise in quantifying, costing and integrating environmental issues into the traditional reporting mechanism. Environmental reporting requires a combination of expertise in different fields that relate to environmental issues (Rahaman, 1999: 21). With the scarcity of qualified staff in most fields (including reporting) in Turkey, this challenge may continue for a long time.

Cost of reporting

The cost of reporting environmental activities is crucial and should be specified clearly. Especially in developing countries, that cost is more important for companies with tight budgets, which as such might prefer to avoid environmental reporting (Rahaman, 1999: 22).

Inadequacy pressure of stakeholders

Stakeholders' pressure is one of the important factors which motivates companies to report their environmental information. In many countries, stakeholders such as investors or governmental organizations play an active role in forcing companies to be environmentally sensitive. For economic reasons, in Turkey, stakeholders play very few roles in this respect. Economic wealth is a priority for Turkish people and environmental challenges are therefore less important for them.

Cultural factors

The Turkish community cannot be regarded as a stakeholder with respect to the protection of natural environment because the Turkish people are largely unaware of the need to preserve natural resources. On the other hand, both community and companies are encouraged to form a kind of environmental culture by the means of education, regulations and laws.

Policy problems

Environmental policies themselves may be at the heart of these accounting problems. The taxation provisions in Turkey clearly discriminate against natural resources.

The common values ignored are loss of soil, degradation of land due to salinity, values of forestry, the value of the assimilative capacity of the environment and so forth. For instance, in the present tax provisions, expenditures on structural improvements for prevention and treatment of land degradation, such as filling erosion gullies and planting of trees and shrubs, could not be depreciated.

Absence of a uniform reporting framework

Inclusion of the environment in any credible manner in documents designed for information and planning purposes undoubtedly requires acceptable reporting methods, computational techniques and indicators. It has been said that there is no standard for environmental reporting in either developed or developing countries. For reporting environmental activities, companies use a few models which were improved by international organizations. However, due to those models being different from each other, most of the environmental reports based on those models are also different. On the other hand, another problem is the lack of regulations requiring corporations to include environmental issues in their annual reports (Rahaman, 1999: 23).

Corporation secrecy

Transparency provides long-term positive impact on a corporation's operation, but besides benefits, corporations must be aware of the risk of disclosing too much information about their operations. There is much competition among corporations to survive for long periods of time, and disclosing too much information can be damaging for corporations. Corporations' secrecy is another reason for corporations to be unwilling to disclose too much information (Muhammad et al., 2004).

7 Conclusion

Environmental reporting in Turkey is voluntary as is also the case in many other developed and developing countries. There is neither a professional standard nor legal framework addressing the issues of environmental reporting. Thus, most Turkish companies disclose only financial information despite growing stakeholder concern and demand for environmental management, sustainable development information and European Union regulations. Only a few companies which were very active exporters, especially to the European Union, report their environmental activities. Based on the result of this study, it can be concluded that the transparency of environmental information reported in Turkish corporations' annual reports is increasing day by day. The examination of ISO 14001–certified corporations' annual reports brought to light that corporations report mostly in qualitative terms. The most reported environmental item in qualitative information is continuous improvement, and never reported in qualitative information are past and future estimates of expenditures and costs. The study also revealed that ISO 14001 certification has an impact on voluntary environmental reporting behaviour, especially environmental preservation and prevention activities and audit works.

The inadequacy of Turkish companies' environmental reporting can be attributed to its voluntary status. Because it is voluntary, companies prefer to report only the information they want to reveal, ignoring issues such as public complaints, legal problems and the like. In addition to this inadequacy, there are not enough legal requirements and qualified personnel. Furthermore, measurement problems, cost of reporting and corporation secrecy are the best-known challenges of environmental reporting for Turkish corporations. As indicated in most studies carried out in developing countries, accountants seem unaware of natural environment issues in their work, and unfortunately the accounting profession has not been yet very active in this field.

Nevertheless, all companies are aware of the importance of environmental protection in Turkey. Turkish efforts to join the EU will most likely encourage environmental reporting in the foreseeable future. For this reason, governmental agencies should instruct companies to attend educational activities (environmental workshops, conferences, lectures) to deepen their understanding of environmental issues and to encourage them to disclose their environmental performance.

Notes

1 For detail see http://borsaistanbul.com/en/indices/bist-stock-indices/sustainability-index-project/.
2 For detail see http://www.cmb.gov.tr/displayfile.aspx?action=displayfile&pageid=88&fn=88.pdf&submenuheader=null/.

References

Ahmad, N. and Gao, S.S. (2005). Corporate environmental reporting in Libya: A study of absence. *Social and Environmental Accounting*, 25(1), 11–13.

Association of Chartered Certified Accountants (ACCA). (2001). *An Introduction to Environmental Reporting*. London: The Certified Accountants Educational Trust.

Department for Environment, Food and Rural Affairs (DEFRA). (2006). Environmental Key Performance Indicators, Reporting Guidelines for UK Business. Queen's Printer and Controller: London. Available at: https://www.gov.uk/government/uploads/system/uploads/attachment_data/file/69281/pb11321-envkpi-guidelines-060121.pdf.

Environmental Protection Agency (EPA). Office of Pollution Prevention and Toxics. (1995). *An Introduction to Environmental Accounting as a Business Management Tool*. Washington, DC: EPA.

Environmental Protection Agency (EPA). (1996). *Valuing Potential Environmental Liabilities for Managerial Decision-Making: A Review of Available Technologies*. Washington, DC: EPA.

Epstein, M.J. and Roy, M.-J. (1998). Integrating environmental impacts into capital investment decisions, in Bennett, M. and James, P. (eds.), *The Green Bottom Line Environmental Accounting for Management*. San Francisco, CA: Greenleaf Publishing, 100–14.

Gray, R. and Kouhy, R. (1996). Accounting for the environment and sustainability in lesser developed countries–an exploratory note. *Research in Third World Accounting*, 2, 387–99.

Gray, R., Owen, D. and Adams, C. (1996). *Accounting and Accountability: Changes and Challenges in Corporate Social and Environmental Reporting*. London: Prentice Hall.

Herath, G. (2005). Sustainable development and environmental accounting: The challenge to the economies and accounting profession. *International Journal of Social Economics*, 32(12), 1035–50.

Hurley, J.F. (1982). Social responsibility accounting for businesses. Unpublished PhD dissertation. Lincoln: University of Nebraska.

Imam, S. (1999). Environmental reporting in Bangladesh. *Social and Environmental Accounting*, 19(2), 12–14.

İnce, O., Orhon, D., Okutan, H., Sözen, S., Ekinci, E. and Arıncı, V. (2007). Environmental Impact Assessment Report for Antalya-Turkey Power Plant. EN-ÇEV: Turkey, December. Available at: http://www.agaportal.de/pdf/nachhaltigkeit/eia/eia_tuerkei_kraftwerk.pdf.

Jahamani, Y. (2003). Green accounting in developing countries: The case of U.A.E. and Jordan. *Managerial Finance*, 9(8), 37–45.

Kavut, F.L. (2010). Kurumsal Yönetim, Kurumsal Sosyal Sorumluluk ve Çevresel Raporlama: İMKB 100 Şirketlerinin Çevresel Açıklamalarının İncelenmesi. *Yönetim / İstanbul Üniversitesi İşletme Fakültesi İşletme İktisadı Enstitüsü Dergisi*, 66(1), 9–43.

Kaya and Durgut. (2008). Turkiye'de cevresel Raporlama Uygulamaları (Environmental Reporting Applications in Turkey). *The Third Business and Economy International Workshop*, pp. 140–156.

Kaya, U. and Karakaya, A. (2008). Sosyal Raporlama Anlayışının Muhasebe Meslek Mensupları Tarafından Algılanması Uzerine Amprik Bir Çalışma. *Muhasebe ve Denetime Bakış*, 7(24), 153–70.

Kaya, U. and Varıcı, I. (2008). Gelişmekte Olan Ülkelerde Çevresel Raporlama: Türkiye Örneği. *MÖDAV*, 4, 209–27.

Lodhia, S.K. (2000). Social and environmental reporting in Fiji: A review of recent corporate annual reports. *Social and Environmental Accounting*, 20(1), 15–18.

Milne, M.J. (1991). Accounting, environmental resource values, and non-market valuation techniques for environmental resources: A review. *Accounting Auditing& Accountability Journal*, 4(3), 81–109.

Muhammad, N., Johari, R.J. and Wan Mustafa, M. (2004). Social responsibility accounting in Malaysia: Challenge and opportunity. The National Conference on Accounting and Finance (NCAF), 23–24 August, Kuala Lumpur.

Nemli, E. (2004). The status of corporate sustainability in Turkish companies. *Second Global Compact Academic Conference*, 16–18 September, Pennsylvania, USA.

Nuhoglu, E. (2003). An exploratory study of website environmental reporting in Turkey. *Social and Environmental Accounting*, 23(1), 1–5.

Okumus, K. (2002). *Turkey's Environment: A Review and Evaluation of Turkey's Environment and Its Stakeholders.* Szentendre, Hungary: The Regional Environmental Center for Central and Eastern Europe.

Pramanik, A.K., Shil, N.C. and Das, B. (2008). Corporate environmental reporting: An emerging issue in the corporate world. *International Journal of Business and Management*, 3(12), 146–54.

Rahaman, A. (1999). Corporate social and environmental reporting in developing nations. *IFAC Quarterly*, 23–34, New York: International Federation of Accountants.

Rajapakse, B. (2002). Environmental reporting practices: Evidence from Sri Lanka. *Social and Environmental Accounting*, 22(2), 3–4.

Savage, A.A. (1994). Corporate social disclosure practices in South Africa: A research note. *Social and Environmental Accounting*, 14(1), 2–4.

Sefcik, S.E., Soderstrom, N.S. and Stinson, C.H. (1997). Accounting through green-coloured glasses: Teaching environmental accounting. *Accounting Education*, 12(1), 129–40.

Skillius, A. and Wennberg, U. (1998). *Continuity, Credibility and Comparability: A Report commissioned by the European Environment Agency.* Lund, Sweden: Lund University.

Steele, A.P., and Powell, J.R. (2002). Environmental accounting: Applications for local authorities to quantify internal and external costs of alternative waste management strategies. Environmental Management Accounting Network Europe, Fifth Annual Conference, Gloucestershire Business School, 11/12 The Park, Cheltenham, United Kingdom.

Sumiani, Y., Haslinda, Y. and Lehman, G. (2007). Environmental reporting in developing country: A case study on status and implementation in Malaysia. *Journal of Cleaner Production*, 15, 895–901.

Sürmen, Y. and Kaya, U. (2003). Environmental accounting and reporting applications in Turkish companies which have ISO 14001 certificate. *Social and Environmental Accounting*, 23(1), 6–8.

UNEP IE. (1994). *Company Environmental Reporting: A Measure of the Progress of Business and Industry towards Sustainable Development.* Technical Report: 24 United Nations Environment Programme Industries and Environment, Paris.

7 Sustainability reporting in the airline industry

The case of Turkish Airlines

John Taskinsoy and Ali Uyar

1 Introduction

Since 1996 the world has witnessed several major global financial and economic crises that have shaken investor confidence in the whole financial system and resulted in financial losses in excess of $20 trillion USD, which is a little more than one-fourth of the world GDP ($79.4 trillion, 2011) (Taskinsoy 2013).[1] These issues, along with 'significant changes in the corporate external reporting environment[,] have led to proposals for fundamental changes in corporate reporting practices' (Beattie, 2000, p. 2).

Just in the US alone, the past decade has seen its good share of corporate misconduct due to accounting irregularities along with unethical business practices by executives; incompetent financial managers who had deliberately overinvested to drive their own perquisites; an inefficient regulatory system which had too many loopholes, allowing companies to engage in fraudulent business practices; and finally, but not the least, an insufficient, biased judiciary process to punish corporate executives who committed fraudulent and criminal acts causing massive financial losses to the investors (Taskinsoy, 2013). Recurring fraudulent and criminal acts by corporate executives forced government officials to create much stronger compliance requirements for publicly listed companies (e.g. Sarbanes-Oxley Act).[2]

The primary objective of this chapter is to provide a descriptive analysis of published academic or non-academic papers and reports about corporate external reporting as well as their 100-plus years' evolution from mere financial statements to complex integrated reporting (Figure 7.1). The chapter looks at sustainability reporting in the airline industry with a specific focus on the case of Turkish Airlines (THY) for the years 2002–2011. We hope that this chapter will contribute to the improvement of sustainability reporting in the airline industry, provide useful information to those who pursue research in the area of corporate reporting, and serve as a gateway to the relevant literature.

The chapter is structured as follows: section 2 describes the evolution of corporate reporting, and is followed by section 3, literature review. The fourth section discusses sustainability reporting in the airline industry. The fifth section presents information regarding the airline industry in Turkey. The sixth section investigates THY's sustainability reporting. The seventh section concludes the paper.

2 Evolution of corporate reporting

Financial reports, in very simple terms, are defined as documents or records prepared by firms to show their stakeholders[3] how companies have performed financially during

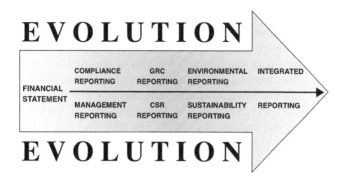

Figure 7.1 Evolution of corporate reporting

Source: Modified from the report by Monterio and Watson (2012).

a specific period (a publicly traded firm's performance is usually measured quarterly). The common financial reports, also referred to as financial statements, used by firms are balance sheet, income statement, cash flow statement, and statement of owners' equity. The ultimate objective of these financial reports is to provide the stakeholders with the firm's financial position so that owners, employees, investors, and creditors can make rational economic decisions. Therefore, firms must ensure that the financial statements are consistent, transparent, relevant, reliable, and understandable. Prior to the advent of the Internet, financial reports as part of the annual reports were in paper form and they were an effective method to communicate information to the firm's various stakeholders; however, with the Internet age, companies are now moving towards electronic financial statements.

The first seeds of corporate reporting evolution in the U.S. were planted nearly a century ago when the Federal Reserve (known as the Fed) published a document called "Uniform Accounting" in an attempt to set standards for how income tax, corporate tax and other financial results were to be reported by corporations. This document lacked enforcement by a functioning regulatory framework, and its ineffectiveness became hugely apparent during the stock market crash of 1929 and the Great Depression, during which many companies had accounting fraud together with top executives engaging in criminal business conduct such as fraud.

The unregulated environment of the 1930s prompted stricter measures out of which two important structural changes took place: first, reporting regulations were massively tightened, requiring publicly traded companies to use independent firms to audit and certify their financial statements before they could be filed on the stock exchange; second, heavy government regulation in the fields of accounting and investing began when the passage of the Securities Act in 1933 and the Securities Exchange Act in 1934 created the Securities and Exchange Commission (SEC), which later passed the responsibility of setting accounting standards to a long list of commissions and boards, the final of which is the current Financial Accounting Standards Board (FASB) established in 1973.

The importance of *compliance reporting* and its enforcement have substantially increased since 2001, especially after the news of several high-profile corporate scandals (e.g.

Enron, WorldCom, Arthur Andersen) hit the markets in the U.S. Compliance, in general, is defined as conforming to a law, policy, rule, regulation (regulatory compliance), or standard. Regulatory compliance can be achieved only if all levels of personnel in the firm are aware of and clearly understand all necessary steps they must take to comply with such laws, regulations, or standards. A long list of national and international regulatory compliance enforcement agencies exists, most prominent of which are the SEC (the U.S. Securities and Exchange Commission), the ISO (the International Organization for Standardization), the FSA (the UK Financial Services Authority), EU legislation, Bill 198 (Canada, also known as C-SOX), the EIA (the U.S. Energy Information Administration under the U.S. Department of Energy), and the IAEA (the International Atomic Energy Agency). Compliance reporting was later integrated into GRC (governance, enterprise risk management (ERM), and compliance with laws, regulations, or domestic and international standards) reporting to avoid redundancy, which leads to inefficient utilization of firms' resources, and to eliminate any conflict, overlap, and uncovered areas throughout the firm.

There are three fundamentally important core disciplines in GRC reporting: governance, risk management, and compliance. Although individual GRC reporting can be implemented in a specific area of the firm (e.g. information technology, finance, operations), a fully integrated GRC (a single framework of control mechanism) is more preferable to avoid overlaps within sections and to save time and money by eliminating conflict and duplicate actions. Each discipline of GRC reporting focuses on four critical components or control points: strategies, technologies, processes, and people. Moreover, all four control points must be seamlessly interconnected through careful analysis in each discipline for the whole structure to produce desired outcomes. Well-functioning corporate governance not only ensures accuracy and timely delivery of critically important information to the top management, but it also monitors how effectively the executive management's decisions are formulated into actions and strategies. Firms are faced daily with various internally or externally generated risks (e.g. political, legal, environmental, regulatory, technological, financial, and more), which must be managed effectively by the firm in order to avoid any adverse impacts on meeting business objectives. Firms must comply with whatever applicable laws, standards, and regulations apply within the area in which they conduct business; in addition, non-compliance by any firm may result in penalty, fine, cancellation of business license, or a combination of these.

The term "corporate social responsibility" (CSR; also referred to as corporate responsibility or CR) has been around little more than half a century; however, closer attention was paid when the definition of stakeholder theory was expanded by R. Edward Freeman[4] in 1984 to include more stakeholders than just the shareholders (owners) of the firm. Since then, CSR reporting has become the 'de facto law for business',[5] which is, contrary to common belief, more than being a good corporate citizen or trying to create corporate conscience. KPMG's "International Survey of Corporate Responsibility Reporting" (2011) findings show that if corporate responsibility is effectively integrated into the business model of the firm, not only can it enhance financial value and promote innovation, but CSR reporting can also foster learning, which can in turn increase organizational value. Most firms today treat CSR reporting as a business imperative rather than a moral obligation to society.[6] KPGM, in its detailed CR reporting survey, analysed 16 different sectors in 34 countries. The survey used the following key components: information systems and processes, assurance (both level and scope), restatements, multiple channel communications, use of Global Reporting Initiative (GRI) standards, and integrated reporting. The survey's results are very interesting. One finding was that firms in the Americas are mainly focused on communication and CR processes are still premature. Most European firms, leading the pack, have been using CR reporting for a decade now and as a result they have demonstrated a competitive advantage in both strong communication and professionalism; nevertheless, the presence in this group of India, with its resilient stand in governance, control, and assurance, comes as a surprise. India excepted, it is not shocking that firms in poorer, emerging, or less developed countries are lagging behind in CR reporting implementations. Another interesting outcome of the survey shows that firms in Asia (China and South Korea) are taking CR very seriously in order to strengthen their credibility and reputation.[7]

3   Literature review

The world's top companies have successfully integrated corporate responsibility into their overall business model and they view this component as indivisible from their corporate culture. Paul Otellini, chief executive officer (CEO) at Intel Corporation, said that '. . . we consider corporate responsibility an inseparable part of our business'.[8] Michael Dell, CEO at Dell Inc., feels that '[s]uccessful, innovative companies tend to aspire to a greater purpose that goes beyond the bottom line'.[9] Apple Inc., the top technology company in the United States, has been ranked number 1 on *Fortune*'s list of "world's most admired companies" (Google is ranked number 2 and Amazon is number 3).[10] Apple's unparalleled growth in terms of both revenue and market cap (over $425 billion at the end of 2012) has put the company in the corporate responsibility spotlight and drawn serious attacks from environmental organizations such as Greenpeace, which has strongly protested against the company for the use of toxic PVC plastics and BFRs (brominated flame retardants) in its products. After 2008 Apple paid greater attention to the social, health, and environmental sustainability of its products and became the first personal computer maker to eliminate the above-mentioned chemicals from its products. Apple has also achieved significant product efficiency where the company's electronics products emit less CO_2 per hour than a 13-watt lightbulb.[11]

Teather (2003) argues that corporate social responsibility should naturally occur as firms carry out their actions with enlightened self-interest rather than by force through "hard" law (legislation or legally binding regulation), and Teather believes this to be commercially unjustified and considers it another form of government tax. Furthermore, Teather (2003) believes that when corporate social responsibility is enforced by law, it is economically inefficient. Caprara and Mallett (2007) see company-supported employee volunteerism as a revolution in corporate citizenship. Nearly half a million employees each year spend close to 10 million hours of their own time for company-supported volunteer work in the U.S. and abroad, which amounts to 40 per cent of companies (Caprara and Mallett, 2007). Carroll and Buchholtz (2006) define corporate social responsibility as expectations that society places on organizations – economic, legal, and environmental. According to Carroll and Buchholtz (2006), firms are expected to produce goods and services to meet customers' needs and wants (economic expectation); in addition, firms are expected to comply with laws, regulations, and standards (legal expectation); and firms are expected to conduct business in ways to avoid any adverse impacts on human health and the environment in which they conduct business.

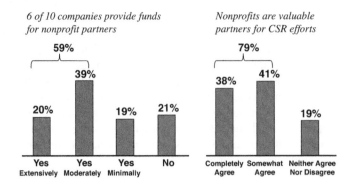

Figure 7.2 Role of non-profit partners in CSR success

Source: Modified from Weber Shandwick's survey of corporate executives (Shandwick, 2010).

Shandwick (2010) conducted a survey of business executives from 216 *Forbes* Global 2000 companies. They were asked various questions designed to gather insight on why corporations invest in corporate social responsibility. About one-third of the respondents see making impact on critical business issues as the number one reason to invest in CSR programs. The key findings of this research include: 1) making an impact on critical issues (30 per cent); 2) demonstrating corporate values in action (26 per cent); 3) smart decision for the corporation (18 per cent); 4) building loyalty among customers (16 per cent); 5) a way of differentiating from competitors (6 per cent); and 6) engaging and retaining employees (4 per cent). Also, 94 per cent of executives strongly feel that vocal support from senior management is crucial to the success of CSR. Moreover, non-profit partners are seen as vital to CSR success and more than three-quarters of executives (80 per cent) say they work with non-profit organizations which bring expertise to their CSR programs. On average, 72 per cent of respondents believe non-profits make CSR investment more effective, provide infrastructure, and help engage customers (Shandwick, 2010).

The graphical representation of Shandwick's (2010) survey provides answers to two main questions: the left side shows the corporate executives' answers to the question of 'Does your company fund non-profit organizations to advance your CSR or pro-social efforts?'; and the right side shows the respondents' answers to the question of 'Do you agree or disagree that nonprofits are valuable partners in CSR efforts?' (Figure 7.2).

KPMG's "International Survey of Corporate Responsibility Reporting 2011"[12] analysed reports of more than 3,400 companies from 16 different sectors, including 250 of the world's largest companies. The important highlights of the 2011 report follow:

> Reporting on CR activities among the 250 largest companies (G250) jumped significantly from 83 per cent in 2008 to 95 per cent in 2011. However, the progress among the top 100 companies (N100) was much stronger: their reporting on CR activities improved from 53 per cent in 2008 to 64 per cent in 2011.
>
> More companies in Europe report on CR activities (71 per cent) than any other regions; Americas (69 per cent), Middle East (61 per cent), and Asia Pacific (49 per cent).

The Nordic countries have enjoyed a remarkable rise in the number of companies reporting on CR activities; Denmark rose from 24 per cent to 91 per cent, Finland climbed from 44 per cent to 85 per cent, and Sweden, more on the moderate side, went from 60 per cent to 72 per cent.

Japan (93 per cent in 2008) and the UK (91 per cent in 2008) have continued domination in 2011; 99 per cent and 100 per cent respectively.

The U.S. and Canada have seen less impressive growth rates in the number of companies reporting on CR activities than Mexico (49 point gain to 66 per cent in 2011), and Brazil (88 per cent).

South Africa has experienced an astounding jump to take the third place in the 2011 leader board; 18 per cent in 2005, 45 per cent in 2008, and 97 per cent in 2011.

More than half of companies in Russia (58 per cent) and China (59 per cent) report on CR metrics. A number of emerging markets are still showing very slow growth rates in reporting: India (20 per cent), Taiwan (37 per cent), Israel (18 per cent), South Korea (48), and Singapore (43 per cent).

The pharmaceutical (65 per cent in 2008), construction (32 per cent in 2008) and automotive (49 per cent in 2008) industries saw growth rates of 39, 33, and 29 percentage points, respectively.

Nearly 70 per cent of the listed companies report on CR activities. Only one-third of family owned or owned by management companies report on CR activities (Figure 7.3).

Close to half of G250 (47 per cent) and less than a third of N100 companies (33 per cent) have already demonstrated financial gains from their CR reporting initiatives.

Out of many reasons why companies choose to report on their CR activities; reputational or brand considerations topped the list (67 per cent, 55 per cent in 2008), and ethical considerations with 58 per cent (69 per cent in 2008) also remained high on the list.

62 per cent of G250 and 45 per cent of N100 companies worldwide claimed offering 'green' or sustainable products.

80 per cent of G250 and 69 per cent of N100 companies are now aligning to the GRI (Global Reporting Initiatives) reporting standards. Remaining G250 companies

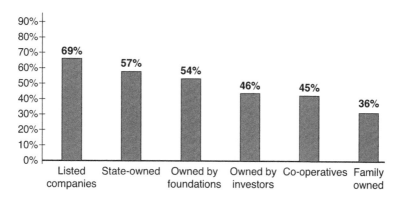

Figure 7.3 Listed companies dominate CR reporting leadership

Source: Modified from KPMG (2011).

used the following ways to report; company developed criteria (21 per cent), national reporting standard (21 per cent), and others (17 per cent).

The Global Reporting Initiative (GRI)[13] is a non-profit organization with the mission of 'providing a trusted and credible framework for sustainability reporting that can be used by organizations of any size, sector, or location'.[14] Economic and financial crises since the late 1990s have increased risks and threats to economic sustainability and created an urgent need for a globally harmonized reporting framework that will ensure transparency about economic, environmental, and social impacts, which are critical components to stakeholder relations. The GRI says that consistent language and metrics are required in order to communicate clearly and openly about sustainability. Since its establishment in 1997, the GRI has profoundly relied on the collaboration of a wide range of diverse stakeholders to continuously improve the reporting framework; this reason alone earned the GRI enormous widespread credibility among all stakeholder groups.

Sustainability reporting can be used for a range of reasons, but three common purposes according to the GRI are benchmarking, demonstrating, and comparing: 'The Sustainability Reporting Guidelines consist of Reporting Principles, Reporting Guidance, and Standard Disclosures (including Performance Indicators). These elements are considered to be of equal in weight and importance [sic]'.[15] The GRI flow chart "Options for Reporting" is divided into two main sections: 1) Principles and Guidance, which has four specific input points: guidance for defining report content, principles for defining report content, principles for ensuring report quality, and guidance for report boundary settings; 2) Standard Disclosures, which after the mentioned inputs provides three outputs: profile, management approach, and performance indicators. The final product at the end of this process is the "Focused Sustainability Report"[16] (Figure 7.4).

4   Sustainability reporting in the airline industry

The aviation industry, which plays an important role in the tourism industry, exerts environmental impacts as well as brings economic benefits to destinations (Mak and Chan, 2007). The environmental impacts include noise pollution, noxious emissions, solid waste, wastewater, and greenhouse gas emissions (Chan and Mak, 2005). As the size of the industry and air traffic increase, the extent of the issue reaches an alarming level. Thus, the aviation industry is expected to take precautionary steps to reduce its harmful environmental impacts. In addition to carrying out environment-sensitive activities, publicizing them through sustainability reporting is also important for the reputation of the firms, for public relations, and for stakeholders. For example, it is important for investors to know that the firm in which they invest is performing its activities and trying to maximize shareholder wealth by behaving in an environmentally conscious way. Reporting environmental activities generally takes one of two forms: embedding it into annual reports or providing stand-alone sustainability reports. Publishing stand-alone sustainability reports is gaining momentum, indicating the seriousness of the issue.

Although studies involving air transportation are rare (Tsai and Hsu, 2008), numerous studies have been published regarding social responsibility and sustainability reporting in manufacturing. Several studies have been conducted within the scope of

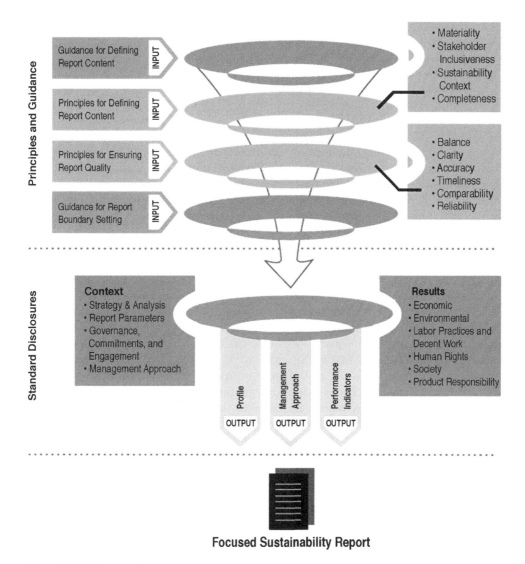

Figure 7.4 GRI options for reporting
Source: Modified from GRI (2011a, p. 4).

sustainability reporting in the airline industry. Some of these studies dealt with corporate social responsibility (Lynes and Andrachuk, 2008; Cowper-Smith and de Grosbois,
2011), while others covered environmental responsibility and reporting (Chan and Mak,
2005; Lynes and Dredge, 2006; Mak and Chan, 2006; Mak and Chan, 2007; Mak et al.,
2007; Lynes and Andrachuk, 2008). Lynes and Dredge (2006) investigated the factors
that shape an airline's commitment to environmental management through a case study

of Scandinavian Airlines, and they determined the following drivers (Lynes and Dredge, 2006, p. 128–9):

- Financial cost-benefit of environmental management
- Regulatory setting
- Desire to be a "good corporate citizen"
- Airline image
- Relationships with the aviation community.

Mak et al. (2007) examined the status of environmental reporting of 10 European and 23 Asian airlines with international flights. They determined that eight European and four Asian airlines published stand-alone environmental reports on a continuous basis; other airlines in the sample produced occasional reports. In addition, reports presented by the European airlines were richer in content than those presented by their Asian counterparts.

A recent study conducted by Cowper-Smith and de Grosbois (2011) investigated the state of adoption of CSR initiatives in 14 airlines out of 41 members of the three largest airline alliances (Star Alliance, Oneworld, and Skyteam). The researchers pointed out a considerable variation in CSR reporting. Most of the airlines focused more on the environmental dimension of CSR than social and economic dimensions; utilizing inconsistent measurements for CSR initiatives makes comparison difficult; and a small number of airlines provided detailed information regarding specific initiatives of CSR, although they noted their achievements of major CSR goals.

Sustainability reporting is the new trend in corporate social responsibility reporting within the airline industry. Every year, a growing number of airlines has been preparing and presenting sustainability reports in line with the framework provided by the GRI (GRI, 2011a; GRI, 2011b). Through a quick Google search, we have determined that some airlines (Asiana Airlines,[17] The SAS Group,[18] Cathay Pacific,[19] Finnair,[20] Air Canada,[21] and Alaska Air Group)[22] have already prepared stand-alone sustainability reports in accordance with the GRI Guidelines.

5   The airline industry in Turkey

The airline industry in Turkey has grown significantly in recent years, especially since 2000. There were various reasons for this rapid development: increasing trading volume as a result of globalization; development of tourism; passengers' desire to reach their destinations more quickly and comfortably; affordable prices and discounts offered by airlines; and new private airlines. Government authorities are also voicing the need for manufacturing aeroplanes in Turkey. Figures also support the development in the aviation industry. As Table 7.1 shows, there are 16 airlines currently operating in Turkey. The table also provides the number of aeroplanes owned by these airlines for the years 2010 and 2011. We observe that the number of aeroplanes owned by airlines increased in 2011 compared to 2010. Moreover, Figure 7.5 also shows the increasing trend in the number of aeroplanes in the industry between 2003 and 2011 comparatively. Table 7.2 and Table 7.3 provide flight and passenger traffic figures for 10 years in the aviation industry. As seen from the tables, there is a consistent and continuous increase in both traffic figures with respect to domestic flights, international flights, and total flights. Currently, Turkish Airlines is the only publicly traded state-owned company in Borsa Istanbul (BIST) (formerly known as

Table 7.1 Number of aeroplanes owned by airlines

Number of Airplanes Owned by Airline Companies	2010	2011
TÜRK HAVA YOLLARI (THY) A.O.	153	179
ONUR AIR TAŞIMACILIK A.Ş.	28	29
ATLASJET HAVACILIK A.Ş.	15	16
PEGASUS HAVA TAŞIMACILIĞI A.Ş.	27	34
GÜNEŞ EKSPRES HAVACILIK A.Ş.	28	23
SIK-AY HAVA TAŞIMACILIK A.Ş.	17	14
MNG HAVA YOLLARI VE TAŞ. A.Ş.	10	7
ULS HAVAYOLLARI KARGO TAŞ. A.Ş.	6	6
HÜRKUŞ HAVA YOLU TAŞ. TİC. A.Ş.	7	6
TURİSTİK HAVA TAŞIMACILIK A.Ş.	7	8
SAGA HAVA TAŞIMACILIK A.Ş.	9	3
IHY İZMİR HAVA YOLLARI A.Ş.	5	7
TURKUAZ HAVA TAŞ. A.Ş.	4	0
ACT HAVAYOLLARI A.Ş.	6	7
TAILWIND HAVAYOLLARI A.Ş.	5	5
BORAJET HAV. TAŞ. UÇAK. BAK.	5	5
TOTAL	332	349

Source: Annual Report of Directorate General of Civil Aviation (DGCA, 2011).

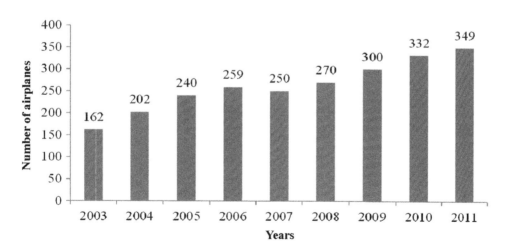

Figure 7.5 Number of aeroplanes over the years

Source: Annual Report of Directorate General of Civil Aviation (DGCA, 2011).

Table 7.2 Flight traffic

Years	Flight Types			
	Domestic	International	Transit	Total
2002	157,953	218,626	155,952	532,531
2003	156,582	218,405	154,218	529,205
2004	196,207	253,286	191,056	640,549
2005	265,113	286,867	206,003	757,983
2006	341,262	286,139	224,774	852,175
2007	365,117	323,471	247,099	935,747
2008	385,764	356,001	268,328	1,010,093
2009	419,422	369,047	277,584	1,066,053
2010	496,865	420,596	294,934	1,212,395
2011	581,271	460,218	290,346	1,331,835

Source: Annual Report of Directorate General of Civil Aviation (DGCA, 2011)

Table 7.3 Passenger traffic (×1000)

Year	Flight Types		
	Domestic	International	Total
2002	8.729	25.054	33.783
2003	9.147	25.296	34.443
2004	14.461	30.596	45.057
2005	20.529	35.042	55.571
2006	28.774	32.880	61.654
2007	31.949	38.347	70.296
2008	35.832	43.605	79.437
2009	41.227	44.281	85.508
2010	50.517	52.189	102.706
2011	58.329	59.018	117.347

Source: Annual Report of Directorate General of Civil Aviation (DGCA, 2011)

the Istanbul Stock Exchange, or ISE). Other than THY, Pegasus Airlines has been listed in BIST recently; however, more airlines are expected to apply to the Capital Markets Board[23] for inclusion in BIST due to the financing needs of private airlines.

6   Sustainability reporting in Turkish airlines

In this study, we adopted case study as the research methodology, selecting Turkish Airlines (THY) since it is the largest airline company in Turkey and it has been operating and publicly traded for a long time. Being a publicly traded corporation makes information easily accessible for researchers as non–publicly-traded corporations have no binding legal or regulatory obligation to publish certain corporate reports. In order to investigate the nature and extent of Turkish Airlines' sustainability reporting, we utilized the content analysis method in the annual reports of Turkish Airlines covering the period 2002–2011. We downloaded annual reports in PDF format from the company's official website (THY, 2012).

The study attempts to answer the following two research questions:

1   *RQ1:* What is the historical status of corporate sustainability reporting in Turkish Airlines between 2002 and 2011?
2   *RQ2:* To what extent does THY's corporate sustainability reporting of 2011 fit into the GRI (G3.1) framework?

In order to find answers to these questions, we carried out two analyses: first, we analysed the contents of THY's annual reports between 2002 and 2011. In this analysis, we determined the disclosure framework based on the content of THY's annual reports and also on prior studies (Holcomb et al., 2007; Inoue and Lee, 2011; Grosbois, 2012). The results of the first-stage analysis are summarized in Table 7.4.

Table 7.4 Brief analysis of sustainability disclosure items of THY 2002–2011

	2002	2003	2004	2005	2006	2007	2008	2009	2010	2011
							Star Alliance membership			
Number of pages in annual report	97	81	102	140	157	145	169	170	164	180
1. Economic	+	+	+	+	+	+	+	+	+	+
Economic performance	+	+	+	+	+	+	+	+	+	+
Market presence	+	+	+	+	+	+	+	+	+	+
2. Environmental										
Environmental sensivity							+	+	+	+
Fuel efficiency							+	+	+	+
3. Community										
Sponsorship								+	+	+
Charity									+	+
4. Human resources										
Occupational health and safety						+	+	+	+	+
Composition of human resources	+	+	+	+	+	+	+	+	+	+
Training and education	+	+	+	+	+	+	+	+	+	+
5. Products and services										
Brand investments									+	+
Awards									+	+
Technical	+	+	+	+	+	+	+	+	+	+
Passenger services	+	+	+	+	+	+	+	+	+	+
Catering				+	+	+	+	+	+	+
Quality management				+	+	+	+	+	+	+
Star Alliance membership					+	+	+	+	+	+
Information technology	+	+	+	+	+	+	+	+	+	+
Fleet information	+	+	+	+	+	+	+	+	+	+

In Table 7.4, we observe five sustainability reporting categories – economic, environmental, community, human resources, and products and services. The results demonstrate that the number of disclosed items is increasing year by year. While some dimensions, such as economic indicators (i.e. traffic results, cargo, investments, sales, profit) are consistently disclosed every year, some other indicators are presented only in recent years. As seen in the table, disclosure of environmental information is a growing field of sustainability reporting in THY. In recent years, sensitivity about the environment and fuel efficiency have gained serious attention in the annual report, which resulted in purchasing environment-sensitive and fuel-efficient aeroplanes. However, some certain topics of environmental disclosure are not mentioned at all, such as materials and water usage and recycling, biodiversity, and so on. Additionally, THY frequently engages in community activities such as charity donations, sponsorship of sports, culture and art programs, tourism, activities that contribute to the development of the aviation industry, and so on. Although recent annual reports document these activities, they are reported more comprehensively under a separate link, named Sponsorship, on the corporate website. Furthermore, regarding human resources, the composition of employees, training, and education-related activities are reported continuously. In recent years, information about occupational health and safety has also been provided. In the last category, indicators of products and services are provided. Information related to technical support, fleet, information technology, and passenger services/satisfaction are among the most frequently disclosed items. However, brand investments, awards, catering, quality, and Star Alliance membership are shown to be growing areas in recent years' reports.

We analysed the THY website as well as the annual report for 2011, and we examined the extent of sustainability reporting based on the GRI (G3.1) framework (see Table 7.5). In this stage of the analysis, we adopted the framework provided for the Airport Operators Sector Supplement (AOSS) by the Global Reporting Initiative (GRI), which provides organizations in the sector with a tailored version of GRI's G3.1 Sustainability Reporting Guidelines (GRI, 2011b). The sustainability performance indicators are organized by economic, environmental, and social categories (GRI, 2011b). Social indicators are further categorized by Labour Practices and Decent Work, Human Rights, Society, and Product Responsibility (GRI, 2011b). Thus, the disclosure list includes six specific sections as denoted in Table 7.5.

Economic indicators

(EC1, EC2, EC3, EC4, EC6, AO1, AO2, and AO3) Economic performance and market presence indicators are covered extensively in the THY annual report. The company's income statement presents how much revenue and profit are generated during the year, as well as any increase in these figures. Furthermore, traffic results regarding number of destinations, fleet size, available seats, total passengers carried, and cargo volumes are documented in great detail. (EC8) The services provided for public benefit are briefly explained under the heading Corporate Communication in the annual report, and the details regarding those services are provided comprehensively on the company's official website under the button Sponsorship, including sports; culture and art; tourism, labour, economics, and society; and aviation. Thus, the coverage of these involvement areas can be provided extensively in future sustainability reports.

(EC9) The company's indirect economic impact could be explained more in depth by pointing out its influence on suppliers, the tourism industry, local communities, national economies of destination countries, and so on.

Table 7.5 Analysis of 2011 annual report of THY based on GRI (G3.1) framework

---

1. Economic

Economic performance	EC1 (pp. 106–10), EC2 (p. 86, p. 90), EC3 (p. 148), EC4 (p. 130)
Market presence	EC6 (p. 100), AO1 (pp. 40–1), AO2 (pp. 40–1), AO3 (pp. 40–1)
Indirect economic impacts	EC8 (pp. 76–7), EC9 (pp. 26–7)

2. Environmental

Materials	
Energy	EN5 (p. 86), EN6 (pp. 85–6)
Water	
Biodiversity	
Emissions, effluents, and waste	EN18 (p. 86, p. 90)
Products and services	EN26 (p. 44, p. 86)
Compliance	
Transport	
Overall	

3. Labour Practices and Decent Work

Employment	LA1 (pp. 80–1), LA2 (p. 81)
Labour/management relations	LA4 (p. 99)
Occupational health and safety	LA7 (pp. 81–2), LA8 (pp. 81–2)
Training and education	LA10 (pp. 62–3), LA11 (pp. 62–3), LA12 (p. 72, p. 82)
Diversity and equal opportunity	LA13 (p. 81)
Equal remuneration for women and men	

4. Human Rights

Investment and procurement practices	
Non-discrimination	HR4 (Code of Ethics, p. 14)
Freedom of association and collective bargaining	
Child labour	
Prevention of forced and compulsory labour	
Security practices	
Indigenous rights	
Assessment	
Remediation	

5. Society

Local communities	SO1 (pp. 76–7)
Corruption	SO3 (p. 103; Code of Ethics, p. 7)
Public policy	SO5 (Public Disclosure Policy)
Anti-competitive behavior	SO7 (Code of Ethics, p. 7)
Compliance	

6. Product Responsibility

Customer health and safety	PR1 (pp. 86–7)
Product and service labeling	PR3 (pp. 26–7, pp. 56–9), PR5 (p. 59, p. 75)
Marketing communications	PR6 (pp. 94–103, pp. 76–7, Public Disclosure Policy, Code of Ethics)
Customer privacy	PR8 (Code of Ethics)
Compliance	

Environmental indicators

Environmental indicators are not presented as much in detail as required by the GRI (G3.1) framework. An insufficient amount of information and indicators regarding energy and emissions are provided. For example, the firm mentions its efforts to use fuels more efficiently in order to reduce greenhouse gas emissions. It also gives figures about the decline in the amount of fuel consumption and CO_2 emissions (EN5, EN6, EN18, EN26).

(EN1 and EN2) The percentages of recycled material content (weight/volume) found in various products used by THY are also expected to be presented in future reports. Materials used that might need to be quantified include food, plastic, paper, textiles, chemicals, glass, and so on .

(EN3 and EN4) Since aviation is a very energy-intensive industry, direct (i.e. jet fuel and other oil products for ground vehicles) and indirect (i.e. electricity and natural gas) energy consumption should be quantified.

(EN8, EN9, and EN10) Even though quantifying water consumption may not be considered as important as energy consumption, usage information can be presented briefly.

(EN11, EN12, EN13, EN14, and EN15) There is no mention about biodiversity in the annual report. The impact of biodiversity on operations, development of strategies, and future plans for managing those impacts of biodiversity might be presented. Engagement in various projects for preserving biodiversity might be reported.

(EN16, EN17, EN18, EN19, EN20, EN21, EN22, EN23, EN24, EN25) Performance indicators regarding emissions, effluents, and waste are provided very briefly. The company has stated that it plans to take necessary initiatives to reduce greenhouse gas emissions, especially a considerable reduction in the amount of CO_2 emissions; it also mentions some achievements in this respect. Therefore, the report should present more information regarding emissions of greenhouse gases, ozone-depleting substances such as nitrogen and sulphur oxides (NO, SO), other significant air emissions, and waste.

(EN26) One adverse environmental effect of air transportation is noise pollution, mainly produced by aircraft (i.e. engine noise and aerodynamic noise). The level of noise pollution and the precautionary steps taken to reduce it can be indicated in the report.

(EN27) This may not be a critical indicator for the company since the airline industry predominantly sells service rather than product.

(EN28) This may be only applicable if it is fined for non-compliance with environmental laws and regulations.

(EN29) Significant environmental impacts arise from thousands of flights in the aviation industry. The environmental impacts resulting from ground operations and the transportation of employees could be marginal when compared with the environmental impacts of flights.

(EN30) Total environmental protection expenditures and investments by type (i.e. waste management, environmental training, and environmental certification) are not reported.

Labour practices and decent work indicators

(LA1, LA2, LA4, LA7, LA8, LA10, LA11, LA12, and LA13) THY is very proud of its dynamic, experienced, and skilled young employees. THY's report provides the composition of employees based on gender, and it provides figures for employee turnover rate and growth of personnel based on positions. It also presents the number of employees to whom company-sponsored health care services are provided. In addition, the report gives statistical figures about the number of job-related accidents, workdays lost due to accidents, average frequency of accidents, and the severity of the average accident. The company also mentions its ongoing health and safety programs (i.e. initiation to obtain OHSAS 18001 Occupational Health and Safety Assessment Series certification) to establish a more secure workplace for its employees. THY has a flight training centre, the Turkish Airlines Aviation Academy, which aims to meet Turkish Airlines' own training needs and support the aviation industry in Turkey as well as take advantage of opportunities in the surrounding region. Training activities given are classified as ground training, flight training, and professional training.

(LA3) There are no indicators presented in relation to benefits provided to full-time employees that are not provided to temporary or part-time employees, by significant locations of operation.

(LA5) Minimum notice periods regarding operational changes are not reported.

(LA6 and LA9) There is no information provided related to workforce represented in formal joint management – worker health and safety committees for monitoring occupational health and safety programs. Furthermore, health and safety topics might not be determined by formal agreements with trade unions.

(LA13 and LA14) Information on diversity of governance and employees, percentage of employees based on gender, and positions of newly hired personnel are presented. Indicators regarding other categories (i.e. age, minority, disability) are not reported. Remuneration based on gender, employee category, and significant locations of operation are not reported.

Human rights indicators

(Indicators from HR1 through HR11) The THY annual report (p. 100) states that the company has its own code and guidelines for suppliers. Whether or not THY performs human rights screening on suppliers is not reported. Compared with other dimensions of sustainability, human rights indicators, like environmental indicators, are mentioned least in the reports. The reason for not reporting might be the irrelevance of related items. Training hours provided on human rights may not be separated from the total training hours given to the personnel. No case of incidents regarding discrimination has been identified because THY states that providing equal employment opportunities and establishing a work environment free of harassment and discrimination are its policies and are also specifically stated in the company's code of ethics.

Society indicators

(Indicators from SO1 through SO10) Society indicators were scattered throughout the contents of three main documents published by THY: annual report, code of ethics, and public disclosure policy. Thus, a sustainability report prepared in the near future will enable stakeholders to view all of these indicators in one document. Moreover, no specific data was provided regarding fines for non-compliance with regulations and laws.

Product responsibility indicators

(PR1, PR3, PR5, PR6, and PR8) In general, THY documents product and service responsibility indicators in its annual report, code of ethics, and public disclosure policy. The company places a great deal of importance to the introduction of its product brands and services to the stakeholders. In addition, Turkish Airlines genuinely tries to adopt all necessary requirements, policies, and standards to provide a secure and risk-free environment to its passengers.

(PR2, PR4, and PR7) Going unreported are the total number of incidents of non-compliance with regulations and voluntary codes concerning health and safety impacts of products and services during their life cycle, product and service information and labelling, and marketing communications. These indicators might not be relevant for reporting.

7   Conclusion

We investigated the state and nature of Turkish Airlines' sustainability reporting for a period of 10 years between 2002 and 2011. We observed that although some dimensions of sustainability are reported every year, other critically important dimensions began to be reported only in recent years. For instance, while economic indicators, fleet information, traffic results, passenger services, and technical and information technology capabilities are reported regularly, environmental indicators, occupational health and safety, brand investments, sponsorship and charity activities have been included only in recent years. We attribute this to several positive key developments, such as firms' and their stakeholders' increasing awareness of sustainability reporting and the growing tendency to use sustainability reporting in all industries together with mounting pressure from the general public for companies to introduce more environmentally sensitive programs. However, we collected all this information from the annual reports and corporate website of THY because the company had not prepared a stand-alone sustainability report when this study was conducted. Therefore, we put the last years' sustainability information collected from the 2011 annual report and corporate website into GRI (G3.1) framework to see what is reported and not reported in terms of the GRI guidelines. As a result of this additional analysis, we provide some implications to THY and to those companies not preparing a sustainability report as of yet:

> Although some indicators are presented fully, some are presented partially. Thus, there needs to be improvement in some certain aspects.
> More quantitative information about some indicators such as environmental and human rights is necessary.
> Designing an information system to gather data regarding sustainability reporting is critically important. It needs to be integrated into the corporate information system, and metrics should be defined and measured.
> In order to take sustainability issue more seriously, it has to be included in the overall corporate agenda as a top-level strategy. The starting point may be assigning a department and personnel for tracking sustainability initiatives and its reporting.
> Practices and reporting styles of other airlines which have already published sustainability reports can give an idea as to how a sustainability report can be prepared according to the GRI guidelines.
> Excellent sustainability reporting may not be achieved easily during the early years of adoption; however, it will improve based on repeated trials.
> The reasons for not reporting some of the performance indicators may be due to the reasons that some indicators may not be substantial enough to warrant reporting, and some indicators may not be applicable to the company.

As THY is an important global player in the airline industry, the issue of sustainability reporting deserves serious discussion at the top management level so that a stand-alone and GRI-based report can be made available to a wide range of stakeholders. This might also help improve THY's local and global image. In presenting the data, tables and graphs might be more helpful for report viewers to get a good grasp of the information and to compare the figures across years and to other airlines.

Notes

1 *Basel III: Road to Resilient Banking: Impact on Turkey's Financial Sector*, Saarbrücken: LAP Lambert Academic Publishing, 2013.

2 With the Sarbanes-Oxley Act of 2002, developed by U.S. Senator Paul Sarbanes and U.S. Representative Michael Oxley, corporate executives will be held accountable for accuracy of financial statements reported by the firms, and executives who engage in any fraud or other criminal acts will be prosecuted.

3 Stakeholders commonly include government, employees, customers, suppliers, creditors, investors, communities, owners (shareholders), and trade or labour unions.

4 See Freeman (1984). Freeman, a professor of business administration at the University of Virginia's Darden School of Business, expanded the traditional stakeholder definition to include shareholders, employees, customers, suppliers, financiers, trade unions, communities, governmental bodies, political groups, and trade associations.

5 See KPMG (2011, p. 2).

6 See KPMG (2011, p. 2).

7 See KPMG (2011, p. 4).

8 See the Intel 2011 Corporate Responsibility Report. Intel Corporation is a US-based technology company which operates in the semiconductor industry. As of this writing, Intel has 105,000 full-time employees.

9 See the Dell 2012 Corporate Responsibility Report. Dell, Inc., is a US-based technology company which operates in the personal computers industry. As of this writing, Dell has 106,700 full-time employees.

10 See the Apple 2012 Corporate Responsibility Report. Apple, Inc., is a US-based technology company which operates in the personal computers industry. As of this writing, Apple has 72,800 full-time employees.

11 See Corporate Responsibility Spotlight: Apple, http://www.fool.com/investing/general/2012/09/14/corporate-responsibility-spotlight-apple.aspx (accessed 1 February 2013).

12 KPMG published its first International Survey of CR Reporting in 1993 and has continued to do so since then. The report has provided a definitive snapshot of the evolving state of CR reporting and continues to deliver unprecedented insight into national, global and industry reporting trends. KPMG's ratings of the 250 largest companies are based on the *Fortune* Global 500 ranking.

13 GRI, the Global Reporting Initiative, was formed as a non-profit organization in 1997 by the US-based Ceres and Tellus Institute with the help of UNEP (the United Nations Environment Programme). The first draft version of the 'Sustainability Reporting Guidelines' was released in 1999, and then the final version came out in 2000. The organization's mission is to promote global economic sustainability. The vision of GRI is to make sustainability reporting used by all companies as routinely and comparably as the financial reporting.

14 See GRI (2011a, p. 2).

15 See GRI (2011a, p. 3).

16 See GRI (2011a, p. 4).

17 https://flyasiana.com/download_file/ASIANA_AIRLINES_SR_2012_Eng_low.pdf (accessed 16 December 2012).

18 http://www.unglobalcompact.org/system/attachments/9789/original/SAS_SustRepGRI2010.pdf?1301667792 (accessed 16 December 2012).

19 http://downloads.cathaypacific.com/cx/aboutus/sd/2011/index.htm (accessed 16 December 2012).

20 http://www.finnairgroup.com/linked/en/konserni/Finnair_CorporateResponsibilityReport_2011.pdf (accessed 16 December 2012).

21 http://www.aircanada.com/en/about/documents/csr_2011_report_en.pdf (accessed 16 December 2012).

22 http://www.alaskaair.com/~/media/Files/PDF/CSR/AAG_CSR_2012.pdf (accessed 16 December 2012).

23 The Capital Markets Board is the only supervisory and regulatory body in Turkey.

References

Allan Cowper-Smith and Danuta de Grosbois. (2011). The adoption of corporate social responsibility practices in the airline industry. *Journal of Sustainable Tourism*, Vol. 19, Issue 1.

Beattie, V. (2000). The future of corporate reporting: A review article. *Irish Accounting Review*, 7(1), 1–36.

Caprara, D.L. and Mallett, R.L. (2007). Corporate Philanthropy 2.0. http://www.brookings.edu/research/opinions/2007/11/28-corporate-volunteering-caprara (accessed 1 February 2013).

Carroll, A.B. and Buchholtz, A.K. (2006). *Business and Society: Ethics and Stakeholder Management*, 6th ed. Mason, OH: Thomson/South-Western.

Chan, W.W. and Mak, B. (2005). An analysis of the environmental reporting structures of selected European Airlines. *International Journal of Tourism Research*, 7, 249–59.

Cowper-Smith, A. and de Grosbois, D. (2011). The adoption of corporate social responsibility practices in the airline industry. *Journal of Sustainable Tourism*, 19(1), 59–77.

de Grosbois, D. (2012). Corporate social responsibility reporting by the global hotel industry: Commitment, initiatives and performance. *International Journal of Hospitality Management*, 31(3), 896–905.

DGCA. (2011). Annual Report of Directorate General of Civil Aviation for the year 2011. http://web.shgm.gov.tr/doc5/2011fr.pdf (accessed 2 December 2012).

Freeman, R.E. (1984). *Strategic Management: A Stakeholder Approach*. Boston, MA: Pitman.

GRI. (2011a). Sustainability Reporting Guidelines Version 3.1. https://www.globalreporting.org/resourcelibrary/G3.1-Guidelines-Incl-Technical-Protocol.pdf (accessed 9 December 2012).

GRI. (2011b). Sustainability Reporting Guidelines and Airport Operators Sector Supplement. https://www.globalreporting.org/resourcelibrary/AOSS-Complete.pdf (accessed 9 December 2012).

Holcomb, J., Upchurch, R. and Okumus, F. (2007). Corporate social responsibility: What are top hotel companies reporting? *International Journal of Contemporary Hospitality Management*, 19(6), 461–75.

Inoue, Y. and Lee, S. (2011). Effects of different dimensions of corporate social responsibility on corporate financial performance in tourism-related industries. *Tourism Management*, 32, 790–804.

KPMG. (2011). KPMG International Survey of Corporate Responsibility Reporting 2011. http://www.kpmg.com/PT/pt/IssuesAndInsights/Documents/corporate-responsibility2011.pdf (accessed 1 February 2013).

Lynes, J. and Andrachuk, M. (2008). Motivations for corporate social and environmental responsibility: A case study of Scandinavian Airlines. *Journal of International Management*, 14(4), 377–90.

Lynes, J.K. and Dredge, D. (2006). Going green: Motivations for environmental commitment in the airline industry: A case study of Scandinavian Airlines. *Journal of Sustainable Tourism*, 14(2), 116–38.

Mak, B. and Chan, W.W. (2006). Environmental reporting of airlines in the Asia Pacific Region. *Journal of Sustainable Tourism*, 14(6), 618–28.

Mak, B.L.M. and Chan, W.W. (2007). A study of environmental reporting: International Japanese Airlines. *Asia Pacific Journal of Tourism Research*, 12(4), 303–12.

Mak, B.L.M., Chan, W.W.H., Wong, K. and Zheng, C. (2007). Comparative studies of standalone environmental reports-European and Asian Airlines. *Transportation Research Part D*, 12, 45–52.

Monterio, B. and Watson, L. (2012). The evolution to integrated reporting: A journey to the next stage of corporate reporting. 24th XBRL International Conference – Abu Dhabi, UAE, March 2012.

Shandwick, W. (2010). Why Corporations Invest in Corporate Social Responsibility: A Survey of Business Executives. http://www.webershandwick.com/resources/ws/flash/SI_CSR_FiveFastFacts.pdf (accessed 1 February 2013).

Taskinsoy, J. (2013). *Basel III: Road to Resilient Banking: Impact on Turkey's Financial Sector*. Saarbrücken: LAP Lambert Academic Publishing.

Teather, R. (2003). Corporate Citizenship: A Tax in Disguise. Ludwig von Mises Institute. http://mises.org/daily/1280 (accessed 1 February 2013).

THY. (2012). Official Website of Turkish Airlines. http://www.turkishairlines.com/tr-tr/ (accessed 2 December 2012).

Tsai, W.H. and Hsu, J.L. (2008). Corporate social responsibility programs choice and costs assessment in the airline industry: A hybrid model. *Journal of Air Transport Management*, 14, 188–96.

8 The internal control system in the prevention of mistakes and fraud

An application in hospitality management

Mehmet Erkan, Ercüment Okutmuş and Ayse Ergül

1 Introduction

The main target of a business is to increase economic performance, profitability, and market value. Therefore, it is necessary that business activity be sustained (Hui, 2008: 452). The aim is not only to make profit but also to make the process sustainable (Steurer et al., 2005).

Management has to measure profitability, efficiency, and success of the business policies as it is growing in a global competitive environment. The sustainability of the organization is associated with close monitoring of the systems of audit and internal control (Kiracı, 2003). Organizations that are changing and developing are also subject to risk. An efficient internal control system is required to minimize risk and maximize sustainability (İbiş and Çatıkkaş, 2012).

The economic crisis that started in 2008 and affected all the world resulted in the reactions to the negative use of the management sources, and the more economic use of these sources are getting more valuable (Akpınar, 2011).

The mistakes and fraud within an organization are not noticed by the organization itself for a long time, and this causes various losses for the organization. Financial scandals that occurred in huge organizations like Enron in the late twentieth century resulted in that the interest of the academicians and the business environment is focused on the tricks and fraud (Dönmez and Karausta, 2011). Accounting fraud which happened in the firms such as Enron, Worldcom, Adelphia, and Xeros gave cause for the losses in terms of both owners of the organizations and investors, employees, loan agencies, government, and audit firms (Pazarçeviren, 2005). The importance of the accounting, audit activities and the internal control systems increases with the regulations in a national and international level (İbiş and Çatıkkaş, 2012).

Fraud is defined as that a person or people deceive an organization to gain profit consciously and deliberately are available in every organization without considering the size of the organization. An efficient internal control system is required to protect the fraud and mistakes in an organization. Designation, establishment, management, and auditing of an internal control system realized with the participation of all the employees and expanded across the whole processes of the organization are in the responsibility of the senior management, and play an important role in the protection of huge losses, mistakes and corruptions. Whether or not the internal control system is run regularly is connected to sustainable internal audit activities, and this affects the sustainability of the organization.

When we looked at the literature in Turkey, we saw that mistakes and fraud in organizations were widely studied. The study called "Efficiency of Internal Control System on Corporate Governance: An Application on Municipal Controlled Firms", published in 2011 by Usul, Titiz, and Ateş, measures the efficiency of internal control systems in municipal management. In the study by Erkan, Özdemir, and Karakoç (2010) named "The Control System in the Process of European Union: The Sample of Pamukkale University", the internal supervision activities applied in Pamukkale University are observed. Özbilgin (2010) evaluates the internal control system of the intermediaries with data published in 2008 by TSPAKB in the study named "The Internal Control System of Brokerage Houses and Evaluation of Related Regulation". In the 2010 study "Corporate Governance, Internal Audit and Independent Audit: Parmalat Case" by Göçen, the case of Parmalat is used as an example of internal control and independent supervision.

In that study, an internal control system was set up, and it worked efficiently after fraud had been identified in a hospitality management organization. The internal control system is still used. When we looked at it from this perspective, we realized the study is important in that it fills a gap in the literature.

The aim of the study is to demonstrate how an internal control system can guard against fraud and mistakes in hospitality management. To this end, we consider a real case of fraud that was exposed via an internal control system.

2   Accounting mistakes and fraud, and their relation to company sustainability

The term "sustainability" as commonly used means to supply the needs of today without compromising the needs of future generations (Harris, 2000). These days, the notion has been used in many disciplines, such as economics, business management, agriculture, tourism, and architecture (Gladwin, Kennelly and Krause, 1995). Sustainability in terms of business science is defined as management of the risks resulting from economic, environmental, and social change and developments. From this viewpoint, the risks which might occur due to the organizational structure and financial conditions of an organization must be manageable to ensure sustainability of the business (Aras, 2014).

The main factors in sustainability of a business are monitoring and auditing, and these are necessarily related to managerial processes. Successful audit activities reflect well upon the management and thus maximize the value of the management (Aras, 2014).

The internal audit is a process that includes all the managerial processes and reports these by evaluating objectively (Aras, 2014). The assurance function of the internal audit is defined as giving sufficient guarantees to the internal and external environments of the management about the existence of an effective internal control system (Korkmaz, 2007). The increase of fraud has become one of the biggest obstacles to enterprise sustainability. The fraud and mistakes keep businesses from reaching their goals and erode confidence, and a business may even go bankrupt (Ertürk, 2010). According to the Association of Certified Fraud Examiners (AFCE), 88.7 percent of the fraud is related to misuse of assets, 27.4% to bribery, and 10.3% to fraudulent financial reports in the US in 2008. Moreover, it is predicted that the loss related to misuse of assets is $150,000, in bribery is $375,000 and in fraudulent financial reports $2 million (ACFE, 2008).

A mistake is defined generally as a fault, deception, or misunderstanding, and does not include deliberateness (Çatıkkaş and Çalış, 2010). An accounting "mistake" is defined as unconsciously taking illegal actions or noncompliance with generally known accounting principles (Bayraklı, Erkan and Elitaş, 2012).

Accounting mistakes arise from ignorance, inexperience, neglect, carelessness, and forgetfulness. They are categorized as qualitative and quantitative, and can also be classified in terms of their reasons and results. The variety of mistakes is separated into mathematics mistakes, record mistakes, transfer mistakes, forgetting and repeating mistakes, and balance sheet mistakes (Bayrakçı, Erkan and Elitaş, 2012).

Others define "mistakes" as faults made unconsciously during accounting processes, while fraud means the activities of management, employees, or third parties to make illegal profit deliberately (Erkan and Arıcı, 2011).

Accounting fraud is called a distortion of the processes, records, and documents of an organization (Çatıkkaş and Çalış, 2010). Accounting fraud includes crimes such as faulty allocation of goods, theft, debit, faulty loading of expense items, and abuse of managerial goods. Fraudulent financial reporting is a crime related to deliberately changing financial tables so that they appear to show next year's revenue as the current year's (Ata, Uğurlu and Altun, 2009).

Accounting fraud is separated into five categories: employee fraud, manager fraud, investment fraud, seller fraud, and customer fraud. Employee fraud is also called occupational fraud and involves theft via debit, meaning that an employee deceives an employer by capturing the assets of an organization or using them illegally. Manager fraud, also called fraudulent financial reporting, occurs when senior management alters financial tables. Investment fraud is selling worthless or nonexistent investments; seller fraud occurs when sellers deceive management alone or with employees; and customer fraud is when a customer deceives management alone or with employees in the organization (Erkan and Arıcı, 2011).

ACFE divides fraud into three categories: corruption, embezzlement, and fraudulent reports. The fraud included in these three categories are *corruption*, defined as conflict of interest, bribery, illegal tips, and economic tyranny; *embezzlement*, defined as appropriating cash and non-cash assets for one's own use; *fraudulent reports*, defined as showing an asset or revenue higher or lower than it is, or fraud in employee documents and internal/external documents (ACFE, 2008).

There are six varieties of accounting fraud: deliberate mistakes, unrecorded processes, records after or before their time, false accounts, documentary fraud, and camouflage of balance sheet (Erkan and Arıcı, 2011).

There are a lot of reasons for accounting fraud. Fraud may be prompted by factors such as pressure, opportunity, and rationalization. According to the "fraud triangle" theory developed by Cressey, these three factors are present in an environment in which fraud occurs (Erkan and Arıcı, 2011). The fraud triangle is shown in Figure 8.1 (Ramos, 2003).

Naturally, rather than discovering fraud and mistakes after they are made, it is preferable to remove the fraud triangle, build an organizational culture which has a high moral code and work ethic, and make publicly known an unequivocal position against fraud (Erkan and Arıcı, 2011).

It can be difficult to prove fraud, but it may be suspected in situations such as change in the life standards of an employee, "loss" of a document, or inconsistency of the accounts. Moreover, determination and proof of fraud can harm an organization and cause material losses (Bayraklı, Erkan and Elitaş, 2012). It is easier to determine fraud in a small organization than a big one, in part because it costs more to investigate a large company than a small one (Erkan, 2012). If a company is fined after fraud is revealed, equities can be reduced, bankruptcy is a possibility, ownership can change, and it may be delisted from the stock market (Carnes and Gierlasinski, 2001).

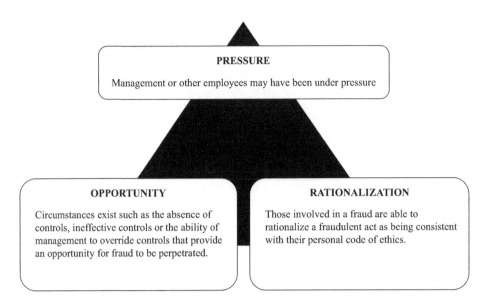

Figure 8.1 The fraud triangle

Fraud committed by management can cause indirect losses in addition to economic losses. Indirect losses may occur when employees who commit fraud are fired, causing a decrease in production; there may be a decrease in profitability after new employees are hired; costs will incur from the legal process; there may be a decrease in the brand value of the business; employee morale may dwindle; and the business may deteriorate because of legal investigations (Bierstaker, Brody and Pacini, 2006). The business management usually focuses on the indirect losses – dignity and brand value – and ignores that the fraud remains without fine; and dissolves the agreement with the employee or the supplier.

Because the determination of fraud is difficult and costly, it is easier and more cost efficient to stop fraud before it starts. Additionally, the precautions of dissuasion, protection, and determination, and programs built by the organization itself can reduce the risk of fraud (Bayraklı, Erkan and Elitaş, 2012). Proactive methods are becoming more important thanks to technological advancements that help to identify potential opportunities for fraud before it occurs (Çatıkkaş and Çalış, 2010). There are three ways an organization can prevent fraud before it happens: build and maintain an organizational culture which has high moral values, use programs to measure and reduce the potential of fraud (Bayraklı, Erkan and Eitaş, 2012), and set up an efficient internal control system.

There also must be an internal audit unit to evaluate the efficiency and profitability of the internal control system; and of course an internal control system is essential to prevent mistakes and fraud (İbiş and Çatıkkaş, 2012). Internal auditing activities contribute to the betterment of an internal control system and aid senior management decision-making. Moreover, auditing makes it possible to identify fraud and mistakes unnoticed by the internal control system (İbiş and Çatıkkaş, 2012). An effective internal control system designed, built, and run regularly and an internal audit are important in terms of management sustainability. The important thing is to use these tools effectively for the whole business (Aras, 2014).

Product ID	Product Code	Product Name	Product Unit	Price	Number of Person	Account Code	Account Name	Rate	Receipt Unit	Outage	Inventory Unit Cost	Receipt Cost	Inventory Marginal Cost	Receipt Marginal Cost
1215	U1060013	Pasa Cousine	Nbr.	37,00	1	1210015	Red Lettuce	0,01	Nbr.	0,00	1,88	0,02	1,88	0,02
						1210024	Cucumber	25,00	Gr	0,00	0,00	0,02	0,00	0,02
						1210026	Onion	35,00	Gr	0,00	0,00	0,04	0,00	0,04
						1320001	Cream	100,00	Gr	0,00	0,01	0,76	0,01	0,76
						1410025	Salt	1,00	Gr	0,00	0,00	0,00	0,00	0,00
						1430001	Red Pepper Powder	1,00	Gr	0,00	0,02	0,02	0,02	0,02
						1430005	Basil	1,00	Gr	0,00	0,02	0,02	0,02	0,02
						1430007	Black Pepper	1,00	Gr	0,00	0,03	0,03	0,03	0,03
												11,78		11,59
1216														
1216	U1060001	Ali Nazik Kebab	Nbr.	32,50	1	1020001	Lambs Leg	200,00	Gr	0,00	0,02	4,00	0,02	4,00
						1210019	Eggplant	200,00	Gr	0,00	0,00	0,30	0,00	0,30
						1330001	Yogurt	100,00	Gr	0,00	0,00	0,24	0,00	0,23
						1410025	Salt	1,00	Gr	0,00	0,00	0,00	0,00	0,00
						1430001	Red Pepper Powder	1,00	Gr	0,00	0,02	0,02	0,02	0,02
						1430010	Black Pepper	1,00	Gr	0,00	0,03	0,03	0,03	0,03
						1520012	Thyme	1,00	Gr	0,00	0,02	0,02	0,02	0,02
						1810002	Hot Sauce	10,00	Gr	0,00	0,06	0,63	0,06	0,63
						1800002	Sunflower Oil	30,00	Gr	0,00	0,00	0,11	0,00	0,11
							Butter	20,00	Gr	0,00	0,01	0,26	0,01	0,26
												5,61		5,60

Figure 8.2 Forming recipe system

3   The internal control system

In this context, "control" is defined as the precautions applied to all levels of management and integrated into business processes to reach the goals determined in advance by the management. "Internal control" means measures for managing risk in achieving those goals (Akpınar, 2011; Candan, 2008). Internal control also may be defined as managerial control over the sustainability of the business goals (Korkmaz, 2007).

"Internal control" is defined in Article 55 of Law No. 5018 as "a whole of financial and other controls including the internal supervision with the organization, method and process formed by the management in order to provide that it runs activities efficiently, economically and profitably, protects the assets and sources, keeps the accounting records clear and complete, and produces financial and managerial information on time and reliably" (Akpınar, 2011; Çavuşoğlu and Duru, 2007).

The control function as one of the managerial functions is realized with the internal control applications, and everything under internal control is evaluated as work under the control function of the management (Güner, 2009). It consists of activities and processes designed in terms of business goals (Candan, 2008). For example, a food and beverage requisition is copied three times. The original remains in the food and beverage department. One copy is sent to the purchasing department, one to the store, and one to the accounting office.

The internal control system consists of five factors: control environment, control activities, risk assessment, information and communication, and monitoring (Kiracı, 2003).

The control environment, which forms the basis of the system, provides internal control discipline and configures control activities. Honesty, ethical values, expertise, the opinion of the top management about the internal control, organization structure, and human resources are the factors which affect the control environment (Akyel, 2010a). An effective control environment contributes to management success by increasing efficiency; transparency prevents fraud and mistakes; and ensures accuracy of the data produced by management (Güner, 2009).

Risk assessment is defined as a process of development of proper responses to the risks, and determination and analysis of them to achieve the goals of an organization. Phases consist of risk determination, risk measurement, determination of the risk capacity of the organization, and developing responses (Akyel, 2010a).

Control activities are policies and procedures set forth to eliminate the risks for the organization to achieve its goals, and these procedures cover all the processes and activities of an organization (Güner, 2009: 189). Delegation of authority, confirmation procedures, separation of the missions, controls over access to the assets, confirmations, agreements, investigations related to the transaction performance, activities, processes, and auditing are on the carpet, and they must become integrated with the other four factors of internal control (Akyel, 2010a).

In a healthy internal control system, punctual, clear, proper, and complete information and qualitative communication are necessary for an organization to achieve its goals (Akyel, 2010a).

Because the internal control system is a dynamic process that has to be integrated with the changes and risks that an organization may meet, monitoring the process is a requirement in terms of goals, environment, sources, and risks (Akyel, 2010a).

Internal control, which is a managerial tool, is not only a case or situation, but also consists of a series of activities reflecting upon all the processes of the management. It is part of everyone's mission directly or indirectly, and all the employees play a role in the formation of an internal control system (Akyel, 2010a). In the formation of the internal control system, determination of mission, authority, and responsibilities of everyone and every department, formation of principal environment and rules in terms of control, revision of the controls that have been applied, risk assessment, information management, and formation of the communication mechanisms, and monitoring the process are necessary (Candan, 2008).

The goals of internal control systems in the management are to enable the efficiency of the activities of the organization, profitability, consistency of the law and regulations, the wholeness of the financial and executive data, and credibility. There is a requirement for an effective internal control system to minimize the risks and prevent the mistakes and fraud that may occur (Elitaş and Özdemir, 2006).

The lack of an internal control system in an organization causes negative results such as losses of money and assets, making faulty decisions, misappropriation and fraud possibility, revenue loss, and failure of the organization to reach its goals. Existence of an internal control system in an efficiently run organization increases credibility of the management, compliance to the regulations and rules, profitability of the activities, and sustainability (Uzun, 2012).

It is necessary to have an effective internal control system which includes the whole of an organization's systems network to provide credibility about whether the organization achieves its own goals in terms of determination and prevention of fraud and mistakes (Akyel, 2010b). Particularly after the 2008 world economic crisis, management must build a healthy internal control system to prevent fraud and mistakes. The main responsibility to identify fraud and mistakes belongs to senior management, and it needs to design, apply, and sustain an effective internal control system to realize this target.

Many internal control systems have been developed as a result of the notorious scandals, and the best-known of these is the Committee of Sponsoring Organizations (COSO) (Erkan, Karakoç and Özdemir, 2010). COSO was founded to support the National Commission on Fraudulent Financial Reporting in 1985. It is an independent private corporation which mentors business professionals about organizational management, work ethic, internal control, institutional risk management, and financial reporting across the world (http://www.coso.org).

COSO aims to evaluate internal control systems with its 1992 report "Internal Control Integrated Framework", and it published *Enterprise Risk Management–Integrated Framework (ERM)* to determine, evaluate, and manage the risks behind the scandals of world's giant corporations in 2004. COSO supports the activities of internal control and combining risk management and internal control systems (Erkan, Karakoç and Özdemir, 2010). As seen, COSO has been contributing the management of the formation of a healthy internal control system in terms of the prevention of mistakes and fraud. Managements can determine the risk of mistakes and fraud that may occur in an organization via these models, which enable effective operation and easier establishment, and prevent them before they happen.

4 The internal control system in the prevention of mistakes and fraud in hospitality management

Hospitality managements are operations which form a unified service combining many sub-services, particularly accommodation and food and beverages. As in other sectors, mistakes and fraud may happen in the hospitality sector, and they can sometimes reach dramatic numbers. Because the hospitality management supply chain is wider than that of other sectors, because it is part of the service sector, and because it is focused on the labor force, it might be regarded as a sector which is more open to mistakes and fraud.

There may diverse fraud in hospitality management, particularly in all-inclusive hotels. This can take place in many areas, such as workers such as selling drinks after the bar is closed, eating and drinking at the restaurants and bars used by costumers, taking advantage of the all-inclusive system, and benefiting from the services by paying cash after midnight, which does not show up on the records. Other areas affected by fraud include the purchasing department or seller deceiving the employer, kitchen management deceiving the organization, customers taking his/her friends or relatives into the hotel, and management fraud on the financial side.

Hospitality management uses various approaches in an attempt to prevent these kinds of fraud. For example, only one member of a family is in charge; management may hire only people who already know each other; or only relatives and close friends are employed in financially important departments such as accounting and purchasing. These temporary precautions are not always enough to prevent fraud, and in fact, these people commit more fraud than others.

An effective internal control system must be overseen by the senior management to prevent potential fraud. First, it is necessary to determine each employee's authority and responsibilities. Additionally, the missions of purchasing, payment, collection, recording, surrender, and operation must be separated from each other, and control is obligatory. Rules must be revised, the shortages must be made up, if necessary, and new rules must be created. Risk assessment is necessary, an efficient mechanism of information and communication must be generated, and the system must be perpetually monitored.

5   Application of the research

The aim and importance of the research

Globalization led to economic crises. The mistakes and fraud that happened in some of the world's largest companies increased the need for internal control systems. This study shows that management must have an efficient internal control system to prevent mistakes and fraud which can lead to huge losses.

The aim of the study is to show the importance of the internal control system so as to prevent the mistakes and fraud that may occur in hospitality management.

Research method

We conducted an internal financial audit of this company in July 2013, at their request. Our research is primarily fieldwork. During the fieldwork, such methods as document control, auditing, investigation, census, and exemplification were used. It was ascertained that some fraud had been committed in the department of food and beverages, and the management had no control system.

After this situation was reported to the management, an effective internal control system was set up at the request of the owner.

The definition of hospitality management in which the application was performed

The hotel for which the internal control system was built was established in the Cappadocia region in 1999, and has 39 rooms. It is currently run as a "boutique hotel", half pension and half bed and breakfast. The customer portfolio consists primarily of well-to-do Americans, Europeans, and Japanese who come for cultural and religious tourism. The hotel is rated one of the top ten hotels in Europe , and also has a prize-winning restaurant. It has won lots of national and international prizes, and is included in international travel guide series such as Frommer's, Lonely Planet, and Mer Noire Turquie de l'oueste, which recommend the best hotels.

The internal auditing activity made in the hotel

The hospitality management asked us to perform an internal audit in July 2013. Before the actual auditing activities began, we met the employees, made ourselves familiar with the activity areas of the hotel, and analyzed the systems which were used manually and virtually; the auditing activities were started afterward.

Activities such as census, controls, agreements, supervision, negotiations, and research via exemplification were made during the internal audit application; fraud was noticed in the department of food and beverages. After a detailed investigation, we determined who made it, how, and why.

Auditing and determination of the fraud

After suspicious activity related to the use of red meat in the department of food and beverages during the internal audit, a fraud investigation was launched. According to the analytic research, when the first seven months of the years 2012[1] and 2013 were compared, there were remarkable differences between two periods related to the use of red meat, although the number of the guests was similar.[2]

The transactions below were made during the fraud auditing related to the use of red meat after the finding determined in the department of food and beverages of the hospitality management:

- Monthly sale amounts of red meat for the first seven months of 2013 were determined based on checks
- Amount of red meat needed for the restaurant's standard recipes was determined
- Menu sales and quantity of red meat used in the standard recipes were calculated for the first seven months of 2013
- Amount of red meat purchased in the first seven months of 2013 was determined from the bills paid by the hotel
- Red meat was inventoried in July 2013, and a negative difference was stated.

Determination of red meat menu sales amount according to checks

The red meat menu sales amount of the food products for the first seven months of 2013 were obtained from the checks by counting. During that period, the number of the products sold which contained red meat was 2,107.

Determination of standard red meat amount that should be used

The amount of red meat required for the restaurant's standard recipes was obtained. The amounts of red meat that were sold in the hotel are given in Table 8.1.[3]

Table 8.1 1 January – 30 July 2013 Sales amount and standard grammages of red meat

Products	Amount of Sales	Standard Grammage (UNIT)	Average KG
Testi kebab	189	0.300	56.700
Adana kebab	138	0.150	20.700
Vadi cuzine	60	0.200	12.000
Saç tava	113	0.200	22.600
Sultan kebab	42	0.200	8.400
Erciyes kebab	192	0.150	28.800
Kiymali pide	12	0.100	1.200
Pacha cuzine	27	0.200	5.400
Ali nazik	119	0.200	23.800
Lamb skewer	86	0.200	17.200
Lamb shank	275	0.350	96.250
Lamb chops	95	0.200	19.000
Gamirasu cuzine	108	0.200	21.600
Lamb steak	6	0.350	2.100
Grilled meatballs	130	0.150	19.500
Half pension	100	0.200	20.000
Filled steak	12	0.350	4.200
Mixed grill	3	0.150	0.450
Total			**379.000**

Determination of the amount of red meat that should be consumed

As seen in Table 8.1, the sales amount of the food products which contained red meat for the first seven months of 2013 was determined from the checks. According to the standard recipes, the red meat amount that should have been consumed for that period was determined to be 379 kilograms.

Determination of the amount of consumed red meat

Purchasing amount of red meat for the first seven months of 2013 was determined to be 1.000,45 kilograms based on the purchasing bills. According to the inventory made at the end of July 2013, the amount of red meat available in the stock was 127,6 kilograms. In accordance with our findings, the difference between them shows the amount of red meat that should have been used in the first seven months of 2013. The actual amount of red meat used for this period is given in Table 8.2.

As indicated in Table 8.2, the hospitality management ordered 1.000,45 kilograms of red meat for the first seven months of 2013. Data related to the kilograms and purchasing prices were obtained from the formal purchasing bills of the hotel.

Table 8.2 1 January – 30 July 2013 Purchasing of red meat

THE OFFICIAL AMOUNTS OF RED MEAT ORDERED AND RECEİVED FROM THE BUTCHER

Item no	Lamb leg	Steak filled	Calf egg	Rib	Lamb arm	Calf mince	Calf meatball	Lamb shank	Lamb chops	Tail	Lamb mince	Calf flake	L.L. BONE	CALF CHOPS	CALF LEG	CAGLAK	CALF	CALF TOTAL
1	14.60	14.60	11.14	6.40	2.50	7.00	1.56	4.75	7,88	2,56	5,00	10,00	5,00	5,00	7,50	2,00	21,50	
2	13.67	21.44	5.95		9.00	6.00		21.00	7,55	2,00		20,00	8,00	5,50	7,50			
3	12.90	12.40	11.25		10.30	5.00		7.00	5,40	2,60		22,50		8,83				
4	7.00	13.94	5.20		7.50	7.00		7.76	5,10			16,41						
5	9.90	21.40	13.60		10.00	5.00		24.60	5,00			20,00						
6	17.10	6.50	15.50			5.00		25.00	5,19									
7	18.60	15.10	5.90			10.00		22.10										
8	12.85	12.00	12.90					23.30										
9	19.44	10.60						23.60										
10	17.50	6.60						25.39										
11	22.27	10.00						24.23										
12		10.25																
13		11.34																
14		12.40																
15		14.20																
16		12.00																
17		22.80																
18		16.60																
Total	165.83	244.17	81.44	6.40	39.30	45.00	1.56	208.73	36.12	7.16	5.00	88.91	13,00	19,33	15,00	2,00	21,50	1.000,45
Unit price (TL)	27.00	40.00	24.00	35.00	26.00	24.00	31.00	22.00	37.00	15.00	30.00	24.00	20,00	37,00	24,00	12,50	24,00	
Grand total (TL)	4.477,41	9.766,80	1.954,56	224.00	1.021,80	1.080,00	48.36	4.592,06	1.336,44	107.40	150.00	2.133,84	260,00	715,21	360,00	25,00	516,00	28.768,88

Stock inventory on 30 July 2013 was done by the department employees under our observation. The results indicated there were 127,6 kilograms of red meat in stock. The inventory results related to the red meat are shown in Table 8.3.

It is necessary to account for the rate of waste in the amount used. Mustafa Nail Özden, the well-known chief cook at the Blue Point Hotel in Alanya, Turkey, was consulted about the predicted rate of waste related to red meat; he determined the rate of waste was 20 percent. Of 379 kilograms of red meat, 75,08 is expected to be wasted given the rate of 20 percent.

Table 8.4 shows the difference between the amount of red meat that should have been consumed in the first seven months of 2013 and the amount that was actually used during the same period. We found a negative difference of 418,77 kilograms.

After the fraud audit, the chief cook was unable to explain this negative difference. We learned that the fraud resulted from an agreement made by the red meat provider, the chief cook, and the purchasing department. Moreover, the meat provider was overbilling, and the difference was shared between the three parties because there was no formal receiving procedure. The material loss was predicted as 12.563,10 Turkish liras (TL) given the price of this meat is about 30 TL.

Table 8.3 30 July 2013 The result of red meat inventory

Products	Amount (KG)	Unit Price (TL)	Total price (TL)
Lamb	8.00	20.00	160.00
Lamb chops	2.60	37.00	96.20
Calf	4.95	40.00	198.00
Calf mince (Fat)	10.80	24.00	259.20
Calf mince (Lean)	8.15	26.00	211.90
Steak fillet	11.45	40.00	458.00
Mincemeat	58.75	19.00	1.116,25
Beef mince	4.90	26.00	127.40
Lamb shank	18.00	22.00	396.00
Calf egg	0.00	24.00	–
Calf shank	0.00	–	–
Lamb mince	0.00	30.00	–
Total	**127.6**		**3.022,95**

Table 8.4 Calculation of the difference in amount of red meat used

Total Red Meat Bought (Table 8.3) +	1000.45 kg
The Red Meat Should Be Used (Table 8.2)–	379.00 kg
Waste (379,00 kg*0,20)–	75.08 kg
Expected Remainder =	*546.37 kg*
Inventory (30 July 2013) –	127.60 kg
NEGATIVE DIFFERENCE =	**418.77 kg**

As a result of the audit, we determined that the hotel had no internal control system, and the management was informed that it was necessary to have an internal control system. The report given to the senior management is reproduced below.

The report of the fraud audit

Dear Sir,

In your Organization, during the fraud audit made for food costs in F&B department states has been determined shown below:

Method

1   Purchasing from İtimat Firm between January and July 2013 has been determined 1000,45 kg from the purchased bills.
2   The amount of red mead food product between January and July 2013 has been determined from the checks.
3   Recipes prepared by the cook Mustafa Göktürk have been provided by the purchase official. The amount of red meat that should be used is calculated 379 kg from these checks.
4   On the date of 30 July 2013 stock inventory has been made and it was determined there was 127,6 kg of red meat in the store.

Within the framework of the above information the calculations are below:

Total Red Meat Bought (Table 3) +	1000,45 kg
The Red Meat Should Be Used (Table 2) –	379,00 kg
Waste (379,00 kg*0,20) –	75,08 kg
Should Be Remained =	*546,37 kg*
Inventory (30 July 2013) –	127,60 kg
NEGATIVE DIFFERENCE =	**418,77 kg**

There is 418,77 kg unexpected loss as calculation result. This case could be explained as:
The responsible cook Mustafa Göktürk either didn't make stock control as part of his job or there could be an unknown abuse.
This report has been prepared to be hand in to İbrahim Baştutan the owner of the hotel. If deemed necessary by the administrator of the hotel, a detailed calculation would be given.

01.08.2013

Auditor: Auditor: Auditor:

The hotel management hired us to set up an internal control system after we concluded our audit, and we built a system to protect the assets of the management and run efficiently. Also, the chief cook was fired. The meat provider paid the difference, and thereafter the hotel stopped purchasing meat from this provider.

General situation of the stocks of food and beverages in the hotel

There was no system to control stocks of food and beverages in the hotel. The goods are taken to storage, and employees would take what they needed without signing any document. Although the stock was inventoried, there was no data to compare. This situation invalidates the stock inventory.

As a result of our research, fraud was determined, and an internal control system was built to prevent it to repeat again. The system is used actively in the hotel.

Setup of the internal control system in the stocks of food and beverages

The first step to provide the internal control system was a prepared food checklist, shown in Table 8.5.

The record of all the food which is served as extra or catering in the conclusion of daily sale of food and beverages is prepared as a checklist in triplicate. For example, it is determined how many portions of Ali Nazik Kebab are sold. If the total is 45 units sold, the line total is 45. The original checklist remains with the chef. The first copy is sent to the front office, and the extra food is charged to the customers. The second copy is sent to the accounting office, where the amount needed for standard recipes is accounted for and the amount of meat that should be used is determined. These amounts are deducted from the stock, and everything is noted in the accounting records. The third copy goes to the purchasing department, and the difference between the amount bought and the amount used is calculated.

Forming recipe system

Dishes (Pasha Cuisine, Ali Nazik Kebab) shown in Table 8.6 are prepared at the restaurant. The values show the amounts uncooked. Wastes are regarded as 20 percent. Preparing the recipes makes it possible to compare the amounts *needed* versus the amounts *used*.

The amount of Ali Nazik Kebab numbered 34 that was sold is shown in the food checklist as 45 units. Under this condition, the amount that should be used daily can be determined by multiplying the unit amount available in the recipe (45 units * 200 gr = 9000 gr/9kg).

Preparing the end-of-month inventory list of food and beverages

Using this inventory list, the hotel can account for what is available at the end of month and food stocks that need to remain can be determined. A second inventory will set forth whether or not there are any differences between the amounts.

Table 8.5 Food checklist

	Income		Kindness		Total	Amount	Explanation
	Document no.					*Date:*	
Salads	*Bed and Breakfast*	*Half pansion*	*Bed and Breakfast*	*Half pansion*			
. . .							
. . .							
. . .							
. . .							
. . .							
Main courses							
28. Gamirasu cuisine							
29. Valley cuisine							
30. Sultan kebab							
31. Erciyes kebab							
32. Potter y kebab (2 persons)							
33. Pasha cuisine							
34. Ali nazik kebab	43		2		45		
35. Lamb skewers							
36. Lamb chops							
37. Lamb shank							
38. Grilled meatballs							
39. Chicken skewers							
40. Chicken with creamed spinach							
41. Sea bass with honey							
42. Grilled fish (sea bass and sea bream)							
43. Crêpe with spinach							
44. Stuffed potato with mushroom							
Desserts							
. . .							
. . .							
Total							

Material issue notes

A person responsible for inventory was identified in the hotel. The amount of food produced and the requisitioned amount are measured and surrendered to the production department.

Table 8.6 Pasha Cuisine and ali nazik kebab standard recipes

Product ID	Product code	Product name	Product unit	Price	Number of persons	Account code	Account name	Rate	Receipt unit	Outage	Inventory unit cost	Receipt cost	Inventory marginal cost	Receipt marginal cost
1215	U1060013	Pasha cuisine	Nbr.	37.00	1	1210015	Red lettuce	0.01	Nbr.	0,00	1,88	0,02	1,88	0,02
						1210024	**Cucumber**	**25.00**	**Gr**	**0.00**	**0.00**	**0.02**	**0.00**	**0,02**
						1210026	Onion	35.00	Gr	0.00	0.00	0.04	0.00	0,04
						1320001	**Cream**	**100.00**	**Gr**	**0.00**	**0.01**	**0.76**	**0.01**	**0,76**
						1410025	Salt	1.00	Gr	0.00	0.00	0.00	0.00	0,00
						1430001	**Red pepper**	**1.00**	**Gr**	**0.00**	**0.02**	**0.02**	**0.02**	**0,02**
						1430005	Basil	1.00	Gr	0.00	0.02	0.02	0.02	0,02
						1430007	**Black pepper**	**1.00**	**Gr**	**0.00**	**0.03**	**0.03**	**0.03**	**0,03**
												11.78		11,59
1216														
1216	U1060001	Ali nazik kebab	Nbr.	32.50	1	**1020001**	**Lamb leg**	**200.00**	**Gr**	**0.00**	**0.02**	**4.00**	**0.02**	**4,00**
						1210019	Eggplant	200.00	Gr	0.00	0.00	0.30	0.00	0,30
						1330001	**Yogurt**	**100.00**	**Gr**	**0.00**	**0.00**	**0.24**	**0.00**	**0,23**
						1410025	Salt	1.00	Gr	0.00	0.00	0.00	0.00	0,00
						1430001	**Red pepper**	**1.00**	**Gr**	**0.00**	**0.02**	**0.02**	**0.02**	**0,02**
						1430010	Black pepper	1.00	Gr	0.00	0.03	0.03	0.03	0,03
						1520012	**Thyme**	**1.00**	**Gr**	**0.00**	**0.02**	**0.02**	**0.02**	**0,02**
						1810002	Hot sauce	10.00	Gr	0.00	0.06	0.63	0.06	0,63
						1800002	**Sunflower oil**	**30.00**	**Gr**	**0.00**	**0.00**	**0.11**	**0.00**	**0,11**
							Butter	20.00	Gr	0.00	0.01	0.26	0.01	0,26
												5.61		5,60

Table 8.7 The end-of-month inventory list of food

	Document no:		Date:
Salads	Amount	Cost	Explanation
. . .			
. . .			
. . .			
. . .			
. . .			
Main courses			
28. Gamirasu cuisine			
29. Valley cuisine			
30. Sultan kebab			
31. Erciyes kebab			
32. Potter y kebab (2 persons)			
33. Pasha cuisine			
34. Ali nazik kebab			
35. Lamb skewers			
36. Lamb chops			
37. Lamb shank			
38. Grilled meatballs			
39. Chicken skewers			
40. Chicken with creamed spinach			
41. Sea bass with honey			
42. Grilled fish (sea bass and sea bream)			
43. Crêpe with spinach			
44. Stuffed potato with mushroom			
Desserts			
. . .			
. . .			
Total			

Conclusion

Change and advancements coming with the globalization result in that the competitive environment takes on a global dimension, and is concentrated; the economic crisis that began in 2008 and affected all around the world, abuse of the managerial sources, and the accounting scandals in the world's giant companies have increased the sustainable importance of the sources, and the managements have required more and more for the internal control and audit systems to maintain and sustain the activities in this change and advancements.

Mistakes and fraud are difficult to identify. Mistakes and fraud cause direct and indirect losses for the companies. Therefore, preventing mistakes and fraud is important to ensure a company's sustainability. One of the most effective tools to combat fraud is an internal control system that the company uses regularly.

It is necessary to determine the mission, authority and responsibilities for each employee in the management of the formation of an internal control system. Also, an internal control system requires principle environment and rules to be formed and revised once the controls are applied. Then the internal control system reforms the fraud and mistakes and builds mechanisms of information management and communication. Therefore, with an internal control system a company runs healthily and the organization is sustainable.

Internal audit activities are required to evaluate the efficiency of the internal control system. As a result of the internal audit, the internal control system can be revised, and assessments are presented to the senior management. Regular operation of the internal control and audit systems will help to prevent mistakes and fraud by eliminating the risk factors.

Like any business, hospitality management is affected by change and advancements, and they must keep up with these. Hotels may serve 1,000–2,000 customers meals three times a day. From this perspective, hotels are at greater risk than other sectors because they are a labor-intensive business. An effective and well-designed internal control system that is used regularly will bolster the sustainability of the management, and the auditing activities will prevent mistakes and fraud.

In this study, an internal audit was performed in a hotel and restaurant in the Cappadocia region. As a result of the internal audit, it was determined that there was no internal control system, the stores were unlocked, the missions were not separated from each other, the accounting records were being falsified, and the quantity of red meat used was an important risk factor for fraud.

All these findings were reported to the senior management, and an internal control system was then built at their request. In the control system, the missions such as acceptance, purchasing, collection, and payment were separated from one another, the stores were locked, the accounting was recorded regularly, stock was inventoried monthly, the missions, authority and responsibilities of the employees were determined, the mistakes in the accounting records were corrected, and insufficient documents such as material issue notes and surrender and order papers were edited from scratch.

The chief cook was fired after the existence of fraud had been determined, and the agreement with the meat supplier implicated in the fraud was cancelled. The internal control system runs perfectly today.

Due to the fact that the mistakes and fraud are difficult for organizations to detect, businesses can suffer considerable damage. Therefore, fraud must be stopped before it starts. From this point of view, we recommend that an internal control system be designed and implemented, an internal auditing system and an organizational culture which has high morale be formed, the fraud risks be accounted for, and the controls be applied to reduce the rate of these risks.

Notes

1 Number of guests staying for the first seven months of 2012 is 7.345, while the number for the first seven months of 2013 is 7.115.
2 The value of red meat used in the first seven months of 2012 is 11.083 Turkish lira, while the value of red meat used for the first seven months of 2013 is 29.403 Turkish lira.
3 The data is taken from the hotel's standard recipes.

References

ACFE (Association of Certified Fraud Examiners). 2008. Report to the nation on occupational fraud & abuse, http://www.acfe.com/uploadedFiles/ACFE_Website/Content/documents/2008-rttn.pdf.

Akpınar, M. 2011. Denetim anlayış ve metodolojisinde değişimin adı: İç denetim, *ZKÜ Sosyal Bilimler Dergisi*, Vol. 7 (14): 285–305.

Akyel, R. 2010a. Tüekiye'de iç kontrol kavramı, unsurları ve etkinliğinin değerlendirilmesi, *Yönetim ve Ekonomi*, Vol. 17 (1): 83–97.

Akyel, R. 2010b. Yönetimde iç kontrol, iç denetim ve dış denetim fonksiyonlarının birbirleri ile ilişkileri ve Türk Kamu yönetiminde uygulanmalarının değerlendirilmesi, *Ç.Ü. Sosyal Bilimler Enstitüsü Dergisi*, Vol. 19 (3): 1–22.

Aras, G. 2014. İşletmelerde sürdürülebilir değer yaratma ve iç denetim, http://www.denetimnet.net/ UserFiles/Documents/isletmelerde%20Surdurulebilir%20Deger%20Yaratma%20ve%20Ic%20 Denetim.pdf.

Ata, H.A., Uğurlu, M., & Altun, M.Ö. 2009. Finansal tablo hilelerinin önlenmesinde denetçi algılamaları, *Gaziantep Üniversitesi Sosyal Bilimler Dergisi*, Vol. 8 (1): 215–230.

Bayraklı, H., Erkan, M., & Eşitaş, C. 2012. *Muhasebe ve Vergi Denetiminde Muhasebe Hata ve Hileleri*, Ekin Basım Yayın Dağıtım, Bursa.

Bierstaker, J.L., Brody, R.G., & Pacini, C. 2006. Accountants' perceptions regarding fraud detection and prevention methods, *Managerial Auditing Journal*, Vol. 21 (5): 520–535.

Candan, E. 2008. Kamuda iç kontrol algılamaları ve uygulamadaki sorunlar hakkında bir değerlendirme (III), http://kontrol.bumko.gov.tr/TR,2213/ic-kontrol-okuma-listesi.html.

Carnes, K.J. & Gierlasinski, N.J. 2001. Forensic accounting skills: Will supply finally catch up to demand? *Managerial Auditing Journal*, Vol. 16 (6): 378–382.

Çatıkkaş, Ö. & Çalış, Y.E. 2010. Hile denetiminde proaktif yaklaşımlar, *Muhasebe ve Finansman Dergisi*, Vol. 45: 146–156.

Çavuşoğlu, M. & Duru, O. 2007. İç Denetim, *Siyasal Vakfı Bülteni*, Vol. 15 (20): 15–20.

Dönmez, A. & Karausta, T. 2011. Çalışanların mesleki hile algısı ve ihbar hattı kullanarak rapor etme eğilimleri üzerine Akdeniz Üniversitesi İktisadi İdari Bilimler Fakültesinde yapılan bir araştırma, *Mali Çözüm*, March–April: 17–41.

Elitaş, C. & Özdemir, Y. 2006. Bankalarda iç kontrol sistemi, *Ticaret ve Turizm Eğitim Fakültesi Dergisi*, Vol. 2: 143–154.

Erkan, M. 2012. *Türk Ticaret Kanununda aile işletmelerinde kurumsallaşma ve iç denetim*, Ekin Basım Yayın Dağıtım, Bursa.

Erkan, M. & Arıcı, N.D. 2011. Hata ve hile denetimi: Sermaye piyasası kuruluna kayıtlı halka açık anonim şirketlere ilişkin düzenlemeler, *Muhasebe ve Denetime Bakış*, January: 29–43.

Erkan, M., Karakoç, M., & Özdemir, S. 2010. İç denetim ve Coso ERM yaklaşımı, 2.Ulusal Kurumsal Yönetim, Yolsuzluk, Etik Ve Sosyal Sorumluluk Konferansı, Büyükada, Adalar, İstanbul.

Erkan, M., Özdemir, S., & Karakoç, M. 2010. Avrupa Birliği sürecinde kamuda iç denetim: Pamukkale Üniversitesi örneği, *Afyon Kocatepe Üniversitesi, İ.İ.B.F. Dergisi*, Vol. 12 (1): 85–109.

Ertürk, A. 2010. *İşletmelerde hata ve hileyi önlemede iç kontrol sisteminin etkinliği ve bir uygulama*, Marmara University, İnstitute of Social Sciences, Unpublished Master Thesis, İstanbul.

Gladwin, T.N., Kennelly, J.J., & Krause, T.S. 1995. Shifting paradigms for sustainable development: Implications for management theory and research, *Academy of Management Review*, Vol. 20 (4): 874–907.

Göçen, A. 2010. Kurumsal yönetim, iç kontrol ve bağımsız denetim: Parmalat Vakası, *Mai, Çözüm*, Vol. 97: 107–130.

Güner, M.F. 2009. Kamu idarelerinin etkin yönetiminde iç kontrol uygulamalarının rolü, *Maliye Dergisi*, July–December (157): 184–195.

Harris, J.M. 2000. Basic principles of sustainable development, *G-DAE Working Paper No. 00–04*: Tufts University, Medford, MA 02155, USA, http://ase.tufts.edu/gdae. http://www.coso.org/aboutus.htm.

Hui, L.T. 2008. Combining faith and CSR: A paradigm of corporate sustainability, *International Journal of Social Economics*, Vol. 35 (6): 449–465.

İbiş, C. & Çatıkkaş, Ö. 2012. İşletmelerde iç kontrol sistemine genel bakış, *Sayıştay Dergisi*, April–June (85): 95–121.

Kiracı, M. 2003. Faaliyet denetimi ile iç kontrol ilişkisi, *Osmangazi Üniversitesi Sosyal Bilimler Dergisi*, Vol. 4 (2): 67–78.

Korkmaz, U. 2007. Kamuda iç denetim (I), *Bütçe Dünyası*, Vol. 2 (25): 4–15.

Özbilgin, İ.G. 2010. Aracı kurumların iç kontrol sistemi ve ilgili düzenlemenin değerlendirilmesi, *Gazi Üniversitesi İktisadi ve İdari Bilimler Fakültesi Dergisi*, Vol. 12 (2): 219–242.

Pazarçeviren, S.Y. 2005. Adli muhasebecilik mesleği, *ZKÜ Sosyal Bilimler Dergisi*, Vol. 1 (2): 1–19.

Ramos, M. 2003. Auditors' responsibility for fraud detection, *Journal of Accountancy*, January (195): 28–35.

Steurer, R., Langer, M.E., Konrad, A., & Martinuzzi, A. 2005. Corporations, stakeholders and sustainable development 1: A theoretical exploration of business–society relations, *Journal of Business Ethics*, Vol. 61: 263–281.

Usul, H., Titiz, İ., & Ateş, B.A. 2011. İç kontrol sisteminin kurumsal yönetimin oluşumundaki etkinliği: Marmara Bölgesi Belediye işletmelerine yönelik bir uygulama, *Muhasebe ve Finansman Dergisi*, January: 48–54.

Uzun, A.K. 2012. İşletmelerde iç kontrol sistemi, http://www.icdenetim.net/makaleler/83-isletmelerde-ic-kontrol-sistemi.

9 Banking and sustainable development in China

Jing Bian

1 Introduction

In the past few years, sustainable development has drawn much attention. Sustainable development has become an institutional necessity in different industrial sectors. Sound business practice in this perspective is required by different governments, non-governmental bodies and individuals. This chapter, written from the Chinese perspective, explores the role of the banking industry in supporting sustainable development. Following a historical review of the evolution of the notion of sustainable development, a brief introduction to the Chinese banking industry will be conducted. Relevant policy and legal framework in this regard are examined. Furthermore, the approaches adopted by the Chinese banking industry in order to achieve and facilitate sustainable development – in particular, the "green credit" – will be studied. Following these, the chapter identifies the key obstacles and shortages in this area. Last but not least, suggestions on the future improvement of sustainable development will be made.

2 Banking industry and sustainable development

The United Nations (hereafter the UN) defined sustainable development as the 'development that meets the needs of the present without compromising the ability of future generations to meet their own needs'.[1] This concept contains three pillars: economic, social and environmental development.[2] More recently, suggestions have been made that a fourth pillar containing a cultural element should be included.[3] This is because it is argued that a complex modern society cannot be reflected by these three dimensions alone.[4] In fact, regardless of number of pillars, the concept of sustainable development is to promote economic development, social well-being, environmental protection and culture sustainability, all at the same time. Figure 9.1 illustrates the systems of sustainable development; it also suggests that the different factors shall, where possible, be integrated and mutually supportive.[5]

One issue that needs to be noticed is that sustainable development cannot be achieved without the business sector's participation. Some, however, feel that opportunities for business may be constrained where sustainability is emphasized; for instance, operating under a strict environmental legal framework or limiting shareholder returns. Nevertheless, from a long-term perspective, this perceived inhibition of growth will be minimized by development of society as a whole. In addition, sustainable development is also able to bring new business opportunities to the various industrial sectors, since by adopting sustainable practices, enterprises can gain a competitive edge, increase their market share and boost

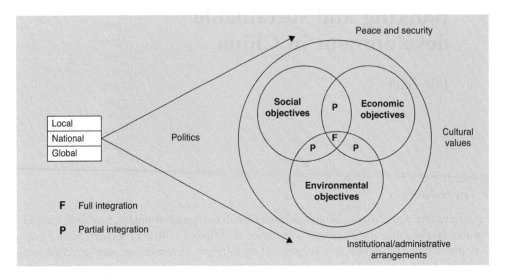

Figure 9.1 The systems of sustainable development
Source: OECD.[6]

shareholder value.[7] Therefore, in order to recognize the important relationship between sustainable development and business participation, sustainable development for business enterprises has been defined as 'adopting business strategies and activities that meet the needs of the enterprise and its stakeholders today while protecting, sustaining and enhancing the human and natural resources that will be needed in the future'.[8]

In terms of banking institutions' participation, two issues are identified. First, what is a bank's role in its own sustainable development? Second, what is a bank's role in supporting other industries and sectors' sustainable development? In fact, banking institutions can contribute to the sustainable development through their own corporate behaviours; for instance, improving their energy efficiency, promoting recycling schemes and fostering ethics or gender equality within their own organizations. Furthermore, banking institutions can also take the lead by incorporating environmental and social considerations into their business plans and marketing strategies. Typically, the banking industry can establish criteria which include environmental and social responsibility standards in their lending policy. For instance, the banks may provide easier access to capital to those who are engaging in environmentally friendly businesses. In this sense, the banking industry becomes a driving force for sustainable development. This can influence conventional business on a large scale.

The banking institutions' participation in this aspect started only in recent years. Since the 1990s this issue has been raised on the banks' agenda. The United Nations Environment Programme Finance Initiative (hereafter the UNEP FI) was launched in 1991. A number of financial institutions, including commercial banks, investment banks, venture capitalists, asset managers and multilateral development banks and agencies participated in the UNEP FI. Furthermore, the UNEP FI promoted the integration of environmental considerations into the financial sector's operations and services, and aimed to foster private-sector investment in environmentally sound technologies and services.[9] The

UNEP Statement of Commitment by Financial Institutions on Sustainable Development suggested that the financial institutions recognize the role of the financial services industry in making the economy and lifestyle sustainable, and commit to the integration of environmental and social considerations into their business operations.[10]

It can be seen from the above that the concept of sustainable development was adopted gradually, and gained recognition slowly from the financial industry. Today, in order to reduce the risks of exposure to environmental liabilities, banks are more cautious about the environmental performance of themselves and their potential clients. It must be admitted that this concept has not been developed from an early stage in China. However, there is fast development in this regard. Some banks are members of UNEP FI; for example, Shenzheng Development Bank, China Merchants Bank Co. Ltd, Industrial Bank Co. Ltd and the China Development Bank.

3   The analysis of Chinese banking industry

The fast development and expansion of the Chinese banking industry in the past few years has drawn the attention of the rest of the world. At the end of 2011 the total assets of China's banking institutions had increased to RMB113.3 trillion; total liabilities rose to RMB106.1 trillion.[11] The concept of banking business in China has evolved from mere deposit taking and loan issuing to today's diversified financial product line. Furthermore, echoing the enlargement of operation scope, the sophistication level of the Chinese banking industry has improved significantly too. Beside the business side, risk management, corporate governance and business ethics and other matters have been addressed by the Chinese banking industry gradually. Notably, the Chinese banking industry focuses not only on providing services to the domestic market but also expanded its overseas business. In 2013 the UK Chancellor George Osborne's visit to Beijing confirmed that the Chinese financial industry would expand the scope of its business for foreign investors by giving London investors the right to buy up to RMB80 billion of stocks, bonds and money market instruments.[12]

Today Chinese banking institutions perform an important and unique role in the socialist market economy. Therefore, in order to maintain financial stability, responsible and accountable banking regulators are needed. The People's Bank of China (hereafter the PBOC) is the central bank in China. The PBOC was established on 1 December 1948; and in September 1983, the PBOC's status was confirmed by the State Council; furthermore, the Law of the People's Bank of China gave the PBOC's central bank status a legal ground.[13] Along with the PBOC, the China Banking Regulatory Commission (hereafter the CBRC) regulates and supervises banking institutions and their business operations.[14] Based on the law and regulations, the banking regulators oversee and monitor the activities of banking institutions.

The development of the Chinese banking industry cannot be separated from the performance of the Chinese banking institutions. Different banks constitute today's banking industry in China. According to the CBRC, at the end of 2011, there were five large commercial banks,[15] 12 joint-stock commercial banks, 144 city commercial banks, 212 rural commercial banks, 190 rural cooperative banks, 2,265 rural credit cooperatives, 1 postal savings bank, 4 banking assets management companies, 40 locally incorporated foreign banking institutions, 66 trust companies, 127 finance companies of corporate groups, 18 financial leasing companies, 4 money brokerage firms, 14 auto financing companies, 4 consumer finance companies, 635 village or township banks, 10 lending companies and 46 rural mutual cooperatives.[16] Apart from the above, the China Development Bank, Export-Import Bank of China, and Agricultural Development Bank of China are the policy banks in China.[17] These institutions together facilitate the development of the national economy.

4   The approaches to improve sustainable banking adopted by the Chinese banking industry

In order to achieve a sustainable banking system, in the past few years, different approaches have been introduced to improve this regime. The concept of sustainable development is recent to China. The enactment of the Company Law (1993) and the Securities Law (1998) started to provide the very general principles and guidelines for corporate governance in China.[18] Following this, the Chinese banking system has tended towards good corporate governance. In this part of the chapter, taking "green credit" as an example, the legal regime of these approaches will be examined in detail.

Generally speaking, a green credit policy refers to using loans as a stimulus for environmentally friendly industries or projects, and requires commercial banks to decline loans to energy-inefficient and polluting enterprises. With the country's rapid industrialization and urbanization, the energy issue has become more severe in China. In order to correct the contradictions of insufficient energy resources and rapid economic development, a series of governmental documents were promulgated. For instance, on 6 July 2007, PBOC issued the "Guiding Opinions of the People's Bank of China on Improving and Strengthening the Work of Financial Service in Energy-saving and Environmental Protection Areas" (Guanyu Gaijin he Jiaqiang Jieneng Huanbao Lingyu Jingrong Fuwu Gongzuo de Zhidao Yijian);[19] the former State Environmental Protection Administration (today Ministry of Environmental Protection, hereafter the MEP), PBOC and CBRC issued the "Guidance on Implementing Environmental Protection Policies and Rules and Preventing Credit Risks" (Guanyu Luoshi Huanjing Baohu Zhengce Fagui Fangfan Xindai Fengxian de Yijian);[20] and on 23 November 2007, the CSRC issued "Guiding Opinions on the Credit Work for Energy Conservation and Emission Reduction" (Jieneng Jianpai Shouxin Gongzuo Zhidao Yijian).[21]

The enactment of these documents suggested a 'green credit wave' had started in China. Chinese regulators established further policies which aimed to provide guidance for banks' risk management on environmental-related risks. Today the commercial banks are actively involved in this regard; for instance, Industrial and Commercial Bank of China (hereafter the ICBC) was the first commercial bank to issue internal "Guidance for Implementing 'Green Credit' Policy"; China Merchants Bank announced it would join the UNEP FI; and the Industrial Bank was the first to adopt the "Equator Principles". (The Equator Principles are a risk management system adopted by financial institutions to determine, assess and manage environmental and social risk in projects. See http://equator-principles. com/.)

Chinese financial regulators have continued their efforts in this regard. A range of measures have been involved in building up the "green credit" system. In 2009 "Guidelines on the Corporate Social Responsibility of Banking Institutions of China" (Zhongguo Yinhangye Jinrong Jigou Qiye Shehui Zeren Zhiyin) was issued in order to enhance the sustainable development of the economy, society and the environment.[22] It states that the corporate social responsibility of banking institutions shall include economic responsibility,[23] social responsibility[24] and environmental responsibility.[25] In particular, with regard to environmental responsibility, the banks shall formulate business strategies, policies and operating rules, optimize the allocation of resources and give support to the sustainable development of society, the economy and the environment.[26] Furthermore, the banking institutions shall use credit and other financial instruments to encourage their customers to save resources and protect the environment, to direct and encourage customers to increase their awareness of social responsibility and to provide customers with environmental protection training, which includes the specific operational procedure for environmental impact assessment and the preparation of green credit documents.[27] It is important to note that this document further requires that banking institutions shall put sustainable development into real practice, by making independent field investigations and examinations of the environmental impact of financing projects, rather than making decisions merely based on environmental impact assessment reports and other materials provided by customers.[28]

Following this, the "Notice of the China Banking Regulatory Commission on Issuing Green Credit Guidelines" (Zhongguo Yinjianhui Guanyu Yinfa Lüse Xindai Zhiyin de Tongzhi) was issued with an aim of enhancing this regime.[29] This document emphasizes that the banking financial institutions shall promote green credit with a strategic perspective, increase the support for the green economy, the low-carbon economy and the circular economy, prevent environmental and social risks and improve environmental and social performance, as well as optimizing credit structures.[30] Apart from the general organization and management,[31] policy system and capacity building,[32] the guidelines set out a detailed work flow,[33] regulations for internal control and information disclosure,[34] and supervision and inspection of this system.[35] In terms of the work flow, the guidelines require that the financial institutions shall strengthen due diligence investigations for credit granting and specify the content of the due diligence investigation for environmental and social risks; shall conduct strict compliance inspections of the clients to be granted credit; shall strengthen the management of the credit granting examination and approval by determining reasonable credit granting authority and examination and approval procedures; shall urge clients to strengthen environmental and social risk management by improving contract clauses; shall strengthen the allocation of credit funds; shall strengthen post-loan management and formulate and carry out pertinent measures for clients with major potential environmental and social risks; and shall strengthen the environmental and social risk management of overseas projects.[36] Furthermore, it requires coordination and cooperation with the relevant competent departments, a sound information-sharing mechanism and improved information services.[37]

In addition, "Notice of the China Banking Regulatory Commission on Issuing the Supervisory Guidelines for Performance Appraisal of Banking Financial Institutions" (Zhongguo Yinahngye Jiandu Guanli Weiyuanhui guanyu Yinfa Yinhangye Jinrong Jigou Jixiao Kaoping de Tongzhi) further emphasizes sustainable development.[38] Several indicators are used to appraise banking financial institutions' risk profile and change tendency. They include credit risk indicators, operational risk indicators, liquidity risk indicators, market risk indicators, reputational risk indicators and others.[39] Furthermore, social responsibility indicators are used to evaluate banks' provision of financial services; support of energy-saving emissions reduction, environmental protection and enhancement of public financial awareness (including the quality of service, fair treatment of consumers, green credit and public finance education); and the overall profile of indicators in this category shall be incorporated into the institutions' social responsibility reports.[40]

These measures have played important roles in establishing a green credit culture. With continuing support and governmental encouragement, green credit has become more popular in China. Notably, this phenomenon is being implemented not only at the central level but also at the provincial level. Up to November 2011 more than 20 provinces and municipalities had issued official documents on implementing green credit loan policies, Hebei and Shanxi among them.[41] A total of 10 provinces and municipalities launched pilot programs for insurance against environmental pollution liability, including Hunan and Jiangsu.[42] Furthermore, Hubei and Guandong, to name two examples, embarked on the reform of the pollutant emission fee charge system.[43] Liaoning, Zhejiang and Hainan, among others, launched pilot programs for ecological compensation for the development of major ecological function zones, drainage basins and mineral resources.[44] Last but not least, more than 10 provinces and municipalities, including Henan and Shandong, issued policy documents on the paid use and trading of emission rights.[45]

Furthermore, from the information platform perspective, over 40,000 entries of information on environmental law violations by enterprises, were recorded in the credit investigation system operated by the PBOC.[46] This was a major reference used for granting credit. Thus, based on the above requirements, the close observation and investigation of clients' environmental performance before formulating the lending and investments decisions has begun to be an important driving force and part of the common practices concerning sustainability in the banking sector.

These documents have significant impacts on the Chinese banking industry. In 2007 the ICBC became the first bank in China to advocate and implement a green credit policy.[47] From 2010 and 2012, ICBC has lent around RMB750 billion to the green economy and provided 7,775 green projects with loans.[48] At the end of 2012, among all the ICBC's domestic corporate customers, over 99.9 per cent were eco-friendly companies or have reached "eco" standards, while the remaining less than 0.1 per cent of the companies were in the process of getting eco-certification.[49] According to the vice president of ICBC, Hongli Zhang, the ICBC, which applies green credit policies in 61 sectors, has been improving its credit classification standard based on the "Equator Principles".[50]

Another example is the China Construction Bank (hereafter the CCB). After the CCB established its marketing guide for green credit, its business transactions sustained fast growth. By 2012 the CCB had loaned around RMB239.6 billion for clean energy, energy-saving and other related environmentally friendly projects.[51]

Currently, the green credit policy is not merely implemented by the state-controlled banks. China Minsheng Banking Corp., Ltd (hereafter the CMBC), the first bank owned mostly by non-government enterprises in China, is actively involved in these activities.[52] In 2008 CMBC developed its internal green credit system, including assessment training for personnel and establishing a management system that controls environmental risks in the credit approval process.[53] In 2009 CMBC introduced "2009 Credit Policy Guidelines".[54] In 2010 it issued the "Green Credit Policy Guide of China Minsheng Bank".[55] And in 2012 the CMBC was awarded the Best Corporate Social Responsibility Practice Award and was ranked first in the Social Responsibility Development Index of the Chinese Banking Industry in the 2012 Blue Paper of Corporate Social Responsibilities, issued by the Chinese Academy of Social Sciences.[56]

5   Problems and limitations

It can be seen from above analysis that green credit has experienced substantial development in China. This has created certain positive impacts. The promoting and implementing of green credit has become more popular in the banking industry and has led to substantial improvements. Nevertheless, many obstacles and difficulties lie ahead.

The chief difficulty is that there is no legislative basis for green credit. Although the aforementioned guidance and measures are playing important roles in this aspect, the laws promulgated by the National People's Congress (hereafter the NPC) have not addressed this issue yet. For instance, there are no relevant provisions in the Environmental Protection Law,[57] the Law of People's Bank of China, the Commercial Bank Law[58] or the Banking Supervision Law.[59] In China, the laws enacted by the NPC prevail over other rules, regulations and guidance. Furthermore, the Constitution Law has not touched upon this issue either, though the protection of the environment and natural resources have been addressed in individual provisions.[60] Therefore, it is crucial to establish a legal basis for the green credit policy.

The weak legal basis is also reflected in the other areas. According to "Notice of the Ministry of Environmental Protection on Issuing the General Planning for the Development of Environmental Protection Legislation and Environmental Economic Policies in China during the 12th Five-Year Plan Period",[61] the following problems are severe: legislative blank spots in certain fields;[62] overlapping environmental supervision systems;[63] weak punishments for environmental law violations;[64] an incomplete legal system for monitoring and overseeing government behaviour;[65] and incomplete legal mechanisms for public supervision over environmental protection.[66] Furthermore, mechanisms for the rational assumption of costs of environmental damage have not been established, which has resulted in the following: the driving force for market players to increase environmental investment and prevent and control environmental risks is weak; a primary driving force is lacking for the effective application of environmental economic policies regarding green credit, insurance against environmental pollution liability and "green securities".[67]

Apart from the legal challenge, the technical difficulties cannot be ignored. Sustainable development, as can be seen from the above analysis, cannot be achieved without coordination and cooperation from the whole of society, and technical support is one of the key issues. The green credit or other future sustainable financial product is or will be based on collaboration between the different industrial sectors; in particular, cooperation from heavy metal–related industries, industries causing serious soil pollution and industries with high environmental risks. Implementing green finance needs a set of accurate and scientific criteria in order to best allocate the funding resources. Techniques to further improve the mechanisms for assessing the environmental risk exposure of the banks' customers, and subsequently to protect banks themselves from potential losses, are required. Currently, the information concerning environmental protection is mainly analysed and dealt with by the Chinese commercial banks. However, the environmental information's political, technical and generally complex nature means that processing such information is very difficult.[68] Based on the above points of view, research is needed on enhancing energy conservation, emission reduction, resources efficiency and replacement of outdated products.

Furthermore, the banks' engagement in sustainable development needs to be further strengthened. In discussion of sustainable development, financial innovation, as a key issue, cannot be ignored. The lack of creative and innovative ability is one of the biggest shortcomings of the Chinese banking industry. Green credit is prompted by the government, based on a very strong administrative management regime, and the market mechanism cannot take the lead in this regard, whether by nature it is supporting or forbidden.[69] This has led to commercial banks that are passively adopting policies but cannot take a decisive lead.[70] Financial products are lagging behind the needs and demands of the market. It is understandable that the Chinese banking industry is taking a cautious attitude towards financial innovation, since such innovation can create certain risks. Nonetheless, these risks can be monitored, controlled or even mitigated with rational preventive steps. If Chinese banking institutions are able to develop and deliver various environmentally friendly products, the role performed by the banking institutions in this area will be enhanced and enlarged. China today has the capacity to generate 6.2 gigawatts of solar power and 68.3 gigawatts of wind power, which is equivalent to about 50 coal-fired power plants[71] Therefore, in order to promote green credit, it is essential that the Chinese commercial banks maintain suitable capacity to address financial innovation. In discussing the financing channels for the lower-carbon and water-related infrastructure in China, it has been suggested that 'a progressive approach is needed that levels the playing field, deters political and policy risk, and develops more efficient, transparent market mechanisms.'[72] An innovative system – for example, the environmental protection bond and environmental securitization – is needed.

The further issue is that commercial banks shall improve monitoring on the use of their loans. Without doubt, the banking institutions provide finance for those who are focusing on environmentally friendly enterprises. However, ensuring the best application of such loans is an important issue. China has witnessed several power plants suffering from losses, such as Suntech Power Holdings.[73] Its China subsidiary has recently filed for bankruptcy. As of this writing, this is the first big Chinese solar group to declare insolvency and the world's biggest such bankruptcy.[74] It may be too early to discuss the reasons behind this corporate failure. Nevertheless, it has been argued that 'cheap loans' and 'preferential government policies' contributed to 'overcapacity after rapid expansion'.[75]

Last but not least, a culture of green credit and sustainable development is yet to be established in China. The appearance of environmental protection on the agenda has only happened in the past few years, and it is in need of further promoting. As for the concept of sustainable development, this is not an issue that has community-wide awareness. Consequently, a public campaign on this issue is compulsory. Moreover, the development of environmentally friendly techniques and industry currently remains a "back-end" approach, that is, prevention and punishment procedures are emphasized while the incentive mechanism of green credit is not well developed. As an example, for those enterprises who engage in environmentally friendly businesses such as new energy, energy-saving and comprehensive utilization of resources, a set of economic incentive policies is absent, as are particular pertinent services.[76] It is not difficult to understand that it will be challenging to achieve a satisfactory result by depending only on the efforts of the commercial banks and particular industries.

6   Conclusion

To promote sustainable development in China, the function of the banking system cannot be ignored. The Chinese banking industry has put great effort into this issue. Green credit has been implemented step by step. Through this approach, banks can support projects initiated by institutions and enterprises engaged in environmentally or socially responsible development.

However, in facing the changing situation internally and externally, promoting this regime needs further reforms. For instance, apart from the aforementioned problems, compared with other types of crime, the relatively low risk of illegal environmental behaviours decreases the efficiency of law and regulation in monitoring and deterring environmental law violations. In addition, more efficient information sharing and communication is needed between the different government departments, industrial sectors and public and private sectors.

It is also important to note that to further improve the banking institutions' participation in sustainable development, a more complete plan is needed for future developments. Environmental financial services have a relatively short history in China, and some gaps and problems remain. Insurance against environmental pollution liability should be promoted and pilot programs for compulsory environmental pollution liability insurance should be launched; the related technical rules for environmental pollution liability insurance should be formulated as soon as possible.[77] In conclusion, the research and experiments in this area could be further encouraged in order to achieve a better solution in the near future.

Notes

1 United Nations (11 December 1987), "Report of the World Commission on Environment and Development", General Assembly Resolution 42/187.
2 United Nations Environment Programme (October 2011), UNEP FI Guide to Banking and Sustainability, p. 12.
3 Jordi Pascual, commissioned by UNESCO Division of Cultural Policies and Intercultural Dialogue (1 September 2009), "Culture and Sustainable Development: Examples of Institutional Innovation and Proposal of a New Cultural Policy Profile". This study examines the relation between culture and sustainable development, and highlights how cities and local governments are incorporating culture into the core of their urban policies.
4 United Cities and Local Governments (2010), "United Cities and Local Governments (UCLG): 'Culture: Fourth Pillar of Sustainable Development'".
5 OECD (2002), *Sustainable Development Strategies: A Resource Book*. London: Earthscan Publications, p. 12.
6 Ibid.
7 International Institute of Sustainable Development, "Business and Sustainable Development", http://www.iisd.org/business/, last accessed 10 November 2013.
8 International Institute of Sustainable Development, in conjunction with Deloitte & Touche and the World Business Council for Sustainable Development, "Business Strategies for Sustainable Development".
9 UNEP FI, "About UNEP FI'", http://www.unepfi.org/about/background/index.html, last accessed 11 November 2013.
10 UNEP FI, '"UNEP FI Statement", http://www.unepfi.org/statements/index.html, last accessed 11 November 2013.
11 CBRC Annual Report 2011, p. 24.
12 Petar Kujundzic (15 October 2013), "Banks Deal Boosts UK Bid to Be Leading China Finance Hub", Reuters, http://uk.reuters.com/article/2013/10/15/uk-china-uk-rqfii-idUKBRE99E06Y20131015, last accessed 8 November 2013.
13 See PBOC, http://www.pbc.gov.cn/publish/english/952/index.html, last accessed 11 July 2012. Law of the People's Republic of China on the People's Bank of China, promulgated 18 March 1995, effective 18 March 1995.
14 The main functions of the CBRC are to formulate supervisory rules and regulations governing banking institutions; to authorize the establishment, changes, termination and business scope of banking institutions; to conduct on-site examination and off-site surveillance of banking institutions, and take enforcement actions against rule-breaking behaviours; to conduct fit-and-proper tests on the senior managerial personnel of banking institutions; to compile and publish statistics and reports of the overall banking industry in accordance with relevant regulations; to provide proposals on the resolution of problem deposit-taking institutions in consultation with relevant authorities. See CBRC, http://www.cbrc.gov.cn/english/info/yjhjj/index.jsp, last assessed 17 July 2013.
15 The Industrial and Commercial Bank of China, Agricultural Bank of China, Bank of China, Bank of Communications and China Construction Bank are the large commercial banks. "Commercial

banks" are enterprise legal persons that are established in conformity with the law and take in deposits from the general public, grant loans, handle settlements and so forth. See Law of the People's Republic of China on Commercial Banks, promulgated 10 May 1995, revised 27 December 2003, Article 2.

16 CBRC Annual Report 2011, p. 24.

17 The policy banks in China were established according to "Decision of the State Council on Reform of the Financial System" to separate policy finance from commercial finance and to solve the problem of national specialized banks executing dual functions. The National Development Bank handles policy loans and discount business for key national construction projects (including capital construction and technical transformation). The Agricultural Development Bank of China (ADBC) undertakes policy loans for state reserves of grain, cotton and edible oil, for contract-purchasing of farm and sideline products and agricultural development, and to appropriate fiscal funds for supporting agriculture and to supervise their use as an agent. The China Import-Export Credit Bank (CIECB) supplies buyers and sellers with credit for importing and exporting large-scale mechanical and electrical equipment and the like. See "Decision of the State Council on Reform of the Financial System", Guofa [1993] No. 91, promulgated 25 December 1993, part 2.

18 Company Law, promulgated 29 December 1993, effective 1 July 1994, revised 27 October 2005. Securities Law, promulgated 29 December 1998, effective 1 July 1999, revised 27 October 2005, effective 1 January 2006.

19 Yin Fa (2007) No. 215.

20 July 2007, Huanfa (2007) No. 108.

21 Yinjinfa (2007) Nol. 83.

22 Issued 12 January 2009, effective 12 January 2009, Article 1.

23 Ibid., Article 3. It requires the bank to maintain a fair, safe and stable competition order in the banking sector and use high-quality professional operations to continually create economic values for the country, shareholders, employees, customers and the general public, conditioned upon abiding by the law.

24 Ibid., Article 3. It requires them to follow the business operation notions meeting the requirements of social ethics and public welfare, actively protect the public interests of consumers, employees and community members, advocate charitable responsibility, actively dedicate themselves to activities for the public good, build up social harmony and promote social development.

25 Ibid., Article 3. It requires them to support the industrial policies and environmental protection policies of the state, save resources, protect and recover the ecological environment and support the sustainable development of the society.

26 Ibid., Article 16.

27 Ibid., Article 20.

28 Ibid.

29 Issued 24 February 2012, effective 24 February 2012.

30 Ibid., Article 3.

31 Ibid., Article 6–9.

32 Ibid., Article 10–4.

33 Ibid., Article 15–21.

34 Ibid., Article 22–4.

35 Ibid., Article 25–8.

36 Ibid., Article 15–21.

37 Ibid., Article 25.

38 Issued 12 June 2012, effective 12 June 2012.

39 Ibid., Article 7.

40 Ibid., Article 10.

41 "Notice of the Ministry of Environmental Protection on Issuing the General Planning for the Development of Environmental Protection Legislation and Environmental Economic Policies in China during the 12th Five-Year Plan Period" (Huanjing Baohu Bu guanyu Yinfa 'Shi'erwu' Quanguo Huanjing Baohu Fagui he Huangjing Jingji Zhengce Jianshe Guihua de Tongzhi), issued 1 November 2011, effective 1 November 2011, Point I.

42 Ibid.

43 Ibid.

44 Ibid.

45 Ibid.

46 Ibid.

47 ICBC Starts in Full Gear to Become A Green Financial Institution http://www.icbc-ltd.com/icbc/newsupdates/icbc%20news/ICBC%20Starts%20in%20Full%20Gear%20to%20Become%20A%20Green%20Financial%20Institution.htm (Accessed on October 23, 2016).

48 "ICBC Disburses Nearly RMB750 Billion in Three Years to Support Green Economy", 5 February 2013), http://www.icbc.com.cn/icbc/newsupdates/icbc%20news/ICBC%20Disburses%20Nearly%20RMB%20750%20billion%20in%20Three%20Years%20to%20Support%20Green%20Economy.htm, last accessed 29 December 2013.

49 Ibid.

50 Yan Meng, Gao Yinan (editor), "China Focus: Banks Boost Green Credit for Green Growth", *People's Daily*, Online, 21 July 2013, http://english.peopledaily.com.cn/90778/8334766.html, last accessed 23 December 2013.

51 Ibid.

52 Established on 12 January 1996 in Beijing, CMBC is a joint stock commercial bank with investments mainly from non-state-owned enterprises. On 19 December 2000 the company was listed on the Shanghai Stock Exchange. On 26 November 2009 the company was listed on the Hong Kong Stock Exchange. See CMBC, http://www.cmbc.com.cn, last accessed 30 December 2013.

53 2008 CMBC Corporate Social Responsibility Report, p. 50.

54 See CMBC, http://www.cmbc.com.cn, last accessed 30 December 2013.

55 2010 CMBC Corporate Social Responsibility Report, p. 50.

56 See CMBC, http://www.cmbc.com.cn, last accessed 30 December 2013.

57 Promulgated 26 December 1989, effective 26 December 1989.

58 Promulgated 10 May 1995, revised 27 December 2003.

59 Promulgated 27 December 2003, revised 31 October 2006.

60 For instance, Articles 9, 10, 22 and 26.

61 Issued 1 November 2011, effective 1 November 2011.

62 Ibid., Point I. For instance, there is no law or regulation enacted in the areas of soil environment protection, nuclear safety, environmental management of dangerous chemicals, environmental monitoring, biological safety or genetic resources protection, as well as electromagnetic radiation, light pollution, heavy metal pollution, persistent organic pollutants and other fields closely related to the living environment of the people. Moreover, there were no implementations governing some important environmental administration systems, such as pollutant discharge permit, total volume control and regional limit approval. Also lacking is related domestic legislation after China signed some international environmental treaties or conventions.

63 Ibid., Point I. For instance, there are more than 20 environmental administration systems in China. However, these agencies overlap one another or even contradict one another in content, which wastes limited legislative resources, results in conflicts of law, increases the difficulties in law revision and causes difficulties in law enforcement.

64 Ibid., Point I. For instance, the existing environmental protection legislation provides for relatively light administrative punishment, excessively narrow scopes of civil compensation and weak criminal punishment.

65 Ibid., Point I. For instance, the regulation of government behaviour by the existing environmental protection laws is insufficient. The legal supervision systems need to be improved for administrative decision-making and administrative execution regarding environmental protection.

66 Ibid., Point I. For instance, it is difficult for the public to play an active role in environment supervision. There is a lack of procedures and channels for public involvement in environmental decision-making and for citizens to maintain their own environmental rights and interests.

67 Ibid., Point I. Such mechanisms mainly include the method for the pricing of products of environmental resources, fee charge and tax collection.

68 Hangying Wu and Ziyuang Zhao, "The Analysis on the Promotion of Green Credit by Commercial Banks" (Qianxi Lüse Xindai zai Shangye Yinhang Tuixing de Zhuangkuang), *Securities and Futures of China* (Zhongguo Zhengquan Qihuo), 2011, Vol. 6, p. 139.

69 Yulan Wang, "The Legal Rules on Practicing Green Credit by Commercial Banks" (Shangye Yinhang Jianxing Lüse Xindai de Falv Guizhi), *Theory Research* (Xue Lilun), 2013, Vol. 23, p. 158.

70 Ibid.

71 Ehren Goossens, "China's Green Strategy Is Awash in Red Ink", *Bloomberg Business Week*, 26 November 2012, p. 61.

72 Andrew H. Chen and Jennifer Warren, "Sustainable Growth for China: When Capital Markets and Green Infrastructure Combine", *Chinese Economy*, September–October 2011, Vol. 44, Issue 5, pp. 86–103.

73 Leslie Hook, "Suntech Unit Declared Bankrupt", *Financial Times*, 20 March 2013. https://www.ft.com/content/c4164d20-916a-11e2-b839-00144feabdc0, last accessed 06 September 2016.
74 Ibid.
75 Ibid.
76 Hong He and Shengwu Wang, "The Experiences of Green Credit of American, British, and Japanese Commercial Banks and their Implication on China" (Mei Ying Ri Shangye Yinghang Lüse Xindai Jingyan dui Woguo de Qishi), *Financial Perspectives Journal (Jinrong Zongheng)*, 2012, Vol. 7, p. 47.
77 "Notice of the Ministry of Environmental Protection on Issuing the General Planning for the Development of Environmental Protection Legislation and Environmental Economic Policies in China during the 12th Five-Year Plan Period," Point III.

References

Chen, A.H. and Warren, J. 2011. Sustainable growth for China: When capital markets and green infrastructure combine. *Chinese Economy*, 44(5), 86–103.

Chen, Andrew H. and Warren, Jennifer. September–October 2011. Sustainable growth for China: When capital markets and green infrastructure combine. *Chinese Economy*, 44(5), 86–103.

China Banking Regulatory Commission. 2011. *China Banking Regulatory Commission Annual Report 2011*, p. 24.

China Minsheng Banking Corporation. 2008. *China Minsheng Banking Corporation Corporate Social Responsibility Report*, p. 50.

China Minsheng Banking Corporation. 2010. *China Minsheng Banking Corporation Corporate Social Responsibility Report*, p. 50.

Goossens, E. 2012. China's green strategy is awash in red ink. *Bloomberg Business Week*, 26 November, p. 61.

He, H. and Wang, S. 2012. The experiences of green credit of American, British, and Japanese commercial banks and their implication on China (Mei Ying Ri Shangye Yinghang Lüse Xindai Jingyan dui Woguo de Qishi). *Financial Perspectives Journal* (Jinrong Zongheng), (07), 47.

Hook, Leslie. 2013. Suntech unit declared bankrupt. *Financial Times*, 20 March 2013. http://www.iisd.org/busines/, last accessed 10 November 2013.

Huanfa. 2007. No. 108.

ICBC. 2013a. Disburses Nearly RMB 750 Billion in Three Years to Support Green Economy, 2013–02–05. http://www.icbc.com.cn/icbc/newsupdates/icbc%20news/ICBC%20Disburses%20Nearly%20RMB%20750%20billion%20in%20Three%20Years%20to%20Support%20Green%20Economy.htm, last accessed 29 December 2013.

ICBC. 2013b. ICBC Pursues with Vigor to be World-Class Green Financial Institution, 2011–04–18. http://www.icbc.com.cn/ICBC/ICBC%20NEWS/ICBC%20Pursues%20with%20Vigor%20to%20be%20World-Class%20Green%20Financial%20Institution.htm, last accessed 29 December 2013.

International Institute of Sustainable Development. 2013. *Business and Sustainable Development.* http://www.iisd.org/business/, last accessed 10 November 2013.

Kujundzic, Petar. 2013. Banks Deal Boosts UK Bid to be Leading China Finance Hub. Reuters, 15 October. http://uk.reuters.com/article/2013/10/15/uk-china-uk-rqfii-idUKBRE99E06Y20131015, last accessed 8 November 2013.

Meng, Y. and Yinan, G. (eds.), China focus: Banks boost green credit for green growth. *People's Daily Online*, 21 July 2013. http://english.peopledaily.com.cn/90778/8334766.html, last accessed 23 December 2013.

OECD. 2002. *Sustainable Development Strategies: A Resource Book*. London: Earthscan.

PBOC. 2012. Law of the People's Republic of China on the People's Bank of China. http://www.pbc.gov.cn/publish/english/952/index.html, last accessed 11 July 2012.

UNEP FI. 2013a. About UNEP FI. http://www.unepfi.org/about/background/index.html, last accessed 11 November 2013.

UNEP FI. 2013b. UNEP FI Statement. http://www.unepfi.org/statements/index.html, last accessed 11 November 2013.

United Nations. 1987. Report of the World Commission on Environment and Development, (11 December 1987), General Assembly Resolution 42/187.

United Nations Environment Programme. 2011. *UNEP FI Guide to Banking and Sustainability: Understanding and Implementing Sustainability in Your Bank Based on the UNEP Statement of Commitment by Financial Institutions on Sustainable Development.* http://www.unepfi.org/fileadmin/documents/guide_banking_statements.pdf, last accessed 23 September 2016.

Wu, H. and Zhao, Z. 2011. The analysis on the promotion of green credit by commercial banks (Qianxi Lüse Xindai zai Shangye Yinhang Tuixing de Zhuangkuang). *Securities and Futures of China* (Zhongguo Zhengquan Qihuo), (06), 139.

Yin Fa. 2007. China Banking Regulatory Commission, State Environmental Protection Administration and People's Bank of China published *Guidelines Regarding Improvement and Enhancement of Financial Service in Energy Saving and Environmental Protection Sectors,* no. 215.

Yinjianfa. 2007. No. 83, *Guiding Opinions on the Credit Work for Energy Conservation and Emission Reduction* (Jieneng Jianpai Shouxin Gongzuo Zhidao Yijian).

Yulan Wang. 2013. The legal rules on the practicing green Credit by Commercial Banks (Shangye Yinhang Jianxing Lüse Xindai de Falv Guizhi). *Theory Research* (Xue Lilun).

10 Ethical issues in business administration and their effects on social and economic development

Rasim Abutalibov, Rufat Mammadov and Seymur M. Guliyev

1 Introduction

In a market economy, enterprises produce and sell products and services in order to meet the demand of customers, make a profit, and continue their existence. While producing, they make some flaws knowingly or unknowingly, and this, in turn, leads to socio-economic problems. Thus, unfair competition, difficulty in preventing bribery, damages caused by irresponsible behavior, indifferent treatment of customers and environment, manufacturing of dangerous products, breaching employee rights, and discrimination are just some of the problems in business ethics. Of course, the existence of such problems increases the importance of business ethics. Common current issues in the world include hazardous workplaces, work-related injuries and death, destruction and pollution of the environment, the exploitation of workers, dangerous products, bribery, financial scandals, abuse of power, corruption, and child labor. In most countries, these issues are at the top of the agenda.

Even though laws exist to prevent such problems, good business ethics are always necessary. A person who is aware of ethical values becomes responsible towards himself and society, and pays attention to his behaviors. Companies must ensure that employees are well trained in ethical business practices and establish confidential procedures for whistle-blowing. Corporations are also required to protect whistle-blowers and are prohibited from retaliating against them (American Management Association, 2006):

> Ethics refers to the value system by which a person determines what is right or wrong, fair or unfair, just or unjust. It is expressed through moral behavior in specific situations.
>
> (L. Dennis et al., 2010)

Business ethics is always positively related with socio-economic development. Either social or economic development is virtually guaranteed if ethical issues are obeyed in a society. At the same time, the opposite also applies: social or economic development is virtually impossible in a society where ethical issues are ignored. The ethical values are more likely to be heeded in socio-economically developed countries than in developing ones.

2   Approaches to business ethics

Here we would like to approach the issue in two ways:

Business ethical issues concerning the external environment of the enterprise and the society

- Ethical issues concerning the natural and socio-cultural environment
- Ethical issues concerning the government bodies
- Ethical issues concerning the competition
- Ethical issues concerning the consumers
- Ethical issues concerning the suppliers and other organizations (wholesalers, retailers, credit organizations, unions, and so on).

Business ethical issues concerning the internal environment of the enterprise and the society

- Ethical issues concerning the shareholders
- Ethical issues concerning the attitudes of managers towards the employees and the organization
- Ethical issues concerning the employees (damaging the property, indifferent or irresponsible work habits, lack of technical skills, chronic absenteeism or lateness, work slowdowns, and so on)
- Ethical issues concerning the relationships among the employees.

All these ethical issues, external and internal, of an enterprise have great socio-economic effects on the society. Ethical issues concerning the natural environment are socio-economically important not only for one country but for the whole planet. Here we may include such issues as pollution and destruction of the environment, inefficient use of resources, global warming, and the like. These issues are the most important ones in the globalizing world.

When it comes to the ethical issues concerning the socio-cultural environment, then we may include diminishing social and moral values, corruption, and so on. One of the most powerful factors resulting in socio-economic problems is corporate tax evasion and manipulation of the tax code. Payment of taxes on time and in correct form can lead to sound formulation of a national budget and thus provide for the socio-economic development of the nation.

In recent years, Turkish media reported that according to research, the number of private taxis in Turkey had risen to 50,000 and the total cost of annual tax evasion was 100,000,000 Turkish liras. Taxi stations that gained customers through the Internet reportedly had revenue of 300,000 Turkish liras per month (http://www.taksinet.com/taksihaber/8866 07.02.2012).

And this is only one example. If we relate this to all business sectors, then we may expect mass tax evasion from state budget. Such cases seriously damage a nation's economy as well as organizations financed by state budget.

In the book *Cultural Industry: Three Mistakes and One Accurate,* Abdurrahman Celik, the general manager of copyrights and cinema, showed the damage to the music sector caused by piracy (illegal duplication of recorded product). According to him, the music sector loses $200 million every year because of pirated products and the copying of music via Internet (http://www.on5yirmi5.com/genc/haber.55366/korsan-yilda-200-milyon-dolar-caliyor.html).

3   Business cases from the world

There is a strong business case for running companies in an ethically responsible way and for finance professionals to facilitate this. A socially and environmentally ethical approach ensures a company's ability to thrive in the long term by protecting its reputation, its license to operate, its supply chain, its relationships with partners, and its ability to recruit talent. Business ethics is about avoiding corporate collapse as a result of litigation or fraud.

Of the 28 companies that fell out of the world-leading S&P 500 index in the past 10 years, comparatively few casualties were claimed by shifts in technologies and markets. More were victims of massive fraud (as with Enron and WorldCom) or had leaders who had failed to create a sustainable business model. This was most evident in the financial services industry, with the likes of Lehman Brothers, Bear Stearns, and Wachovia choosing huge short-term gains at the cost of their long-term survival. Similarly, UK electronics company Marconi was brought down by it its unsustainable business plan (Smart, Barman and Gunasekera, 2010: 6).

When we look at the world experience, we see that many factors affect the sustainable development of enterprises. These factors include efficiency and effectiveness. Efficiency is the measurement of how an enterprise uses the current resources optimally in reaching its organizational goals. Effectiveness is the measurement of how the enterprise reaches its goals (Abutalibov and Mammadov, 2009: 37).

We will focus on effectiveness. Many managers think that creating sustainability means keeping prices lower and the business's efficiency and quality high. Thus they forget about effectiveness. But when we look at the organizations mentioned below, we see that though they were once mighty enterprises, they collapsed. They lost their effectiveness in market and management systems.

We may show efficiency as A and effectiveness as B, thus $A*B$ = sustainability; here A and B are interdependent from each other. No matter that A is positive and B is negative – the result will be negative. At the same time, the reverse is also possible. That is why these two elements should be taken into consideration. The ethical issues arising from managers will always affect a company's effectiveness. We think that the main reason for collapse of the mentioned enterprises is lack of effectiveness.

The big businesses discussed below did not have good business ethics, and as a consequence they faced many problems. One of them is Enron Corporation. This publicly owned American company dealt with energy, commodities, and services, and in fact was one of the leading companies in electricity, natural gas, communications, and the pulp and paper industries. But because of accounting fraud, Enron announced bankruptcy in 2001. The Enron scandal was the base for the Sarbanes–Oxley Act in 2002.

Another example is Ahold. Ahold is one of the major supermarket operators in the world. The company's headquarters is in Amsterdam, the Netherlands. Its attempt at global expansion came to an end with an accounting scandal in 2003 in one of its U.S. subsidiaries. As a result, the CEO and CFO resigned. From that time, the company's income started to plummet.

Our last example is Parmalat SpA, an Italian international dairy and food corporation. The company was famous for its ultra-high-temperature milks. But it, too, was also faced with accounting fraud and collapsed. In 2003 the company announced bankruptcy with a deficit of €14 billion in its accounting.

Worldcom, Inc., Xerox, and Ericsson

Three more examples are Worldcom, Inc., Xerox, and Ericsson. Of course, all these events not only damaged the companies but also affected the society, the country, and as the whole everyone who came in contact with these enterprises. The attempts to do illegal business by companies or specific people cause increased social problems, such as unemployment, poverty, fraud, robbery, gender exploitation, and so on. Another factor is ethical issues concerning the competition. Greed makes the enterprise or the business professional break laws and do unethical things. Such cases can be seen every day in our society. When we say "ethical issues concerning the competition", we mean the way in which companies that produce the same or different products act towards one another. Selling its own product in large quantities, pricing out market rivals, and producing cheap and low-quality products can lead to unwanted results. These results include:

- Consumers buying poor quality or even dangerous products believing they are products of high quality.
- Businesses form a monopoly and sell products to consumers at high prices and dictate their own rules.
- If we take into consideration the fact that every member of the society is a consumer, then the ethical issues concerning the consumers are frequently faced. We may face such ethical issues either in market or in public transportation.
- Suppliers and other agents (wholesalers, retailers, credit organizations, unions, and so on) have direct influence on the existence of the enterprises. If the agents mentioned above fail to obey ethical principles, destruction of the enterprises may result and hundreds or even thousands of people may become unemployed.

The main issues in ethics concerning an enterprise's internal environment relate to its shareholders. The managers are appointed by the owners of the enterprise. But some managers are overpaid or disloyal, and this can take an enterprise into bankruptcy.

Other important internal ethical issues are as follows: the ethical issues of managers towards employees and the ethical issues towards the company (negative socio-psychological corporate culture, unhealthy or dangerous work environment, failing to provide workers with health insurance, paying workers poorly, meaningless criticism of workers, and so on) (Adam, 2005). All these ethical issues are regulated, and if the enterprises are organized by ethical rules, then they will create harmony and a sound environment. But if a company ignores business ethics, it will likely face unwanted consequences (embezzlement or theft, inattention or outright hatred towards the work, inefficient use of technology, and so on).

In some cases, managers try to improve the internal environment of the organization and treat the employees well, but some employees abuse this treatment. In this case, the ethical issues concerning the employees can include damaging company property, indifferent or irresponsible work, inefficient use of technology, chronic lateness and absenteeism, and work slow-downs. In order to prevent such cases, managers must create a disciplined workplace with a code of practice, where employees obey the internal rules. Otherwise such cases can cost the enterprises a lot of money, and sometimes take the enterprises into bankruptcy.

Figures 10.1 and 10.2 show the main reasons for ethical issues in sustainable development. For companies of all sizes, compliance with legal and regulatory conditions is the critical sustainability driver. For large companies, government grants or other incentives are the least powerful sustainability driver, but for small and medium-sized companies, supply chain vendor requirements are the least powerful driver for sustainable development.

One of the most important factors in poor ethical values is that citizens do not know their rights (David, 1990). The employee must know what his or her rights are under law at the time of employment, otherwise he or she may learn there is no health insurance, or he/she may work with no contract and face an uncertain future. Great responsibilities lie

To what extent are the following factors driving your company's sustainability efforts?

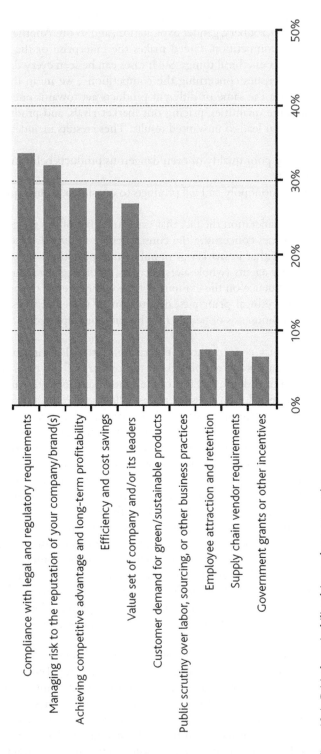

Figure 10.1 Critical sustainability drivers – large companies

Source: Evolution of corporate sustainability practices, AICPA, CICA and CIMA research study, 2010.

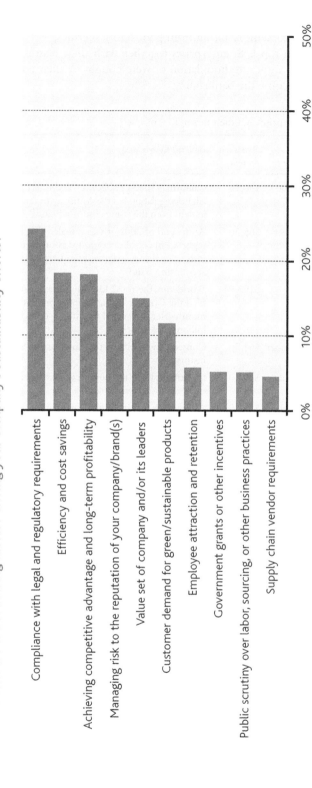

To what extent are the following factors driving your company's sustainability efforts?

Figure 10.2 Critical sustainability drivers – small and medium-sized enterprises (SMEs)

Source: Evolution of corporate sustainability practices, AICPA, CICA and CIMA research study, 2010.

on the shoulders of the government and every member of the society in order to prevent such socio-economic problems resulting from poor business ethics.

Table 10.1 shows ten top U.S. enterprises together with their reason for bankruptcy. Some of the enterprises went into liquidation or were bought by their competitors in the market in order to overcome the bankruptcy.

Table 10.1 10 top U.S. enterprises and their reason for collapse

Company name	Date of bankruptcy	Assets (in billions)	Bankruptcy reason
Pacific Gas and Electric Co.	6 April 2001	$36.15	California's largest publicly owned utility filed for bankruptcy after deregulation led the company to incur billions of dollars in debt from the rising cost of wholesale energy.*
Enron Corporation	2 December 2001	$65.50	At the end of 2001, it was revealed that the company's reported financial condition was sustained largely by institutionalized, systematic, and creatively planned accounting fraud.
Worldcom, Inc.	21 July 2002	$103.91	Worldcom, the no. 2 U.S. long-distance phone company, filed for Chapter 11 bankruptcy protection nearly one month after it revealed that it had improperly booked $3.8 billion in expenses.**
Conseco, Inc.	17 December 2002	$61.39	Conseco, Inc., became the third-largest U.S. bankruptcy in history.***
Lehman Brothers Holdings, Inc.	15 September 2008	$691.06	Investment bank fell prey to the credit crisis.****
Washington Mutual, Inc.	26 September 2008	$327.91	Although it was its home loan business that caused it to go on life-support, it was an old-fashioned, panic-driven run on deposits from its retail banking side that delivered the death knell.*****
Chrysler LLC	30 April 2009	$39.30	On 10 June 2009 Chrysler emerged from bankruptcy proceedings with the United Auto Workers pension fund, Fiat, and the U.S. and Canadian governments as principal owners.
Thornburg Mortgage, Inc.	1 May 2009	$36.52	Based in Santa Fe, New Mexico, this company struggled with liquidity problems beginning in summer 2007, when the value of mortgages on its balance sheet began to tumble.
General Motors Corporation	1 June 2009	$91.05	According to GM's bankruptcy filing, the company has assets of $82.3 billion, and liabilities of $172.8 billion. That would make GM the fourth largest U.S. bankruptcy on record, according to Bankruptcydata.com, just behind the 2002 bankruptcy of telecom WorldCom.******
CIT Group Inc.	1 November 2009	$71	A 101-year-old commercial lender, this company filed for bankruptcy to cut $10 billion in debt after the credit crunch dried up its funding and a U.S. bailout and debt exchange offer failed.

Source: http://amazingimageworld.blogspot.com/2009/11/top-10-us-bankruptcies.html.

* http://content.time.com/time/specials/packages/article/0,28804,1841334_1841431_1841356,00.html.
** http://money.cnn.com/2002/07/19/news/worldcom_bankruptcy/.
*** http://www.foxnews.com/story/2002/12/18/conseco-files-for-chapter-11-bankruptcy-protection/.
**** http://content.time.com/time/specials/packages/article/0,28804,1841334_1841431_1841342,00.html.
***** http://useconomy.about.com/od/businesses/p/wamu.htm.
****** http://money.cnn.com/2009/06/01/news/companies/gm_bankruptcy/.figuConclusion.

4   Conclusion

The cases mentioned above make it obvious that ethical issues are important for sustainable development and management of enterprises. However, ethical issues in big enterprises have an impact on the economy of the country at a macro level. Thus, bankruptcy results in a reduction in tax collection, reduction in gross domestic product, and increased unemployment. All together, these lead to crises in the country's economy.

The research on ethical issues and sustainable development shows that it is very important not only for big enterprises but also for small to medium-sized enterprises to address ethical issues, especially as they relate to corporate finance.

Taking into consideration all these factors, much attention must be given to prevention of such ethical issues at either the enterprise or national level. This in turn will lead to sustainable development of enterprises and prosperity of the economy. It must be made clear that the business success depends on more than just ethical issues. Here we tried to show the importance of ethical issues especially in the financial field. Together with ethical issues, the managerial role, the competitiveness, and the sustainability of the enterprise must be treated equally.

References

Abutalibov, R. and Mammadov, S. (2009). Idare Etmenin Esaslari. Baku, Azerbaijan: Nurlar Publication.

Adam, S. (2005). The Dynamics of Socio-Economic Development: An Introduction. Cambridge: Cambridge University Press.

AICPA, CICA and CIMA research study. (2010). Evolution of Corporate Sustainability Practices. http://www.cimaglobal.com/Documents/Thought_leadership_docs/CIMA_AICPA_CICA%20sustainability_report.pdf

American Management Association. (2006). The Ethical Enterprise: A Global Study of Business Ethics 2005–2015. http://www.amanet.org/images/HREthicsSurvey06.pdf

David, J. (1990). Levels of Socio-Economic Development Theory. New York: Praeger.

Ferrell, O.C., Fraedrich, J. and Ferrell, L. (2012). Business Ethics: Ethical Decision Making and Cases. Mason, OH: Cengage Learning.

Hartman, L. and DesJardins, J. (2010). Business Ethics: Decision-Making for Personal Integrity & Social Responsibility. New York: McGraw-Hill.

Parsons, J. Patricia (2004). Ethics in Public Relations: A Guide to Best Practice. London: Kogan Page.

Smart, V., Barman, T. and Gunasekera, N. (2010). Incorporating Ethics into Strategy: Developing Sustainable Business Models. CIMA Report. http://www.cimaglobal.com/Documents/Thought_leadership_docs/Sustainability%20and%20Climate%20Change/ethics_reportFINAL.pdf

Wilcox, D.L., Cameron, G.T., Ault, P.H. and Agee, W.K. (2009). Public Relations Strategies and Tactics. 9th edition. Boston: Allyn & Bacon.

Yanez- Arancibia, A., Davalos, S.R., Day, J.W. and Reye, E. (2013). Ecological Dimensions for Sustainable Socio Economic Development. Boston: WIT Press/Computational Mechanics.

Websites

http://amazingimageworld.blogspot.com/2009/11/top-10-us-bankruptcies.html [Access date 1 November 2013].

http://content.time.com/time/specials/packages/article/0,28804,1841334_1841431_1841356,00.html [Access date 1 November 2013].

http://content.time.com/time/specials/packages/article/0,28804,1841334_1841431_1841342,00.html [Access date 3 November 2013].

http://www.foxnews.com/story/2002/12/18/conseco-files-for-chapter-11-bankruptcy- protection/ [Access date 3 November 2013].

http://money.cnn.com/2002/07/19/news/worldcom_bankruptcy/ [Access date 1 November 2013].
http://money.cnn.com/2009/06/01/news/companies/gm_bankruptcy [Access date 4 November 2013].
http://www.on5yirmi5.com/genc/haber.55366/korsan- yilda- 200-milyon-dolar-caliyor.html [Access date 13 August 2013].
http://www.taksinet.com/taksihaber/8866 07.02.2012 [Access date 15 August 2013].
http://useconomy.about.com/od/businesses/p/wamu.htm [Access date 4 November 2013].
World Socialist Web site: http://www.wsws.org/articles/2004/jan2004/parm-j06.shtml [Access date 15 August 2013].

11 Integrated sustainability and social responsibility communication

Duygu Türker and Huriye Toker

1 Introduction

In parallel to the growing number of social and environmental problems, business organizations start to adopt more sustainable and socially responsible ways of doing business. From the "business case" approach for sustainability (Salzmann, Ionescu-Somers, and Steger, 2005; Schaltegger, 2008) and corporate social responsibility (CSR) (Carroll and Shabana, 2010; Weber, 2008), a firm can also leverage its involvement in sustainability and social responsibility activities. Despite this, the link between these corporate activities and financial performance is still inconsistent (Margolis and Walsh, 2003). The literature indicates that corporate sustainability and social responsibility can affect a company indirectly by increasing its competitiveness (Burke and Logsdon 1996; Porter and Kramer, 2002) and reputation (Lewis, 2003), positively affecting employees' commitment (Peterson, 2004; Turker, 2009), or attracting prospective employees (Turban and Greening, 1997). However, while some organizations can take the advantage of their social and sustainability concern, others cannot build their own "business case" at all. The underlying reason of this significant variability among firms is partly related to a company's overall communication strategy. The problem is not usually related to the amount or quantity of communication; it is mainly related to how they can communicate such involvement effectively (Dawkins, 2004; Morsing, 2006a) and how they can strategically use their communication efforts to increase stakeholder involvement. Corporate sustainability and social responsibility communication (SSRC)[1] is a long-term process that requires an organizational awareness for the changing needs, expectations, and interests of all stakeholders and a willingness to increase their participation in the decision-making process to achieve more balanced organizational decisions and actions. This process relies on establishing sound external and internal communication.

Due to its increasing relevance to companies and investors, recently SSRC has been broadening in its scope and quality, and the media becomes the central forum to disseminate the related information to the various stakeholders. For instance, while the number and length of sustainability and social reports are increasing, some companies are paying more attention to their stakeholder communication by increasing the quality of their reporting system. The study of Brown, Guidry, and Patten (2010) indicated that the quality of sustainability reporting can change a company's reputation positively and most companies start to focus on quality and quantity simultaneously. Therefore, companies increasingly need to adopt an *integrated* sustainability and social responsibility communication (ISSRC) that will ensure the transmission of their overall message to all stakeholders and provide a strategic position among its competitors (Isenmann, 2006). Moreover, this integrated perspective is particularly important to consider the diverse interests of all stakeholders from an ethical standpoint (Turker and Altuntaş, 2013), to manage communication inflows and outflows effectively (Morsing, 2006a; Morsing and Schultz, 2006), and to combine all efforts within the organization towards sustainability and social responsibility (Dawkins, 2004; Morsing and Schultz, 2006).

The current study attempts to articulate why and how managers can integrate their SSRC through using the components of communication and considering cross-cultural differences. Deriving from the perspectives of stakeholder approach and critical theory, first, a theoretical framework is provided to explain why the notion of communication is important to increase stakeholder participation and make more sustainable and socially responsible decisions in the organization. Then, four ways of integration in the SSRC are explained as the integration of all stakeholders, communication inflows and outflows, organizational efforts, and components of communication. Considering the increasing attention to this last way of integration, the next section provides an analysis of SSRC components and an explanation of the traditional and technology-oriented ways of corporate communication. In the last section, the cross-cultural differences in SSRC, which emerge due to the differences in the notions of communication, sustainability, and social responsibility across various cultures and countries, are discussed through reviewing the empirical studies in the literature.

2   Organizational communication with stakeholders

Depending on the shift in the focus of organizational theory towards the organization-environment interface, it has been increasingly recognized that an organization is not an *island* (Hakansson and Snehota, 1989) and should consider its environment (Hall et al., 1977: 457; Laumann, Galaskiewicz, and Marsden, 1978). From a sociological point of view, the process of attaining organizational goals can be viewed as 'a relation between a system (in this case a social system) and the relevant parts of the external situation in which it acts or operates' (Parsons, 1956: 64). Starting from this 'early and limited' form of systems theory thinking, which ties the organization to its environment (Carper and Snizek, 1980), organizations start to be conceptualized as *open systems* that continuously interact with their environment (Katz and Kahn, 1966). Since the 1960s, systems theory (Thompson, 1967) has shed light on the organizational life and evokes many productive ideas, concepts, and approaches to the relations of businesses with their environment.

As one of these approaches, the stakeholder management approach is nourished by systems thinking, as well as corporate planning, corporate social responsibility (CSR), and organizational theory, and provides a significant strategic perspective for managers (Freeman and McVea, 2001). According to this approach, an organization is conceptualized in the nexus of its relations with the stakeholders (Freeman, 2010) in the task and general environment (Bourgeois, 1980; Dill, 1958). Stakeholders can be defined as any people, group, or entity that can affect or be affected by the achievement of organizational objectives (Freeman, 1984). Based on this comprehensive definition, an organization should coordinate the 'multiple and not always entirely congruent' interests and purposes of its stakeholders (Donaldson and Preston, 1995: 70). Drawing from stakeholder-agency theory, since managers are the only group that has direct control over the decision-making process, they are responsible for strategic decisions and resource allocation of an organization in order to balance the diverse interests of stakeholders (Hill and Jones, 1992). Considering the increasing environmental and social problems caused by business organizations, the current managerial decision-making structure falls short of capturing the complexity of this stakeholder relationship.

According to Deetz (1995a: 278), the increasing power of organizations should drive managers to rethink their organizational decisions and actions. When making decisions, they have to use this business power more responsibly and consider the economic, environmental, and social impacts of business operations on various stakeholders. These organizational decisions and actions can be best articulated within the framework of CSR and sustainability. In his famous definition, Carroll (1979: 500) states that 'social responsibility of business encompasses the economic, legal, ethical, and discretionary expectations that society has of organizations at a given point in time'. As recently defined by the European Commission (EC) (2011: 6), CSR is 'the responsibility of enterprises for their impacts on society' through integrating 'social, environmental, ethical human rights and consumer concerns into their business operations and core strategy in close collaboration with their stakeholders'.

It can be seen that there is a natural fit between the concepts of social responsibility and stakeholders (Carroll, 1991: 43), and organizations need to recognize the interests of each stakeholder for their sustainability and social responsibility involvement. Husted and Allen (2006) state that 'a strategic approach to CSR requires that firms select a CSR strategy contingent upon the demands of salient local and global stakeholders'. Based on the critical theory, the best way of doing this is to ensure the *participation* of all stakeholders in the decision-making process to let them discuss and negotiate their own interests (Deetz, 1995b). A better governance and decision-making system can enable stakeholder participation and communication (Kuhn and Deetz, 2008), and the role of a manager in such an ideal stakeholder model would be to coordinate these conflicting interests instead of managing or controlling the process (Deetz, 2006: 273). Therefore, in order to engage stakeholders in long-term value creation (Andriof et al., 2002) through corporate sustainability and social responsibility activities, managers should manage the relationship with stakeholders – not the stakeholders themselves (Morsing and Schultz, 2006).

Despite some practical shortcomings of critical theory due to possible power inequalities among parties (Griffin, 2009: 273; Turker, 2013), it can provide a theoretical backbone for the centrality of *communication* to increase stakeholder participation in more sustainable and socially responsible business organizations. Communication is the natural linchpin between an organization and its stakeholders. According to Kuhn and Deetz (2008: 91), 'a conception of CSR based in a rich vision of communication has the potential to both expose and incorporate the myriad values present in organizational decision-making'. Therefore, communication can be viewed as the main tenet of the decision-making model, which produces more sustainable and socially responsible decisions. A shift in the decision-making heuristics of managers can start with building *integrated* communication for sustainability and social responsibility efforts.

3   Towards an "integrated" perspective on SSRC

Today, the notions of stakeholder participation and dialogue become critical to reach democratic ideals within the organization and improve corporate self-presentations (Morsing and Schultz, 2006: 325). In doing so, managers should formulate and implement an effective communication strategy around their sustainability and social responsibility involvement. The literature provides various definitions for the communication activities of corporate sustainability and social responsibility activities. CSR communication is usually viewed as 'building and maintaining of favourable reputations and relationships with key stakeholders' (Cornelissen, 2004: 17). However, this definition oversimplifies the scope and function of communication within a sustainability and social responsibility framework. In a wider sense, CSR communication can be defined as 'a process of anticipating stakeholders' expectations, articulation of CSR policy and managing of different organization communication tools designed to provide true and transparent information about a company's or a brand's integration of its business operations, social and environmental concerns, and interactions with stakeholders' (Podnar, 2008: 75). In their study, Signitzer and Prexl (2007) combine the sustainability and social responsibility aspects under the concept of corporate sustainability communication (CSC) and define it as the integration of sustainability issues into existing public relations activities through considering social justice, environmental awareness, and economic success. Based on these previous definitions, SSRC can be defined as a process of strategically interacting with stakeholders on the corporate sustainable and social responsibility activities to achieve more balanced corporate decisions and actions in the way of sustainable development. In this case, SSRC is not the last stage for the announcement of organizational, social, and environmental performance – rather it becomes a strategic and interactive step of an ongoing sustainability and social responsibility involvement process.

Although many business organizations try to communicate their sustainability and social responsibility activities in some ways, their involvement usually lacks an *integrated* perspective. Integration in SSRC can be strategically accomplished in four ways. Following Deetz's critical approach for organizational communication, a company should first integrate *all stakeholders* into the communication process. The literature indicates that managers can pay more attention to some stakeholders over others. They can prioritize the stakeholder interests depending on the power of these stakeholders over the firm, the legitimacy of their relationship to the firm, or the urgency of their claim on the firm (Mitchell, Agle, and Wood, 1997), or simply the urgency or importance of their claim (Carroll, 1991). However, the growing pressure of environmental and social problems requires managers to obtain a wider sense in their stakeholder conception and take into account the interests of *other* stakeholders as well; because 'whatever the magnitude of their stake, each stakeholder is a part of the nexus of implicit and explicit contracts that constitutes the firm' (Hill and Jones, 1992: 134). In their study, Turker and Altuntaş (2013) refer to stakeholders who are usually neglected by managers as "indirect stakeholders". Including the natural environment, non-human species, and future generations, these indirect stakeholders should be recognized by the decision-makers from an ethical standpoint to take a strategic position for the future (Turker and Altuntaş, 2013).

Moreover, despite their importance, most companies ignore the role of their employees in this process and usually fail to engage them into the communication process. Since employees as a group are some of the most sensitive stakeholders to CSR involvement (Peterson, 2004; Turker, 2009) and the potentially powerful advocates of such activities (Dawkins, 2004) to outsiders, managers should ensure whether the internal communication process is working well enough to disseminate the core communication message among the internal stakeholders. According to Morsing (2006b), 'communicating corporate CSR efforts via external stakeholders is one of the current most powerful communication strategies available to improve member identification, or cause disidentification' among internal stakeholders. Therefore, there is a need for integration of external and internal communication efforts to cover all stakeholders of an organization.

The second integration is about the direction of communication. Morsing (2006a: 239) states that CSR communication is usually seen as a 'one-way process of informing stakeholders about corporate intentions and activities'; however, this approach is not sufficient to satisfy the stakeholders' expectations and so a company should integrate their stakeholders into 'a two-way approach' in which 'the company can stage and encourage to enhance stakeholder dialogue and thereby increase understanding of stakeholder expectations'. Morsing and Schultz (2006: 326–7) base the first CSR communication strategy on the public information approach and call it an informing strategy. The main purpose is to disseminate information 'to inform the public as objectively as possible about the organization's CSR decisions and actions' (Morsing and Schultz, 2006: 326–7).

Morsing and Schultz (2006) classify the two-way approach of communication as stakeholder response and stakeholder involvement strategies; despite the fact that the former is mainly focusing on convincing the stakeholders of corporate attractiveness, the latter assumes a *dialogue* with stakeholders. Drawing from the critical theory of communication on the stakeholder management approach, the dialogue is the key phenomenon for sustainability and social responsibility communication. 'Dialogue is about communication among stakeholders in ways that take serious account of expressed views' and it can pave the ways of possible partnerships towards a more sustainable development (Holliday, Schmidheiny, and Watts, 2002: 150–2). Besides informing stakeholders about CSR efforts, an organization should continuously evaluate and respond to stakeholder attitudes and demands. In this way, communication becomes a circular process that permits information inflows and outflows. In doing so, SSRC can increase the accuracy of information and ensure the transparency of communication process. Morsing (2006a: 239) suggests the integration of both one-way and two-way communication approaches 'to make stakeholders positively connote to the corporate CSR efforts'.

The third way is integration and coordination among the organizational units that are working in sustainability, social responsibility, and communication. In corporate communication, Cornelissen (2008: 122–3) suggests managers to consolidate their communication efforts in a central department, locate this department close to the decision-makers in the organizational structure, and follow a cross-functional coordination between this department and other units of organization. These recommendations become particularly relevant in the management of SSRC. Against the challenges of the increasing complexity of business operations and increasing competition, managers should ensure, at least, a moderate degree of coordination among organizational units that are working for the accomplishment of sustainability and social responsibility activities. The empirical study of Pollach et al. (2012) indicates that CSR and communication departments are usually engaging in a close collaboration in their CSR communication. Although Black and Härtel (2004) find the skills of the public relations department critical in CSR communication, the ability of other functional managers is also important to incorporate stakeholder concerns and social factors into the decision-making process (Bronn, 2010: 317). A more participative model of stakeholder relationship can be best achieved with the integration of all functional managers into the process – rather than just the efforts of public relations and marketing managers (Morsing and Schultz, 2006: 325). According to Dawkins (2004: 118), cross-functional involvement can be important 'in winning space for corporate responsibility messages; this of course includes corporate communications or public affairs, but also functions ranging from marketing to human resources to investor relations'. Therefore, SSRC should be accomplished through the integrated efforts of all related units within the organization.

The last approach is integration among all tools and components of corporate communication strategy. According to stakeholder involvement strategy (Morsing and Schultz, 2006), there is a strong requirement for a well-designed communication strategy and implementation of organizational communication based on stakeholder expectations. Stakeholders have ascribed increased value to CSR, and they have come to see it as a social responsibility of the business. The basics of communication – message, content, channel, and feedback – are important for the outcomes of communication. Communication outcomes are variable and depend on the stakeholder characteristics. Since creating stakeholder conscience and managing stakeholder perceptions towards a company's sustainability and social responsibility activities are key factors for planning, controlling, and managing strategic benefits, it is important for managers to evaluate and understand the key issues related to CSR communication. These issues are similar to communication basics including the content and channel of message as well as using loud or silent communication tools. Integration among all these components of SSRC is particularly important to ensure the consistency of all processes. Since there is a growing interest of practitioners and scholars in these components, we explain them in detail in the next section.

3   Components of ISSRC

There are a variety of communication channels through which information about a company's sustainability and social responsibility activities can be disseminated. A company can communicate its CSR activities through official documents such as an annual CSR report or press releases, dedicate a section of its official corporate website to CSR, purchase TV commercials, magazine or billboard advertisements, or use social media. To consider the best channel and the most effective SSRC, we need to divide the communication means into "traditional" (i.e. CSR reports, press conferences, brochures, presentations, advertisements) and "technology-driven tools" (i.e. CSR electronic forums, emails, website FAQs, blogs, electronic newsletters, Intranets, audio and video podcasts) and use them in the appropriate time and place.

In fact, in the CSR communication strategy, CSR reporting and official company websites are the most common tools to disseminate CSR-related information to various stakeholder groups. CSR reporting seems the most attractive medium, and it has grown significantly in recent years (Toker, 2013). Nowadays, almost all companies try to reach their stakeholders via CSR reports. As an international project, Global Reporting Initiative (GRI) tries to provide a common reporting framework for organizations within 97 indicators of sustainability performance (GRI, 2013). Depending on the increasing popularity of such reporting frameworks in the business community, companies pay significant attention to the number and length of these reports and try to reach a wide range of stakeholders. Moreover, creative communication alternatives are used to communicate corporate sustainability and responsibility messages. For instance, some awarding and appraisal schemes, like the Association of Chartered Certified Accountants' (ACCA) Sustainability Reporting Awards (ACCA, 2013), are designed to commend the best companies. This is certainly a new way of obtaining a competitive edge. Except for this reporting system, the other traditional communication tools, like personal contacts, public meetings, interviews, workshops, presentations, and business dinners, are usually considered *outdated*. These tools are not suitable for the different groups of society (Isenmann, 2006: 253). However, in an integrated SSRC process, traditional tools can be used effectively to interact with some stakeholder groups. For instance, an organization can use strategic conversations to learn about stakeholder concerns, improve its CSR strategy (Miles, Munilla, and Darroch, 2006), and convert these expectations into governance objectives, targets, and indicators (Castka, Bamber, and Sharp, 2004).

Today, CSR communication is in a phase of transition and entering a new digital online stage. In order to overcome the inadequacy of traditional communication tools (Isenmann, 2006: 247), companies need to adopt specific responses to use the online area effectively. The idea behind Internet-based communication is to open windows for advanced CSR communication and to reach as many stakeholders as possible. Online availabilities, downloads, external CSR documents, feedback opportunities and interactivity, contact details, automatic order forms, CSR electronic forums, search engines, and hyperlinks are just some of the content capabilities that companies can use. Furthermore, companies are expanding CSR responsibilities on a global scale with the help of Web 2.0 social media applications. Internet-based tools provide interactivity and dynamic transparency, including emails, web forms, website FAQs, blogs, audio and video podcasts, electronic newsletters, Intranets, and social media applications such as Facebook, Twitter, LinkedIn, Flickr, and so on. Such tools can be target-group-tailored, individualized, even personalized: reports, press releases, newsletters, brochures, leaflets, and presentations that are accessible to all (Toker, 2013).

Although these traditional and technology-driven tools exist, companies are not getting full credit and support for their social responsibility initiatives due to the varied information needs and expectations of different stakeholder groups, among them non-governmental organizations (NGOs), shareholders, media, mass audiences, and employees, in different contextual settings. For example, while the British public considers child labour, education, and environmental issues particularly important for companies to address, the Norwegian public considers environment-related issues as far more important than anything else. Therefore, on corporate responsibility as on other topics, 'tailoring messages to the different interests, information needs and preferred channels of different stakeholders is crucial to effective communications', which can be successful with a well-designed communication strategy (Dawkins, 2004: 110). On the other hand, some communication vehicles can be more powerful and effective than others. For instance, in most cases, 'marketing communications tools . . . are not perceived in a positive light by consumers or, to a large extent, by businesses' (Jahdi and Acıkdilli, 2009: 106). Furthermore, stakeholders respond differently to the various communication channels available. For example, a mass audience may not be aware of the greenwashing activities of a company, but the NGOs in the field and the media naturally pay a lot more attention. Therefore, managers should admit that there are specific challenges in communicating such corporate activities due to the scepticism towards company messages, negative attitude to this type of advertising ("advertorials"), and potentially hostile reactions from the media, campaign/lobby groups, and others. Considering the sensitive nature of this communication, corporate sustainability and social responsibility activities cannot be advertised in the same way as a company's products or services (Pomering and Dolnicar, 2009: 288). Morsing and Schultz (2006) find that consumers prefer such initiatives to be communicated through 'silent' channels, such as annual reports and websites. Sometimes a silent traditional channel is less aggressive and even less eye-catching for the stakeholders who are searching for the information.

As discussed here, corporate responsibility communications are not yet being effectively and strategically tailored according to the needs and characteristics of different stakeholders. Therefore, communication still remains the missing link in the practice of corporate responsibility. As a result, companies need to differentiate online and traditional communication tools on CSR for different stakeholders. Information supply evolves from a "traditional" strict, one-way, company-controlled mechanism towards a more interactive, transparent, and participatory approach using online communication tools. The latter can reach a greater audience, trying to get feedback from a number of stakeholders, and then providing CSR communication tools that exactly meet their requirements. The Internet has the potential to provide interactive, customized, or even personalized communication tools, and offers a platform for dialogue between companies and stakeholders. However, technology is not the only solution for sustainable corporate communication requirements.

4   Cross-cultural differences

SSRC is one of the most context-sensitive fields of business operations due to the changing meanings of sustainability, CSR, and communication concepts across cultures. Since communication is closely aligned with the culture of a society, it has been difficult to provide a single definition for the concept (Griffin, 2009: 6). On the other hand, the way sustainability and CSR is defined, practised, and communicated in different parts of the world is also related to the specific cultural and social contexts (Chapple and Moon, 2005; Golob and Bartlett, 2007). Although the concepts of sustainability and social responsibility originated in the West, they have become a worldwide issue through globalization. As Stohl, Stohl, and Popova (2007: 34) point out, 'a global CSR is responsive to the multiple cultures, value sets, and communicative practices of different nations while recognizing that (inter) organizational contexts are no longer bounded by the nation-state'.

In spite of globalization argument, there is also another viewpoint which accepts CSR as the product of the specific social and cultural context from which it emerges. As May and Zorn (2003: 595) argued, '[C]orporate social responsibility is, at its core, about the simultaneously contested and consensual nature of the relationship between organizations and culture(s)'. From this point of view, scholars have started to examine how CSR is practised in different social and cultural contexts (e.g. Sriramesh et al., 2007). A brief literature review shows that cultural characteristics affect the audience's perception significantly and result in a diversity of SSRC practices among organizations. The studies show that while companies in the United States are usually motivated by a business case approach in engaging in CSR communication, their European counterparts are more concerned with competitive ranking (Klein et al., 2005). The former try to justify the use of CSR by focusing on the economic aspects of sustainability via a financial discourse, and the latter focus on the concepts of citizenship, accountability, or moral commitment (Hartman, Rubin, and Dhanda, 2007). A study by Maignan and Ralston (2002) analyses CSR communication in websites of companies in France, the Netherlands, the United Kingdom, and the U.S., and finds that 'different countries hold substantially different perspectives on: (1) how important it is to be publicly perceived as socially responsible; and (2) which CSR issues are more important to emphasize'. For instance, this study reveals that 'French and Dutch businesses were not as eager as their Anglo counterparts to convey good citizenship images on the web', partly because of the differentiation in the role of businesses in society.

Due to the predominantly Western focus in the literature (Tang and Li, 2009; Whelan, 2007), most of the strategies and recommendations on SSRC are designed for companies in this context. However, sustainability and CSR have become a global phenomenon and most companies in developing countries are starting to adopt a sustainable and socially responsible approach. In their study, Jamali and Mirshak (2007) analyse CSR activities in

Lebanon and find that these companies also use different stakeholder management techniques internally, via the company intranet, newsletters, bulletin boards, and staff meetings, to affect employees positively, and also externally, via partnership arrangements and collaborative projects. In Hungary, national media is very negative to CSR and treats it as implicit advertisement, so most companies try to convey their messages through regional and local media or publish their CSR or sustainability reports. Hungarian companies pay less attention to internal communication; employers very rarely ask their employees for input before making decisions, and instead deliver only one-way messages (Ligeti and Oravecz, 2009: 148).

On the other hand, in a Chinese context, companies are usually seen as the major source of social and environmental problems, so there is disregard for and scepticism towards CSR activities. However, an increasing number of companies are involving themselves in CSR and communicate it on their websites using one of these three approaches: CSR as ad hoc philanthropy, CSR as strategic philanthropy, and CSR as ethical business conduct (Tang and Li, 2009). Similarly, leading companies in Turkey have increasingly recognized the importance of social and environmental reporting when communicating their sustainability and social responsibility activities. However, a study by Altuntaş and Turker (2012) on the reports of supply chain activities of Turkish companies shows that despite their emphasis on social and environmental aspects of sustainability, they built their supply chain activities around economic concerns.

5   Conclusion

Considering the increasing scepticism about companies and their social and environmental involvement, managers must communicate their activities in a sincere, responsible, and ethical manner. Based on the incorporated perspectives of the stakeholder management approach and critical theory, the overarching aim of all these activities is to increase the stakeholder inclusion in the decision-making process and so achieve more sustainable and socially responsible business operations. In doing so, it becomes critical to follow a deeper sustainability and social responsibility philosophy and reflect what is actually done by the organization. Although it is known that 'CSR efforts are driven not just by ideological thinking that corporations can be a powerful and positive force for social change, but more by the multi-faceted business returns that corporations can potentially reap from their CSR endeavors' (Du, Bhattacharya, and Sen, 2010), an organization can engage in sustainability and social responsibility in a conscientious and proactive manner (Bovee and Thill, 2011: 130), follow a "dark green" (activist) approach (Freeman, Pierce, and Dodd, 1995), and become a leader company that proactively recognizes 'its responsibilities, ambitious targets, and extensive reporting' (Hahn, 2012). Developing such a sincere approach to a company's social and environmental involvement and communicating all these activities truthfully will ultimately improve corporate reputation and prestige among its stakeholders.

The current study attempts to provide an overview on ISSRC. Future studies can particularly focus on the cross-cultural differences in the application of SSRC and try to provide insight for companies in developing countries. Moreover, the differences among organizational responses towards SSRC should be explored considering the organizational variables. For instance, studies show that CSR can be communicated differently depending on the industry (Sweeney and Coughlan, 2008) or the customer target of companies (B2B or B2C) (Tang and Li, 2009). On the other hand, despite the useful efforts of international initiatives like GRI, there is a need for the development of common frameworks that will guide organizations when communicating sustainability and social responsibility. The voluntary nature of all these company involvements can turn into an obligatory framework in the near future.

Note

1 Although the concepts of sustainability and social responsibility can be distinguished in many ways (see Van Marrewijk, 2003), they can be unified within the corporate communication framework. For instance, Signitzer and Prexl (2007: 3–4) suggest using "corporate sustainability communication" as an umbrella term that covers similar conceptions, including CSR as well. In the current study, these two closely related concepts are combined in SSRC to provide a comprehensive perspective.

References

Altuntaş, C. and Turker, D. (2012). Sustainable supply chains: A content analysis of sustainability reports. *Dokuz Eylül Üniversitesi Sosyal Bilimler Enstitüsü Dergisi*, 14(3), 39–64.

Andriof, J., Waddock, S., Husted, B. and Rahman, S.S. (eds.). (2002). *Unfolding Stakeholder Thinking: Theory, Responsibility and Engagement*. Sheffield: Greenleaf.

Association of Chartered Certified Accountants (ACCA) (2013). http://www.accaglobal.com/en.html [accessed on 21 May 2013].

Black, L.D. and Härtel, C.E. (2004). The five capabilities of socially responsible companies. *Journal of Public Affairs*, 4(2), 125–44.

Bourgeois, L.J. (1980). Strategy and environment: A conceptual integration. *Academy of Management Review*, 5(1), 25–39.

Bovee, C.L. and Thill, J.V. (2011). *Business in Action*. New York: Pearson.

Bronn, P.S. (2010). Reputation, communication, and the corporate brand. In R.L. Heath (ed.), *Handbook of Public Relations*. Thousand Oaks, CA: Sage, 307–20.

Brown, D.L., Guidry, R.P. and Patten, D.M. (2010). Sustainability reporting and perceptions of corporate reputation: An analysis using fortune. In Freedman, M. and B. Jaggi (eds.), *Sustainability, Environmental Performance and Disclosures* (Advances in Environmental Accounting & Management, Vol. 4). Bingley: Emerald, 83–104.

Burke, L. and Logsdon, J.M. (1996). How corporate social responsibility pays off. *Long Range Planning*, 29(4), 495–502.

Carper, W.B. and Snizek, W.E. (1980). The nature and types of organizational taxonomies: An overview. *The Academy of Management Review*, 5(1), 65–75.

Carroll, A.B. (1979). A three dimensional conceptual model of corporate social performance. *Academy of Management Review*, 4, 497–505.

Carroll, A.B. (1991). The pyramid of corporate social responsibility: Toward the moral management of organizational stakeholders. *Business Horizons*, 34(4), 39–48.

Carroll, A.B. and Shabana, K.M. (2010). The business case for corporate social responsibility: A review of concepts, research and practice. *International Journal of Management Reviews*, 12(1), 85–105.

Castka, P., Bamber, C. and Sharp, J.M. (2004). *Implementing Effective Corporate Social Responsibility and Corporate Governance: A Framework*. London: BSI Publications.

Chapple, W. and Moon, J. (2005). Corporate social responsibility (CSR) in Asia: A seven-country study of CSR web site reporting. *Business and Society*, 44(4), 415–41.

Cornelissen, J.P. (2004). *Corporate Communications: Theory and Practice*. London: Sage.

Cornelissen, J.P. (2008). *Corporate Communication*. London: Sage.

Dawkins, J. (2004). Corporate responsibility: The communication challenge. *Journal of Communications Management*, 9(3), 108–19.

Deetz, S. (1995a). Transforming communication, transforming business: Stimulating value negotiation for more responsive and responsible workplaces. *International Journal of Value-Based Management*, 8, 255–78.

Deetz, S. (1995b). *Transforming Communication, Transforming Business: Building Responsive and Responsible Workplaces*. Cresskill, NJ: Hampton.

Deetz, S. (2006). Corporate governance, corporate social responsibility, and communication. In S.K. May, G. Cheney and J. Roper (eds.), *The Debate over Corporate Social Responsibility*. Oxford: Oxford University Press, 267–78.

Dill, W.R. (1958). Environment as an influence on managerial autonomy. *Administrative Science Quarterly*, 2(4), 409–43.

Donaldson, T. and Preston, L.E. (1995). The stakeholder theory of the corporation: Concepts, evidence, and implications. *Academy of Management Review*, 20(1), 65–91.

Du, S., Bhattacharya, C.B. and Sen, S. (2010). Maximizing business returns to corporate social responsibility (CSR): The role of CSR communication. *International Journal of Management Reviews*, 12(1), 8–19.

European Commission (EC) (2011). A renewed EU strategy 2011–14 for corporate social responsibility. http://eur-lex.europa.eu/LexUriserv/LexUriserv.do?uri=COM:2011:0681:FIN:EN:PDF [accessed 5 June 2013].

Freeman, R.E. (1984). *Strategic Management: A Stakeholder Approach*. Boston, MA: Pitman.

Freeman, R.E. (2010). *Strategic Management: A Stakeholder Approach*. New York: Cambridge University Press.

Freeman, R.E. and McVea, J. (2001). A stakeholder approach to strategic management. Working Paper No. 01–02. http://papers.ssrn.com/paper.taf?abstract_id=263511 [accessed 18 May 2013].

Freeman, R.E., Pierce, J. and Dodd, R. (1995). *Shades of Green: Ethics and the Environment*. New York: Oxford University Press.

Global Reporting Initiative (GRI). (2013). https://www.globalreporting.org/Pages/default.aspx [accessed 21 May 2013].

Golob, U. and Bartlett, J.L. (2007). Communicating about corporate social responsibility: A comparative study of CSR reporting in Australia and Slovenia. *Public Relations Review*, 33, 1–9.

Griffin, E. (2009). *A First Look at Communication Theory*. Singapore: McGraw-Hill.

Hahn, R. (2012). ISO 26000 and the standardization of strategic management processes for sustainability and corporate social responsibility. *Business Strategy and the Environment*, 22(7), 442-455 [Online – DOI: 10.1002/bse.1751].

Hakansson, H. and Snehota, I. (1989). No business is an island: The network concept of business strategy. *Scandinavian Journal of Management*, 5(3), 187–200.

Hall, R.H., Clark, J.P., Giordano, P.C., Johnson, P.V. and Rockel, M.V. (1977). Patterns of interorganizational relationships. *Administrative Science Quarterly*, 22(3), 457–74.

Hartman, L.P., Rubin, R.S. and Dhanda, K.K. (2007). The communication of corporate social responsibility: United States and European Union multinational corporations. *Journal of Business Ethics*, 74(4), 373–89.

Hill, C.W. and Jones, T.M. (1992). Stakeholder–agency theory. *Journal of Management Studies*, 29(2), 131–54.

Holliday Jr., C.O., Schmidheiny, S. and Watts, P. (2002). *Walking the Talk: The Business Case for Sustainable Development*. Sheffield: Greenleaf Publishing.

Husted, B.W. and Allen, D.B. (2006). Corporate social responsibility in the multinational enterprise: Strategic and institutional approaches. *Journal of International Business Studies*, 37(6) [Three Lenses on the Multinational Enterprise: Politics, Corruption and Corporate Social Responsibility], 838–49.

Isenmann, R. (2006). CSR online: Internet based communication. In J. Jonker and M.C. Witte (eds.), *Management Models for Corporate Social Responsibility*. Germany: Springer, 247–54.

Jahdi, S.K. and Acıkdilli, G. (2009). Marketing communications and corporate social responsibility (CSR): Marriage of convenience or shotgun wedding? *Journal of Business Ethics*, 88(1), 103–13.

Jamali, D. and Mirshak, R. (2007). Corporate social responsibility (CSR): Theory and practice in a developing country context. *Journal of Business Ethics*, 72(3), 243–62.

Katz, D. and Kahn, R.L. (1966). *The Social Psychology of Organizations*. New York: John Wiley.

Klein, A., et al. (2005). Accounting for good: The global stakeholder report 2005. In *The Second World-Wide Survey on Stakeholder Attitudes to CSR Reporting*. Germany: Pleon Kohtes Klewes GmbH. http://www.jussemper.org/Newsletters/Resources/Pleon_GSR05_en.pdf [accessed 23 September 2016]

Kuhn, T. and Deetz, S. (2008). Critical theory and corporate social responsibility: Can/should we get beyond cynical reasoning? In A. Crane, A.M. Williams, D. Matten, J. Moon and D. Siegel (eds.), *The Oxford Handbook of Corporate Social Responsibility*. Oxford: Oxford University Press, 173–96.

Laumann, E.O., Galaskiewicz, J. and Marsden, P.V. (1978). Community structure as interorganizational linkages. *Annual Review of Sociology*, 4, 445–84.

Lewis, S. (2003). Reputation and corporate responsibility. *Journal of Communication Management*, 7(4), 356–66.

Ligeti, G. and Oravecz, A. (2009). CSR Communication of corporate enterprises in Hungary. *Journal of Business Ethics*, 84(2), 137–49.

Maignan, I. and Ralston, D.A. (2002). Corporate social responsibility in Europe and the US: Insights from businesses self-presentations. *Journal of International Business Studies*, 33(3), 497–514.

Margolis, J.D. and Walsh, J.P. (2003). Misery loves companies: Rethinking social initiatives by business. *Administrative Science Quarterly*, 48(2), 268–305.

May, S. and Zorn, T. (2003). Forum introduction. *Management Communication Quarterly*, 16, 595–8.

Miles, M.P., Munilla, L.S. and Darroch, J. (2006). The role of strategic conversations with stakeholders in the formation of corporate social responsibility strategy. *Journal of Business Ethics*, 69(2), 195–205.

Mitchell, R.K., Agle, B.R. and Wood, D.J. (1997). Toward a theory of stakeholder identification and salience: Defining the principle of who and what really counts. *Academy of Management Review*, 22(4), 853–86.

Morsing, M. (2006a). Strategic CSR communication – the challenge of telling others how good you are. In J. Jonker and M.C. Witte (eds.), *Management Models for Corporate Social Responsibility*. Germany: Springer, 237–45.

Morsing, M. (2006b). Corporate social responsibility as strategic auto-communication: On the role of external stakeholders for member identification. *Business Ethics: A European Review*, 15(2), 171–82.

Morsing, M. and Schultz, M. (2006). Corporate social responsibility communication: Stakeholder information, response and involvement strategies. *Business Ethics: A European Review*, 15(4), 323–38.

Parsons, T. (1956). Suggestions for a sociological approach to the theory of organizations-I. *Administrative Science Quarterly*, 1(1), 63–85.

Peterson, D.K. (2004). The relationship between perceptions of corporate citizenship and organizational commitment. *Business & Society*, 43(3), 296–319.

Podnar, K. (2008). Guest editorial: Communicating corporate social responsibility. *Journal of Marketing Communications*, 14(2), 75–81.

Pollach, I., Johansen, T.S., Nielsen, A.E. and Thomsen, C. (2012). The integration of CSR into corporate communication in large European companies. *Journal of Communication Management*, 16(2), 204–16.

Pomering, A. and Dolnicar, S. (2009). Assessing the prerequisite of successful CSR implementation: Are consumers aware of CSR initiatives? *Journal of Business Ethics*, 85(2), 285–301.

Porter, M.E. and Kramer, M.R. (2002). The competitive advantage of corporate philanthropy. *Harvard Business Review*, 80(12), 56–65.

Salzmann, O., Ionescu-Somers, A. and Steger, U. (2005). The business case for corporate sustainability: Literature review and research options. *European Management Journal*, 23(1), 27–36.

Schaltegger, S. (2008). Managing the business case for sustainability. Proceedings of EMAN-EU Environmental and Sustainability Management Accounting Network, Budapest.

Signitzer, B. and Prexl, A. (2007). Corporate sustainability communications: Aspects of theory and professionalization. *Journal of Public Relations Research*, 20(1), 1–19.

Sriramesh, K., Ng, C.W., Soh, T.T. and Luo, W. (2007). Corporate social responsibility and public relations: Perceptions and practices in Singapore. In S. May, G. Cheney and J. Roper (eds.), *The Debate over Corporate Social Responsibility*. New York: Oxford University Press, 119–34.

Stohl, C., Stohl, M. and Popova, L. (2007). A new generation of global corporate codes of ethics? Paper presented at the Annual conference of International Communication Association, San Francisco, California.

Sweeney, L. and Coughlan, J. (2008). Do different industries report Corporate Social Responsibility differently? An investigation through the lens of stakeholder theory. *Journal of Marketing Communications*, 14(2), 113–24.

Tang, L. and Li, H. (2009). Corporate social responsibility communication of Chinese and global corporations in China. *Public Relations Review*, 35(3), 199–212.

Thompson, J.D. (1967). *Organizations in Action*. New York: McGraw-Hill.

Toker, H. (2013). Media CSR forum. In S.O. Idowu, N. Capaldi, L. Zu and A. Das Gupta (eds.), *Encyclopedia of Corporate Social Responsibility*. Berlin and Heidelberg: Springer-Verlag, 1643–50.

Turban, D.B. and Greening, D.W. (1997). Corporate social performance and organizational attractiveness to prospective employees. *Academy of Management Journal*, 40(3), 658–72.

Turker, D. (2009). How corporate social responsibility influences organizational commitment. *Journal of Business Ethics*, 89, 189–204.

Turker, D. (2013). Analyzing relational sources of power at the interorganizational communication system. *European Management Journal* [available online 22 July 2013, ISSN 0263–2373, http://dx.doi.org/10.1016/j.emj.2013 June 007].

Turker, D. and Altuntaş, C. (2013). Ethics of social responsibility to indirect stakeholders: A strategic perspective. *International Journal of Business Governance and Ethics*, 8(2), 137–54.

Van Marrewijk, M. (2003). Concepts and definitions of CSR and corporate sustainability: Between agency and communion. *Journal of Business Ethics*, 44(2–3), 95–105.

Weber, M. (2008). The business case for corporate social responsibility: A company-level measurement approach for CSR. *European Management Journal*, 26, 247–61.

Whelan, G. (2007). Corporate social responsibility in Asia: A Confucian context. In S. May, G. Cheney and J. Roper (eds.), *The Debate over Corporate Social Responsibility*. New York: Oxford University Press, 105–18.

12 Sustainability in airlines

Hesam Shabaniverki

1 Introduction

Airlines play significant roles is shaping economic, political, and social effects of the communities they serve and in which they originate. Yet week after week, month after month, year after year, they are limited and significantly restricted by global rules.

The airline industry, much like any large industrial complex, produces unintended consequences on the natural environment. Airlines are considered one of the most valuable transportation commodities. They involve a wide range of activities determined by how they are managed. To explore this further, we must first agree on some definitions. Specifically, what do we mean by "strategy" and "sustainable development"?

Strategy

Strategy refers to the key issues of an organization's future state, the long-term direction of an organization. For instance, strategy is how an airline manages its entry into the market and how it survives in the market (Johnson and Fowler, 2011). Strategic management was established and started to grow in the late twentieth century, mainly in the field of economics. The strategy of an organization cannot be predicted or predestined. Its study must start with defining the strategy, the process, and the environment and how it is analysed in the airline industry (Harrison and Enz, 2005).

This chapter examines different definitions related to strategy in order to differentiate and explain an organization's strategy. Below are strategy definitions from three theorists in strategy, namely Alfred Chandler and Michael Porter from Harvard Business School, and Henry Mintzberg from McGill University. Each defines strategy distinctively. Chandler focuses on a logical flow from determining goals and objectives to allocation of resources. Porter emphasizes deliberate choices, differences, and competition. Mintzberg uses word patterns to accept the fact that strategies do not always follow a chosen and logical plan but can emerge in more ad hoc ways (Johnson and Fowler, 2011).

According to Chandler (Kirschner, Ayres, and Chandler, 2011), strategy is the determination of the long-run goals and objectives of an enterprise, the adoption of courses of action, and the allocation of resources necessary for carrying out these goals. Michael Porter looks at competitive strategy as being about being different. To him, strategy means to deliberately choose a different set of activities to deliver a unique mix of value. However, Henry Mintzberg defines strategy as a pattern in a stream of decisions. Thompson and Strickland (Thompson, 2003) refer to a company's strategy as consisting of the competitive efforts and business approaches that managers employ to please customers, compete successfully, and achieve organizational objectives.

The term "strategy" has been used for many years. One of the definitions in the 1980s was that of Andrew. He defined strategy as 'the pattern of decisions in a company that determines and reveals its objectives, purposes, or goals'. Strategy produces the principal policies and plans for achieving those goals and defines the range of business activities the company is to pursue. Strategy also determines the kind of economic and human organization the company is or intends to be, and the nature of economic and non-economic contribution it intends to make to shareholders, employees, customers, and communities (Johnson and Fowler, 2011). The above definitions bring out the important elements of strategy, which will be useful to give concrete understanding to its meaning. An examination of the definitions will give a better understanding of what is involved in strategy and how it can be related to the airline industry.

Sustainable development in both public and private sectors has brought many challenges to management, since the sustainable development concept is variously defined by different authors. The public and private sectors started facing these challenges as a result of the development of company policies on such issues as gender equity, occupational health and safety, and results-based management. Sustainable development entails the integrated processes of leadership, planning, implementation, monitoring, and review. Dalal-Clayton and Bass (2002) identified sustainable development as a new pattern of government or organization policy-making.

2 Sustainability

Sustainability concerns can be traced to the eighteenth and nineteenth centuries when there were issues of scarcity of resources due to the increasing shortage of population energy. Care about the environment during that time focused on health hazards caused through industrialization. The term "sustainability development" was used during the 1980s by the International Union for Conservation of Nature and Natural Resources (IUCN). This group later conceived the World Conservation Strategy, which aimed at conservation of natural resources with a focus on ecological sustainability, thus linking sustainability to social and economic aspects (Hezri and Dovers, 2006).

Definition

"Sustainability" was best defined by Brundtland (1987), who at the time was the prime minister of Norway. He later chaired the UN Conference on Environment and Development in Brazil in 1992 (Hezri and Dovers, 2006). Brundtland defined "sustainable development" as development that meets the needs of the present without compromising the ability of future generations to meet their own needs (Lowitt, 2011). According to Lowitt (2011), the value of sustainability of an organization should not be based on the balance of economic and social performance with economic aspects, but rather the environmental and social aspects should drive the economic factors.

"Economic sustainability" refers to maintaining the integrity of life support systems such as biodiversity and ecosystems. It is a fundamental requirement for all the other sustainability aspects. There is a need to consider how we use resources from the land, sea, and air so we don't deplete these resources or destroy the Earth now or in the future. It is essential to make sure all forms of life, including animals, plants, and their habitats, are cared for. This will ensure that all ecosystems in both natural and man-made environments are maintained so that all the different forms of life can coexist. An organization's carbon emissions, consumption of water, waste sent to landfill, and energy consumption through normal operations (Lowitt, 2011) are all regarded as environmental aspects of an organization.

Social sustainability

Social sustainability focuses on equity within and between generations, ethnicities, and social groups. This aspect of an organization embraces development of the mental and physical well-being of people and the cohesion of their communities. All people are considered equal regardless of culture, age, or social group, and they all have the same right to exist and grow in a supportive community and a healthy environment. Facets of social sustainability include knowledge, technology, financial, and capital resources, which are provided by an organization to local communities (Lowitt, 2011).

Economic sustainability

Economic sustainability looks into the utilization of resources to provide products and services for the well-being and aspirations of the present generation and for generations to come. Financially, shareholders have a right to a return on their investment. It is critical, then, that we maintain a strong balance sheet so that we retain the capability to invest and the capability to give shareholders profitable returns (Andersson, 2012).

However, Brundtland's definition of sustainable development illuminated how an organization can embrace sustainable practices in order to have some value in the future. Sustainability does not only focus on keeping the environment green, but rather emphasizes an ongoing, unchanging commitment in which an organization can balance its returns financially due to environmental and social impacts (Lowitt, 2011).

Strategic development gives an organization growth opportunity while at the same time reducing its risk to legal and resource exposure. Sustainability has helped companies pay more critical attention to the efficacy and future viability of their operations. This has led to an increase in brand value and revenue, and has reduced risks and costs, which is valuable for investors. Nowadays, due to the growing demand and expectation from stakeholders, an organization cannot survive and operate without having a sustainability strategy. For an organization, customers, employees, shareholders, authorities, and partners cannot be ignored. The sustainability strategy of an organization must reflect its values, aspirations, and the main business strategy. Some organizations' sustainability strategy and growth innovation strategy are regarded as similar strategies, according to Lowitt (2011). However, as he points out, '[I]t is advisable that sustainable strategy should begin with corporate strategy without distractions from other projects'(Lowitt, 2011).

3   Airline industry

The global airline industry operates services all over the world, creating an international economy. The airline industry contributes to the economy through its operations and related industries such as aircraft manufacturing and tourism. The industry also affects economically its external participants, such as government policy, media, and other investors with an interest in air travel. The international airline industry's development led to technological advancement in the 1950s, and the introduction of the jet aircraft led to commercial airlines. Later, in the 1970s, this advancement was followed by wide-body jumbo jet aircraft.

Despite this trend, some airlines did create value for their investors in the past two years. Some airlines from most regions of the world and includes long-haul network airlines, regional airlines, low-cost carriers, and other business models. They are, though, the exception and are few in number (IATA, 2012).

Regulations and deregulation

Airline industry deregulation was established into law in 1978 with an aim to encourage an air transportation system that relies on competitive market forces as the basic determinant of commercial airline operations (Sweet, Woyat, Koblinski, and Bramhall, 2009). Prior to that time, the Civil Aeronautics Board controlled airline routes and ticket prices in order to serve the interest of the public. Domestic airlines were allowed to fly domestic routes only if they were approved by the Department of Transportation (DOT). The DOT changed its role from making sure the airline operations were in accordance with public interest to deciding whether airlines were operating according to safety standards and standard operating procedures. In the 38 years since route schedules and airline pricing were deregulated, major regulations in other areas of the industry are still in place. Local governments have been able to institute regulations in their regions, since they own and manage airports. They are able to control airport services such as accessibility to runways and boarding gates.

In most cases, airport commissions in a region allocate gates without any formal market mechanism, such as a bidding process. They often require concrete proof that the airline will operate in the best interest of the public. However, deregulation in global routes has gradually changed. Negotiated bilateral open-skies agreements have allowed airline companies from two different countries the right to fly between those countries without restrictions. These open-skies agreements do not develop a competitive market, since they do not permit foreign aircraft to transfer passengers within a country or vice versa. Regulations designed to avoid congestion at a country's busiest airports have lagged behind market realities. Service to small, isolated markets also is subsidized and regulated by the government. However, though the end-consumer for airline tickets faces a market-driven menu of prices and services, key inputs into the industry are allocated using non-market mechanisms. Gowrisankaran, in 1980, stated that 22 years after deregulation, the airline market is still partly regulated. As a result of airline mergers, this partial regulation has reduced costs and increased market share. Nevertheless, price-fixing has forced small airlines out of business. By increasing the numbers of seats and reducing competition in other markets, as evidenced by the dismantlement of some regional airlines by bigger ones, big corporations are known for their monopolistic acts and predatory pricing (Sweet et al., 2009).

4   Finnair: strategic development and sustainability

History of Finnair

Finnair was founded in 1923 by Consul Bruno Lucander, as managing director, Gustaf Snellman, and Fritiof Åhman. It was operated under Aero O/Y, located at the time in Helsinki, Finland. Finnair owned its first aircraft in 1924, named the Junkers F 13 D-335. An agreement between the manufacturers of the aircraft and Aero O/Y gave the manufacturers a 50 per cent holding in Aero in exchange for one aircraft plus technical help and personnel. In March 1924, Aero O/Y operated its first commercial flight, carrying 162 kilos of mail from Helsinki to Tallinn. The aircraft carried 269 passengers.

Aero became a member of the International Air Transport Association (IATA) in 1927. During the years 1924–1929, Aero received six more Junkers aircraft. Aero O/Y lost Bruno Lucander when he suddenly died. Due to the agreement, Junkers Flugzeugwerke A.G., the aircraft manufacturer, became a shareholder of the airline, owning a 50 per cent share. Later in the 1930s, investors in Finland managed to buy the shares from Junkers, which resulted in Aero becoming a Finnish-owned company. During the Second World War, the Aero O/Y was used for military control. This was a challenging time for the airline since air routes were closed and fuel was scarce. Things changed in 1952 when Finland hosted the Olympics. This brought success to the airline industry, due to an increase in passengers. During the same year, the airline moved its operations to Seutula. In 1953 Aero O/Y was officially named Finnair (Beck et al., 2008).

Finnair current operations

Finnair is regarded as one of the most innovative, safest, and longest-operating airlines internationally. The airline specializes in operating flights between Asia and Europe, and desires to be the leading airline in the Nordic region, with a focus on the Asian market. It strives to be one of the three big operators in transit traffic between Asia and Europe, including transfers during the trip. Its growth strategy focuses on the rapid flight connections to the growing Asian market. Finnair owns other business groups related to the airline business, aviation services, and travel services, which employ approximately 7,000 personnel. Finnair subsidiaries provide support services directly to the airline or operate closely in the related areas. The major shareholder of the airline is the Finnish government, which holds 55.8 per cent of shares. Other shareholders include public bodies, financial institutions, private companies, and households (Virtanen, 2013).

Finnair is responsible for domestic and international scheduled flight operations, route planning, product development, sales and marketing, cooperation with other airlines, and fleet management. Other subsidiaries and business units under Finnair operations include the Commercial Division, Flight Operations, Production Management, Finnair Cargo Ltd, Finnair Cargo Terminal Operations Ltd and Finnair Aircraft Finance Ltd. Finnair subsidiaries employed over 4,252 employees with a turnover of $1.736 billion in just one year alone. This was 3 per cent better than the previous year. With its scheduled flights, Finnair saw an increase in passengers in 2008 to 7 million. However, due to a demand for a cheaper fare class, its revenue actually fell by 5.1 per cent as compared to the previous year. On the other hand, Finnair's cargo operations in 2008 were a success, mostly due to good fares and efficient operations. However, the cargo operations subsequently dropped drastically, due to the global recession. It is predicted to continue more successfully in the near future (Beck et al., 2008).

The airline's fleet is a subsidiary of Finnair, managed by Finnair Aircraft Finance. Finnair operated 45 aircraft by the end of 2012, with 15 wide-body and 30 narrow-body aircraft. Finnair's balance sheet indicated 24 aircraft operations owned by the airline by Flybe Finland. The estimated age of the fleet operated by Finnair was 9.8 years at the end of 2012. The estimated age of the fleet operated by other airlines is 4.1 years. Finnair also has eight leased aircraft, which it has subleased and which are operated by other airlines. The details are provided in Table 12.1.

Table 12.1 Finnair aircraft fleet on 31 December 2012

	Seats	Pcs	Own	Leased	Finance leasing	Average age	Change from 31 Dec 2011	Ordered	Add options
European Traffic									
Airbus A319	123–38	9	7	2		11.5	−2		
Airbus A320	165	10	6	4		10.4	−2		
Airbus A321	196	6	4	2		12.0		5	
Embraer 170*	76	1	1			6.4	−4		
Embraer 190	100						−12		
Long-Haul Traffic									
Airbus A330	297/271/263	8	4	1	3	3.2			
Airbus A340	270/269	7	5	2		10.0			
Airbus A350	Na.							11	8
Leisure Traffic									
Boeing B757	227	4	0	4		15.0			
Total		45	27	15	3	9.8	−20	16	8

Finnair strategies

Finnair's objective is to be the leading airline in the Nordic region. Its desired route is Asia and Europe. The airline aims to increase its revenue from Asian traffic from 2010 until 2020. Finnair's growth strategy implementation focuses its core business on building a more extensive network of partners while being committed to creating added value for its customers and shareholders. Finnair has numerous strengths. One strength is having a clear strategy. It also has a sustainable competitive advantage over other airlines due to its geographical location. It operates a modern, fuel-efficient fleet and offers a top-class service product. Finnair is regarded as northern Europe's best airline, with excellent operational quality and efficiency. Moreover, the quality and capacity of the Helsinki-Vantaa Airport is superb, not to mention the company's excellent financing position for implementing future fleet investments (Virtanen, 2013).

Finnair's strategy focus is to make sure they take advantage of the potential for routes between Asia and Europe. Their strategy is based mainly on providing the growing Asian market with the fastest connections between Asia and Europe. They hope to do this by offering high-quality service, being the most efficient airline in the industry, and being cost-efficient. Due to Helsinki's geographical location, Finnair has a competitive advantage compared to other cities in northern Europe, resulting in fast connections to Asia.

Finnair operates for both business and leisure travellers with a combination of cargo for the Asian market. This is an advantage for Finnair compared to other European airlines that don't operate directly to Asia. It is estimated that 20 million people travel annually to Asia and European destinations through Finnair, including transfer passengers without direct connections to the destination. Due to Asia's large population, growth of just 1 per cent in travel between Europe and Asia would potentially bring about 200,000 new passengers every year. According to a forecast by Airbus, there is an expectation of growth of 4.1 per cent per year in revenue passenger kilometres between Europe and Asia between

Table 12.2 Finnair goals

Profitable growth	Cost competitiveness	Customer experience	International winning team
New Asian destination Chongqing, decisions on new routes to Hanoi and Xi'an	Structural change and cost-reduction programmes	Increased automation in customer service process	Leadership development
New ancillary services like advance seat reservations offered to customers	Procurement Increased automation in customer service process	Service identity – peace of mind	
New ticket types			

2012 and 2031. This provides Finnair with a huge opportunity to grow its Asian operations. Finnair experienced a structural reform in 2011, which made the airline focus on its main objectives to provide services in support of other airline businesses and European feeder traffic (Andersson, 2012).

This reform led to the establishment of partnerships with world-class operators. Strategic partnerships are a part of Finnair's strategy to improve the quality of its operations while reducing costs that are essential for the industry. Finnair has been able to adjust its operations and cost level more flexibly, according to the prevailing market conditions, by focusing on its main business.

Finnair's growth strategy focuses on investing in and charting new market possibilities. Their strategy includes improving profitability, developing customer service and leadership, maintaining a well-managed staff, and promoting superb customer satisfaction. Finnair's goal is to be an active and valuable partner. The airline is part of the Oneworld Alliance, a leading airline industry group. Finnair holds a strong position as an expert in traffic between Asia and Europe (Virtanen, 2013). The details are provided in Table 12.2.

Finnair sustainability

Finnair sustainability measures account for the financial, social, and environmental sustainability of their enterprise. As early as 1997, it became one of the first airlines to report on sustainability. Since 2008 Finnair has followed standards set by the Global Reporting Initiative, the most widely recognized international authority on sustainability reporting (Andersson, 2012).

Economic sustainability

Finnair's objective is to make sure that it creates sustainable economic value to the economy and business by operating flight services more profitably and cost-competitively, and meeting the needs of the environment and society. Embracing responsible operations is the key to its business profitability. Finnair, as a public limited company with an objective to earn profit for its shareholders, distributes its profit through dividend policy. The airline takes into account its operations and financial decisions on its environment and society. These are assessed by the corporate, social responsibility, and risk management departments. The airline's interest in society and the environment has also been of interest to tour operators interested in promoting sustainable tourism. The airline offers its financial report online in order to provide, as transparently as possible, information about Finnair's financial position and development. The airline industry is sensitive to cyclical fluctuations in the world economy as well as the economy of individual countries. Since the airline relies on earnings generated from people's need to travel for business or leisure and for cargo carriage, the infrastructure forms part of the country's economy.

Aviation is a very important industry for Finnish society and the country's economy. The Finnish airline industry generates 3–5 per cent of GDP, employment for society, and tax revenue. Easy accessibility by the airlines is vital for the country's world competitiveness. Finnair's Asian strategy is the key area of the country's GDP contribution, with an estimated value of 12 billion euros. Finnair implements structural changes to improve its profitability in this competitive industry. The airline developed a "career gate" concept, which assists employees in finding work more efficiently. The most important change in airline operations has been the deep alliance it has made to increase cost-effectiveness in order to reduce costs for all its operations. Worldwide airline traffic has changed in recent years, and there have been structural changes as well. This has spurred market liberalization, growth in competition, overcapacity, consolidation, alliances, and specialization. Furthermore, the international consolidation of the airline industry is predicted to keep going and Finnair aims to take advantage of all of these developments (Andersson, 2012).

Capturing Asian traffic has been Finnair's core strategy to pursue as the leading airline in the Nordic region. They are accomplishing this by cooperating with strong partners. Partnership is essential since small and medium-sized firms cannot do everything by themselves. Due to the increase in competition in the airline industry, there has been an ongoing improvement in cost-competitiveness and quality, requiring specialization and large-scale cooperation. A major increase in oil prices took place in 2011, as well as a growth in market capacity. During this time, the industry had expectations of market growth due to increase in demand. But since the world economy declined in recent years, there has been a tight, competitive situation which has affected airlines' passenger and cargo business. Finnair, unlike other airlines, managed to increase its market share in traffic between Asia and Europe on the routes it operates despite the oil price increase (Andersson, 2012).

Social sustainability

The airline industry, in general, is very strict with regulations. Finnair regularly takes part in discussions concerning its operating conditions. The airline engages in an ethical, sustainable business through its views and perspectives. Finnair aims to strengthen its relationship with authorities and the government. It does this through negotiations regarding transportation policies and transport operations. It also participates in relevant negotiations and the operations of advocacy organizations. For example, it is an active member of many air transportation associations, such as Association of European Airlines (AEA) and IATA (Andersson, 2012; Virtanen, 2013).

Finnair's mission is to be transparent, honest, and timely in communication with its investors. This involves regulations governing operations in accordance with the Finnish Act. Finnair also respects all viewpoints. Airline responsibility must be reflected in its strategy and brand building in order to maintain a positive image for the company. Finnair interacts with all employees and other important investors that have interest in the company's operations. In order to create a good work environment that enables freedom of discussion, people in leadership roles must communicate goals, operations, and results to their own work community. One of Finnair's social responsibilities is to never accept corruption of any kind or form. Towards this goal, the airline identifies and evaluates corruption risk using surveys in all of its business areas.

Finnair's procurement program likewise follows ethical guidelines and supports an expectation that its stakeholders be treated fairly. Finnair does not accept or give bribes. The giving and accepting of business gifts is politely avoided while maintaining good manners. The airline's workforce is not allowed to accept gifts or services which exceed the maximum set by the organization at a given period of time. Suspected cases of bribery are reported to the company's Internal Auditing Department, which is responsible for retraining new hires.

Finnair's policy in business operations is to adhere to competition law. The airline industry has a constant flow of new competitors in this highly competitive market. The Internal Auditing Department makes sure that there is compliance with competition law. It audits foreign sales units and reviews issues relating to compliance with competition law.

Mostly, Finnair business operations are based on official regulations and solid supervision. Individuals approved by the authority in question are responsible for compliance with official regulations. Finnair has internal control procedures that include managers in each unit. They have management control in their own department and are responsible for documenting internal control principles in accordance with the company's values and ethics. The findings of the Audit Committee are reported to Finnair's Board of Directors, who confirm that controls are exercised effectively, property is maintained, and operations are conducted appropriately in accordance with the group's goals and objectives. The priorities of the internal auditors are determined in accordance with the group's risk management strategy. Information regarding control requirements is communicated through guidelines, policies, and procedures. The results of the Audit Committee's control work, in the form of observations, recommendations, and proposed decisions and measures, are continuously reported (Andersson, 2012).

Environmental sustainability

Finnair's mission is to become one of the leading environmental airlines in the world. Finnair takes environmental issues seriously in all of its operations. It strongly supports the International Air Transport Association (IATA) zero emission target for aviation. The airline complies with ongoing current environmental legislation. In their environmental work, they wish to be a leader in evaluating, reporting, and reducing environmental impacts (IATA, 2012).

Finnair recognizes its corporate responsibility and acknowledges environmental management in its strategy. The company employs personnel responsible for environmental training on a corporate level. They train the entire workforce in appropriate practices for both internal and external campaigns. The airline's environmental practice is to maintain a fleet of recent aircraft. Currently the company uses the Airbus A320 and Embraer aircraft. The average life of the fleet is 7.2 years. The aim is to lower fuel consumption to less than 3 litres per hundred kilometres per passenger. As part of developing its technologies, Finnair has become involved in biofuel projects. The airline operated its first biofuel flight in the summer of 2011, and it aims to continue with biofuel projects and flights (Virtanen, 2013).

5 Case study Iran air: strategic development and sustainability

Brief description of Iran

Iran, also known as Persia but officially named the Islamic Republic of Iran since 1980, is a country in western Asia. It is bordered on the north by Armenia, Azerbaijan, and Turkmenistan, with Kazakhstan and Russia across the Caspian Sea; on the east by Afghanistan and Pakistan; on the south by the Persian Gulf and the Gulf of Oman; on the west by Iraq; and on the northwest by Turkey. Comprising a land area of 1,648,195 square kilometres (636,372 sq. mi), it is the second largest nation in the Middle East and the eighteenth largest in the world. With over 77 million inhabitants, Iran is the world's seventeenth most populous nation. It is the only country that has both a Caspian Sea and Indian Ocean coastline.

History of Iran Air

In 1946 a group of businessmen founded Iran's first flag carrier under the name of Iranian Airways. Operations covered domestic and regional passenger and freight services, plus a weekly freight service to Europe. The fleet consisted of Douglas DC-3s initially, supplemented by Douglas DC-4 and Vickers Viscount aircraft later on. In 1954 the privately owned airline Persian Air Services (PAS) was established. It initially operated only freight services, followed by passenger operations between Tehran and other major cities in Iran. In 1960 PAS initiated service to several European destinations, including Geneva, Paris, Brussels, and London, using Douglas DC-7C aircraft, leased from Sabena.

On 24 February 1962, Iranian Airways and PAS merged to form the Iran National Airlines Corporation, known as Iran Air. It was a public sector venture that combined the assets and liabilities of the two predecessor air carriers. Among the aircraft used were Avro York, Douglas DC-3, Douglas DC-6, and Vickers Viscount. The carrier became a full member of IATA in 1964.

Iranian Airways was established in May 1944 and flew its first passenger flight after the Second World War from Tehran to the holy city of Mashhad. Within a period of 17 years, from 1945 to 1962, the airline developed into a major domestic carrier with a few international flights per week.

The board of ministers ratified a proposal to establish a national airline on 10 February 1961. Following this decision, on 24 February 1961, Iranian Airways and Pars Airways, a private airline established in 1954, merged to form a new airline called Iran Air, using the HOMA bird as a symbol. The Iran Air logo, which was designed by Edvard Zahrabian (1961), was chosen as the best airline logo worldwide (Abrahamian, 2008). For more details, refer to Table 12.3 and Table 12.4.

Expansion

In 1965 Iran Air bought its first jet aircraft, the Boeing 707 and the Boeing 727-100. This was followed by the Boeing 737-200 in 1971, the stretched Boeing 727-200 in 1974, and three variants of Boeing 747s (747-100, 747-200 and SP), starting in 1978–1979. By the mid-1970s Iran Air was serving cities in Europe with non-stop and one-stop flights (there were over 30 flights per week to London alone).

Table 12.3 Aircraft operated by Iran Air as of November 2012

Iran Air Fleet							
Aircraft	*In service*	*Orders*	*Passengers*			*Year of entry*	*Notes*
			C	*Y*	*Total*		
Airbus A300B4	8	0	30	248	248	1980	
Airbus A300–600R	4	0	30	248	278	1991	
Airbus A310–200	1	0	0	200	200	2001	
Airbus A310–300	2	0	0	200	200	2000	
Airbus A320–200	6	0	0	147	147	2005	
Boeing 747–100B	1	0	22	427	449	1976	
Boeing 747–200BM	2	0	0	291	291	2000	
Boeing 747–200	3	0	22	427	449	1976	
Boeing 747SP	4	0	22	283	305	1979	
Boeing 727–200	3	0	0	153	153	1975	
Fokker 100	16	0	0	104	104	1991	
Tupolev Tu-204	0	35	TBA	TBA	210	To be delivered between 2014–2015	5 to be given to Iran Airtour
Iran Air Cargo Fleet							
Airbus A300B4F	2	0	Cargo			1978	
Boeing 747–200F	1	0	Cargo			1980	
Boeing 747–200C	1	0	Cargo			2008	
Total	54	35					

Note: C = Business; Y = Economy

On 8 October 1972, Iran Air placed an order with British Aircraft Corporation for two Concorde supersonic jets, plus one option. One was leased for a few flights from Tehran to Kish Island, but never appeared in Iran Air livery. These orders were cancelled in April 1980, in the wake of the Iranian Revolution, making Iran Air the last airline to cancel its Concorde orders.

On 29 May 1975, the Tehran to New York City route was inaugurated, first with Boeing 707s, making a stop-over at London Heathrow Airport. Shortly thereafter, the route was converted into a nonstop flight using Boeing 747SPs, making Iran Air the second Middle Eastern carrier (after El Al), to offer non-stop service to New York. With this flight, Iran Air set a new world record in time and distance for a nonstop, scheduled long-haul flight (12 hours and 15 minutes, 9,867 km – 6,131 mi – 5,328 nm). In 1978, the airline acquired six Airbus A300B2k aircraft for use on its domestic trunk and busy regional routes. By the end of that year, Iran Air was serving 31 international destinations stretching from New York City to Beijing and Tokyo. Plans were made to offer direct services to Los Angeles and to Sydney, for which the airline's long-range Boeing 747SP aircraft were ideally suited. This would have allowed Iran Air to use Tehran as a midway point between East and West, because of its home base's favourable geographical location. These plans were never realized (Abrahamian, 2008).

Table 12.4 Aircraft operated by Iran Air as of January 2014

Iran Air Fleet

Aircraft	In service	Orders	Passengers			Year of entry	Notes
			C	*Y*	*Total*		
Airbus A300B2	4		18	234	254	1980 2 Stored at Tehran-Mehrabad	
Airbus A300B4	4		18	236	254	2006	
Airbus A300–600R	4		22	239	261	1994	
Airbus A310–200	2		12	188	200	2001	
Airbus A310–300	2		14	198	212	2000	
Airbus A320–200	6		12	144	156	2009	
Boeing 727–200Adv	2		12	134	146	1973	
Boeing 747–200	3		22	427	449	1977	
Boeing 747SP	4		22	283	305	1976	
Fokker 100	16		0	104	104	1990	
Tupolev Tu–204	0	35	TBA	TBA	210	To be delivered between 2014–2015	5 to be given to Iran Airtour
Iran Air Cargo Fleet							
Airbus A300B4F	2		Cargo			2008	
Boeing 747–200F	1		Cargo			2008	
Total	51	35					

Note: C = Business; Y = Economy

By the late 1970s Iran Air was the fastest-growing airline in the world and one of the most profitable. By 1976 Iran Air was ranked second only to Qantas as the world's safest airline, having been accident-free for at least 10 consecutive years. Although both airlines were accident free, Iran Air came in second only because of fewer operational hours flown than those flown by Qantas. Prior to this ranking, a fatal accident occurred on 25 December 1952, in which 27 of the 29 passengers on board a Douglas DC-3 perished, when their aircraft crashed on landing (Abrahamian, 2008).

After the Iranian Revolution

In the wake of the Iranian Revolution in February 1979, Iran Air began to reorganize its international operations, discontinuing service to a range of foreign destinations. Tehran was designated as the only official gateway to Iran, while Shiraz could be used as an alternate, only in case of operational requirements. All other cities in Iran lost their international status. However, in recent times, many of Iran's major city airports have regained a minor international status. These direct international flights, using airports in other major Iranian cities, currently serve regional countries. The last departure from New York was on 7 November 1979. The last scheduled flight from Tehran to New York City on

8 November 1979 was diverted at the last minute to Montreal, prompted by an embargo suddenly imposed by the U.S. government. Subsequently, the Boeing 747SPs were used on the airline's European and Asian routes.

After the start of the Iran–Iraq War in September 1980, Iran Air's domestic and international operations were often subject to cancellation and irregularity, in line with the wartime situation. This continued until August 1988, when a cease-fire agreement took effect. Right from the start of the Iran–Iraq War, Abadan, the gateway to Iran's oil-producing region, lost all its air links, because the airport had to be closed.

The year 1981 saw the formal name of the airline changed to "The Airline of the Islamic Republic of Iran". Iran Air carried 1.7 million passengers in that year. In 1990 the first of six Fokker 100 jets was added to the fleet, and five more were added later on. In 2001 the airline bought six second-hand Airbus A310 aircraft (five 200 and one 300 series), since the U.S. authorities blocked the planned purchase of any new Airbus A330 units. In 2005 the carrier bought two Airbus A300–600s from Olympic Airlines. In the wake of the growing tension between the U.S. and Iranian governments over Iran's nuclear program, a plan to supply Boeing spare parts or aircraft to upgrade Iran Air's aging fleet was blocked by the United States and members of the EU. However, a new agreement between Iran and the United States at the end of 2006 changed that and allowed an overhaul of Iran Air's fleet. The airline is wholly owned by the government of Iran and has 7,500 employees.

Iran Air current operations

Iran Air's average fleet age was 25.7 years (as of 26 August 2012) and 25.8 years (as of January 2014). Aircraft acquired by Iran Air must have less than 10 per cent of U.S.-manufactured components on board and must not have belonged to a U.S. airline since its registration.

As most Airbus aircraft are powered by General Electric, CFM, Pratt and Whitney, or Rolls-Royce engines, Iran Air has not been able to acquire many of their aircraft. Current U.S. sanctions do not prevent Iran Air from leasing American or European aircraft, but Iran Air prefers purchasing in order to be able to perform all maintenance and remain up to date with technological advances. Since purchasing from American or European manufacturers is directly prohibited under U.S. and EU sanctions, Iran Air turns to third-party airlines as well as Russian manufacturers (Noush, 2001).

On 20 December 2006, Iran Air put back into operation one of its Boeing 747SP aircraft that had been out of operation for many years, after putting it through a major overhaul by the Fajr Aviation and Composites Industry (Noush, 2001). In June 2007 Iran Air leased one A340–200 aircraft from Conviasa Airlines of Venezuela. This marked the first time a leasing operation was completed by an all-Iranian team led by Capt. Daryoush Khorasani to set up the A340 fleet for two months (Airliners, 2007).

On 14 August 2007, it was reported that Iran Air had overcome sanctions imposed by the west and that their fleet of A310s are ready to resume service.

On 21 May 2008, it was reported that Iran Air may become subject to a new EU sanction, banning all its flights from landing in EU airports. According to Iran Air's managing director Saeed Hesami, EU is citing Iran Air's technical and safety shortcomings as the reason for the imminent ban.

While the U.S. no longer supports and maintains any American-made planes of Iran Air, the airline's American-made planes could use parts made in non–European Union countries such as Russia or China. For instance, the 747 fleet of Iran Air is fully examined and maintained by Chinese technicians when it flies to Beijing, since China is one of Iran's most powerful allies.

6   Conclusion

Airline sustainable strategies discuss issues and exchange information regarding all aspects of airline operations, including the origination and history, regulation and deregulation, facilities, aircraft types, and age and environmental effects. Moreover, managers and governments can consider the long-term financial benefits too. They must offer a variety of programs, such as an educational program for the airline managers and employees, presenting an opportunity to publicize the airline industry and its influence on society, the environment, and the economy.

Sustainable airlines can participate in many fields for sustainable development too, among them special events, education, safety, emergency plan and rescue activities, charity and volunteer activities, and environmental activities.

Once sustainability is identified, the level of participation must be identified for each airline in a country. For example, in Iran, there are some private airlines that must join Iran Air in identifying how the group of airlines as a whole can attain sustainability. Another example is Finland, where, because of the European Commission, airlines can work for sustainability with other airlines in Europe.

In addition, not all airlines need to be involved all aspects of sustainability. A country's central government or an airline association must define a matrix that will show different aspects of sustainability and each airline's role in achieving the goals. Types of participation can be:

* Inform
* Consult
* Involve
* Collaborate

The world recent critical show that we need to redesign the development way in a sustainable mode that one of the important parts is transportation. Because of importance of air transportation, airlines can act as an eco-social system are suitable for sustainable development for different countries. Human life quality can be start from airports by airlines.

Acknowledgement

The author would like to acknowledge Mr Khalilallah Memarzadeh of Iran and also Mrs Leanne Thomas of the United States for their great help. Special thanks to Prof. Dr. Kıymet Çalıyurt for the opportunity that she provided.

References

Abrahamian, E. (2008). *A History of Modern Iran*. Cambridge: Cambridge University Press.
Aircraft, N. (2001). Iran Air Rare and Exclusive. *Kian Noush*, 68.
Aircraft, November 2001, Iran Air Rare and Exclusive, *Kian Noush*, 69.
Airliners. (2007). Conviasa A342 Flying for Iran Air. http://www.airliners.net/aviation-forums/general_aviation/read.main/3684798/ (Retrieved on June 30, 2013).
Andersson, S. (2012). Finnair: Innovating interactivity. *eTourism Case Studies*, 293.

Beck, P., Bartlett, D., Bilski, P., Dyer, C., Flückiger, E., Fuller, N. and Spurny, F. (2008). Validation of modelling the radiation exposure due to solar particle events at aircraft altitudes. *Radiation Protection Dosimetry*, 131(1), 51–8.

Brundtland, G. (1987). *Our Common Future: The World Commission on Environment and Development.* Oxford: Oxford University Press.

Dalal-Clayton, D.B. and Bass, S. (2002). *Sustainable Development Strategies: A Resource Book* (Vol. 1). London: Earthscan.

Harrison, J.S. and Enz, C.A. (2005). *Hospitality Strategic Management: Concepts and Cases.* Hoboken, NJ: Wiley.

Hezri, A.A. and Dovers, S.R. (2006). Sustainability indicators, policy and governance: Issues for ecological economics. *Ecological Economics*, 60(1), 86–99.

International Air Travel Association (IATA). (2012). *Statistics.* http://www.iata.org/services/statistics/air--transport-stats/Pages/index.aspx (Retrieved on September 23, 2016).

Iran Air, http://ucan-motorlu.tr.gg/iran-air.htm (Accessed on October 14, 2016)

Iran Air, http://ucan-motorlu.tr.gg/iran-air.htm (Accessed on October 24, 2016).

IUCN, U. WWF. (1980). *World Conservation Strategy.* Gland, Switzerland: World Conservation Union, United Nations Environment Programme, Word Wide Fund for Nature.

Johnson, D.D. and Fowler, J.H. (2011). The evolution of overconfidence. *Nature*, 477, 317–20.

Kirschner, P.A., Ayres, P. and Chandler, P. (2011). Contemporary cognitive load theory research: The good, the bad and the ugly. *Computers in Human Behavior*, 27(1), 99–105.

Lazzarini, S.G. (2015). Strategizing by the government: Can industrial policy create firm-level competitive advantage? *Strategic Management Journal*, 36(1), 97–112.

Lowitt, E. (2011). *The Future of Value: How Sustainability Creates Value through Competitive Differentiation.* New York: John Wiley & Sons.

Quinn, J.B. (1999). Strategic outsourcing: Leveraging knowledge capabilities. *MIT Sloan Management Review*, 40(4), 9.

Sweet, K.M., Woyat, C.J., Koblinski, D.M. and Bramhall, D.A. (2009). Aviation security: An evaluation of the 'opt-out' option for airport operators. *Journal of Airport Management*, 4(1), 51–71.

Thompson, A.A. (2003). *Strategy: Core Concepts, Analytical Tools, Readings.* New York: McGraw-Hill.

Virtanen, A. (2013). Strategic Development and Sustainability of Airline Industry: Case study: Air Malawi, Laurea University of Applied Sciences, Laurea Kerava, Finland.

13 Sustainability reporting

Çağatay Akarçay and Ayça Akarçay Öğüz

1 Introduction

Enterprises consume resources in the name of acquiring these resources. Although consumption is an indispensable part of human life and business enterprises, consuming more than required and even consuming unconsciously is considered unfavourable (Önce and Marangoz, 2012). Mass production, which started with the industrial revolution, has caused unconscious consumption of resources and post-production wastes that harm the environment. As a result, the concept of sustainability has generated interest for conserving the resources so that future generations will have some left (Öztel, Köse and Aytekin, 2012). 'The development that meets the needs of the present without compromising the ability of future generations to meet their own needs' as stated in the Brundtland Report, is the most widely accepted definition of sustainable development.

The concept of sustainability has emerged with environmental protection and focused on the preservation of natural resources. One of the main reasons for business neglecting environmental issues is that the "business environment" has been identified as an environment in which economic, social, political and technological factors affect the performance of an enterprise, with no attention paid to nature. Enterprises consider customers, employees, government and suppliers as their stakeholders, excluding the natural environment. In recent years, managers have begun to realize that the world is running out of natural resources. Some companies have begun to act responsibly, recycling or reusing what was previously considered waste, using environmentally friendly technologies in production and embracing environmental protection as a philosophy instead of a legislative requirement (Nemli, 2001).

Commercial enterprises should accept and use the values that prioritize the activities that increase the economic profitability of the organization instead of the activities that aim to increase accounting profit. The financial expectations of the past are being joined by social expectations. Although the financial expectations remain intact, enterprises engaged in socially responsible activities that help to safeguard environmental and societal values have gained a competitive advantage (Kuşat, 2012). Pressure from investors and the public combined with regulations are forcing enterprises to document and report their responsibilities to keep the environment clean, to treat their employees humanely and to achieve economic goals. These reports are referred to as sustainability reports. Information provided in sustainability reports has become important to internal and external decision-makers. A lot of companies consider the sustainability reports necessary tools to increase corporate value and to sustain their profits in the long term (White, 2005).

This chapter aims to reveal the importance of sustainability reporting in terms of the enterprises and their stakeholders. For this purpose, concepts of sustainability, sustainable development and corporate sustainability are analysed in the section headed "Sustainability". The next section, headed "Sustainability Reporting", deals with the evolution of sustainability reporting, its contributions and the types of sustainability reports.

2   Sustainability

Sustainability is one of the widely used concepts in recent times. The word "sustainability" derives from "sustain", which itself is derived from the Latin *sustinere*. One definition of "sustain" is "to keep going" or "to support" (Monto, Ganesh and Varghese, 2005).

The concept of sustainability can be defined as a participative process that entails conservative use of social, cultural, scientific, natural and human resources and forms a social view based on respecting this (Gladwin, Kennelly and Krause, 1995). Sustainability can also be defined as a community, ecosystem or any other system continuing its functions into an unspecified future without exhausting its main resources (Özmehmet, 2012).

Sustainability has many meanings to different individuals. However, any definition of sustainability should include the condition known as equality among generations (Yıldıztekin, 2009).

Sustainability can be revealed as a concept that requires a change in the style of thinking without reducing the quality of life. The essence of this change is to curtail our habit of unbridled consumption and refocus our efforts toward environmental management, social responsibilities and economic solutions that benefit everyone (Özmehmet, 2012).

The environment and ecology movement, which emerged in the 1960s and became more widespread in the 1970s, was the reason for the establishment of the World Commission on Environment and Development by the United Nations in 1983. The publication of the report titled "Our Common Future" in 1987, prepared by the World Commission on Environment and Development, also known as the Brundtland Commission, drew attention to the concept of sustainable development. This report marks the beginning of interest in the relationship between environmental issues and sustainable development (Quental, Lourenço and Silva, 2011). The foundations of the concept of corporate sustainability, emphasizing the role of businesses in sustainable development, are in the summit meeting that were held in Rio de Janeiro, Brazil, in 1992 and in Johannesburg, South Africa, in 2002. According to the commonly held view of sustainable development, continuous satisfaction of human needs is possible. The equivalent of this view at the entity level is corporate sustainability (Dyllick and Hockerts, 2002). In the literature, the concepts of sustainable development and corporate sustainability are used interchangeably from time to time.

2.1   Sustainable development

The concept of sustainable development, which creates a balance between economy, society and environment, provides a conceptual framework as guidance for global, national, regional and corporate level applications (Altuntaş and Türker, 2012). In terms of the concept's historical development, it attracted greater attention with the publication of the Brundtland Report in 1987, although it had been used in the earlier years. The World Commission on Environment and Development (WCED) was established by the United Nations with participants from 20 countries. The Brundtland Report stated that a relationship has to be established between environmental and economic development, and the development of this relationship should be sustainable (Quental, Lourenço and Silva,

2011). The concept of sustainable development was officially defined for the first time in this report, and this definition has become the most widely accepted. As stated in the Brundtland Report, '[S]ustainable development is development that meets the needs of the present without compromising the ability of future generations to meet their own needs'.

The UN Conference on Environment and Development (UNCED) was held in Rio de Janeiro in 1992 with 178 participant countries. In this conference, also known as the Earth Summit, the focus was on humankind at the centre of the concerns for sustainable development, and it was stated that people have a right to live a productive life in harmony with nature. The concept of sustainable development was demonstrated in a detailed and comprehensive way, securing its acceptance by the United Nations, governments and other organizations and institutions. In 1997 the Rio+5 Summit was held by the United Nations, during which the participants recommended taking responsibility and cooperating for the protection of the environment.

In the World Summit on Sustainable Development, also known as Rio+10, held by the United Nations in 2002, under discussion were the degree of application, usefulness, problems and measures to be taken on the topics covered by the Rio Report, Agenda 21 and Rio+5 Summit (Carr and Norman, 2008). In the same year, principles set by Agenda 21 were improved by the Organisation for Economic Co-operation and Development (OECD) Parliamentary Commissioner for the Environment, placing responsibility on business entities regarding economic development to make the world a better place (Tokgöz and Önce, 2009).

Rio+20, the United Nations Conference on Sustainable Development, was held in Rio de Janeiro in 2012. To renew the agreement on sustainable development, to support an economically, socially and environmentally sustainable future, high-level government representatives, even heads of state, attended this conference. At the end of the conference, "The Future We Want" was approved as the outcome document (http://sustainabledevelopment. un.org).

Although the concept of sustainable development has been dealt with from different angles in past meetings and conferences, it essentially aims to provide justice among generations and to secure the long-run permanence of social and ecological systems. Prominent common points of these conferences include the following ideas (Aksoy, 2013):

- Sustainable development practices should focus not only on environmental issues but also on the fulfilment of human needs.
- Each generation should be able to benefit fairly from the heritage of the previous generations and to guarantee the fulfilment of the needs of the future generations.
- Economic, social and environmental developments are the building blocks of sustainable development. Each one should be given equal attention.

2.2 Corporate sustainability

Business enterprises are the main actors that contribute to economic, social and environmental welfare. Their role in sustainable development was emphasized in the 1992 Rio and 2002 Johannesburg summits, and business enterprises have been accepted as important stakeholders of sustainable development (Özsözgün Çalışkan, 2012a). Corporate sustainability can be defined as the concept of sustainable development reduced to or transferred to the enterprise level. The generally accepted definition of sustainable development can be adapted for business as the enterprise meeting the needs of its direct and indirect stakeholders without endangering the ability to meet the needs of its future direct and indirect stakeholders (Dyllick and Hockerts 2002). It is possible to come up with some basic assumptions from this definition (Altuntaş and Türker, 2007):

- Each business enterprise aims to survive. It is impossible for an unsustainable business enterprise to meet the needs of the current and future stakeholders within the framework of the sustainable development goals.
- The common objective of all business enterprises is to meet the needs of people. While carrying out this function, business enterprises not only use resources to produce goods that will ultimately become waste, but they also create needs for people and thereby affect their consuming behaviours and lifestyles.
- Business enterprises should meet the needs of their direct and indirect stakeholders in the best way possible. How the enterprises continue their activities and how the community accepts them are the most important elements in ensuring their legality.

Corporate sustainability can be explained as an enterprise's economic, social and environmental responsibility to focus on both profit and non-profit success (Sananuamengthaisong, 2013). This concept is a new and developing alternative to the traditional understanding of good management as based on growth and profitability. In this approach, equal importance is given to corporate growth and profitability and pursuing communal goals such as environmental protection, social equality, justice and economic development. In other words, corporate sustainability is an understanding that the enterprises carry on with their activities by harmonizing their products and services with their stakeholders and hence creating economic, environmental and social value (Özsözgün Çalışkan, 2012b).

Corporate sustainability accepts that growth and profitability are important for enterprises but also requires them to go after societal goals that are related to sustainable development. The concept of corporate sustainability takes some elements from other concepts: sustainable development, corporate social responsibility, stakeholder theory and corporate accountability theory. Sustainable development provides a goal for corporations to work toward ecological, social and economic sustainability. Corporate social responsibility provides ethical arguments and stakeholder theory provides business arguments as to why enterprises and corporate managers should work toward sustainable development. Corporate accountability provides a rationale for sustainability reporting (Wilson, 2003).

Evaluating economic, social and environmental sustainability as one unit and using the resources efficiently is called the triple bottom line (Elkington, 1997). The triple bottom line concept has three dimensions: people, planet and profit. This approach suggests first the traditional measurement of enterprise – profit; second, the measurement of the human aspect of the enterprise – social responsibility; and third, the measurement of the world aspect of the enterprise – environmental responsibility. In summary, the triple bottom line recommends measuring the financial, social and environmental performance of the enterprises in certain periods (Bakoğlu, 2010). The core characteristics of the triple bottom line include accepting accountability, being transparent, integrating planning and operations, committing to stakeholder engagement, and multidimensional measurement and reporting (Goel, 2010). Environmental justice, social equality and business ethics depend on how economic, social and environmental capital is used. According to this approach, business enterprises are responsible not only for their financial earnings but also for the environmental protection and the health of people in the community (Aksoy, 2013).

The concept of sustainability has become important for several reasons (Yalçınkaya, Durmaz and Adiller, 2011):

- Globalization has brought additional responsibilities, social and environmental, to enterprises. Enterprises have a role to play in these areas, which formerly were considered to be the responsibility of only the governments.
- The integrated way of doing business has caused enterprises to act responsibly along the entire supply chain process.
- A negative development about an enterprise in almost any country can be heard around the globe in a very short time due to advances in the communication technologies. As a result, enterprises should act responsibly in all the regions that they operate in.
- Investors evaluate the social and environmental performance of the enterprise as well as its financial performances in making investment decisions. Enterprises acting accordingly are believed to create value for their stakeholders in the medium and long term.
- Customers and consumers now expect enterprises to act responsibly in providing products and services. This has forced the enterprises to act accordingly.
- All stakeholders require transparency, accountability and corporate governance from the enterprises. Transparency asks for the disclosure of the social and environmental effects of the enterprise products and services rather than solely the basic financial statements.
- Global climate changes and environmental disasters force businesses to pay attention to these issues.

Enterprises can meet their goals of corporate sustainability if they keep their performances high in all dimensions (Aksoy, 2013).

2.3 Dimensions of sustainability

Looking at the varying definitions of sustainability, we can see that the term is interpreted broadly and affects all units of the community. What is common to all those definitions is that the concept has three dimensions. Although the environmental dimension is in the foreground, it is necessary to consider sustainability as the whole of economic, environmental and social dimensions (Altuntaş and Türker, 2007). When these three dimensions are handled together, objectives can be described under the same concept, as can be seen in Table 13.1 (Soubbotina, 2004).

Table 13.1 Objectives of sustainable development

Economic objectives	Social objectives	Environmental objectives
Growth	Full employment	Healthy environment for humans
Efficiency	Equity	Rational use of renewable resources
Stability	Security	Conservation of non-renewable natural resources
	Education	
	Health	
	Participation	
	Cultural identity	

Source: Soubbotina (2004, p. 9)

2.3.1   Environmental dimension of sustainability

The environmental dimension of sustainability anticipates that biological and physical systems can be balanced. The aim is to ensure that ecosystems adapt to changing conditions (Tıraş, 2012). There are renewable and non-renewable resources in the world and people have to be careful in the consumption of these resources. To ensure sustainability, the consumption rate of renewable resources should be lower than their renewal rate. Renewable resources that serve the same function should be preferred instead of non-renewable resources. The important point here is to use the renewable resources as much as needed, without stocking them, so that the future generations can also benefit from these resources.

Ecosystems have a limited capacity to renew themselves, and accordingly careful and responsible consumption of natural resources, such as soil, air, water, forests, oil and minerals, is required. With the increased population, factors such as excessive consumption, environmental pollution and rapid depletion of natural resources pose a threat to the carrying capacity of the world and therefore to environmental sustainability (Nemli, 2004).

Regulating the consumption of the resources will affect the economic performance of an enterprise for sure. Enterprises must get the same output with lower intake of resources. The main difference between the environmental and economic factors is that environmental factors are outside the enterprise. Nevertheless, they are very important for management and the organization. In the long-run, resource consumption and production techniques will contribute a lot to value creation in the enterprises (Aras and Crowther, 2008a).

2.3.2   Economic dimension of sustainability

The economic dimension of sustainability is related to the use of scarce resources. An economically sustainable system is a system that can produce goods and services continuously, that can avoid sectoral instability, which harms agricultural and industrial production, and that can ensure the sustainability of internal and external debts at a manageable level (Tıraş, 2012).

Economic sustainability is related to the benefit-cost analysis of the enterprise aiming to be profitable while producing goods and services that contribute to society. This approach aims to create long-term value for the stakeholders by evaluating the opportunities and risks associated with economic, environmental and social development (Nemli, 2004).

2.3.3   Social dimension of sustainability

The social dimension of sustainability focuses on humans. A socially sustainable system is a system that provides adequate and equally allocated social services and conditions such as education and health, gender equality, political responsibility and participation (Tıraş, 2012).

Humans comprise the social dimension of sustainability. Enterprises should take them into consideration in their mission and vision activities and their plans for the future.

3   Sustainability reporting

3.1   Concept of sustainability reporting

Traditional financial accounting and enterprise financial reporting have been criticized as insufficient in terms of sustainability and the stakeholders. One of the criticisms is that financial accounting gives priority to profits and profitability, leaving social and environmental aspects in the background. Another criticism is that accrual basis, consistency and conservatism principles have some flaws in evaluating company activities that have ecological implications. Money being used as the common measurement unit of accounting is also criticized, since prioritizing money may not be sufficient to provide a whole picture of all the opportunities and risks that are present for the organization. To summarize, financial accounting has been criticized for being insufficient to explain the corporate, environmental and social indications. Additional disclosures are required regarding the environmental and social performance of the enterprise. In order to overcome the inadequacy of traditional accounting, the concept of sustainability accounting and reporting has emerged (Özsözgün Çalışkan, 2012b).

Corporate sustainability reporting started in the late 1980s in the United States, with external reports addressing environmental issues. Sustainability accounting received attention in the accounting literature with Gray's work in the early 1990s, and gathered momentum with the launch of the environmental reporting awards of the Association of Chartered Certified Accountants and the release of Agenda 21 in the 1990s. This trend continued with the release of the Sustainability Reporting Guidelines in 2002 at the World Summit on Sustainable Development (Daizy, Sen and Das, 2013; Lamberton, 2005).

'Sustainability reporting is the practice of measuring, disclosing, and being accountable to internal and external stakeholders for organizational performance toward the goal of sustainable development' (Mintz, 2011, p. 27). Sustainability reporting is also known as non-financial reporting, triple bottom line reporting, corporate social responsibility reporting and more.

Sustainability reporting should include the three dimensions of sustainability: economic, environmental and social. Economic viability, social responsibility, corporate governance, ethical culture and environmental awareness should be covered by sustainability reporting (Daizy, Sen and Das, 2013). A sustainability report provides information about the sustainability performance of a reporting organization. The report should include both positive and negative contributions (Goel, 2010). A sustainability report communicates the economic, environmental, social and governance performance of an organization (https://www.globalreporting.org). A sustainability report differs from an environmental report, since it includes the enterprise's economic and social performance and provides a more thorough image of the non-financial activities of the enterprise (Berthelot, Coulmont and Serret, 2012). Transparency, inclusiveness, auditability, completeness, relevance, accuracy, neutrality, comparability, clarity and timeliness are the qualities that support sustainability reporting (Painter-Morland, 2006).

Enterprises may choose to prepare sustainability reports for many reasons: in order to ease the application of environmental strategies, to create environmental awareness throughout the organization, to gain credibility by increasing transparency, to obtain the necessary licenses to continue certain activities, to improve the organization's reputation, to create cost advantage, to meet customer demands for ecological products and processes, to increase efficiency, to gain competitive advantage, to be included in the sustainability indexes, to act in conformity with the voluntary international standards and to meet legal obligations and strict regulations (Özsözgün Çalışkan, 2012b).

Sustainability reporting can provide internal and external benefits for companies and organizations (Goel, 2010; https://www.globalreporting.org). These can include:

- Increased understanding of risks and opportunities
- Showing the link between financial and non-financial performance

- Affecting long-term business plans, strategy and policy of the management
- Avoiding being implicated in publicized environmental, social and governance failures
- Benchmarking and evaluating sustainability performance
- Comparing sustainability performance internally and between different organizations
- Improving brand loyalty and company reputation
- Demonstrating how the organization influences, and is influenced by, expectations about sustainable development

3.2   Sustainability reports

There are two approaches to preparing sustainability reports. Enterprises claim that corporate sustainability performance can be reported more efficiently using the voluntary reporting approach. On the other hand, unions and governmental institutions claim that mandatory reporting should be used in order to improve the transparency, accountability and objectivity of sustainability performance reporting (Aksoy, 2013).

Unlike the International Accounting and Financial Reporting Standards that are accepted globally for financial accounting practice, there is no one set of universal standards for sustainability reporting. Principles and frameworks for the preparation of sustainability reports are set by various global organizations and local legislations. In some countries it is mandatory to prepare sustainability reports using the national standards and principles; however, in other countries it is optional to prepare sustainability reports and the enterprises are free to choose from any set of principles and guidelines. The most widely preferred and used guidelines are the ones issued by the Global Reporting Initiative.

3.2.1   Global Reporting Initiative

Global Reporting Initiative (GRI) is an organization with a mission of making sustainability reporting standard practice by providing guidance and support to organizations. GRI has developed a Sustainability Reporting Framework, which is widely used around the globe.

GRI was founded in 1997 as a project division of the Coalition for Environmentally Responsible Economies (CERES) for developing a framework and guidelines for disclosure of sustainability information. The first version of the guidelines was released in 2000. G2, the second generation of the guidelines, was launched at the World Summit on Sustainable Development in Johannesburg (Rio+10) in 2002. The guidelines were not produced with the intention of replacing Generally Accepted Accounting Principles (GAAP); rather, they were designed to provide a basis for credible and precise non-financial reporting that complements GAAP. In the same year, GRI became an independent and international non-profit organization, being formally accepted as a United Nations Environment Programme (UNEP) collaborating organization. The third generation of the guidelines, G3, was released in 2006. Following the release of G3, formal partnerships were established with other organizations, Sector Guidelines were created for diverse industries, and educational and research-and-development publications were produced. The fourth generation of the guidelines, G4, was launched in 2013 (Crawford, 2005; https://www.globalreporting.org).

GRI has three governance bodies: the Board of Directors, the Stakeholder Council and the Technical Advisory Committee. The Technical Advisory Committee administers the development of the GRI's Reporting Framework content, the Stakeholder Council provides advice on strategic issues and proposed changes to the framework content and the Board of Directors makes the final decision regarding the release of the framework content (https://www.globalreporting.org).

GRI has strategic partnerships with many other organizations, among them the Organisation for Economic Co-operation and Development (OECD), the United Nations Global Compact (UNGC), the United Nations Environment Programme (UNEP), the International Organization for Standardization (ISO), the Carbon Disclosure Project (CDP), the United Nations Conference on Trade and Development (UNCTAD), the International Finance Corporation (IFC) and Earth Charter (https://www.globalreporting.org).

GRI provides globally applicable guidelines for voluntary use by organizations to report their sustainability performance and reveal the economic, environmental and social dimensions of their activities. The framework aims for organizational accountability and transparency (Aras and Crowther, 2008b; https://www.globalreporting.org).

The GRI Sustainability Reporting Guidelines include Reporting Principles, Standard Disclosures and an Implementation Manual. All organizations, regardless of their size, sector or location, can use the guidelines to prepare their sustainability reports. Multinational enterprises, small and medium-sized enterprises, public agencies, non-governmental organizations and trade associations can use the guidelines. 'The Guidelines are developed through a global multi-stakeholder process involving representatives from business, labour, civil society, and financial markets, as well as auditors and experts in various fields; and in close dialogue with regulators and governmental agencies in several countries' (https://www.globalreporting.org).

The GRI Sustainability Reporting Guidelines are reviewed periodically to provide up-to-date guidance. G4 was planned and developed as part of the review process and the fourth generation of the guidelines was launched in May 2013. The objectives of G4 include providing guidance that can be applied to all organizations around the world and that integrates with other internationally accepted standards (GRI, 2013; https://www.globalreporting.org).

Preparing the sustainability report is a process that starts with obtaining an overview. The next step is choosing the preferred "in accordance" option. The guidelines offer two options for organizations to prepare their sustainability reports in accordance with the guidelines. The core option involves the basic elements of a sustainability report, disclosing the economic, environmental and social and governance performance of an organization. The comprehensive option requires additional disclosure of the strategy and analysis, governance, and ethics and integrity of the organization. After deciding on a compliance level, the organization prepares its General Standard Disclosures and then its Specific Standard Disclosures. The final step of the process is preparing the sustainability report (GRI, 2013).

When preparing sustainability reports, organizations need to exercise the guidelines' Reporting Principles to attain transparency. Principles for Defining Report Content include stakeholder inclusiveness, sustainability context, materiality and completeness. Balance, comparability, accuracy, timeliness, clarity and reliability are among the Principles for Defining Report Quality (GRI, 2013).

GRI provides detailed guidelines on how to report and what to report by defining overall objective and content, and regulating the content using standard disclosures and sector supplements. The disclosures also provide guidance on assurance (Joseph, 2012). The guidelines address two types of Standard Disclosures: General Standard Disclosures on Strategy and Analysis, Organizational Profile, Identified Material Aspects and Boundaries,

Stakeholder Engagement, Report Profile, Governance, Ethics and Integrity; and Specific Standard Disclosures Including Disclosures on Management Approach in Three Categories, Economic, Environmental, and Social, and Indicators. 'General Standard Disclosures offer a description of the organization and the reporting process. Specific Standard Disclosures offer information on the organization's management and performance related to material Aspects' (GRI, 2013, p. 92).

3.2.2   *Other reporting principles and guidelines*

Although guidance set by the Global Reporting Initiative is the most preferred and widely used by enterprises worldwide, there are other principles and guidelines that can also be used.

- United Nations Principles for Responsible Investment (UNPRI): In 2005 an investor group of 20 people from 12 countries invited by the United Nations Secretary-General came together with a group of experts from the industry and civil society to determine the six Principles for Responsible Investment. These were put into play at the New York Stock Exchange in 2006. According to these principles, the performance of investment portfolios can be affected by environmental, social and corporate governance issues (http://www.unpri.org).
- OECD Guidelines for Multinational Enterprises: These guidelines, first adopted in 1976, are recommendations for multinational enterprises to improve their contribution to sustainable development. The guidelines encourage multinational enterprises to disclose timely and reliable information regarding their social, environmental and financial performance (http://mneguidelines.oecd.org).
- United Nations Global Compact (UNGC): provides a framework for the development, implementation and disclosure of sustainability policies and practices. Enterprises are asked to accept, support and use the Ten Principles, a set of globally accepted values in the areas of human rights, labour standards, environment and anti-corruption. Voluntary UNGC members are expected to report their activities in these areas and share their performance with the public (http://www.unglobalcompact.org).
- ISO 26000 Social Responsibility Standard: not a certified standard, it was developed by stakeholders around the world and launched in 2010. The standard provides guidance to all types of organizations regarding social responsibility and how they should act in an ethical and transparent way to contribute to society (http://www.iso.org/iso/iso26000).
- AA100 Accountability Principles Standard and AA100 Assurance Standard: These are principle-based standards set by AccountAbility, a professional institute, to help organizations become more accountable, responsible and sustainable. The AA100 Accountability Principles Standard, which has been used since 2008, provides a framework for corporate sustainability. The AA100 Assurance Standard, on the other hand, was developed to assure the quality and credibility of sustainability performance and reporting (http://www.accountability.org).

3.2.3   *Sustainability Accounting Standards Board*

The Sustainability Accounting Standards Board (SASB) is a non-profit organization, developed and incorporated in 2011, that is responsible for creating sustainability accounting standards for use by U.S. publicly listed corporations in disclosing material sustainability issues. SASB defines sustainability as 'environmental, social and governance factors that have the potential to affect long-term value creation and/or are in the public's interest' (http://www.sasb.org).

Sustainability accounting standards are intended to complement the financial accounting standards set by the Financial Accounting Standards Board (FASB). The standards issued by SASB must be relevant, useful, applicable, cost-effective, comparable, complete, directional and auditable. SASB issues standards that are applicable to all investors, pertinent and relevant across an industry, focused on driving value creation, expected to bring benefits that exceed the perceived costs, actionable by companies, easily verified, objective and support decision-making, highest quality possible at any given time, reflective of the views of stakeholders, determined to support the shift to integrated reporting, and determined to support the convergence to international accounting standards (http://www.sasb.org).

Investors, analysts, auditors, companies and consultants can use SASB standards. The standards enable investors to compare peer performance on material sustainability issues, understand the relative sustainability positioning of companies to one another, direct capital toward the most sustainable corporations and industries and understand sustainability risks and opportunities across portfolios. With SASB standards, companies can measure, manage and disclose sustainability impacts according to industry-specific performance indicators, and they can compare their performance with competitors and industry benchmarks (http://www.sasb.org).

SASB aims to develop standards for more than 80 industries in 10 sectors. SASB issued standards for the health care sector on 31 July 2013 applicable to such industries as biotechnology, pharmaceuticals, medical equipment and supplies, health care delivery, health care distributors and managed care. Another set of standards for use by companies and investors was released on 25 February 2014 for industries in the financials sector. Companies in such areas as commercial banking, investment banking and brokerage, asset management and custody activities, consumer finance, mortgage finance, security and commodity exchanges, and insurance can apply these standards in addressing environmental, social and governance issues.

SASB has released all the standards on the remaining eight sectors, including Technology and Communications, Non-Renewable Resources, Transportation, Services, Resource Transformation, Consumption, Renewable Resources and Alternative Energy, and Infrastructure as of 31 March 2016 (http://www.sasb.org).

Focusing on U.S. public equities and creating industry-specific sustainability accounting standards differentiates SASB from the other sustainability reporting entities. Although they share the same goal – the advancement of corporate sustainability reporting – GRI and SASB have their differences. GRI provides guidance on an international scale, within a general scope for public and private companies to prepare voluntary reports for a target audience of all stakeholders. SASB, on the other hand, provides industry-specific standards that require mandatory filing by the public companies traded on US exchanges for investors (http://www.sasb.org).

3.2.4 Sustainability indexes

In recent years, a lot of changes and improvements have been developed for publicly listed companies to disclose their sustainability practices. These aim to increase transparency and to create awareness regarding sustainability. Integrating sustainability criteria among the quotation rules, presenting awards for the successful sustainability practices, publishing sustainability guides and developing sustainability indexes are among these (www.borsaistanbul.com).

Sustainability indexes have been developed by the leading stock markets of the world to compare enterprises' sustainability activities. The first sustainability index, Domini Social Index, was developed by Amy Domini, an employee of KLD Rating Company, in the United States in 1990. Four hundred leading (in terms of social environmental and ethical aspects) US corporations are listed in this index. In 2001 the first sustainability index of the United Kingdom, FTSE4Good Index, was launched (Aksoy, 2013). This is a socially responsible investment index designed to reflect the performance of socially responsible enterprises (Tokgöz and Önce, 2009).

The Dow Jones Sustainability Index, started in 1999, provides a tool for investors and financial analysts to evaluate firms according to their sustainability performance. Dow Jones Sustainability Indexes serve as benchmarks for investors (http://www.sustainability-indices.com). The underlying logic is that financial analysis cannot be complete without taking non-financial factors into consideration.

London, National Association of Securities Dealers Automated Quotations (NASDAQ) and Euronext are among the leading stock markets in regard to sustainability indexes. Sustainability indexes were created in 2007 in Germany and in 2008 in Spain, Austria, Denmark, Sweden and Norway. A few developing countries have also considered sustainability as an important concept and have launched sustainability indexes, including in 2009 in Korea and Indonesia and in 2010 in Egypt (borsaistanbul.com).

In the case of Turkey, a cooperation agreement has been signed between Borsa Istanbul and the Ethical Investment Research Services Limited (EIRIS) to create the BIST Sustainability Index to evaluate enterprises on their environmental, social and corporate governance performances. This index was launched on November 4, 2014 (borsaistanbul.com).

4   Conclusion

We live in a system in which corporations have changed their perspectives; they care about not only their own interests but also the interests of society. Traditional financial reporting emphasizes economic profits as enterprises' main objective. Economic profitability, or the result of the entity's activities, indicates that company assets and resources are efficiently used, preserved and well managed. However, the world has changed and advanced, increasing expectations. Traditional financial reporting has become inadequate to meet the needs of enterprises and their stakeholders. Of course, the profit approach remains, but we now expect enterprises to claim responsibility for social and environmental issues. Reporting the economic, environmental and social implications of company activities is known as sustainability reporting. Sustainability reporting has emerged as an alternative to traditional financial reporting. Since sustainability reporting contains social and environmental components, it is also referred to as non-financial reporting.

Sustainability reporting has a lot of benefits for enterprises, such as decreasing costs, creating competitive advantage, improving the company's reputation, increasing innovative activities, improving employee loyalty and increasing profit margins with qualified recruitment. In terms of society as a whole, enterprises acting responsibly to their all stakeholders and sustaining their continuity by maximizing their reputation and profits at the same time will contribute to the development of the national economy.

Sustainability practices and reports should not be limited to only some enterprises but should be applied to the entirety of the business world. Although these reports are mainly prepared by multinational and large industrial enterprises, it would be beneficial to generalize sustainability reports to even small and medium-sized enterprises. Led by academia and with the full support of the business world, this can be achieved through conducting seminars, meetings and workshops to express the importance and the necessity of sustainability reports.

References

Aksoy, Ç. (2013). Sürdürülebilirlik Performansının Değerlendirilmesine Yönelik Ölçek Önerisi ve Türkiye'deki İşletmelerde Uygulaması Yayımlanmamış Doktora Tezi. Retrieved from https://tez.yok. gov.tr/UlusalTezMerkezi/tarama.jsp.

Altuntaş, C. and Türker, D. (2007). Sürdürülebilir Tedarik Zincirleri: Sürdürülebilirlik Raporlarının İçerik Analizi. *Dokuz Eylül Üniversitesi Sosyal Bilimler Enstitüsü Dergisi*, 3(14), 39–64.

Altuntaş, C. and Türker, D. (2012). http://dergipark.ulakbim.gov.tr/deusosbil/article/view/5000064122/5000059993

Aras, G. and Crowther, D.A. (2008a). Governance and sustainability: An investigation into the relationship between corporate governance and corporate sustainability. *Management Decision*, 46(3), 443–8.

Aras, G. and Crowther, D.A. (2008b). Evaluating sustainability: A need for standards. *Issues in Social and Environmental Accounting*, 2(1), 19–35.

Bakoğlu, R. (2010). *Çağdaş Stratejik Yönetim*. İstanbul: Beta Basım Yayım Dağıtım.

Berthelot, S., Coulmont, M. and Serret, V. (2012). Do investors value sustainability reports? A Canadian study. *Corporate Social Responsibility and Environmental Management*, 19, 355–63.

Carr, D.L. and Norman, E.S. (2008). Global civil society? The Johannesburg world summit on sustainable development. *Geoforum*, 39, 358–71. Retrieved from http://geog.ucsb.edu/carr/DCarr_Publications/Carr_Norman_Geoforum_08.pdf.

Crawford, D. (2005). Managing and reporting sustainability. *CMA Management*, 78(9), 20–6.

Daizy, J., Sen, M. and Das, N. (2013). Corporate sustainability reporting: A review of initiatives and trends. *The IUP Journal of Accounting Research & Audit Practices*, 12(2), 7–18.

Dyllick, T. and Hockerts, K. (2002). Beyond the business case for corporate sustainability. *Business Strategy and the Environment*, 11, 130–41.

Elkington, J. (1997). *Cannibals with Forks: The Triple Bottom Line of 21st Century Business*. Oxford: Capstone.

Gladwin, T.N., Kennelly, J.J. and Krause, T.-S. (1995). Shifting paradigms for sustainable development: Implications for management theory and research. *Academy of Management Review*, 20(4), 874–907.

Goel, P. (2010). Triple bottom line reporting: An analytical approach for corporate sustainability. *Journal of Finance, Accounting and Management*, 1(1), 27–42.

GRI. (2013). *G4 Sustainability Reporting Guidelines*. www.gri.org (Retrieved on Feb 2, 2014).

Joseph, G. (2012). Ambiguous but tethered: An accounting basis for sustainability reporting. *Critical Perspectives on Accounting*, 23, 93–106.

Kuşat, N. (2012). Sürdürülebilir İşletmeler İçin Kurumsal Sürdürülebilirlik ve İçsel Unsurları. *Afyon Kocatepe Üniversitesi İ.İ.B.F. Dergisi*, 14, 227–42.

Lamberton, G. (2005). Sustainability accounting: A brief history and conceptual framework. *Accounting Forum*, 29, 7–26.

Mintz, S.M. (2011). Triple bottom line reporting for CPAs: Challenges and opportunities in social accounting. *The CPA Journal*, 81(12), 26–33.

Monto, M., Ganesh, L.S. and Varghese, K. (2005). *Sustainability and Human Settlements: Fundamental Issues, Modeling and Simulations*. New Delhi: Sage.

Nemli, E. (2001). Çevreye Duyarlı Yönetim Anlayışının Gelişimi. *İstanbul Üniversitesi Siyasal Bilgiler Fakültesi Dergisi*, 23(4), 211–24.

Nemli, E. (2004). *Sürdürülebilir Kalkınma: Şirketlerin Çevresel ve Sosyal Yaklaşımları*. İstanbul: Filiz Kitabevi.

Önce, A.G. and Marangoz, M. (2012). Pazarlamanın Sürdürülebilir Gelişmedeki Rolü, 389–96. Retrieved from www.eecon.info/papers/435.pdf.

Özmehmet, E. (2012). Dünyada ve Türkiye Sürdürülebilir Kalkınma Yaklaşımları. *Journal of Yasar University*, 3. Retrieved from http://Journal.yasar.edu.tr/wp-content/uploads/2012/11/vol_3_no_12_Ecehan_OZ_Makale.pdf.

Özsözgün Çalışkan, A. (2012a). İşletmelerde Sürdürülebilirlik Ve Muhasebe Mesleği İlişkisi. *İSMMMO Mali Çözüm Dergisi*, 112, 133–60.

Özsözgün Çalışkan, A. (2012b). Sürdürülebilirlik Raporlaması. *Ankara SMMMO Muhasebe ve Vergi Uygulamaları Dergisi*, 5(1), 41–68.

Öztel, A., Köse, M.S. and Aytekin, İ. (2012). Kurumsal Sürdürülebilirlik Performansının Ölçümü İçin Çok Kriterli Bir Çerçeve: Henkel Örneği. *Karabük Üniversitesi Tarih Kültür ve Sanat Araştırmaları Dergisi*, 4(1), 32–44.

Painter-Morland, M. (2006). Triple bottom-line reporting as social grammar: Integrating corporate social responsibility and corporate codes of conduct. *Business Ethics: A European Review*, 5(4), 352–64.

Quental, N., Lourenço, J.M. and da Silva, F.N. (2011). Sustainable development policy: Goals, targets and political cycles. *Sustainable Development*, 19, 15–29.

Rio Declaration on Environment and Development. (1992). Retrieved from http://www.unesco.org/education/nfsunesco/pdf/RIO_E.PDF.

Sananuamengthaisong, M. (2013). Corporate social responsibility strategy and corporate sustainability of food businesses in Thailand. *IABE Journal of Business & Economics*, 13(4), 155–166.

Soubbotina, T.P. (2004). *Beyond Economic Growth: An Introduction to Sustainable Development*. Washington, DC: World Bank.

Tıraş, H. (2012). Sürdürülebilir Kalkınma ve Çevre: Teorik Bir İnceleme. *Kahramanmaraş Sütçü İmam Üniversitesi İ.İ.B.F. Dergisi*, 2, 57–73.

Tokgöz, N. and Önce, S. (2009). Şirket Sürdürülebilirliği: Geleneksel Yönetim Anlayışına Alternatif. *Afyon Kocatepe Üniversitesi İ.İ.B.F. Dergisi*, 11, 249–75.

WCED. (1987). *Our Common Future*. Retrieved from http://www.un-documents.net/our-common-future.pdf.

White, G.B. (2005). How to report a company's sustainability activities. *Management Accounting Quarterly*, 7(1), 36–43.

Wilson, M. (2003). Corporate sustainability: What is it and where does it come from? *Ivey Business Journal*, March/April67(6). and Adiller, L. (2011). Sürdürülebilir Kalkınma ve Kurumsal Sürdürülebilirlik için Yeni Ölçümleme: Üçlü Performans. 9th International Conference on Knowledge, Economy& Management Proceedings, s.3320–3332. Retrieved from http://www.academia.edu/4503476/SURDURULEBILIR_KALKINMA_VE_KURUMSAL_SURDURULEBILIRLIK_ICIN_YENI_OLCUMLEME_UCLU_PERFORMANS.

Yalçınkaya, Durmaz and Adiller, Sürdürülebilir Kalkınma ve Kurumsal Sürdürülebilirlik İçin Yeni ölçümleme: Üçlü Performans, Uluslararası 9. Bilgi, Ekonomi ve Yönetim Kongresi, 23–25 Haziran 2011 Saraybosna-Bosna Hersek.

Yıldıztekin, İ. (2009). Sürdürülebilir Kalkınmada Çevre Muhasebesinin Etkileri. *Atatürk Üniversitesi Sosyal Bilimler Enstitüsü Dergisi*, 13(1), 367–90.

Websites

http://www.accountability.org
http://www.borsaistanbul.com
https://www.globalreporting.org
http://www.iso.org/iso/iso26000
http://mneguidelines.oecd.org
http://www.sasb.org
http://sustainabledevelopment.un.org
http://www.unglobalcompact.org
http://www.unpri.org

Part III

Sustainability and management in the Far East

14 Ethical issues characteristics and their relevance to auditors' ethical decision-making in Malaysia

Razana Juhaida Johari, Zuraidah Mohd Sanusi,
Rashidah Abdul Rahman and Normah Omar

1 Introduction

The area of accounting ethics has gained significant interest since the turn of the millennium thanks to various global accounting scandals. Such accounting scandals as those of Lehman Brothers, Enron and WorldCom in the West and a series of financial irregularities in Malaysian firms such as Sime Darby Berhad, PKFZ Berhad and Transmile Berhad have highlighted the concern about ethical conduct among auditors. Historically, auditors have been recognized as a group of individuals who practice honest principles and perform efficient and valuable services for their respective clients and public at large. However, the recent occurrences have led citizens to question auditors' ethical responsibilities in performing their duties. Exploring how people act in an ethical conflict, Rest (1986) developed a Four Component Model of the ethical decision-making process. The model comprises four steps – ethical sensitivity, ethical judgement, ethical intentions and ethical behaviour – that must occur for ethical manners to take place.

Empirically, research in accounting has addressed the influences of individual, situational and organizational factors on the ethical decision-making process (Jones, Massey and Thorne, 2003; Craft, 2013). However, the assessment of ethical issues and influences on the ethical decision-making process have received less attention in accounting studies (Leitsch, 2004). The importance of ethical issues characteristics (i.e. moral intensity) on the ethical decision-making process has been highlighted by Jones (1991) in his model. According to Jones (1991), the moral intensity of the issue captures the heightened feelings and emotions of a particular ethical conflict and significantly influences all the sequential steps of an individual's ethical decision-making process. He also argues that ethics-related situations vary in terms of moral intensity of the issue itself.

2 Understanding the concepts of ethical issues characteristics and ethical decision-making

The ethical issues characteristics (referred to as "moral intensity construct" in Jones' [1991] model) refers to 'the extent or degree of issue-related moral imperative in a situation'. Craft (2013), in her recent reviews of the empirical ethical decision-making literature, stated that this construct is one of the two most prevalent models used to support ethical decision-making research. This construct is added to Rest's (1986) model to consolidate the prior ethical decision-making models. There are six components of the ethical issues characteristics: magnitude of consequences, social consensus, temporal immediacy, proximity, probability of effect and concentration of effect (Jones, 1991).

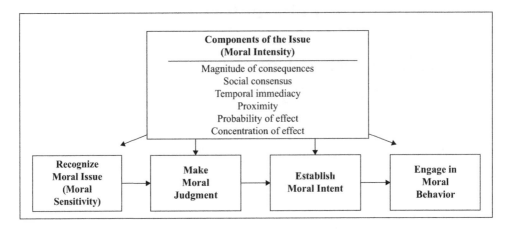

Figure 14.1 Jones' (1991) model

These components change in concept as moral intensity is thought to increase or decrease the moral imperative inherent in a situation. For example, if an action is perceived to cause serious consequences, it should be more "morally intense" than an action with less serious consequences.

Jones' (1991) model (Figure 14.1) is based on Rest's (1986) model. Rest (1986) specified four distinct sequential processes of ethical decision-making. The first stage, recognition of moral issues (moral sensitivity), represents the stage at which one recognizes that a situation presents an ethical dilemma. The second stage, moral judgement, represents the stage at which one uses a variety of strategies to determine which courses of action are morally right or wrong. The third stage, moral intention, represents the stage at which one decides to behave in an ethical or unethical manner. Finally, the fourth stage, moral behaviour, represents the stage at which one engages in ethical or unethical action. Jones (1991) posited that the components of the moral issue significantly affect the process of ethical decision-making. He argued that the moral intensity of an issue would influence the recognition of an issue as an ethical problem and the subsequent behaviour in which the decision-maker engages.

Prior to Jones' (1991) model, many models were proposed to explain ethical decision-making within the context of business ethics (e.g. Hunt and Vitell, 1986; Rest, 1986; Trevino, 1986). These models included a variety of individual (e.g. cognitive moral development, locus of control and ethical philosophy) and situational/organizational/cultural characteristics (e.g. managerial influences, referent others and competition), but none included variables related to the issue itself. Jones (1991) argued that by neglecting the influence of the ethical issue components, previous models only suggested the same process for any dilemma faced by an individual. For instance, Jones (1991) claimed that there is no difference in making the ethical decision for a dilemma involving the theft of a few supplies from an organization and a dilemma involving the release of a dangerous product to market. Since moral problems do not all bring out the same response, Jones claimed that investigating the components of ethical issues will clarify the ethical decision-making process. By investigating the components of the issue, researchers can

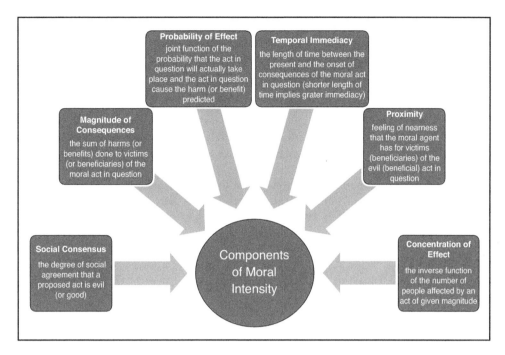

Figure 14.2 Components of moral intensity (Jones, 1991)

learn more about what triggers individuals to pay attention to certain ethical problems and ignore other ethical problems. The six components of moral intensity construct are illustrated in Figure 14.2 above.

Magnitude of consequences

"Magnitude of consequences" refers to 'the sum of harms (or benefits) done to victims (or beneficiaries) of the moral act in question' (Jones, 1991). Moral intensity increases as the amount of harm increases. According to Bird and Gandz (1991), people are more motivated to respond to ethical issues if the issues have serious consequences on a large number of people.

Social consensus

Social consensus is 'the degree of social agreement that a proposed act is evil (or good)' (Jones, 1991). The greater the agreement that an act is wrong, the greater the moral intensity. Individuals in a social group or culture may share values and standards that influence their perception of the goodness of various behaviours. However, these values and standards vary across cultures. People's actions are often kept within the established conventions set by social norms, principles and habits (Bird and Gandz, 1991).

Probability of effect

"Probability of effect" of an act refers to the 'joint function of the probability that the act in question will actually take place and the act in question cause the harm (or benefit) predicted' (Jones, 1991).The greater the likelihood of the act taking place and causing harm, the greater the moral intensity.

Temporal immediacy

"Temporal immediacy" refers to 'the length of time between the present and the onset of consequences of the moral act in question (shorter length of time implies grater immediacy)' (Jones, 1991). The shorter the time between the act and the resultant consequences, the greater the moral intensity. Jones argued that future consequences of events would be discounted. If the impact of an issue is discounted, the issue may not be readily recognized as a moral issue.

Proximity

Proximity of a moral issue refers to the 'feeling of nearness that the moral agent has for victims (beneficiaries) of the evil (beneficial) act in question' (Jones, 1991). The moral intensity increases as closeness increases. There are four aspects of proximity: social, cultural, psychological and physical. People show more concern and care for family members and friends (people whom they feel close to) than they do for strangers. People are motivated to respond to ethical issues to the extent that the issues personally affect them (Bird and Gandz, 1991).

Concentration of effect

Concentration of effect refers to 'the inverse function of the number of people affected by an act of given magnitude' (Jones, 1991). For example, an act that causes $100,000 in harm that affects 100 people, so that each incurs $1,000 of damage, is of greater moral intensity than an act that causes the same $100,000 in harm, but instead affects 100,000 people, so that each incurs $1 of damage. In addition, an act that causes harm to an individual is of greater moral intensity than an act that causes harm to a corporation (Jones, 1991).

3   Empirical studies of ethical issues characteristics and ethical decision-making

Initial empirical studies indicate that moral intensity construct influences ethical decisions on various business and marketing-related dilemmas (Singhapakdi, Vitell and Kraft, 1996; Barnett and Valentine, 2004). Since its introduction in 1991, this construct has been the subject of several published research studies. Few studies examined all six dimensions of moral intensity on the ethical decision-making process. For example, Singhapakdi et al. (1996)'s survey of marketing professionals showed that the six dimensions of moral intensity influenced ethical judgement and intention. In another study, Wright, Cullinan and Bline (1997) provided a significant result of interacting effect between ethical intensity and ethical sensitivity on ethical issue recognition. In addition, May and Pauli (2002) contributed to the literature when their study found that the probability of negative

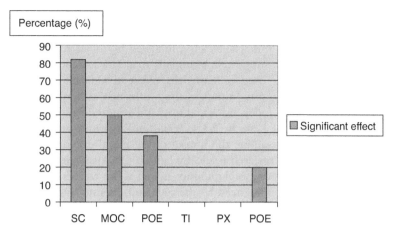

Figure 14.3 Significant effect of moral intensity components
Source: McMahon and Harvey (2007).

consequences is positively associated with ethical issue recognition. This finding supported the previous findings of Singhapakdi et al. (1996) but not the results of Chia and Mee (2000).

In 2007 McMahon and Harvey made an overview of the studies done on moral intensity constructs and ethical judgement from 1992 to 2001. Figure 14.3 represents the statistics of McMahon and Harvey's overview. From the review, it is indicated that social consensus (SC) seems to be the most robust of the six moral intensity components, having a significant effect in 9 of the 11 studies (82 per cent) in which it was examined. For the magnitude of consequences (MOC), from the 12 studies, this component provided a significant effect in the six studies (50 per cent). Out of eight studies, probability of effect (POE) had a significant effect in three studies (38 per cent). On the other hand, temporal immediacy (TI) was not significant in seven studies, but did show some significance in one study (significance varied by scenario). Similarly, proximity (PX) was also found to be not significant in four studies, but did show some significance in two studies (significance varied by scenario). Finally, the last component, concentration of effect (COE), was found significant in one of the five studies (20 per cent).

In light of the problems and concerns that have generated interest in the auditing profession, an increased stream of academic research on accounting ethics emerged that provided some empirical studies on accounting-related dilemmas. The inclusion of the moral intensity components within accounting ethics research has been offered by a few researchers, such as Karcher (1996), Leitsch (2004; 2006), Cohen and Bennie-Martinov (2006), Sweeney and Costello (2009) and Johari (2013). For example, Karcher (1996) found out the strong effect of the ethical issue in her study. The propensity to mention the ethical issue differed significantly between issues (level of intensity) included in the study, and subjects (auditor) were more likely to mention an ethical issue if the circumstances surrounding it were more severe. A survey of the moral intensity effects on auditors was also conducted by Cohen and Bennie-Martinov (2006) and Johari (2013). In their study, Cohen and Bennie-Martinov (2006) suggested that all six moral intensity components were considered important at each of the four stages of ethical decision-making. The importance rating and ranking of the six moral intensity components across the four stages of the ethical decision-making process was stable, with the magnitude of consequences considered the most important factor, followed by social consensus and probability of effect. These results supported arguments made by Karcher (1996) regarding the possible components of the moral intensity that affect an auditor's judgement. On the other hand, Johari (2013) supported the mediating influences of moral intensity on the relationship between auditors' independence threats and ethical decision-making.

Alternatively, the studies of Leitsch (2004; 2006) and Sweeney and Costello (2009) used accounting students to examine the impact of the moral intensity components on ethical decision-making. The research results by Leitsch (2004) suggested that a student's perception of the components of moral intensity as well as the various stages of the moral decision-making process was influenced by the type and intensity of the moral issue. A more recent study conducted by Sweeney and Costello (2009) further supported the previous findings concerning the influence of the moral intensity of the situation on the ethical decision-making process. In addition, in their study, the social consensus emerged as the most strongly moral intensity component related to the ethical decision-making process. This is consistent with the previous studies, which suggested that when dealing with student groups, social consensus was the most important component but, when dealing with manager groups, magnitude of consequences emerged as the most important component (Barnett and Valentine, 2004).

The research findings presented above have extended current understanding on the influence of moral intensity components on ethical decision-making particularly in developed countries. Noting the usefulness of the moral intensity construct in explaining the differences of ethical decision-making process taken by individuals, this current study is carried out to examine the effect of this construct pertaining to developing countries such as Malaysia. The involvements of Malaysian auditors in unethical behaviours are becoming the restless issues argued by the public in these recent years. For example, in 2002, one of the audit firms in Malaysia, Arthur Andersen, was sued for RM500 million by Cold Storage for negligently giving a clean report (Sujatani, 2002). In addition, another two audit firms, Johari Abas and David Low See Keat, were also sued by their clients due to the auditors' failure to detect wrongdoing of their client companies in the course of the auditors' normal duties (Mohamad Adam, Maisarah and Ainun, 2002). The case of Transmile Group may be the highest-profile casualty amongst the spate of Malaysian firms to announce accounting irregularities. The company inflated its revenue by RM75 and RM158 million for the years 2005 and 2006, when in fact the company was at a net loss of RM370 million and RM126 million, respectively (Kang, 2007). The auditors Deloitte and Touche failed to detect these actual losses in their audit.

4   Current study on the effect of ethical issue characteristics on auditors' ethical decision-making in Malaysia

The objective of the current study are twofold; first, to identify the relevant components of ethical issue characteristics (i.e. moral intensity components) in predicting auditors' ethical decision-making process; and second, to examine the different level of moral intensity of the issue on the auditors' ethical decision-making process. The respondents of the study are the auditors who are currently working in audit firms in Malaysia. The response rate of the study is 23.5 per cent, or 191 respondents. The study utilized a scenarios approach in measuring the moral intensity components and the three stages of auditors' ethical decision-making process. Two auditing scenarios were adapted into this current study. Each of the scenarios represents a different level of moral intensity issues, with scenario 1 (under-reporting time) indicating a low moral intensity issue and scenario 2 (non-compliance) demonstrating a high moral intensity issue.

The results of the study, shown in Table 14.1, indicated that of the six components of moral intensity, only two components, social consensus and proximity, are significantly related to ethical sensitivity in both of the scenarios. Similarly, the components of social consensus and proximity also played a significant role between moral intensity and the auditors' ethical judgement. Both of these components significantly influenced the auditors' ethical judgement in both scenarios. However, the component of temporal immediacy is found to be significantly related to ethical judgements only in Scenario 2. Finally, the components of social consensus and proximity were also found to be significantly associated with ethical intentions in Scenario 1 but not in Scenario 2 (only the proximity component). Therefore, from the results we identified that moral intensity components were differently related to the ethical decision-making process based on the scenario given. The most two dominant components which constantly have a significant relationship to the ethical decision-making process were social consensus and proximity, followed by temporal immediacy.

In addition, the study examined how a different level of moral intensity issues could influence the auditors' perceptions on each of the ethical decision-making processes. As previously mentioned, Scenario 1 (underreporting time) represents the low moral intensity issue and Scenario 2 (non-compliance) demonstrates the high moral intensity issue. For ease of explanation, the level of score was analysed into three categories, namely

Table 14.1 Regression analysis

	Ethical sensitivity	*Ethical judgements*	*Ethical intentions*
Scenario 1:			
Magnitude of Consequences	−0.016	−0.033	.056
Social Consensus	.118a	.168a	.187a
Probability of Effect	.086	−0.155	.097
Temporal Immediacy	−0.029	.020	.087
Proximity	.321b	.134a	.244b
Concentration of Effect	.024	.211	.032
R2	10.8%	10.4%	38.7%
Scenario 2:			
Magnitude of Consequences	−0.011	.150	.012
Social Consensus	.112a	.142a	.002
Probability of Effect	.020	−0.086	.082
Temporal Immediacy	.062	.126a	.012
Proximity	.450b	.160a	.147a
Concentration of Effect	−0.027	.004	.050
R2	22.3%	23.7%	22.0%

Table 14.2 Means of ethical decision-making process

	Scenario 1* (Low moral intensity)		Scenario 2* (High moral intensity)	
	Mean	Score's level	Mean	Score's level
Ethical decision-making process:				
Ethical sensitivity	4.88	69.7%	5.17	73.9%
Ethical judgement	4.62	66.0%	5.11	73.0%
Ethical intention	4.45	63.6%	5.26	75.1%

high (> 66.67 per cent), moderate (33.33–66.66 per cent) and low (< 33.32 per cent). As depicted in Table 14.2, respondents reported relatively high levels (above 66.67 per cent) of ethical sensitivity for each scenario, which validates the ethical nature of the issues addressed in the scenarios. However, Scenario 2 is regarded as having higher level of auditors' ethical sensitivity as compared to Scenario 1 (73.9 per cent for Scenario 1 and 69.7 per cent for Scenario 2). Thus, this reflects the earlier notation in the current study that the issue of non-compliance (Scenario 2) is regarded as having more ethical concern among the auditors as compared to the issue of underreporting of time (Scenario 1). Notably, the auditors' ethical judgements and auditors' ethical intentions were also marked higher in Scenario 2 as compared to Scenario 1. These findings also revealed the fact that in a more ethical concern situation, respondents tend to make more ethical judgement, which will directly influence their intention to act ethically.

The results revealed that the auditors' perceptions for each of the moral intensity components appeared to vary between each scenario and their perceptions on the ethical decision-making process are influenced by the level of the ethical issue presented in the respective scenarios. The above findings clearly supported Jones' (1991) theory that individuals tend to perceive some situations as more 'morally intense' than others. In other words, the moral intensity of the issue itself does have a significant role and could influence the auditors in the ethical decision-making process as their attention to the issue is being directed by the embedded intensity level of the respective issues.

5   Conclusion

The results of the current study revealed that all the ethical issue characteristics (i.e. moral intensity components) measured were significantly different between the scenarios. These findings indicated that the auditors' perception for each of the moral intensity components appeared to vary between each scenario and were consistent with results by Leitsch (2006) and Sweeney and Costello (2009). However, the effects of certain moral intensity components on the ethical decision-making process are different as compared to previous studies (e.g. Singhapakdi et al., 1996; Leitsch, 2006; Sweeney and Costello, 2009). In both of the scenarios, the magnitude of consequences was found not significantly related in any of the three stages of the auditors' ethical decision-making process. On the other hand, social consensus has been identified as the most important component, and significantly affected the three stages of the auditors' ethical decision-making process (except for the impact on the ethical intentions in Scenario 2).

The importance of social consensus indicates that respondents' perceptions of society's attitudes to issues influence their decisions, and this is consistent with lower levels of cognitive moral development (Kohlberg, 1969; Rest, 1986). In addition, Barnett (2001) also pointed out that for respondents around the age of 20, it is expected that their beliefs about societal opinion would be a very important influence. The results of the current study are supported by the fact that more than half of the respondents (71 per cent) comprised the audit staff (audit assistant and audit senior) and had worked as an auditor for less than six years with an average age of 24 years old. Therefore, with these auditors' background, as being recognized by the Kholberg theory (1969) and Barnett (2001), their actions are being guided by perceived societal acceptance. Thus, this argument reasoned out the justification of having contradictory findings regarding the impact of the magnitude of consequences and social consensus on the three stages of Malaysian auditors' ethical decision-making process.

Another moral intensity component which significantly correlated with all three stages of auditors' ethical decision-making process in both scenarios is proximity. The results revealed that proximity has the strongest relationship throughout the three stages of the auditors' ethical decision-making process, which is inconsistent with previous studies (e.g. Singhapakdi et al., 1996; Sweeney and Costello, 2009). Jones (1991) claims that people care more about other people who are close to them (socially, culturally, psychologically or physically) than they do for people who are distant. Based on this assertion, Malaysian auditors seem to place a higher consideration on the proximity components as compared to other components of moral intensity. This might be due to the notion that Malaysian people are more considerate in making judgements when the consequences will affect the people who are close to them. The ethical values which Malaysian respondents held might be used to explain this finding. Malaysians are associated with such ethical values as respect for elders, maintaining harmonious relationships by not hurting others, being sensitive towards others' feelings and being tolerant (Asma, 1992). Therefore, these arguments supported the significant impact of proximity on the three stages of auditors' ethical decision-making (ethical sensitivity, ethical judgement and ethical intentions).

In conclusion, this current study extends the previous work on moral intensity by examining the influence of moral intensity components on the first three stages of the auditors' ethical decision-making process (i.e. ethical sensitivity, ethical judgement and ethical intentions) in a developing country. The findings presented above add to the existing accounting ethics literature by adding up the different effects of certain components on auditors' ethical decision-making as a result of the differences in environment and culture of the respondents. These findings suggest that future research needs to be done to further examine the possible effect of moral intensity construct on auditors' ethical decision-making. In other words, the results extend our understanding of moral intensity components' influence on the ethical decision-making process, particularly for the auditing profession. These findings can be used to enhance ethics coursework and training programs in educational settings and audit firms by highlighting the significant aspects of moral intensity components that could influence auditors in making ethical decisions, particularly in developing countries.

References

Asma, A. (1992). The influence of ethnic values on managerial practices in Malaysia. *Malaysian Management Review*, 27(1), 3–18.

Barnett, T. (2001). Dimensions of moral intensity and ethical decision-making: An empirical study. *Journal of Applied Social Psychology*, 31(5), 1038–57.

Barnett, T. and Valentine, S. (2004). Issue contingencies and marketers' recognition of ethical issues, ethical judgments and behavioral intentions. *Journal of Business Research*, 57, 338–46.

Bird, F. and Gandz, J. (1991). *Good Management: Business Ethics in Action*. Scarborough, ON: Prentice Hall.

Chia, A. and Mee, L.S. (2000). The effects of issue characteristics on the recognition of moral issues. *Journal of Business Ethics*, 27(3), 255–69.

Cohen, J.R. and Bennie-Martinov, N. (2006). The applicability of a contingent factors model to accounting ethics research. *Journal of Business Ethics*, 68, 1–18.

Craft, J.L. (2013). A review of the empirical ethical decision-making literature: 2004–2011. *Journal of Business Ethics*, 117, 221–59.

Hunt, S.D. and Vitell, S.J. (1986). A general theory of marketing ethics. *Journal of Macromarketing*, 6(1), 5–16.

Johari, R.J. (2013). Ethical decision making of Malaysian auditors. Doctoral thesis, Universiti Teknologi, MARA, Selangor, Malaysia.

Jones, J., Massey, D.W. and Thorne, L. (2003). Auditors' ethical reasoning: Insights from past research and implications for the future. *Journal of Accounting Literature*, 22, 45–103.

Jones, T.M. (1991). Ethical decision-making by individuals in organizations: An issue-contingent model. *Academy of Management: The Academy of Management Review*, 16(2), 366–95.

Kang, S.L. (2007, July 27). Steps to improve accounting firms. *New Straits Times*, 43.

Karcher, J.N. (1996). Auditors' ability to discern the presence of ethical problems. *Journal of Business Ethics*, 15, 1033–50.

Kohlberg, L. (1969). Stage and sequence: The cognitive-development approach to socialization, in D. Goslin (ed.), *Handbook of Socialization Theory and Research* (pp. 347-380). Chicago, IL: Rand McNally.

Leitsch, D.L. (2004). Differences in the perceptions of moral intensity in the moral decision process: An empirical examination of accounting students. *Journal of Business Ethics*, 53, 313–23.

Leitsch, D.L. (2006). Using dimensions of moral intensity to predict ethical decision-making in accounting. *Accounting Education*, 15(2), 135–49.

May, D.R. and Pauli, K.P. (2002). The role of moral intensity in ethical decision-making: A review and investigation of moral recognition, evaluation, and intention. *Business and Society*, 41(1), 85–118.

McMahon, J.M. and Harvey, R.J. (2007). The effect of moral intensity on ethical judgment. *Journal of Business Ethics*, 72, 335–357.

Mohamad Adam, B., Maisarah, M.S. and Ainun, A.M. (2002). Ethics and the accounting profession in Malaysia. Paper presented in AAAA Conference, 28–31 October, Nagoya, Japan.

Rest, J. (1986). *Moral Development: Advances in Research and Theory*. New York: Praeger.

Singhapakdi, A., Vitell, S.J. and Kraft, K.L. (1996). Moral intensity and ethical decision-making of marketing professionals. *Journal of Business Research*, 36(3), 245–55.

Sujatani, P. (2002). Andersen sued for RM350m. *The News Straits Times*, 30 June, pp. 1.

Sweeney, B. and Costello, F. (2009). Moral intensity and ethical decision-making: An empirical examination of undergraduate accounting and business students. *Accounting Education*, 18(1), 75–97.

Trevino, L.K. (1986). Ethical decision-making in organizations: A person-situation interactionist model. *The Academy of Management Review*, 11(3), 601–17.

Wright, G.B., Cullinan, C.P. and Bline, D.M. (1997). The relationship between an individual's value and perceptions of moral intensity: An empirical study. *Behavioral Research in Accounting*, 9, 26–41.

15 Human capital, governance and firms' performance in public listed companies in Malaysia

Is there a relationship?

Roshima Said and Noorain Omar

1 Introduction

One of the most extensively discussed topics in academic literature, the media and speeches by government regulators concerns how to properly structure the organization and put into place effective human capital and corporate governance characteristics to improve the firm's performance.

The current financial performance of many companies in Malaysia is worrying the government. More and more companies are experiencing bankruptcy, financial distress and being de-listed from the Bursa Malaysia. According to a report from Bursa Malaysia, many listed companies are not in a financially sound position. Even though at the date of listing, these companies must fulfil the Listing Requirements of Bursa Malaysia, given time, the company's financial position and business direction can change for better or for worse.

The listed companies that are in financial distress are classified by Bursa Malaysia as PN17. PN17 stands for Practice Note 17/2005 and is issued by Bursa Malaysia. PN17 companies need to submit a proposal to the Approving Authority to restructure and revive the company in order to maintain their listing status.

Human capital and corporate governance characteristics are believed to improve a firm's performance. Due to this belief, firms in developed and developing countries are putting more emphasis on human capital development. Firms are investing more resources in developing their human capital in expectation of improving the firm's performance.

Human capital development is a significant component of an overall effort to achieve cost-effectiveness and to improve a firm's performance. Hence, firms need to be aware of human capital characteristics that would improve employee satisfaction and improve a firm's performance (Marimuthu et al., 2009).

The importance of having good corporate governance has been a long-debated issue. Poor corporate governance has led to the collapse of many well-established companies, mainly in the USA and in the UK. In Malaysia, the corporate governance issue has become a significant focus following the 1997 Asian financial crisis (Shamsul Nahar, 2006).

Human capital is getting wider attention with the rise of globalization and also the diffusion of the job market due to the recent recession in the various economies of the world. Most countries around the world are devoting more time and effort to developing human capital in order to accelerate economic growth. Human capital can have a significant impact on a firm's performance.

Apart from human capital, good or bad corporate governance affects a firm's performance. This study investigates the relationship between human capital, corporate governance characteristics and a firm's performance.

2 Literature review

Past studies have found significant relationships between human capital and a firm's performance. Bontis and Fitzenz (2002) found that human capital has a direct relationship between intellectual capital assets and higher financial results per employee. The development of human capital is significantly influenced by the employee's educational level and satisfaction and eventually has a significant impact on the ROI of the firm.

Seleim et al. (2007) found that human capital indicators such as training and teamwork had a positive association with the performance of software companies. Additionally, results from a survey of 131 listed companies in China's small and medium-sized enterprises (hereinafter SME) board by Liu et al. (2010) supported the positive relationship between human capital and firm's performance.

The economic turmoil experienced by most Asian countries in 1997 and 1998 was believed to open the eyes of the corporate world to the importance of corporate governance. Subjects like transparency, accountability and disclosure received more attention than previously among government, the business community and the public. Corporate governance is the process and structure used to direct and manage the business and affairs of a company towards increasing profit and corporate accountability with the ultimate objective of realizing long-term shareholder value while taking into account interests of other stakeholders (MCCG, 2000). Good corporate governance is believed to reflect the image and values of a company and is one way to attract and restore the investors' confidence.

Adams and Mehran (2003) found that a higher number of outside directors on a corporate board has a positive effect on a firm's performance because the independent directors act as effective monitors of managers. However, Ponnu and Karthigeyan (2010) discovered that there no relationship between outside directors and corporate performance. The result of their study revealed that the number of outsiders did not improve a firm's performance.

Vethanayagam et al. (2006) examined the relationship between non-executive directors, managerial ownership and a firm's performance in Malaysian public listed companies. Their study used Tobin's Q as a measurement of a firm's performance in Malaysian public listed companies. The result of their study showed a nonlinear relationship between managerial ownership and firm's performance. Their study also revealed that the number of independent non-executive directors on the board did not contribute to the firm's performance.

Theoretical framework

Based on the literature review above, there is a need to study the relationship between human capital and corporate governance characteristics and its effect on a firm's performance. The conceptual framework below offers the conceptual foundation to examine and explore the relationship between human capital, corporate governance and a firm's performance.

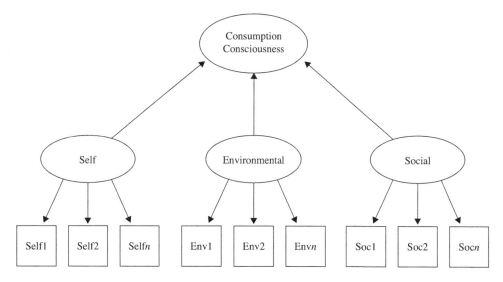

Figure 15.1 A proposed theoretical framework for factors influencing a firm's performance

In view of the literature that has been briefly reviewed, the following hypotheses were formulated to guide the study:

H1: The age of the chairman does have a significant impact on the firm's performance.
H2: The age of the CEO does have a significant impact on the firm's performance.
H3: The knowledge background of chairman does have a significant impact on the firm's performance.
H4: The knowledge background of the CEO does have a significant impact on the firm's performance.
H5: The proportion of female directors does have a significant impact on the firm's performance.
H6: The board size does have a significant impact on the firm's performance.
H7: The board independence does have a significant impact on the firm's performance.
H8: The managerial ownership does have a significant impact on the firm's performance.
H9: The top 10 largest shareholders do have a significant impact on the firm's performance.

3 Research methodology

This study uses correlational research design with which the association or correlation between two or more variables is established. It is a fact that when two or more variables are associated, it does not necessarily mean that one is a cause of the other(s). In addition, the study is cross-sectional, in which data is collected at one point in time.

Population and sampling

The population of this study comprises of all Main Market companies of Bursa Malaysia for the year ended 2009. This study will include all sectors in the Main Market. All financial companies will be excluded from this study due to dissimilar regulatory framework and governance environment.

The proportional stratified random sampling method is used in this study to determine the sample size of each sector of public listed companies in Main Board Companies in Malaysia. Using the recommended sampling method, 137 samples have been selected from the population of 863 of listed companies on Bursa Malaysia.

Unit of analysis

The unit of analysis of the study is the annual report of public listed companies in Main Market of Bursa Malaysia. The annual reports in 2009 were selected and examined. We analysed annual reports because they offer relevance and expedient proxy. In addition, the annual report is a highly useful source of information because managers commonly signal what is significant through the reporting mechanism. The annual report is also commonly recognized as the principal means for corporate communications.

Sample size

This study used a proportionate stratified random sampling of 137 Malaysian public listed companies. Sekaran (1992) states that:

> Stratified random sampling involves stratifying the elements along meaningful lines and taking proportionate or disproportionate samples from the strata. This sampling design is more efficient than the simple random sampling design because, for the same sample size, we get more representativeness from each important segment of the population and obtain more valuable and differentiated information with respect to each group.

Additionally, Roscoe's 'rules of thumb' are used to decide the sample size of the study. According to Roscoe (1975), the sample size should be not less than 80 companies. This study satisfied the rules of thumb since 137 companies were selected as a sample size, thus leading to, on average, about 28 per cent of companies for each sector in the Main Market of Bursa Malaysia (see Table 15.1).

The study is based on secondary data collected from the annual reports of companies in the Main Market of Bursa Malaysia Berhad. The sample data selected is from non-financial companies listed on the Main Market of Bursa Malaysia in 2009. In the study we selected five sectors to represent the sample data: Consumer Products, Industrial Products, Trading and Services, Construction and Technology.

Table 15.1 Sample size determination based on stratified sampling method

Sector	Total listed companies	Number of selected	Percent
Consumer Products	113	34	30%
Industrial Products	183	55	30%
Trading and Services	119	30	25%
Construction	43	10	23%
Technology	27	8	30%
Total	485	137	137/485=28%

Table 15.2 Measurement of dependent, independent and control variables

No	Independent variables	Measurement
1	Chairman/CEO age	Age
2	Chairman/CEO knowledge background	1 = SPM/ Diploma 2 = Degree 3 = Master/ Professional 4 = PhD
3	Proportion of female directors	Number of female directors divided by total number of board directors
4	Board size	Number of board members (Cheng and Courtenay, 2006; Said et al., 2009)
5	Board independence	Number of independent non-executive directors divided by total number of directors on board (%) (Eng and Mak, 2003; Gul and Leung, 2004; Haniffa and Cooke, 2005; Said et al., 2009)
6	Ownership concentration	Top 10 largest shareholders (Haniffa and Cooke, 2002; Mohd. Ghazali and Wheetman, 2006)
7	Firm's size	Total asset
8	Profitability	Return on asset (ROA), return on equity (ROE) and net profit margin (NPM) (Ho and Wong, 2001; Bliss and Balachandran, 2003; Eng and Mak, 2003; Mohd. Nasir and Abdullah, 2004; Haniffa and Cooke, 2005; Willekens et al., 2005; Barako et al., 2006).

Measurement of variables (dependent, independent and control variables)

The measurement of each variable is described in Table 15.2.

4   Data analysis

Statistical techniques

For the purpose of data analysis and hypothesis testing, the data collected were entered into Statistical Package for Social Sciences (SPSS) software. By using SPSS for Windows Release 12.0, several statistical techniques were used, such as descriptive statistics, correlation and hierarchical regression, and other appropriate methods, in order to test the hypothesis.

Regression analysis

Multiple regressions analysis was used to test the hypothesized relationships between the independent variables (predictor) and the dependent variables (criterion) (Hair et al., 2006). According to Pallant (2005), multiple regressions is not just one technique but a family of techniques that can be used to explore the relationship between one continuous dependent variable and a number of independent variables. Thus, in order to test the hypotheses, regression analysis is used to find how much of the variance of firm's performance is explained by the corporate governance and human capital characteristics.

In this study, hierarchical multiple regression analysis was carried out to examine the strength of the relationship between corporate governance and human capital characteristics with a firm's performance, as controlled by the firm's size in Malaysian public listed companies for the year ended 2009. Incorporating all these variables, the formula for the regression is as follows:

FP = $\beta_0 + \beta_1$BD SIZE + β_2NED + β_3 CONCERN + β_4MGR OS + β_5AGECHAIR + β_6AGECEO + β_7KNLDGECHAIR + β_8KNLDGECEO + β_9PROPFEMALE + β_{10}TA + $\bar{e}$

FP: FIRM'S PERFORMANCE

β_1BD SIZE: Board Size

β_2NED: Percentage of non-executive directors to total directors

β_3 CONCERN: Ownership concentration

β_4MGR OS: Managerial ownership

β_5AGECHAIR; Age CHAIR

β_6AGECEO: Age CEO

β_7KNLDGECHAIR: Chairman's knowledge background

β_8KNLDGECEO: CEO's knowledge background

β_9PROPFEMALE: Percentage of female director to total directors

β_{10}: TA proxy for firm's size

$\bar{e}$: Error term

---

5   Findings of the study

Descriptive analysis

The descriptive statistics of the independent variables and control variables are given in Table 15.3; it comprises presentation of frequencies, mean, maximum, minimum and standard deviation of metric variables. The independent variables are net profit, total assets, return on assets, total of equity, return on equity, sales, net profit margin, age of chairman, age of CEO, board size, total of female directors, proportion of female directors to total directors, total of independent directors, proportion of independent executive directors to total directors, managerial ownership and top 10 ownership concentration.

In Table 15.3, the descriptive statistic of board characteristics shows that the board size varies from 4 to 13 with a mean of 7.365. The proportion of independent directors varies from 0 to 75 percent. The mean of proportion of independent directors, 39.54 per cent, revealed that the proportion of independent non-executive directors fulfils the listing requirement in Malaysian Code of Corporate Governance, i.e. one-third of board directors are independent directors. The chairman age ranges from 35 to 87 with a mean value of 60.13, and the CEO age ranges from 36 to 80 with a mean value of 54.28. The proportion of female directors ranges from 0 to 34 per cent with a mean value of 8.91 per cent. This shows that Malaysian public listed companies have a higher proportion of males in the boardroom. The control variable, represented by total assets of the company, shows that the range is from RM2,717,545.00 to RM5,261,184,000.00 with a mean value RM215,370,312.28.

Table 15.3 Descriptive statistics for independent variables and control variables

	N	Minimum	Maximum	Mean	Standard Deviation
NP	137	−139654000.00	1375476000.00	17326099.85	124648873.10
TOTASSETS	137	2717545.00	5261184000.00	215370312.28	464076610.85
ROA	137	−38.81	1.78	−.2765	3.33437
CSEQUITY	137	7954397.00	3814949000.00	152710010.26	331247483.33
ROE	137	−4.84	5.14	.021	.72
SALES	137	3200.00	1375857000.00	72916535.40	163016011.63
NPM	137	−191.72	10.24	−3.65	23.26
AGECHAIR	137	35.00	87.00	60.13	8.78
AGECEO	137	36.00	80.00	54.28	8.01
BDSIZE	137	4.00	13.00	7.365	1.83
FEMALEDIR	137	.00	3.00	.58	.78
PROPFEMALE	137	.00	0.34	.09	.15
BDINDEP	137	.00	6.00	2.83	.98
PROPINDEP	137	.00	.75	.10	.13
MGRIALOWN	137	.00	58.79	14.57	15.71
OWNCONCERN10	137	21.94	98.32	63.45	15.95

Table 15.4 Model summary

Model	R	R Square	Adjusted R Square	Standard Error of the Estimate	Change Statistics					Durbin-Watson
					R Square Change	F Change	df1	df2	Sig. F Change	
1	.540[a]	.292	.285	1.34102	.292	39.572	1	96	.000	
2	.644[b]	.414	.340	1.28844	.123	1.800	10	86	.073	2.249

***p < 0.01, ** p < 0.05, * p < 0.10

a Predictors: (Constant), logtotalassets
b Predictors: (Constant), logtotalassets, FEDIR, AGECHAIR, KBCHAIR, OC10, MGRIALOWN, AGECEO, BDSIZE, KBCEO, PROPFE
c Dependent Variable: logNP (Firm's Performance)

Hypotheses testing

The result of regression in Table 15.4 indicated that the estimated equation is statistically significant at less than 1 per cent level (p < 0.01) with F value for all models ranging from 1.80 to 39.52. This indicates that the model as a whole for Model 1 and Model 2 is significant. The reported D-W value is 2.249 (which is close to 2) in Table 15.4 and suggests that the residuals are reasonably independent of each other.

Model 1 shows regression analysis with one control variable, namely the firms' size (natural log total assets). The model is significant with R square 0.0.292, adjusted R square = 0.285,

R square change = 0.292 and F value = 39.57. The result showed that the control variable, namely total assets (β = +0.542, p < 0.01), was found to be significant at p < 0.01.

In Model 2, the independent variables are included in the model together with the control variables. The model shows the evidence of direct relationship between independent variables and dependent variables after statistically controlling for the four control variables total assets (natural log total assets). The model improved significantly with R square = 0.414, adjusted R square = 0.340, R square change = 0.123, F value = 1.80. The result shows that the control variable, namely total assets (β = +0.510, p < 0.01), were found to be significant at p < 0.01. In this model, the most significant independent variable that influenced the firm's performance is the chairman's knowledge background, and it is positively correlated with β = +0.18, p < 0.10. The chairman's age is positively correlated with β = +0.16, p < 0.10. The result indicates that the more knowledgeable the chairman and the older the chairman, the higher the firm's performance.

However, the result showed that the age of the CEO, the knowledge background of the CEO, the board size, the proportion of female directors, the managerial ownership and the ownership concentration do not significantly relate to the firm's performance. Therefore, the hypotheses H1 and H3 are accepted, while hypotheses H2, H4, H5, H6, H7, H8 and H9 are rejected.

In Model 2, by adding the model variables together with the control variable, the R square has increased to 12.2 per cent and the R square change is 5.50 per cent and is significant. This implies that the additional 5.5 per cent of the variation in a firm's performance is explained by model variables. In addition, the R square change of 5.50 per cent means that the model variables explain an additional 5.50 per cent of the variance in firm's performance even when the effect of firm's size is statistically controlled for.

6   Discussion and conclusion

Discussion

The current study extends the prior studies on the inclusion of human capital characteristics as a factor that influences a firm's performance. As for the relationship between human capital characteristics, corporate governance characteristics and a firm's performance, the most significant variables that influence the firm's performance are the knowledge background of the chairman and the age of the chairman. These two variables are the element of human capital characteristics. Knowledge background in this study refers to the academic qualifications of the chairman such as SPM degree, master's degree or PhD. Greater age is believed to be strongly related to wider experience and a higher level of expertise.

The results of this study are consistent with the findings of Hambrick and Mason (1984), Bontis and Fitzenz (2002) and Seleim, Ashour and Bontis (2007). The characteristics of a chairman such as age and knowledge background play an important role in ensuring the success of the business. An older, more educated chairman is wise in planning and drafting strategy to ensure better performance and long-term survival of the company. In fact, Part 2: Best Practices in Corporate Governance, of the Malaysian Code of Corporate Governance states under appointments to the board that the nominating committee should recommend the candidate who possesses the most skills, knowledge, expertise, experience, professionalism and integrity.

In this study, it can be noticed that corporate governance characteristics are no longer significant in influencing a firm's performance compared to a decade ago. In Malaysia, the Code of Corporate Governance was introduced in 2000. It has been well developed in most companies, which are already aware of the importance of good corporate governance. Hence, the corporate governance characteristics are no longer significant.

Based on the above argument, we can see that human capital characteristics do enhance a firm's performance directly and indirectly. This study intends to integrate human capital as a predictor of a firm's performance in Malaysian listed companies. As an important mechanism in achieving competitive advantage and improving a firm's performance, human capital must be continuously improved.

Implications

This study has some important implications that are relevant in many countries irrespective of whether they are developing or developed countries. It provides strong evidence to show that the age and knowledge of the chairman are significant variables in ensuring a firm's performance. This study is useful to search committees in Malaysia in identifying the person to be appointed as chairman in the future.

Limitations

The main limitation of the study is small sample size, which may affect the degree of representation of the population. For future research, it is suggested that the sample size is increased so that it becomes a better representation of the population. In addition, the future researcher should also include other variables such as a firm's characteristics or conduct the study by comparing a firm's performance of Shari'ah and non-Shari'ah compliance companies.

References

Adams, R.B. and Mehran, H. (2003). Is corporate governance different for bank holding companies? Working paper, Federal Reserve Bank of New York.

Barako, D.G., Hancock, P. and Izan, H.Y. (2006). Relationship between corporate governance attributes and voluntary disclosures in annual reports: The Kenyan experience. *Financial Reporting, Regulation and Governance*, 5(1), 1–26.

Bliss, M. and Balachandran, J. (2003). CEO duality, audit committee independence and voluntary disclosures in Malaysia. Paper presented at International Conference on 'Quality Financial Reporting and Corporate Governance-Building Public Trust, Integrity and Accountability', Kuala Lumpur, Malaysia.

Bontis, N. and Fitzenz, J. (2002). Intellectual capital ROI: A casual map of human capital antecedents and consequents. *Journal of Intellectual Capital*, 3(3), 223–47.

Cheng, E.C.M. and Courtenay, S.M. (2006). Board composition, regulatory regime and voluntary disclosure. *The International Journal of Accounting*, 41, 262–89.

Eng, L.L. and Mak, Y.T. (2003). Corporate governance and voluntary disclosure. *Journal of Accounting and Public Policy*, 22(4), 325–45.

Gul, F.A. and Leung, S. (2004). Board leadership, outside directors' expertise and voluntary disclosures. *Journal of Accounting and Public Policy*, 23, 351–79.

Hair, J.F., Black, W.C., Babin, B.J., Anderson, R.E. and Tatham, R.L. (2006). *Multivariate Data Analysis*, 6th edn. Upper Saddle River, NJ: Pearson/Prentice Hall.

Hambrick, D. and Mason, P. (1984). Upper echelons: The organization as a reflection of its top managers. *Academy of Management Review*, 9(2), 193–206.

Haniffa, R.M. and Cooke, T.E. (2002). Culture, corporate governance and disclosure in Malaysian corporations. *Abacus*, 38(3), 317–48.

Haniffa, R.M. and Cooke, T.E. (2005). The impact of culture and corporate governance on corporate social reporting. *Journal of Accounting and Public Policy*, 24, 391–430.

Ho, S.M. and Wong, K.S. (2001). A Study of the relationship between corporate governance structures and the extent of voluntary disclosure. *Journal of International Accounting, Auditing & Taxation*, 10, 139–56.

Liu, D., Liang, Y., Zhang, L. and Zhang, Y. (2010, June). The effects of human capital on competitive strategies and performance: Evidence from listed companies in China's SME Board. In *Management of Innovation and Technology (ICMIT), 2010 IEEE International Conference in Singapore on* (pp. 670-675).

Marimuthu, M., Arokiasamy, L. and Ismail, M. (2009). Human capital development and its impact on firm performance: Evidence from developmental economics. *The Journal of International Social Research*, 2(8), 265–72.

Mohd. Ghazali, N.A. and Wheetman, P. (2006). Perpetuating traditional influences: Voluntary disclosure in Malaysia following the economic crisis. *Journal of International Accounting, Auditing and Taxation*, 15(2), 226–48.

Mohd. Nasir, N. and Abdullah, S.N. (2004). Voluntary disclosure and corporate governance among financially distressed firms in Malaysia. *Financial Reporting, Regulation & Governance*, 3(1), 1–44.

Pallant, J. (2005). *SPSS Survival Manual: A Step by Step Guide to Data Analysis Using SPSS for Windows Version 12.* Crows Nest, NSW: Allen & Unwin.

Ponnu, C.H. and Karthigeyan, R.M. (2010). Board independence and corporate performance: Evidence from Malaysia. *African Journal of Business Management*, 4(6), 858–68.

Roscoe, J.T. (1975). *Fundamental Research Statistics for the Behavioural Sciences*, 2nd edn. New York: Holt Rinehart & Winston.

Said, R., Omar, N. and Nailah Abdullah, W. (2013). 'Empirical investigations on boards, business characteristics, human capital and environmental reporting', *Social Responsibility Journal*, 9(4), pp. 534–553. doi: 10.1108/srj-02-2012-0019.

Sekaran, U. (1992). *Research Methods for Business.* New York: John Wiley.

Seleim, A., Ashour, A. and Bontis, N. (2007). Human capital and organizational performance: A study of Egyptian software companies. *Management Decisions*, 45(4), 789–801.

Shamsul Nahar, A. (2006). Board structure and ownership in Malaysia: The case of distressed listed companies. *Corporate Governance Journal*, 6(5), 582–94.

Vethanayagam, K., Yahya, S. and Haron, H. (2006). Independent non-executive directors, managerial ownership and firm performance in Malaysian public listed companies. Paper presented at 5th One Day Symposium on Accountability, Governance & Performance: Achieving Excellence, Sofitel, Brisbane. Retrieved 13 August 2006, from http://www.griffith.edu.au/school/gbs/afe/symposium/2006/proceedings/.

Willekens, M., Bauwhede, H.V., Gaeremynck, A. and Van De Gucht, L. (2005). Internal and external governance and the voluntary disclosure of financial and non-financial performance. Paper presented at BAA Auditing SIG Conference 2005, 15th National Auditing Conference. Aston Business School, Birmingham, UK, March 11–12.

Part IV

Sustainability and management in Australia, the USA and Brazil

16 A narrative on teaching sustainability

Maria Lai-ling Lam and Martha J.B. Cook

1 Introduction

Back in the olden days, this author taught what was called a mixed fifth and sixth grade – the overflow of the regular fifth grade and sixth grade classes. She was new to the school, so she didn't know that she had been given the students the other teachers didn't want. One of those fifth grade students fit well into the broad example of sustainability. He wore glasses that were given to the family by the Lions Club, a community service group which commonly donates eyeglasses to the needy. They were much too large for his face, so his peers called him 'Old Owl Face'. The teacher suspected the unwanted nickname provoked the boy to act up. On this particular day, during an arithmetic lesson, the teacher was just behind the boy's seat when he took off his hated glasses and threw them at the chalkboard, which illustrated a problem he couldn't solve. As he left his seat, she grasped his shirt collar and with her best bowling swing she aimed for his derriere. Then she made the mistake of letting go of his collar. Suddenly, his body wasn't there to offset her swing! She fell flat on her face on the wooden floor, hitting her nose, which started to bleed. The class was deathly quiet except for some tippytoe steps coming toward her. She looked up just as Old Owl Face looked down at her. He said to her, 'Teacher, you are going to have to get faster or else I am going to have to slow down'. Trying hard not to laugh, she said, 'I will remember that'. The profound dialogue between student and teacher held a message that contained an insightful thought: today, young people will have to slow down and old people will have to keep pace if we expect to sustain equilibrium (Cook, 2013).

Most definitions of sustainability in marketing education draw on the definition of sustainable development given by the Brundtland Commission: 'Sustainable development is development that meets the needs of the present without compromising the ability of future generations to meet their needs' (World Commission on Environment and Development, 1987: 7). Many scholars and educators have proposed a transformative paradigm in sustainability and explored the role of marketing in fostering the adoption of sustainable products and practices (Carlson on Sustainability conference, 2010; Cook and Lam, 2012; Ehrenfeld, 2008; World Economic Forum, 2010). Marketing educators are called to help individuals, organizations, and societies move from incremental to a transformative sustainability future through more 'innovative, interdisciplinary, practice-oriented, and eternal communication efforts' (Starik, Rands, Marcus, and Clark, 2010: 382). In this chapter, the authors will adopt a narrative approach as the research methodology. Our definition of sustainability is 'to educate our students to know how to build on the best of the past, adapt and meld it with the present and sustain it for the future'. We will share insights to develop students' knowledge, skills, and practices to become responsible consumers and decision-makers. This book chapter is grounded on our combined total of 80 years in management education, insights, and extensive literature review. It covers five areas: literature review, our professional experience (i.e., research methodology), our beliefs (i.e., prescriptive knowledge), pedagogical strategies (i.e., normative knowledge), and reflections and discussion (i.e., contribution and future research).

2   Literature review on pedagogy of sustainability management education

Several management educators have urged students to pursue triple bottom lines: economic, environmental, and social sustainability through experiential learning, multidisciplinary teaching, transformation paradigms, new metaphors, holistic education, system-thinking, and innovative collaborative approaches (Bradbury, 2003; Gundlach and Aivnuska, 2010; Kurland, Michaud, Best, Wohldmann, Cox, Pontikis, and Vasishth, 2010; Welsh and Murray, 2003). They all propose various pedagogies such as system-thinking, interactional expertise, critical pedagogy, and learner-centred pedagogies for sustainability education. However, our current quantitative, technical, or economical approaches to teaching and learning within a marketing curriculum do not correspond with sustainability, which is based on the whole-person approach, stakeholders' perceptions, and clarification of values (Benn and Marin, 2010; Lam, 2005). Furthermore, many proven pedagogies in the aforementioned research of management education for sustainability need to be re-examined with regard to their impact on the sustainability of the brain. Sustainability marketing education may not sustain the students' brain when many basic values and practices necessary to sustain life are not well managed (Pruzan, 2008; Vaill, 1996, 2003, 2007). Being mindful of the values and practices of sustaining the brain in human history will enable students and educators to use technology wisely in their sustainability education (Eshelman, Lam, and Cook, 2012). Sustainability of the brain requires that learners acquire the ability to focus (Tippett and Diamond, 2009).

Sadly, human beings tend to be measured according to their consumption power in our marketing curriculum. Seniors are valued, not by their wisdom, but by their purchasing power. The learning experiences that seniors can sustain for over 70 years need to be explored and respected in an American society that faces many unprecedented changes. We, two professional educators, propose that sustainability must utilize the brains of all generations, not just the existing target generations described in American marketing textbooks. According to research on U.S. age trends, marketers mainly target five major numerically classified generations: seniors (born before 1946), baby boomers (born between 1946 and 1964), generation X (born between 1965 and 1976), generation Y (born between 1977 and 1994), and teens (born between 1995 and 2000). The last two generations are also called millennials, and many are involved in changing the world through environmental sustainability (Kerin, Hartley, and Rudelius, 2011: 71). We advocate the broader view of sustainability that includes the development and collaboration of the brain of each generation, including preschoolers, if we really want "sustainability" to be not just a buzzword but a major part of our lives. Each person has been gifted with a brain and each must appreciate, sustain, or lose it as he or she matures.

3   Professional experience of two authors

Author Cook from a Western culture is a professor and has more than 60 years of classroom experience in the development of the potential of future generations to flourish and to comprehend and demonstrate a deep understanding of sustainability in terms of personal growth, interpersonal relationships, community participation, and conservation. Her research work on bibliotherapy (Cook, 1979) and her book entitled Grammar toward Professionalism (Cook, 2006) used comparative ideas and "scaffolding" to increase the effectiveness of our human brains in the journey toward sustainability. She has written a grammar book, *Grammar toward Professionalism* (Cook, 2006), not the most popular subject in education, but she used the concept of sustainability throughout the book: memorizing the kind of nouns c2ap (common collective abstract proper) is a sustainable 'hint' acronym using a chemistry formula to provide a memory scaffold; she uses facts to teach sentences which contain knowledge for other academic subjects (A kangaroo is a marsupial); she uses colour coding to emphasize what should be taught each year of formal education (pink and blue are kindergarten and first grade); she uses Maslow's Hierarchy of Needs as a pattern for basics to useful sustainability (words, phrases, sentences, punctuation, organization, presentation); she keys her comments on an evaluated paper to the page number in the book so that the user must do research to learn the 'why' of the error and its correction. There is little sustainability unless there is 'scaffolding' to recall facts necessary to sustain, recall, or research information throughout life. As previously stated, we all have been gifted with a human brain and we must appreciate, sustain, or lose it.

The other author has an Eastern culture background and has taught business education at the U.S. undergraduate and graduate levels for more than 10 years. Since 2006 she has presented papers at numerous sustainability conferences globally, and has spent seven years researching the practices of foreign multinational enterprises' corporate social responsibility in a developing country (Lam, etc., 2006, 2010; Lam, 2006; 2007a; 2007b; 2008a; 2008b; 2009; 2010a; 2010b; 2010c; 2011a; 2011b; 2011c; 2012a, 2012b). She has asked her undergraduate and graduate students to reflect upon the challenges of learning sustainability in marketing courses. Many students are overloaded with conflicting information about sustainability and feel they do not know how to choose and practice sustainability in a quick-paced, efficiency-oriented environment. They perceive that the university education does not acknowledge the importance of sustainability of the body, mind, and resources. Sadly, the resource of technology is not regarded as a tool but as an end for sustainability. To use technology at a faster rate is how people are considered to be better consumers (Hoyer and MacInnis, 2007: 431). There is no question about personhood or human beings working properly in the efficient system (Eshelman, Lam, and Cook, 2012). As one author, coming from a developing country, treasures education and practices yoga every day, she has seen so much waste in many young people's lives when they are handling multiple tasks at a faster speed and are conditioned to be bombarded by many technical designs. The experiences of silence and deep breaths are very rare to her students.

The authors have had an ongoing discussion for the past three years about our students' learning and the challenges of teaching sustainable development. One co-author edited another author's graduate students' papers concerning sustainability. Our in-depth discussion in the area of sustainability enables us to know how to maintain liberal arts and moral education as a core in our teaching institution when the complexities and uncertainties of the business world have been trivialized and decontextualized by the prevalent analytical models and reductionist paradigms in our current marketing education.

4   Our beliefs

The prominent concepts of sustainability tend to be constrained to materialistic matters. Not often do we think of the brain as one of those sustainable resources which needs further thought. When one thinks of the brain, there are usually derogative nouns such as nerd, geek, square, wise guy, smart alec, and, now and then, positive words such as 'intellectual' or 'gray matter.' Let us consider that wonderfully created organ as we would our biceps, derriere, mammary endowment or our entire 'bod.' Is it possible to convince people that sustainability of the brain needs constant exercise to meet the acceleration of the technologies? We have a biological organ that meets all specifications for sustained learning; are we going to replace it or diminish it with machine intelligence? Can't one enhance the other if the exercise is equally distributed and in chronological order – biological first; machine second? Some parts of the body cannot be flexed in front of the mirror and for that reason some parts, equally necessary, are not exercised because of 'hidden viewability' and even worse 'verbal negativity.' We believe that teaching sustainability in marketing needs to address how to guide students to exercise their brains before they use the machines. One author's dissertation (Cook op. cit.) about acceptance of death and dying has proved statistically that one has a greater emotional platform to solve emotional problems by reading about how others have been helped. We believe that the power of the printed word, sustained in the human brain, is one of the most powerful tools for solving problems. The power has been elaborated more in a testimony in Appendix A. Sustaining our brains through printed words increases our resilience to many changes that assault our values in business organizations. Sustainability is also related to our spirituality development (Pruzan, 2008; Vaill, 1996, 2007). Brain and body must be coordinated and complemented. Do we underestimate the capability and usefulness of the brain and overemphasize the capability of the viewable body in neo-American culture in contrast to the mature culture of older countries?

As professional educators, we believe the inherent potentialities of human beings and the reflective abilities of our students will lead them to find multiple alternatives toward solving existing problems. Our interpretation of sustainability includes the perspective of continual exercising of basic assets and conservatively or prudently using the existing resources for the greater good. Students need to learn to know how to sustain their lives, personal relationships, communities, organizations, and environment through reciprocal experiential learning exercises. We also believe that honest marketing can play a significant role in bringing sustainable solutions to consumers and other stakeholders; the effectiveness of teaching sustainability in management education needs to examine the previous and existing education students have. The two authors believe that we need to educate our students to know how to build on the best of history, adapt and meld it with reality, and sustain it for the future. This can be accomplished in many ways and with many tools but the tools must be used constructively and chronologically – no shortcuts.

We don't spend all our lives in the classroom; there is life after formal education. Statistically people are living longer, so this becomes as important as the preservation of water, the conservation of the soil, and global health issues which need to be solved by sustainability. All ages of people need to be informed. Never stop learning! The brain needs to be exercised even more when years make the biceps, the derriere, the mammary endowment, and the looks of the 'bod' not so important. Now, priceless experiences, informative reading, comprehensive listening, and discretional viewing should become prevalent so that the brain keeps active commensurate with the length of life. We also believe that pedagogical strategies complemented with physical 'workouts' should be concomitantly practised.

5   Pedagogical strategies

The basic focus of our pedagogical strategies is to affirm each student's worth and to inspire him or her to form the desire for sustainability and exercise his or her brain. There are four basic learning strategies: learning from the past, from service, from mentors, and from critical research. These strategies are grounded on the principles of self-reflection, listening, and constructive collaborative learning. Students are also guided to learn how to develop multiple dialogues with multiple stakeholders, integrate multiple perspectives, and reflect what personal values individuals treasure in the business world and beyond. When students are provided many opportunities to work with people who are different from themselves, they exercise their brains and develop deeper insights about the complexity of practising sustainability in organizations.

6   Learning from history

In a major activity, undergraduate students were asked to visit two museums of interest to them and reflect on how a new understanding of sustainable consumption behaviour had changed their attitudes and behaviours in their personal and professional lives. Students presented their experiences and reciprocally changed the attitudes of other students in taking care of things (sustainability) and not trying to keep up with all things that are trendy (fads). Through the learning of history, including sports history, in our local museums, one student interpreted sustainability as teamwork and persistence. One student planned to eat more locally grown food and to avoid wasting food by planning ahead. One student perceived that she could infuse sustainability concepts into her fashion business. In summation, the theme of "caring" emerges among all students' presentations. They learn that sustainability has diversified dimensions, both physically and mentally. Basic examples of their perceptions may clarify the term "sustainability" differently:

> Student #1: Sustainability means to be frugal, to take care of things, and to be grateful.
>   Student #2: Sustainable consumption means taking good care of what you have, to make what you have last by making the most of what you have and not wasting any resources.
>   Student #3: Feel grateful for what you have.

After the presentations, students chose two museums as their service-learning projects and developed collaborative work with the clients. The process is to help students learn how to meet the needs of the present by examining the past and through museum learning projects, relating the best of the past to the present and sustaining development of learning into the future.

7   Learning from service

One author guided her undergraduate and graduate students to serve the local community through more than 40 client-based marketing projects. These projects focused on helping those in need. They included the topics of cultivating community gardens, encouraging corporate wellness programs, using horses for therapy, identifying and helping homeless people, organizing veterans' events, and serving other disadvantaged groups in the community. Students are asked to serve the community through the development of relevant marketing plans for clients. They present their literature reviews and marketing solutions to the clients through two presentations. Some undergraduate and graduate students learn how they are trapped in the industrial agricultural system and become conscious of their unsustainable lifestyles. Many students learn the joy of seeking something bigger than themselves and learn to be grateful to the community when they are marketers. Through these service-learning projects, they can develop a proactive attitude towards the solidarity of a community and are inspired to seek the common good of the residents with a sense of personal and communal growth. Furthermore, they also understand how to mobilize people to have pro-social behaviour through community service projects. The collaborative learning experiences lead them to appreciate different perspectives, and the know-how to establish harmonious relationships among people in a learning community. They learn how to respectfully confront people in the process of solving conflicts and to include people of different abilities in their projects. The habit to do service will become their second nature if their future employers will develop sustainability through community service projects. This student quotation summarizes well the reflections of the majority:

> Now that our class has ended, I want to extend my thanks for your work in the class. It was a difficult class that required significant effort, but the hardest part for me was choosing between letting the learning change my life or just getting through the material and assignments and moving on. I decided to open myself to learning what God was teaching me and acknowledged that I had unsustainable areas in my life that needed to change. I have begun to change and realize that the changes need to be for the rest of my life. (student #4)

8   Learning from mentors

At the beginning of this undergraduate business course, students are encouraged to find mentors from whom they can learn sustainable management initiatives that they want to cultivate in an educational relationship during the semester. They have to interview for at least half an hour a successful business person and learn how the chosen mentor integrates faith with his or her professional and personal life. Most students interview their parents or close friends and appreciate the opportunity to understand in depth about their mentors. They learn that these mentors are imperfect human beings but are proud of doing sustainable business. They are asked to think about what kind of person they would like to be, to imagine the future situations in which they can use their learning, and to describe their personal vision and professional code of ethics.

Before they submitted their final papers, they discussed their drafts with their peers and had opportunities to articulate their own insights to their peers. They also publicized their code of ethics in the class and learned to internalize positive values. In the meantime, one author encouraged them to review an ethics statement given by the founder of Chick-fil-A, or previous classmates, and some sustainable organizations. She also challenged them to think in depth about their own values and their identities when she commented on their papers. Furthermore, she encouraged students to contact these mentors again and reflect on their own personal growth. Students learned why these mentors liked to help young people to be successful and had hope and faith in them. These multigenerational interactions showed them the meaning of sustainability in their lives. Thus, the process of meeting mentors and writing their own papers is designed to awaken their conscience and affirm their own worth in the journey of sustainability. This quotation summarizes well the reflections of many undergraduate students in this assignment:

> In the interview, I learned some very valuable knowledge about business. In all of my classes . . . we are told stories of the unethical practices businesses perform in today's markets. It seems that in most illustrations in our books that the company owners are often depicted as greedy, faithless, mean people. However, in my interview, I found that business owners can be very friendly, caring people who care for their employees more than their profit. (student #7)

Students also learn why they are energized by good business practices of their mentors. They learn to discern what kinds of organizations in which to work so that their gifts and talents can be nurtured and developed. They also learn the importance of sustaining the best of their lives through the values and organizations. When they can find an organization that does the kind of work in which they really believe and is needed in a resource-constrained world, then they can find it rewarding to be leaders in that context (Vaill, 2003). They are also encouraged to revise their papers and ask for feedback from their mentors. The experience of reciprocity is also a way to learn sustainability. Indeed, many of students' experiences were a part of their training from birth through their prior schooling. Now, through these exercises, in their mind "sustainability" has culminated in a mature outlook.

9   Learning from critical research

The buzzword "sustainability" must involve a decision about what we want to sustain, how we want to sustain it, and what we need to sustain it. How are power and the language of sustainability being used to perpetuate the existing operational paradigm – the high-input/high-output efficiency model – without treating the Earth as an asset in our balance sheet? Critical research leads students to question the assumptions of existing market mechanisms, their values, and many "green-washing" activities. Undergraduate and graduate students must be critical and reflective concerning sustainable business practices. They are exposed to the problems of current operation paradigms in consumption and production behaviour through experiential learning and videos, including *The Story of Stuff* (Leonard, 2007). Later, they have to examine the basic assumptions in the existing operation paradigm – the maximization of shareholders' interests – in their individual assignments and group projects.

Graduate students are usually employed adults and are thus generally more mature than undergraduate students. In addition, they have more in-depth experiences and opportunities to examine their own companies' sustainable practices. Through their research papers concerning the best sustainable practices of companies in their industry, they gain more knowledge and understanding of the limitations of their companies' practices in the existing operation paradigm. They can challenge existing assumptions and learn the complexity of implementing sustainability in their organizations. The more students can relate the practices of sustainability to their life experiences, the more receptive they are to the idea of sustainability and the more they realize that sustainability has been around for a long time.

10   Reflections

Aging is a natural teacher of sustainability. From birth, one's future depends on environment (atmospheric and familial); health issues (genetic and self-imposed); nourishment (physical and mental); intellect (used and misused). In the pre-classroom through post-classroom, sustainability becomes a recall of past learning, a present with new adventures, and a future based on what we sustained from birth. The parallel of sustainability in the classroom is much more controllable than in the business world. Decisions based on marketing of products take on a new meaning of sustainability.

> Have we equipped the brain with judgement of essentials – I need as opposed to I want?
> Have we been taught tolerance, patience, self reliance, and priorities?
> These may seem to be abstractions until we look at the use of our time as we age.

Digital information has challenged the productivity and longevity of the brain. Moderation now seems to be the correct abstraction to become a 'buzz' word as how we recognize, materialize, and supervise the use of modern 'short cuts.' Marketing entices – 'I want'; brainpower chooses – 'I need.' Turn off the cell phone when not needed; prioritize the use of the computer to put family matters first. Limit multitasking to a maximum of two items and only when absolutely necessary. The brain is 'wired' to adapt but not beyond its original genetic possibilities; aging takes its toll in sustainability; use the brain or lose it; moderation in all things; sustainability in necessities.

As the field of sustainable development emerges, it needs students to be more exposed to good practices in this area and develop a keen interest before they are committed to becoming leaders. Whenever we choose to practice sustainability in our marketing education, we must embrace the brains of all generations. It needs more courage and faith of business educators to teach transformative sustainability when the domain of knowledge is emerging and can easily be overshadowed by the accessibility of technology. The dynamic and complex nature of sustainable development will never be understood by one discipline or one generation. Many instructors at many levels of education need to keep on learning and leading students to know how to discern what information needs to be treasured and to be explored in depth. Unfortunately most people do not consciously realize that each individual is equipped with a brain and that it needs exercise throughout life.

Professional educators need to question the assumption that students know how to transfer their education into the business world. We also need to examine many questions of education in our students' lives and think about what kinds of habits they have accumulated when they come to our courses in higher education. What basic skills have been missed or forgotten? What basic skills have been stored in the brain and need retrieved to judge the existing operating paradigm? Will our students rely on the easiest and cheapest ways to function with the illusion of the power of technology in their journey of sustainability? Professional management educators need to reflect the practices that may be repeating the same operating paradigm – efficiency at the expense of innate assets, especially our brains. Do we model to our students that there is no shortcut path to learning? Do we lead our students to have basic knowledge etched in their left and right sections of the brains (Thompson, 2010)? Do we tell our students to use the brain storage first, machine storage second? Do we use traditional educational methods, such as reading parables and biographies, memorizing chemistry formulae, printing as well as cursive writing, memorizing multiplication tables, and then sustaining the knowledge to complement the use of machines? In the journey of sustainability, we should ask more educational questions and examine our practices which will provide room for transformative sustainable practices – if we really want to solve the real-world problems through marketing education.

11   Discussion

In this chapter, we shared our thoughts on sustainability and our practices of sustainability education in marketing. We invite marketing educators to sustain the brain in sustainability education. But will sustainability education lead students to more unsustainable consumption behaviour or production decisions when this information is not paced, managed, and reflected?

In this chapter, we do hope readers think about the issues of multigenerational equity, cross-cultural equity, and corporate sustainability in the marketing education. We propose the following research question for sustainability in marketing:

1   Multigenerational equity in sustainability:

    a   How do educators facilitate students to learn from the older generation and pass the best to the future generation in marketing?

    b   How does the young generation communicate with the older generation when they do not understand the technical vocabulary in communication?

    c   What are the learning experiences of seniors that can be sustained for at least 70 years? How do their experiences inspire sustainable consumption behaviour? How does this consumption behaviour inspire manufacturers to have better design in the product and production of sustainability education?

2   Cross-cultural equity in sustainability:

    a   What skills do students in the United States need to develop to communicate with people of different age, social, economic, and political background in virtual communities?

3   Corporate sustainability:

    a   How do marketing executives facilitate dialogues among multiple functional areas in their companies and among various stakeholders when corporate sustainable development programs are implemented?

In this chapter, we invite marketing educators to know how to sustain students' brains by knowing how to build on the best of the past, adapting and melding it with the present, and sustaining it for the future. Educators may reflect the skills we should facilitate in the development of an interest in sustainability in our students or learn to be mindful of values and practices behind our pedagogies. You may discover that current marketing sustainability education may teach more unsustainable consumption behaviour when the basic values and practices necessary to sustain life are not well managed in education. Let us keep an open climate for questioning our practices of sustainability education. No one way is the answer; no shortcut is the solution; the brain needs multiple exercises, collaboration of devices, and flexibility of choices.

Appendix A

Personal experience

A teenager came into a high school counsellor's office unannounced and very disrespectfully declared with decibels beyond privacy, 'I'm going to run away from home.' Practising my training, I used reflective counselling and said, 'Oh, you are going to run away from home.' Timing is very important in counselling so I said no more; the silence became an embarrassment. She could stand it no longer so she said, 'Yes, my mother makes me do all the work; she says she's sick but she's not; she just uses that as an excuse; so I am going to run away.' Silence again. This time I broke the silence and selected a book from my desk library which I had just discussed in my accelerated senior English class. It was *Ethan Frome*. She looked at me as though I hadn't heard her but I alleviated her disgust by saying, 'You don't need to read this; all I want you to do is to place this book where your mother is apt to find it. In a week or so I want you to come back and let me know how things are going at home.' She took the book and left abruptly as though this conference was useless. I was stalling for time by asking her to return and she unbeknowingly was 'setting her mother up' with information that just might solve the problem. I won't go into the book review but the woman in the book paralleled her mother in actions and told what happens sometimes when people try to 'dupe' others. In fact, we had discussed this very fact in my English class; one young man asked, 'Is this that Tom Sawyer deal?' The power of the printed word sustained in the human (bibliotherapy) is one of the most powerful tools for solving problems (Cook, 1979).

References

Benn, S. and Marin, A. (2010). Learning and change for sustainability reconsidered: A role for boundary objects. *Academy of Management Learning and Education*, 9(3), 397–412.

Bradbury, H. (2003). Sustaining inner and outer worlds: A whole-system approach to developing sustainable business practices in management. *Journal of Management Education*, 27(2), 172–87.

Carlson on Sustainability Conference (2010). Retrieved 17 February 2012. http://www.csom.umn.edu/sustainability/agenda.aspx.

Cook, M. (1979). Bibliotherapy. Unpublished dissertation, Akron University.

Cook, M. (2006). *Grammar toward Professionalism*. Pittsburgh, PA: RoseDog Publishing.

Cook, M. and Lam, M. (2012). Challenge of teaching sustainability in education of management. Proceedings of the NAMS (North American Management Society) of MBAA International Conference, Chicago, Illinois. March 29, 2012, U.S.

Ehrenfeld, J. (2008). *Sustainability by Design: A Subversive Strategy for Transforming our Consumer Culture*. New Haven, CT, and London: Yale University Press.

Eshelman, G., Lam, M. and Cook, M. (2012). Three contributing factors to effective utilization of technology in management education and practice: Personhood, mindfulness, and meditation. *Journal of the North American Management Society*, 6, 24–34.

Gundlach, M.J. and Aivnuska, S. (2010). An experiential learning approach to teaching social entrepreneurship, triple bottom line, and sustainability. *American Journal of Business Education*, 3(1), 19–28.

Hoyer, W. and MacInnis, D. (2007). *Consumer Behavior*, 4th edn. Boston, MA: Houghton Mifflin.

Kerin, R., Hartley, S. and Rudelius, W. (2011). *Marketing*, 10th edn. New York: McGraw-Hill/Irwin.

Kurland, N., Michaud, K., Best, M., Wohldmann, E., Cox, H., Pontikis, K. and Vasishth, A. (2010). Overcoming silos: The role of an interdisciplinary course in shaping a sustainability network. *Academy of Management Learning and Education*, 9(3), 457–76.

Lam, M. (2005). Moral character development and marketing education. Paper presented at Marketing Management Association 2005 Spring Conference Proceedings, March 17, 2015, Chicago, IL, US.

Lam, M. (2006). A study of the transfer of corporate social responsibility from multinational enterprises to Chinese subsidiaries: Implications for Christian business educators. Proceedings of the 22nd Christian Business Faculty Association Annual Conference, Cedarville University, Dayton, Ohio, US.

Lam, M. (2007a). Increasing corporate social responsibility of multinational enterprises in China. *The Journal of International Business Research and Practice*, 1, 161–73.

Lam, M. (2007b). A study of the transfer of corporate social responsibility from well-established foreign multinational enterprises to Chinese subsidiaries. In J. Hooker, J. Hulpke and P. Madsen (eds.), *Controversies in International Corporate Responsibility*. International Corporate Responsibility Series, Vol. 3. Pittsburgh, PA: Carnegie Mellon University, 343–63.

Lam, M. (2008a). Non-government organizations as the salt and light in the corporate social responsibility movement in China. Proceedings of the 2008 Christian Business Faculty Association Annual Conference, Indianapolis, US, Nov. 6–8.

Lam, M. (2008b). Beyond credibility of doing business in China: Strategies for improving corporate citizenship of foreign multinational enterprises in China. *Journal of Business Ethics*, 87, 137–46.

Lam, M. (2009). Sustainable development and corporate social responsibility of multinational enterprises in China. In S. Ivanaj, V. Ivanaj and J. McIntyre (eds.), *Multinational Enterprises and the Challenge of Sustainable Development*. Cheltenham, UK, and Northampton, MA: Edward Elgar, 230–44.

Lam, M. (2010a). Political implications of the corporate social responsibility movement in China. *The Journal of International Business Research and Practice (JIBRP)*, 4, 125–34.

Lam, M. (2010b). Managing corporate social responsibility as an innovation in China. In A.-H. Latif and J. Chen (eds.), *Innovation in Business and Enterprise: Technologies and Frameworks*. Hershey, PA: IGI Global Publications, 224–38.

Lam, M. (2010c). Beyond legal compliance: Toward better corporate citizenship of foreign multinational enterprises in China. *Journal of Biblical Integration in Business*, 13, 100–9.

Lam, M. (2011a). Successful strategies for sustainability of foreign multinational enterprises in China. *The Journal of International Business Research and Practice*, 5, 89–100.

Lam, M. (2011b). Becoming corporate social responsible foreign multinational enterprises in China. *The Journal of International Business Research and Practice*, 5, 47–61.

Lam, M. (2011c). Challenges of sustainable environmental programs of foreign multinational enterprises in China. *Management Research Review*, 34(11), 1153–68.

Lam, M. (2012a). An alternative paradigm for managing sustainability in the global supply chain. *International Journal of Social Ecology and Sustainable Development*. 3(4), 1–12, October-December, IGI Global, Forthcoming.

Lam, M. (2012b). A best practice of corporate social responsibility: Going beyond words on a page and a check. In Jared A. Jaworski (ed.), *Psychology of Social Responsibility*. Advances in Sociology Research, Vol. 13. New York: Nova Science Publishers, chapter 8, 157–64.

Lam, A., Lam, M. and Lam, L. (2006). A study of human rights non-government organizations (NGOs) as social movement organizations (SMOs) in Hong Kong, China: Implications for higher education. *The International Journal of the Humanities*, 3(9), 105–17.

Lam, M., Lam, A. and Lam, L. (2010). The importance of non-government organizations in the corporate social movement in China. *The International Journal of Humanities*, 7(12), 101–14.

Leonard, A. (2007). *Story of Stuff* (video). Retrieved 27 September 2011 from http://www.storyofstuff.com/.

Pruzan, P. (2008). Spirituality as a firm basis for corporate social responsibility. In A. Crane, A. McWilliams, D. Matten, J. Moon and D. Siegel (eds.), *The Oxford Handbook of Corporate Social Responsibility*. Oxford: Oxford University Press, 552–9.

Starik, M., Rands, G., Marcus, A. and Clark, T. (2010). From the guest editors: In search of sustainability in management education. *Academy of Management Learning and Education*, 9(3), 377–83.

Thompson, C. (2010). *Anatomy of Soul: Surprising Connections between Neuroscience and Spiritual Practices that Can Transform Your Life and Relationships*. Carol Stream, IL: Tyndale House Publishers.

Tippett, K. and Diamond, A. (2009). Learning, doing, being: A new science of education. [Podcast]. 19 November. MP3 audio file Retrieved from http://being.publicradio.org/programs/2009/learning-doing-being/.

Vaill, P.B. (1996). *Learning as a Way of Being: Strategies for Survival in a World of Permanent White Water*. San Francisco, CA: Jossey-Bass.

Vaill, P.B. (2003). Riding the rapids: A conversation with Peter Vaill. *Leadership in Action*, 22(6), 7–11.

Vaill, P.B. (2007). Organizational epistemology: Interpersonal relations in organizations and the emergence of wisdom, in E. Kessler and J. Bailey (eds.), *The Handbook of Managerial and Organizational Wisdom*. Thousand Oaks, CA: Sage, 327–55.

Welsh, M.A. and Murray, D.L. (2003). The ecocollaborative: Teaching sustainability through critical pedagogy. *Journal of Management Education*, 27(2), 220–36.

World Commission on Environment and Development (1987). *Our Common Future*. Oxford: Oxford University Press.

World Economic Forum (2010). Redesigning business value: A roadmap for sustainable consumption. Retrieved 7 November 2011 from http://www.weforum.org/reports/redesigning-business-value-roadmap-sustainable-consumption.

17 Sustainability and the consumer-citizen's consumption consciousness

Julie E. Francis and Teresa Davis

1 Introduction

The sustainability imperative is likely to have a profound influence on marketing practice and theory (Kotler, 2011). Sustainability garners much attention from academics, governments, businesses, and non-governmental organizations. Much of this attention focuses on the role of governments and businesses in fostering sustainability through public policy and corporate social responsibility. For instance, in the public policy arena, governments encourage and sometimes mandate more sustainable options through education, incentives, legislation, and taxes. Meanwhile, businesses are urged to manage the triple bottom line of economic, environmental, and social responsibility. Nevertheless, the problems associated with unsustainable consumption continue to grow, and greater attention must be paid to the role of consumers (e.g., Kotler, 2011; Prothero et al., 2011).

Consumers have a crucial role in driving and using the change to a more sustainable future through their purchase demands and decisions. There is a long history of people showing concern for the implications of their consumption, from the ancient followers of Epicurean philosophy (Botton, 2000) (not to be confused with modern conflations of Epicurus and hedonism) through to contemporary down-shifters and anti-consumers. Increasingly, though, such consumption consciousness is shifting from the margins to the mainstream. For example, the LOHAS (lifestyles of health and sustainability) segment now includes 19 per cent of American adults (Kotler, 2011). Thus, marketers must develop a better understanding of the consumers' perspective of sustainability – to understand their concerns, to effectively segment and target consumption-conscious citizens, and to help mitigate the gap between sustainable attitudes and unsustainable behaviour.

There are various avenues through which researchers may contribute to addressing the gaps in our understanding of the sustainability-concerned consumer. In particular, there is much to gain from establishing a framework for the consumer equivalent of the triple bottom line – a framework that enables systematic theory development and testing. Subsequently, this chapter proposes and conceptualizes *consumption consciousness* as that equivalent notion. The discussion begins by examining the role and agency of consumers in sustainability. Next, the chapter defines, explicates, and conceptualizes the construct of consumption consciousness. The content domain of the construct is then determined by performing a review and synthesis of relevant consumer studies. Finally, the chapter concludes by describing the marketing and research applications of the proposed conceptualization.

2   Role and agency of consumers

There have always been consumers who, for ideological reasons, actively reject certain forms of consumption or particular products. In the current era, researchers examine such consumers under a variety of banners, including voluntary simplicity, anti-consumption, ethical consumption, and market activism. These topics are enjoying a wave of heightened interest, as is demonstrated by the recent series of special issue journals (e.g., *European Journal of Marketing,* 2010; *Journal of Business Research,* 2009; *Journal of Consumer Behaviour,* 2010; *Journal of Macromarketing,* 2013; *Journal of Marketing Management,* 2012; *Journal of Social Marketing,* 2013). Notably, though, such work tends to focus on that which consumers reject or dislike, as opposed to the larger dynamic of everyday consumption choices and trade-offs. Often, too, the topics prioritize the margins or extremes whereas the underlying considerations are shifting to the mindset of mainstream consumers.

Consumers today are increasingly empowered and responsibilized to consider the implications of their consumption. On the empowerment side, consumers have greater information and flexibility: communication technology (e.g., Internet and social media) provides ready access to extensive information about products, brands, businesses, and purchases alternatives, while e-commerce (e.g., Internet retailing and mobile marketing) dramatically expands consumers' ability to exercise purchase choice (Kotler, 2011). On the responsibilization side, public policy variously employs education (e.g., awareness campaigns), incentives (e.g., solar power rebates), and legislation (e.g., carbon tax schemes) to encourage the use of sustainable alternatives. Meanwhile, the pervasive influence of bio-power, as proposed by Foucault, politicizes consumption such that multiple media vehicles explicitly or implicitly call on consumer-citizens to exercise self-regulation in the marketplace (Rose, 2000).

Thus, consumers increasingly play the dual roles of actors and agents in the shift towards more sustainable practices through their everyday choices and demands. In turn, marketers and researchers need to develop a better understanding of the new consumer-citizen (Kotler, 2011; Prothero et al., 2011). This endeavour requires a framework for identifying, measuring, benchmarking, and monitoring consumers' consciousness of sustainability considerations. As a step in this direction, Sheth, Sethia and Srinivas (2011) proposed a consumer equivalent of the business triple bottom line. The authors put forth the construct of *mindful consumption,* which they describe as the consumer's consciousness in thought and behaviour of consumption consequences. They also identify *self, nature,* and *community* as the three dimensions of mindful consumption, in parallel to the economic, environmental, and social dimensions of the business-centric triple bottom line.

The intent and direction of Sheth, Sethia and Srinivas' (2011) proposal has much to support. Nevertheless, their conceptualization raises four concerns. First, although the construct label of mindful consumption is intuitively appealing, there is potential for confusion and incongruence with the field of mindfulness psychology. Second, the authors aggregate attitudes and behaviour. A widely recognized paradox is the gap between consumers' sustainable attitudes and unsustainable behaviour (Prothero et al., 2011). Thus, aggregating mindset and actions poses theoretical and practical restrictions. Third, where the authors broadly describe the domain of each dimension, a systematic and comprehensive literature review is required to identify the content domain as operationalizable criteria. And fourth, their work does not fully specify the structural nature, or type, of construct. Such specification is crucial to understanding the construct-dimension-indicator relationships, developing suitable measures of the construct and subsequent theory testing (Churchill, 1979; Diamantopoulos and Winklhofer, 2001; Francis, 2009; Lee and Hooley, 2005; Mowen and Voss, 2008; Rossiter, 2002).

Given the critical role and agency of consumers in sustainability, and the need to better understand the new consumer-citizen, this paper addresses the limitations of the mindful consumption construct by proposing and more fully conceptualizing the alternative of consumption consciousness. The procedures for doing so apply the recommendations of various measurement scholars, such as those cited above, while also drawing from research into the concerns of ideologically motivated consumers.

3   Initial conceptualization

We propose and define "consumption consciousness" as a person's awareness and concern for the sustainability implications of their consumption. This definition has three elements that set the scope of what the construct does and does not include. First, the "awareness and concern" part establishes that the construct includes the cognitive (thoughts and beliefs) and affective (feelings and emotions) aspects of attitude but does not include actual consumption behaviour – for the previously discussed theoretical and practical reasons. Researchers could, and later should, examine actual behaviour as a parallel construct. But given the prevalence of attitude-behaviour gaps, conflating the two at this stage is problematic.

Second, the "sustainability implications" aspect refers to the spectrum of antecedents and consequences that factor into a product's sustainability. The business-centric model divides such implications into the areas of economic (the entity's own well-being and capacity to prevail), environmental (the physical world and resources), and social (people, communities, and future generations) (Byrch et al., 2007; Froschhesier, 2009; Kyro, 2001). In the consumer-centric model we replace the economic dimension with a *self* dimension to capture the consumer's (as opposed to the entity's) own well-being. Then, analogous to the business model, we retain the dimensions of *environmental* and *social*. This trio of dimensions is also comparable to Sheth, Sethia and Srinivas' (2011) dimensions of self, nature, and community but with more conventional labels for the latter two. The following section will examine the suitability and completeness of these three initial consumer dimensions.

The third aspect of the definition, the "consumption" part, takes the construct beyond the scope of anti-consumption by including the rejection of that which is considered to be unsustainable as well as the acceptance of that which is considered to be sustainable – and any trade-offs or evaluations in between. In this way, anti-consumption considerations factor into consumption consciousness but are not the sum total of the construct. Notably, too, when taking the "consumption" part in the context of the whole definition, the construct deals with the thoughts and feelings that precede consumption, as opposed to the subsequent consumption behaviour which may or may not be consistent with those thoughts and feelings.

Conceptualizing a construct also involves specifying the construct type, or measurement model (Diamantopoulos and Winklhofer, 2001; Mowen and Voss, 2008; Rossiter, 2002). This step establishes the proposed relationships between a construct and the parts of that construct, and has substantial implications for measuring and testing theories about the phenomenon. Because constructs are theoretical abstractions, the specification of a construct's type can be subjective and sometimes debated (e.g., Diamantopoulos and Winklhofer, 2001; Francis, 2009). However, we propose that consumption consciousness is best conceptualized as a second-order formed construct with reflective first-order indicators and formative second-order indicators. Diamantopoulos describes this type of construct, and Figure 17.1 depicts the model applied to the current construct.

This model indicates that consumption consciousness is a composite of (formed by) the three causal dimensions (i.e., self, environment, society), in much the same way as

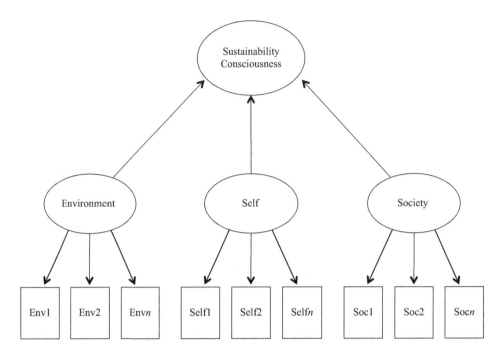

Figure 17.1 Conceptual model of consumption consciousness

socio-economic status is a composite of income plus education plus occupation. This implies that consumption consciousness does not inherently exist in the way that personality and IQ exist but is instead a theoretical combination of otherwise existing phenomena. The model also specifies that self, environment, and society are latent variables that are not directly observable but that they elicit (cause) manifest reflective indicators. For instance, a consumer's consciousness of environmental implications is reflected in their consciousness of different aspects of the environment. The following section of this chapter reviews relevant consumer studies to determine what the different aspects (content domain) of each dimension include, and examines the suitability of the three proposed dimensions.

4   Content domain

To identify the content domain of the sustainability implications about which consumers are aware and concerned, we examined empirical studies of ideologically motivated consumers. The sample of 22 journal articles included rejection-oriented studies (e.g., anti-consumption, brand avoidance, market activism, boycotts, and consumer resistance) plus acceptance-oriented studies of that which the consumers deem suitable (e.g., ethical consumption, voluntary simplicity, down-shifting, and green consumption). The literature review identified the issues and concerns (the criteria) that participants raised. Next, we sorted the criteria into the thematic categories of self, environmental and social, and assessed the extent to which those categories suitably and completely housed said criteria – which they did. Expanding the pool of consumer studies was not necessary because multiple sources supported each criterion and informal reviews of further studies did not reveal any additional issues to include. The results are summarized in Table 17.1 and described below.

Self

The self dimension houses concerns relating to the direct personal implications of consumption choices. The domain includes five considerations: independence, authenticity, psychological well-being, personal growth, and physical health. More specifically, independence involves freedom from marketplace pressures to consume and freedom from debt. Authenticity refers to expressing and maintaining an authentic self-image and identity, as opposed to creating or altering one's identity through material possessions. Psychological well-being involves considering whether consumption will contribute to or detract from leading a peaceful, meaningful, and well-balanced life. The personal growth element reflects concerns about improving self-worth and wisdom through self-actualization. Finally, physical health deals with maintaining a healthy lifestyle and natural diet.

Environmental

The domain of environmental consciousness covers four core issues: conservation, eco-damage, harm to animals, and connectedness. The conservation aspect relates to minimizing waste, recycling, and conserving natural resources. The eco-damage considerations deal with avoiding harm, destruction, or genetic interference with nature. Harm to animals involves choosing products that have not caused or will not cause direct and/or

Table 17.1 Dimensions and domain of consumption consciousness

Dimension	Content domain	Empirical studies*
Environment	Conservation	1, 2, 4, 6, 7, 10, 11, 13, 14, 15, 18, 20, 22
	Eco-damage	4, 7, 10, 11, 15, 17, 18, 19, 20, 21, 22
	Harm to animals	1, 2, 19, 20
	Connectedness	4, 11, 14, 18, 19, 22
Self	Independence	1, 2, 3, 4, 7, 10, 11, 13, 14, 18, 19, 20, 22
	Authenticity	4, 9, 10, 11, 12, 16, 17, 22
	Psychological well-being	1, 4, 6, 7, 10, 21, 22
	Personal growth	1, 3, 6, 10, 11, 14, 18, 19
	Physical health	1, 10, 11, 13, 15, 19, 20, 21
Society	Community well-being	6, 8, 10, 11, 14, 18
	Cultural damage	4, 7, 16, 17, 21
	Capitalism	1, 4, 5, 8, 12, 14, 15, 17, 18, 19, 20, 21
	Inequity	4, 7, 11, 12, 17, 19, 20

*Empirical Studies

1. Bekin, Carrigan and Szmigin (2005)
2. Bekin, Carrigan and Szmigin (2007)
3. Cherrier (2002)
4. Cherrier (2009)
5. Close and Zinkhan (2009)
6. Craig-Lees and Hill (2002)
7. Etzioni (1998)
8. Hoffman and Muller (2009)
9. Hogg, Banister and Stephenson (2009)
10. Huneke (2005)
11. Kozinets and Handelman (2004)
12. Lee, Motion and Conroy (2009)
13. Leonard-Barton (1981)
14. McDonald et al. (2006)
15. Peattie and Peattie (2009)
16. Piacentini and Banister (2009)
17. Sandikci and Ekici (2009)
18. Sharma (1981)
19. Shaw et al. (2005)
20. Shaw and Newholm (2002)
21. Varman and Belk (2009)
22. Zavestoski (2002)

indirect harm to animals. Finally, the connectedness element captures the desire to foster a general respect for, and affiliation with, nature.

Social

The social dimension of consumption consciousness captures concerns and considerations relating to community well-being, cultural damage, capitalism, and inequity. More closely, the community well-being aspect deals with preserving community values, harmony, and economic viability. The cultural damage aspect reflects broader concerns about Westernized or Americanized consumption practices diluting and reshaping otherwise unique cultures. Concerns with capitalism focus on perceived excesses of power, corporate self-interest, market manipulation, and opportunism among large, often multinational, corporations. Finally, this dimension also includes inequity concerns relating to the human rights and well-being of all people, especially those in developing nations.

5   Discussion

The need to shift to more sustainable consumption practices raises an abundance of opportunities and challenges for marketers and researchers. Kotler (2011) outlines his vision of the implications for marketing theory and practice while Prothero et al. (2011) identify the most urgent directions for research and public policy. A common thread in these and other similar discussions is the call to develop a comprehensive and systematic understanding of the new consumer-citizen. This call recognizes the crucial role and agency of consumers in driving the change to greater sustainability through their purchase demands and decisions. Central to developing and subsequently applying an understanding of the new consumer-citizen is the construction of a theoretical framework of the consumer's sustainability concerns.

To this end, the current authors proposed and conceptualized the notion of consumption consciousness. We defined and delineated that which is and is not consumption consciousness. A model of the construct's components and the relationships between those components was developed. We also reviewed empirical studies of ideologically motivated consumers to identify their specific issues of concern, thereby identifying the construct's content domain. These procedures were theory-driven, directed by construct specification and measurement principles. The outcome is a framework that parallels the business-oriented notion of a triple bottom line and addresses the limitations of earlier consumer-oriented efforts of this kind. Moreover, the consumption consciousness framework delivers an operationalizable conceptualization of the new consumer-citizen's sustainability considerations.

Thus, an initial application of the framework is to develop a consumption consciousness measurement scale. At the first-order level, Table 17.1 identifies the item criteria for each component, while Figure 17.1 indicates the need to apply reflective measurement principles. At the second-order level, where the components (i.e., self, environmental, and social) are formative indicators, one would not necessarily expect consistency across component scores. For instance, a consumer may score highly on self but produce a low score on the environmental dimension. However, the aim is not to produce an overall consumption consciousness score (e.g., high, medium, or low). Rather, this model works towards identifying consumer typologies from the various combinations of component scores. For example, one type may be low on the first two dimensions but high on the third, whereas another type may be high on dimensions one and two but low on the third.

In turn, measuring consumption consciousness this way has applications for researchers, marketers, and policy makers. On the research side, the opportunities include performing profile analysis and benchmarking consumer attitudes. Theory testing could then, with a parallel measure of behaviour, quantify the gap between sustainable attitudes and unsustainable behaviour, and examine the factors that contribute to this gap. For marketers, survey findings could inform segmentation, targeting, and positioning activities. They may also use the dimensions and content domain of consumption consciousness as a checklist for assessing the sustainability rating of their brand or product offering. Meanwhile, policy makers can use such survey results to identify the sustainability issues for which awareness and education initiatives are required, and to monitor the effectiveness of such initiatives.

A further consideration – and one that is relevant to researchers, marketers, and policy makers alike – is the need to similarly develop a better understanding of the child's perspective. Mainstream marketing has long recognized the importance of studying child consumers. Children form a powerful segment of consumers: they direct billions of dollars each year through their own purchases and by influencing the purchase decisions of their parents (Carey, Shaw and Shiu, 2008; Nadeau, 2011). Childhood is also the period of consumer socialization in which young people acquire the consumption knowledge, skills, values and motives that they will carry into adulthood (Benn, 2004; John, 1999; Strong, 1998). As current and future consumers, children are a substantial part of the sustainability imperative. However, with the exception of environmental education programs, children rarely factor into discussions of sustainability. Thus, we also recommend developing and similarly using a child-centric model of consumption consciousness.

References

Bekin, C., Carrigan, M. & Szmigin, I. (2005). Defying market sovereignty: voluntary simplicity at new consumption communities. *Qualitative Market Research: an International Journal*, 8(4), 413–429.

Bekin, C., Carrigan, M. & Szmigin, I. (2007). Beyond recycling: commons-friendly waste reduction at new consumption communities. *Journal of Consumer Behaviour*, 6(Sep-Oct), 271–286.

Benn, J. (2004). Consumer education between consumership and citizenship: experiences from studies of young people. *International Journal of Consumer Studies*, 28(2), 108–116.

Byrch, C., Kearins, K., Milne, M., & Morgan, R. (2007). Sustainable "what"? A cognitive approach to understanding sustainable development. *Qualitative Research in Accounting & Management*, 4(1), 26–52.

Carey, L., Shaw D. & Shiu, E. (2008). The impact of ethical concerns on family consumer decision-making. *International Journal of Consumer Studies*, 32(5), 553–560.

Cherrier, H. (2002). Drifting away from the consumption spiral: trait aspects of voluntary simplicity. Asia Pacific Advances in Consumer Research, Eds Ramizwick and Tu Ping, Valdosta GA, 5, 280–281.

Cherrier, H. (2009). Anti-consumption discourses and consumer resistant identities. *Journal of Business Research*, 62(2), 181–190.

Churchill, G.A. (1979). A paradigm for developing better measures of marketing constructs. *Journal of Marketing Research*, 16(February), 64–73.

Close, A.G. & Zinkhan, G.M. (2009). Market-resistance and Valentine's day events. *Journal of Business Research*, 62(2), 200–207.

Craig-Lees, M. & Hill, C. (2002). Understanding voluntary simplifiers. *Psychology and Marketing*, 19(2), 187–210.

de Botton, A. (2000). *The Consolations of Philosophy*. Penguin Books: New York.

Diamantopoulos, A., Riefler, P. & Roth, K. P. (2008). Advancing formative measurement models. *Journal of Business Research*, 61(12), 1203–1218.

Diamantopoulos, A. & Winklhofer, H.M. (2001). Index construction with formative indicators: an alternative to scale development. *Journal of Marketing Research*, 38 (May), 269–277.

Etzioni, A. (1998). Voluntary simplicity: characterization, select psychological implications, and societal consequences. *Journal of Economic Psychology*, 19(5), 619–643.

Francis, J.E. (2009). Is C-OAR-SE best for internet retailing quality? *Managing Service Quality*, 19(6), 670–686.

Froschhesier, L., (2009). Business sustainability: the strategies to achieve, the leadership that makes it happen. *SuperVision*, 70(4), 3–4.

Hoffman, S. & Muller, S. (2009). Consumer boycotts due factory relocation. *Journal of Business Research*, 62(2), 239–247.

Hogg, M.K., Banister, E.N. & Stephenson, C.A. (2009). Mapping symbolic (anti-)consumption. *Journal of Business Research*, 62(2), 148–159.

Huneke, M.E. (2005). The face of the un-consumer: an empirical examination of the practice of voluntary simplicity in the United States. *Psychology and Marketing*, 22(7), 527–550.

John, D.R. (1999). Consumer socialization of children: a retrospective look at twenty-five years of research. *Journal of Consumer Research,* 26(December), 183–213.

Kotler, P. (2011). Reinventing marketing to manage the environmental imperative. *Journal of Marketing,* 75 (July), 132–135.

Kozinets, R.V. & Handelman, J.M. (2004). Adversaries of consumption: movements, activism, and ideology. *Journal of Consumer Research*, 31(3), 691–704.

Kyro, P. (2001). To grow or not to grow? Entrepreneurship and sustainable development. *International Journal of Sustainable Development and World Ecology*, 8(1), 15–28.

Larsson, B., Anderson, M. & Osbeck, C. (2010). Bringing Environmentalism Home: Children's Influence on Family Consumption in the Nordic Countries and Beyond. *Childhood,* 17(1), 129–47.

Lee, N. & Hooley, G. (2005). The evolution of classical mythology within marketing measure development. *European Journal of Marketing*, 39(3/4), 365–385.

Lee, M.S.W., Motion, J. & Conroy, D. (2009). Anti-consumption and brand avoidance. *Journal of Business Research*, 62(2), 169–180.

Leonard-Barton, D. (1981). Voluntary simplicity lifestyles and energy conservation. *Journal of Consumer Research*, 8(3), 243–252.

McDonald, S., Oates, C.J., Young, C.W. & Hwang, K. (2006). Towards sustainable consumption: researching voluntary simplifiers. *Psychology and Marketing*, 23(6), 515–534.

Mowen, J. C. & Voss, K. E. (2008). On building better construct measures: Implications of a general hierarchical model. *Psychology and Marketing,* 25 (6), 485–505.

Nadeau, M. (2011). *Food Advertising Directed at Children: Review of Effects, Strategies and Tactics.* Quebec: Quebec Coalition on Weight-Related Problems.

Peattie, K. & Peattie, S. (2009). Social marketing: a pathway to consumption reduction? *Journal of Business Research*, 62(2), 260–268.

Piacentini, M.G. & Banister, E.N. (2009). Managing anti-consumption in an excessive drinking culture. *Journal of Business Research*, 62(2), 279–288.

Prothero, A., Dobscha, S., Freund, J., Kilnourne, W. E., Luchs, M. G., Ozanne, L. K., & Thogersen, J. (2011). Sustainable consumption: opportunities for consumer research and public policy. *Journal of Public Policy and Marketing,* 30 (1), 31–38.

Rose, N. (2000). Government and Control. *British Journal of Criminology*, 40(2), 321–339.

Rossiter, J.R. (2002). The C-OAR-SE procedure for scale development in marketing. *International Journal of Research in Marketing*, 19(4), 305–35.

Sandikci, O. & Ekici, A. (2009). Politically motivated brand rejection. *Journal of Business Research*, 62(2), 208–217.

Sharma, A. (1981). Coping with stagflation: voluntary simplicity. *Journal of Marketing*, 45(Summer), 120–134.

Shaw, D., Grehan, E., Shiu, E., Hassan, L. & Thomson, J. (2005). An exploration of values in ethical consumer decision making. *Journal of Consumer Behaviour*, 4(3), 185–200.

Shaw, D. & Newholm, T. (2002). Voluntary simplicity and the ethics of consumption. *Psychology and Marketing*, 19(2), 167–185.

Sheth, J. N., Sethia, N. K. & Srinivas, S. (2011). Mindful consumption: a customer-centric approach to sustainability. *Journal of the Academy of Marketing Science,* 39, 21–39.

Strong, C. (1998). The impact of environmental education on children's knowledge and awareness of environmental concerns. *Marketing Intelligence and Planning*, 16(6), 349–355.

Varman, R. & Belk, R.W. (2009). Nationalism and ideology in an anti-consumption movement. *Journal of Consumer Research*, 36(December), 686–700.

Ward, S. (1974). Consumer Socialization. *Journal of Consumer Research,* 1 (September), 1–14.

Zavestoski, S. (2002). The social-psychological bases of anti-consumption attitudes. *Psychology and Marketing*, 19(2), 149–165.

18 Marketing's role in the future of corporate sustainability efforts

Ravi Parameswaran, Krishna Parameswaran,
Steven Kooy and Susan Kuzee

1 Introduction

The 1987 World Commission on Environment and Development report "Our Common Future", also referred to as the Brundtland Commission Report, defines sustainable development as development that 'meets the needs of the present without compromising the ability of future generations to meet their own needs' (Brundtland 1987). Sustainable development is thus an intergenerational compact in which the current generation meets its needs in such a manner that does not hinder the ability of future generations to meet their needs.

Stigson (1998) noted: 'Sustainable development is built on three pillars: economic growth, ecological balance and social progress. It is a continuingly evolving process in which society gradually moves to a position where the three elements of sustainable development act in a sustainable manner. For a company to become sustainable, it must be able to strike the right balance between these three pillars. This balance is referred to as "the triple bottom-line," and increasingly it is about strategic positioning and staying ahead of the competition'.

Any activity is sustainable when it is conducted in a manner that balances economic, environmental, and social considerations, that is, by paying attention to the triple bottom line. Sustainable practices are those that promote this balance. The triple bottom line concept, according to Bhagwat (2005), involves 'the addition of environmental values and social values to the economic value to form the decision-making bottom line'. He goes on to note that the concept 'requires companies to minimize harm from the economic activity and to increase environmental and social values, or at least to not diminish them. This involves consideration of costs as well as benefits, called "externalities." Negative externalities are costs not currently borne by the consumer of the product. Positive externalities are benefits that are enjoyed but not paid for by the consumer'. Sustainability is also described as consideration of the 3 *Es* (economic, environment, and equity) or the 3 *Ps* (people, planet, and profit) and paying attention to corporate social responsibility. Another analogy is that of a three-legged stool: all three legs have to be balanced for it to serve its purpose.

Over the past two and a half decades, sustainable development concepts have been applied to various activities, including extractive industries like mining, and to manufacturing, agriculture, and forestry. In attempting to apply these concepts certain apparent contradictions emerge. In a field like open-pit mining of metals, Muth and Parameswaran (1998) and Rajaram and Parameswaran (2005) have discussed how sustainability concepts are applicable, although at first blush it appears that mining cannot be compatible with sustainable development. The reason for such views is that no mine lasts forever, because mineral resources are finite and non-renewable. The other reason is that historic mining practices, which are no longer acceptable, have had negative impacts on the environment. The counter argument is that mining is important for the economic development of many nations. In addition (the counter argument continues), every item in modern commerce is made from something that is either mined or grown and it is impossible to foresee sustainable development, or for that matter, any development that is not to some extent based on mineral development. Some of the contradictions discussed by these authors are:

- Non-renewable resource. The life of an individual mine is not relevant because, as Pring (1998) notes, sustainability constitutes more than the continuing availability of a resource, and because the resource is non-renewable it is even more important to take other sustainability considerations into account. Furthermore, mining companies have robust exploration programs that add to the resource base. Technological advances also add to the inventory of economically mineable reserves. Such considerations are equally applicable to other extractive industries such as oil and gas production as well as to agriculture, where the green revolution has allowed for the vast expansion in food supply.
- Recycling of metals is another action contributing to sustainability. Many metals once produced are capable of being recycled, smelted time and again to their original elemental form, and refined to demanding specification. Furthermore, recycling can conserve energy, since recycling processes are much less energy-intensive than the production of primary metals. Recycling also contributes to the conservation of natural resources by providing an above-ground virtual mine. As a result of recycling, the majority of all copper mined is still in use, as is at least 99 per cent of the gold ever produced, and upward of 60 per cent of the silver mined is still in existence as bullion, coins or fabricated products. Metals are, through recycling, almost infinitely renewable and, therefore, useful as a store of value to future generations. Again, such considerations are equally applicable to forestry and agriculture, where reforestation and replanting crops contribute to sustainability.

In applying sustainability principles to these diverse activities, certain common elements emerge: conservation of natural resources and energy, mitigation of environmental impacts, and engagement of stakeholders. Conservation of natural resources that are not renewable can be accomplished by replenishing them through exploration programs and advances in technology. In the case of energy it can also be achieved by substitution with renewable sources. Mitigation of environmental impacts could involve improvements in pollution control technologies, adoption of cleaner technologies, and reduction in waste generation. Societal considerations involve evaluating and addressing impacts of the activity on the community and general public, as well as transparent communications with various stakeholders that are likely to be affected by the activity.

The preceding discussion focused on sustainability considerations applied to two of the four basic economic activities within a society (Goodwin et al. 2006) – resource maintenance (enhancing an economy's productivity by preserving or improving its stock of capital resources – natural, manufactured, human, social, and financial) and production (conversion of resources into useful goods and services). However, in order for sustainability to be comprehensive, it has to address all four basic activities within the society (Goodwin et al. 2006). Therefore, sustainability can be enhanced by concentrating on the remaining two basic economic activities – namely, distribution (the sharing of products and resources among people through exchanges and transfers) and consumption (the process by which goods and services are put to final use by the society at large). In contemporary business, these activities are commonly associated with the marketing function. In its broadest interpretation, marketing may be viewed as encompassing all human activities undertaken to optimize societal consumption needs. Marketing, with its generally perceived focus of stimulating demand for products (goods and services), events, experiences, persons, places, properties, organizations, information, and ideas (Kotler and Keller 2009), can also at first blush be unfavourably viewed as fostering unsustainable levels of consumption, but market mechanisms can be used to address environmental and social concerns.

Kotler and Keller (2009) state that 'marketing is about identifying and meeting human and social needs'. They further add that 'one of the shortest good definitions of marketing is "meeting needs profitably" and that ". . . marketing savvy . . . turn(s) a private or social need into a profitable business opportunity". The American Marketing Association formally defines marketing as 'an organizational function and a set of processes for creating, communicating, and delivering value to customers and for managing customer relationships in ways that benefit the organization and its stakeholders'. Burns and Bush (2010) state that the role of marketing is shifting away from the view of optimizing profits through efficient promotion, distribution, and pricing decisions once a physical product is created to a service-oriented view. This conceptual framework was first enunciated by Vargo and Lusch (2004), and includes the following: '(a) identify core competencies – the fundamental knowledge and skills that may represent a potential competitive advantage; (b) identify potential customers that can benefit from these core competencies; (c) cultivate relationships with these customers that allow customers to help in creating values which meet their specific needs; and (d) gauge feedback from the market, learn from the feedback, and improve the values offered to the public'. In other words, the role of marketing has shifted from a purely value delivery mode to value exploration, value creation and value delivery foci (Kotler, Jain and Maesincee 2002). Value in this context refers to the value chain first expounded by Porter (1985). Figures 18.1 (a) and 18.1 (b) are modified representations of the value chain concept, expressed in our conceptualization of stakeholder interests without and with consideration of sustainable development objectives respectively.

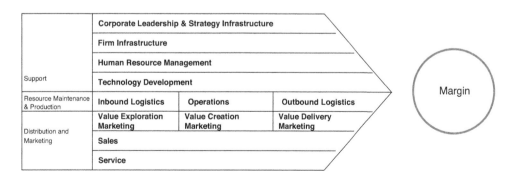

Figure 18.1a Without sustainable development: Porter's Value Chain

Source: Porter, M. E. (1985) Competitive Advantage: Creating and Sustaining Superior Performance. New York, NY: The Free Press.

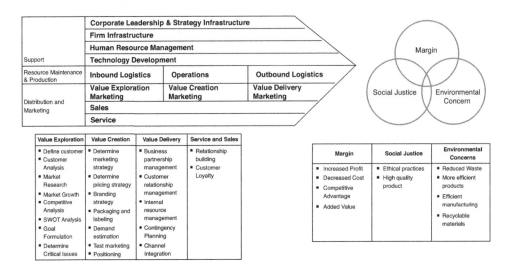

Figure 18.1b With sustainable development: Modification of the Porter's Value Chain

As the central and critical nature of marketing in the business domain is being increasingly appreciated, the dual role of marketing has crystallized. In addition to marketing's role as a function within the organization, it is also recognized as a set of values and processes that all functions within the organization participate in implementing (Moorman and Rust 1999). This recognition of marketing as 'the function of business' (Haeckel 1997) is known as the firm's marketing orientation. Therefore marketing is both a function and an orientation within an organization. Moorman and Rust (1999) illustrate the impact of marketing with the following diagram.

Through a case study on Haworth, Inc. (Haworth), a Michigan-based global leader in the design and manufacture of office furniture and organic workspaces, we examine how sustainability concepts emanating from within the organization can be channelled through the marketing function to evolve as a "top of consciousness" corporate aspiration permeating the organization and the world beyond. Such a role for marketing in sustainability would alleviate the criticism that environmental, social, and humanitarian goals (Chabowski, Mena and Gonzalez-Padron 2011), being externalities in an organizational context and driven as a buzzword or mission (Closs, Speier and Meacham 2011), are 'necessary but not sufficient conditions' for driving sustainability in an organizational context. In his editorial for the *Journal of the Academy of Marketing Science* special issue on sustainability, Hult (2011) states, 'Sustainability is an appealing concept for a variety of fields, but marketing, in particular, has an opportunity to contribute significantly to the understanding of sustainability, its boundaries, its merits, and its viability as a focus for organizations' future operations'. He further adds that marketing '[may be] in a unique position to elevate its focus from managing relationships with customers to strategically managing a broader set of marketplace issues. . . . Overall, an organization achieves market-based sustainability to the extent that it strategically aligns itself with the market-oriented product needs and wants of customers and the interest of multiple

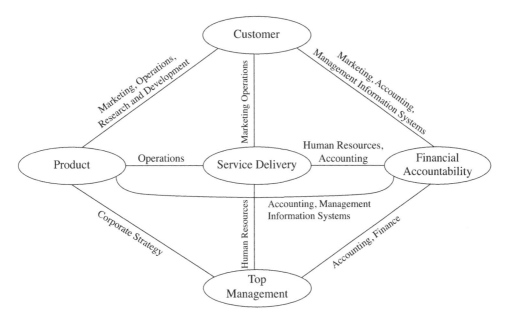

Figure 18.2 Functional influences on the connections between central elements of the firm
Source: Mooreman, C. & Rust, R. T. (1999) The Role of Marketing, *Journal of Marketing*, Vol. 63, Special Issue.

stakeholders concerned about social responsibility issues involving economic, environmental, and social dimensions'.

2 Is marketing compatible with sustainable development?

Kilbourne and Beckmann (1998) reviewed research on marketing and the environment from 1971 to 1997. They categorized the literature into three research streams: the first dealt with characterization of the 'environmentally conscious' or 'green' consumer, attempting to profile them in terms of demographic, psychographic, and personality variables, to measure their 'social consciousness' and 'environmental concerns' and their attitudes towards environmental issues such as recycling, 'green' products, and pollution. They noted that although results of these efforts were often inconclusive, there was nevertheless a brief period of introduction of "green" products and "green" advertisements.

In the second stream, the early 1980s through 1995, the focus shifted to energy conservation and legislative initiatives such as packaging laws. Although the sophistication of the analysis improved, the focus was still on how behaviour was influenced by environmental beliefs, knowledge, and attitudes. Again, the results were inconclusive in relating individual attitudes to environmentally responsible behaviour. Since 1995 the scope of research has broadened considerably, from the individual attitudes and behaviour to deeper examination of the individual's motivation, including perceived consumer effectiveness, cooperative behaviours, and strategic alliances. The research objectives included attempting to distil more general environmental beliefs and environmental values and identifying institutional factors influencing these values and beliefs. The authors characterize this development as a critical turn, as previously held assumptions were questioned and research moved 'to the larger question of system sustainability'. They also see this as a shift from micromarketing to a macromarketing perspective.

Peattie (2001) refers to three ages in the evolution of the relationship between marketing and the environment. He refers to the first age of ecological "green" marketing arising from social and environmental consciousness during the 1960s and early 1970s following the publication of Rachel Carson's (1962) *Silent Spring* and the Club of Rome's *Limits to Growth* (1974), which pointed out the finiteness of natural resources and that a business-as-usual scenario would eventually deplete the natural resources and systems necessary for our well-being. The focus was on specific environmental issues such as air and water pollution, depletion of oil reserves, oil spills, and ecological impacts of synthetic pesticides such as DDT. During this time there was increased environmental regulation, requiring "end-of-pipe" controls, a source of increased cost and, in general, a constraint on marketing. However, companies like Body Shop, Ben and Jerry's, and 3M embraced social and environmental values driven more by the vision of their founders than by consumers or the market.

The second age of environmental green marketing during the latter part of the 1980s was influenced by events such as the Bhopal gas tragedy in 1984, the discovery of the Antarctic hole in the ozone layer in 1985, the Chernobyl nuclear accident in 1986, and the *Exxon Valdez* oil spill in 1989. Media coverage of these events elevated public concern, bringing environmental issues to the forefront, and this was reflected in public opinion surveys. Companies started developing environmental policies and paid attention to environmental performance. At the same time, other important ideas about business and the environment were put forth, the most important of which was sustainability. This idea was important because it integrated environmental, societal, and economic considerations and recognized the need for balancing these factors. It also gave diverse stakeholders such as companies, governments, and environmental groups a common platform, even though the trade-offs they would make would be entirely different.

One of the other developments that occurred during this period was a movement from end-of-pipe controls to the development of "clean technology". It involved the design of new products or production processes in which pollution or waste was minimized or, where feasible, eliminated at the design stage. "Take-back" programs by manufacturers for used products such as automotive batteries strengthened the recycling chain, and the concept of "product stewardship" – i.e., that manufacturers were responsible for their products after sale for satisfaction in use and proper disposal after use – began to take hold. Another idea that gained vogue was that socio-environmental performance could be turned into a strategic competitive advantage for companies. An outgrowth of this development was a measurement of eco-performance, if companies were to differentiate themselves from their competition on environmental grounds. The task of measuring eco-performance is difficult because it seeks to capture various environmental attributes of a product and production measures in a few relevant metrics, and, not surprisingly, many companies found themselves subjected to criticism. Finally, companies implemented quality and environmental management systems to measure and monitor environmental performance.

The implication for marketing during this period was that the focus turned from a few industries with direct impact on the environment, such as oil, mining, agro-chemicals, and automobiles, to more global concerns, such as resource scarcity, depletion of the ozone layer, loss of biodiversity, protection of endangered species, protection of sensitive ecosystems, and global warming and climate change. The focus also turned to consumer products and services such as tourism and banking – i.e., "green" investment funds. There was a spotlight on packaging, since discarded packaging was a large contributor to waste problems from litter to ever-diminishing landfill space. Reduction of over-packaging or utilizing recycled materials without affecting product attribute or performance was easy to implement and resulted in cost reduction.

Peattie (2001) also observed that developing competitive advantage from good environmental performance had run into 'the corporate green wall'. This is because in the initial stages environmental improvement was achieved through cost reduction projects that saved energy or reduced wastes. Further improvement required more radical changes, which became much more difficult to implement. He concluded that the second age of environmental marketing affected marketing practices and that considerable progress has been made in business-to-business and organizational marketing. Large companies have used their purchasing power to get their suppliers to improve their environmental performance and back it up with audits. Governments have also used specifications on tenders to get their suppliers to improve their environmental performance. Many organizations have implemented environmental management systems that commit to conservation of natural resources and pollution prevention programs.

Despite the improvements, Peattie (2001) notes that our economies and societies (and the environment on which they depend) are no more sustainable than they were when the Brundtland report was published. Although the concept of sustainability appears straightforward, implementing it is not. He correctly observes that 'although the general principles of sustainability have been widely endorsed by governments and major companies, agreeing about what it means and how to achieve it has proved difficult' (Peattie 2001). He concludes that the next step in the evolution process, 'moving from environmental marketing to sustainable marketing, will be a monumental one, both in terms of the difficulty and its importance. It means moving from evolutionary changes which reduce environmental damage, towards radical changes in the way we live, produce, market and consume.' (Peattie 2001).

More recent work by Chabowski, Mena and Gonzalez-Padron (2011) examines the structure of sustainability research in marketing from 1958 to 2008, concluding that while 1,320 sustainability-focused articles in 36 journals were identified, there was a paucity of research on the topic in premier marketing journals.

Finally, marketing can promote sustainability by educating the ultimate consumers or users of the product in conservation, making appropriate choices, choosing more sustainable products to less sustainable ones, making the value chain more efficient in terms of sustainability.

3   Case study: Haworth, Inc.

Haworth, Inc., is a global leader in the design and manufacture of office furniture and organic workspaces, including raised access floors, movable walls, systems furniture, seating, storage, and wood case goods. Haworth serves markets in more than 120 countries through a global network of 600 dealers. The company, headquartered in Michigan, had net sales of US$1.38 billion in 2011.

Over the past several years Haworth has made significant strides in designing and manufacturing products that attempt to comport with the definition of sustainability in the Brundtland Report (1987), as reflected in its vision statement:

> Haworth will become a sustainable corporation. We engage our employees in more sustainable practices; we initiate and use processes that are neutral or improve our

environment; and we utilize our resources in ways that create adaptable and sustainable workspace solutions for our customers. We do all of this globally to protect and restore our environment, create economic value, and support and strengthen our communities.

Haworth's executive management has the ultimate responsibility for ensuring that the company's sustainability goals and objectives are met. A cross-functional steering committee sets company-wide goals and performance metrics for these goals. Twice a year, a global sector meeting takes place at which the chief financial officer (CFO) and the chief executive officer (CEO) review the implementation of the sustainability plan.

The company's policy statement identifies seven objectives, as follows:

- *Sustainable Product and Workspace Design:* Understand, reduce, and eliminate the negative environmental impacts from the manufacture, use, and end-of-life management of Haworth products and workspaces.
- *Energy Management:* Increase energy efficiency and utilize renewable energy alternatives to become climate neutral, with the long-term objective of utilizing 100 per cent renewable energy.
- *Green Transportation:* Eliminate harmful emissions associated with the distribution of Haworth products and services and member business travel.
- *Zero Waste and Emissions:* Eliminate waste and emissions associated with corporate operations and the production of products and services. This includes elimination of all greenhouse gases.
- *Green Building and Sustainable Site Management:* Use green building design and practices to construct new buildings and interior renovations for all Haworth facilities worldwide and ensure sites in use are managed for sustainability.
- *Social Responsibility:* Support the communities in which we conduct business and operate as an ethical organization.
- *Stakeholder Engagement:* Engage all Haworth stakeholders in our path toward sustainability.

While the manufacturing function has driven the "Zero Waste to Landfill" policies, the design function has driven integrated, adaptable, and more sustainable solutions, engineering has defined and utilized life cycle thinking, and marketing has altered its procedures as well.

Haworth's commitment to sustainable development also includes supplier engagement. The supply chain goals include meeting diversity and other social responsibility goals. Beyond diversity, each supplier is required to meet the company's standard code of conduct policy and sign off, stating they adhere to socially responsible practices such as labour rights, child labour laws, basic pay requirements, and so on.

Haworth demonstrates its adherence to sustainability concepts, as discussed below.

Sustainable product development

Haworth's product development team adopted the sustainability concepts of nontoxic materials, high recycled content, product take-back, and seeking eco-labels from third-party certification companies. Haworth and its competitors first sought differentiation by embracing specific sustainability attributes. Cleaner products with a smaller ecological footprint warranted special attention in marketing materials, magazine articles, and third-party certification.

Table 18.1 Case: Haworth, Inc.

Corporate Leadership Strategy Infrastructure Vision Statement Policy Statement Global Reporting Initiative Social Responsibility Stakeholder Engagement	Value Exploration Leverages innovative sustainability activities by its marketing team to promote either goodwill/ best in class abilities or reduce competition. Building a network of green non-governmental organizations (NGOs) that support and enhance the Haworth brand.	Marketing, Operations, and Research and Development Implementation of key sustainability features in new product design. Knowledge, research, and sustainability goals provide requirements for designers and engineers.
Other Support Function Infrastructure Green Building Marketing (Concept and Implementation) LEED Certification	Value Creation Sustainable Product Development Green Building Marketing Initiative (Education) Sustainability Document Related to Product	Marketing, Accounting and Management Information Systems None Marketing and Other Units Communications by marketing, communications and sustainability team with all other business units through FAQs, e-blasts, webinars, and newsletters explaining complex matters, such as Forest Stewardship Council (FSC) certification requirements
Resource Maintenance and Production Sustainable Product and Workspace Design Energy Management Green Transportation Zero Waste and Emissions Green Building and Sustainable Site Management	Value Delivery Organic Workspace Operating Showroom Educating Clients and Influences	
	Sales Product Marketing Sustainability Communications Conference and Trade Exhibitions	
	Service Global Sustainability Report	

Beyond the marketing "arms race" toward the most sustainable product, Haworth and its customers acknowledged the lack of education in terms of choosing the right path toward sustainability. Naturally, stakeholders focus on specific sustainability characteristics such as recycled content or recyclability. Once educated on the complexity of a product's relationship to the environment via supply chain, material extraction, end of life, and the like, stakeholders sought third-party certifications with a single score or rank. Third-party certifications are provided by third-party certifiers such as McDonough Braungart Design Chemistry Cradle to Cradle Certification (C2C) review multiple attributes, seeking a much more holistic view of the product's impact on the environment and society.

With the advent of product certifications came other certifications. Companies, non-governmental organizations (NGOs), and certifying bodies alike sought recognition for their contributions or priorities in sustainable product design. For example, the Forest Stewardship Council (FSC) focuses on forest management. FSC certification provides Haworth and its customers third-party validation that the wood supplied is harvested from a sustainably managed forest. FSC certification endorses Haworth's work in supporting a sustainable supply chain for wood. Manufacturing, toxicity content, recyclability, and other attributes must be addressed via marketing materials or other product certifications.

Rather than set a sustainable product development goal of achieving a certain certification, Haworth seeks to first meet internal strategic sustainability goals like nontoxic materials and recycled content and utilizes certifications as additional validation.

Value exploration

In the context of value exploration, the Haworth sales and marketing team leverages innovative sustainability activities to promote either goodwill/best in class abilities or improve the quality of competitive bids by requiring sustainability certifications as part of a bid.

Other activities supporting value exploration include building a network of green nongovernmental organizations (NGOs) that support and enhance the Haworth brand. By partnering with NGOs and offering product, human resources, and financial support, the company receives additional visibility and goodwill. This represents a win–win–win situation; that is, the non-profit wins, Haworth receives recognition, and the environment, society, or economy are positively influenced.

Outbound logistics

Haworth's logistics team leverages existing programs to ensure that its carriers align with the company's sustainability goals with the ultimate objective of reducing the carbon footprint related to transportation. In 2008 Haworth was one of the first in the industry to join the U.S. Environmental Protection Agency's (EPA) SmartWay Transport Partnership program. In 2011 over 85 per cent of the company's shipment was with SmartWay transporters.

In addition, Haworth partners with area shippers to consolidate shipments through ride share programs. The goal is to keep trucks fully loaded, meet schedules, and travel minimum distances to our destinations. Increased trailer efficiencies save fuel and reduce CO_2 emissions. In 2010 ride sharing saved over 2,000,000 pounds of CO_2. By leveraging collaboration among local businesses and service providers, Haworth also helps reduce costs and relieve road congestion.

SAP Improved Transportation Systems Applications and Products (SAP) was implemented in 2010 to help streamline the company's transportation documents. The SAP packing list gives customers better information while requiring less paper than the previous system. Plus, emailing shipping documents helps eliminate printing and faxing when necessary. Overall, a 25 per cent reduction in paperwork is anticipated. In addition, transportation within SAP is based on a delivery date rather than ship date. Having delivery information sooner in the process allows Haworth to use more bulk packs, reduce packaging, and make better decisions about the type of transport required.

In order to further reduce packaging material and waste, a custom boxing machine was purchased in 2011. Making boxes on demand on site reduces inventory and the need to recycle. It was predicted that the new machine would save the equivalent of one to two trips per week.

Starting in November 2011, Haworth Asia Pacific changed standard polyethylene packaging for biodegradable, chemically safe packaging. The new packaging helps mitigate the issue of sending plastic packaging and waste to landfills, which is especially significant for densely populated countries like China and India.

Green building marketing initiatives

The renovation of One Haworth Center, the corporate headquarters, represented the achievement of a significant milestone on the road to the company's sustainability by putting into practice a number of forward-thinking design and construction concepts, including connecting Haworth team members with the natural environment. The facility utilized a broad array of sustainable materials and technology highlighted by a 45,000-square-foot modular green roof. The renovated headquarters provides most team members with outdoor views and daylight, literally bringing nature into the workplace.

The renovation of One Haworth Center was an attempt to break through the "green wall" by radically altering the facility's daily use. Early in the project, Haworth realized the process of building a more sustainable building was of equal importance to the end result. Haworth also considered it important to share the knowledge behind the decision-making. The result was a multidisciplinary marketing and communication approach.

Haworth conducted "hard hat tours" to educate internal and external stakeholders on green building practices such as construction waste recycling, under floor air construction, and energy efficient heating, ventilation and air conditioning (HVAC). This behind-the-scenes look at sustainable construction provided a holistic view of what is required to create a sustainable workspace.

The completed space illustrates sustainability concepts such as occupant comfort and productivity, movable walls, raised floors, and recycling concepts supporting Haworth's "zero waste to landfill" goals. Architects, clients, and designers learn how Haworth implemented a triple bottom line approach creating a flexible, user-focused workspace in action adaptable to change with minimal waste created.

Haworth operates showrooms in 50 major cities around the world. Periodically the showrooms move, allowing facilities to choose new locations, layouts, and so forth. A goal of the showroom is to share its Organic Workspace strategy and product portfolio with clients. Haworth shows how its solutions affect green office practices through Leadership in Energy and Environmental Design (LEED) certification. Haworth renovates showrooms to LEED standards. To date Haworth has certified eight North American showrooms and two showrooms in Asia to LEED standards, demonstrating the company's leadership, knowledge, and commitment to sustainability.

Upon completion of renovation projects, Haworth submits documentation required by the US Green Building Council (USGBC) to register as a LEED certified space. The documentation includes green education materials. Similar to One Haworth Center, but on a smaller scale, the documentation outlines the environmental and social benefits of the space formatted to the LEED green building standard. Internal training as well as external education sessions are conducted to share knowledge associated with the design and construction of the space.

Haworth's contribution to value creation means creating a product or suite of products with sustainability in mind, allowing Haworth to address the client's present and future needs, including their sustainability goals. The value proposition is that the client sees that Haworth is meeting future needs and markets appropriately. Marketing these items often requires the sustainability team and the marketing team to review product data such as carbon footprint, material utilization, or energy savings and translate those into a value proposition for the client.

Product marketing: Informing customers of our product attributes

For the past 10 years, Haworth customers have increasingly asked for sustainability documentation related to its products. In response, Haworth has increased web content focused on a product's sustainability attributes. Specific information related to USGBC's LEED certification program highlights how its product contributes to their LEED project.

As a global company, Haworth receives inquiries from a diverse group of stakeholders with an equally diverse set of interests. Therefore, a product's relationship to LEED is only one of the attributes and is generally not sufficient.

Haworth created Product Environmental Data sheets to capture all sustainability-related information. These documents share product attributes such as toxicity information, recyclability, material content, and carbon footprint.

In situations where electronic documentation does not meet the customer's needs, Haworth implemented sustainable strategies for brochure materials. In early 2004 brochure paper was changed to a highly recycled paper and then upgraded to an FSC (Forest Stewardship Council) certified paper that comes from a mill using wind energy to operate. FSC certification guarantees the paper was harvested from a sustainably managed forest.

Global marketing initiatives: Publication of sustainability reports

Haworth's global sustainability report, first published in 2006 (for 2005) to the Global Reporting Initiative (GRI) standards, was the first in the industry. These standards were developed by CERES, a US NGO and the UN Environmental Programme to improve the quality, rigor, and utility of sustainability reporting. These were formalized in the GRI 2000 Sustainability Reporting Guidelines and were revised in 2002 and released as the GRI 2002 Reporting Guidelines at the World Council for Sustainable Development Conference in Johannesburg in August 2002. The company's sustainability reports for 2006 and subsequent years are available at http://www.haworth.com/en-us/About-Us/Sustainability/Pages/Vision.aspx.

These reports publicly communicated the company's vision, policy, and objectives. The reports also stated goals and provided metrics to support progress made in meeting them. Highlights of the report include a letter from leadership and stories on product design, green building, green manufacturing, and social responsibility.

Building relationships and marketing through sustainability achievements and knowledge sharing

Haworth seeks to promote leadership by educating clients and their influencers – architects and designers – on sustainability trends. Continuing education units (CEUs) are offered in green building and environmental certifications. Haworth also provides speakers for sustainability events globally.

Members of the Haworth sustainability team have presented internally and externally in various countries in person or using video, WebEx, or conference calls. Internally Haworth requires that all members undergo training, and manufacturing staff participates in International Organization for Standardization (ISO) training.

The basis of the education is Haworth's experience or a Haworth client's experience. As clients look for sustainable solutions, the questions are often the same. What is our product's impact on the environment? How much will it cost to implement a sustainable solution?

Haworth seeks to answer these questions providing real examples and lessons learned. Furthermore, the goal is to shift the focus from simply "checking the sustainability box" to changing the approach in order to reach a sustainable a solution. Put another way, previous designs, cost analyses, and purchasing behaviours must be altered to meet the company's triple bottom line goals.

Web-based marketing and social media is key to the company's delivery of sustainable marketing messaging and is an important component of value delivery. Haworth's showrooms are also key marketing tools and an avenue for the company to not only show its commitment to sustainability but to demonstrate that it practices what it preaches. The tools Haworth creates directly support its mission for global company, supply chain, products developed, and services rendered.

Integration with other organizational functions

Sales and communications activities include creating a list of key sustainability activities for highlighting in client proposals; issuing press releases and email messages to key clients and their influencers emphasizing these achievements; attending conferences and trade exhibitions to promote Haworth products and sustainability activities; and providing "knowledge series" events where clients and influencers can learn from Haworth, special guest speakers, and/or fellow attendees.

Service activities involving the company's dealer network include scoring dealers on their activities promoting sustainable operations on both large and small items. For example, recycling of packaging materials at the installation site greatly enhances the company's sustainability story. Likewise, product take-back or recycling facilitations through our dealers further supports our "zero waste to landfill" strategy. Small items, such as client promotional items, are sourced with sustainability in mind. This eliminates the potential for conflict. For example, these gifts are often made of recycled wood or wood from sustainably managed sources rather than sourcing from unknown suppliers that may have used illegally harvested wood.

New product development is one main area where many teams/organizational functions are pulled together. Knowledge, research, and sustainability policies and goals provide requirements for designers and engineers. The Haworth marketing team often captures that knowledge through various interactions with the marketplace to ensure that key sustainability features are implemented in new designs.

Haworth's move to Forest Stewardship Council (FSC) certified wood is another area requiring close coordination with most aspects of its business. The marketing and communications team, in conjunction with the sustainability team, created frequently asked questions and e-blasts (emails to influencers regarding news items), webinars, and newsletter articles explaining the program. Given the complexity of FSC certification, Haworth will need to continue explaining the program in more depth via periodic updates.

4 Conclusion: Looking toward the future

Since the turn of the millennium, customers and manufacturers have focused on improving a product's or company's sustainability attributes. Likewise, marketing material supported this through product certifications, publicizing case studies, and the like. These activities remain important as much more improvement is necessary.

In the future, sustainability marketing and communication must expand beyond the characteristic or activity-based marketing into the "root use" of the product or services offered. Rather than compare two products against each another, the stakeholders must ask much more probing questions, such as why is it needed? What is needed? How will the product be used now and in the future? We believe accounting for future use, including future generations, advances sustainability much farther than a side-by-side product comparison.

Going forward, challenges to the marketing discipline in incorporating sustainability concepts include the fact that marketing has been concerned about delivering satisfaction to customers and profitability to investors. The focus, however, has been on the current generation and it is not clear how the interests of future consumers and investors can be considered. In this regard, Peattie's (2001) caution, 'If current production and consumption systems are unsustainable, then the choices available to future generations may be limited,' is just as valid today.

Another challenge in addressing sustainability arises due to the disparity in incomes and consumption between industrialized nations and the developing world. In this regard, we must find a way to address need, whereas contemporary marketing is focused on addressing wants.

We hope that this chapter is a starting point towards addressing the need Hult (2011) alludes to for a more rigorous theoretical foundation, delineation, and connection to strategic marketing thought.

References

Bhagwat, S. (2005). Economics of sustainable mining. In V. Rajaram, S. Dutta and K. Parameswaran (eds.), *In Sustainable Mining Practices: A Global Perspective*. Leiden: A.A. Balkema Publishers, 54–61.

Burns, A.C. and Bush, R.F. (2010). *Marketing Research*, 6th edn. Upper Saddle River, NJ: Prentice Hall.

Carson, R. (1962). *Silent Spring*. New York: Houghton Mifflin.

Chabowski, B.R., Mena, J.A. and Gonzalez-Padron, T.L. (2011). The structure of sustainability research in marketing, 1958–2008: A basis for future research opportunities. *Journal of the Academy of Marketing Science*, 39, 55–70. doi:10.1007/s11747–010–0212–7.

Closs, D.J., Speier, C. and Meacham, N. (2011). Sustainability to support end-to-end value chains: The role of supply chain management. *Journal of the Academy of Marketing Science*, 39, 101–16. doi:10.1007/s11747–010–0207–4.

Goodwin, N., Julie A.N. and Jonathan, M.H. (2006). Environmental dimensions of macroeconomic measurement, Environmental and Social Issues in Economics, Encyclopedia of Earth.

Haeckel, S.H. (1997). Preface. In D. Lehmann and K. Jocz (eds.), *Reflections on the Futures of Marketing*. Cambridge, MA: Marketing Science Institute, ix–xvi.

Hult, T.M. (2011). Market-focused sustainability: Market orientation plus! *Journal of the Academy of Marketing Science*, 39, 1–6. doi:10.1007/s11747–010–0223–4.

Kilbourne, W.E. and Beckmann, S. (1998). Review and critical assessment of research on marketing and the environment. *Journal of Marketing Management*, 14, 513–32.

Kotler, P., Jain, D. and Maesincee, S. (2002). *A New Approach to Profits, Growth, and Renewal*. Boston, MA: Harvard Business School Press.

Kotler, P. and Keller, K. (2009). *Marketing Management*, 13th edn. Upper Saddle River, NJ: Prentice Hall.

Meadows, D., Meadows, D., Randers, J. and Behrens III, W. (1974). *The Limits to Growth: A Report for the Club of Rome's Project on the Predicament of Mankind*. New York: Universal Books.

Meadows D.H., Meadows D.L., Randers J., Behrens III, W. (1974). *The Limits to Growth*. Universe Books.

Moorman, C. and Rust, R.T. (1999). The role of marketing. *Journal of Marketing*, 63, 180–97.

Muth, R.J. and Parameswaran, K. (1998). The 21st century: Challenges and opportunities in the mining industry. In *Proceedings International Symposium on Environmental Management of Mining and Mineral*

Industries (EMOMAMI-'98). Bhubaneswar, India: Ed. P.K. Jena, Organized by Natural Resources Development Foundation and Institute of Advance Technology & Environmental Studies, 84–104.

Peattie, K. (2001). Towards sustainability: The third age of green marketing. *The Marketing Review*, 2, 129–46.

Porter, M.E. (1985). *Competitive Advantage: Creating and Sustaining Superior Performance*. New York: The Free Press.

Pring, G. (1998). Sustainable development: Historic perspective and challenges for the 21st century. United Nations Development Programme (UNDP) and United Nations Revolving Fund for Natural Resource Exploration (UNRFNRE), 15–16 October, New York.

Rajaram, V. and Parameswaran, K. (2005). What is sustainable mining? In V. Rajaram, S. Dutta and K. Parameswaran (eds.), In *Sustainable Mining Practices: A Global Perspective*. Leiden: A.A. Balkema Publishers, 1–3.

Stigson, B. (1998). Sustainable business: Performing against the triple bottom line: World Business Council for Sustainable Development (WBCSD). *International Council on Metals and the Environment (ICME) Newsletter*, 6, p. 3.

Vargo, S.L. and Lusch, R.F. (2004). Evolving to a new logic for marketing. *Journal of Marketing*, 68(1), 1–17.

World Commission on Environment and Development. (1987). *Our Common Future*. Oxford: Oxford University Press.

Author note

The co-authors would like to acknowledge the contribution of Christopher Toepper (then graduate assistant at Oakland University) in the early versions of this chapter.

19 Agenda 21 as a tool for managing the relationship between companies and communities

A case study at Petrobras

Rosane Beatriz Juliano de Aguiar Figueiredo,
Osvaldo Luiz Gonçalves Quelhas, Sergio Luiz Braga França,
Marcelo Jasmim Meiriño and Walter Leal

1 Introduction

In recent decades, businesses have undertaken important changes in their strategies for growth. Today, business development must be based on more than just the usual trend of economic activities, though these still constitute a necessary condition. Indeed, business development is now characterized by a complex process that takes into account a number of interrelated dimensions: social, environmental, political, cultural, and economic, as well as institutional factors. A corporation's performance in all these areas (and not just an economic dimension) forms the basis of corporate recognition. For continued business growth, new relationships are needed, relationships derived from models where sustainability plays a leading role.

To promote sustainability in business, companies must skilfully manage their relationships with their customers and communities (Boechat, Grassi, and Soares Filho, 2006). As Resende and Kamel (2007) pointed out, the dialogue should not be dictated by economic power and institutional hierarchy, dialogues in which companies would set all the rules. To make themselves more sustainable, companies are being called on to establish new forms of relationships with their stakeholders.

Management proposals geared to stakeholders are now raising elements of responsibility as a whole (Leal Filho and Rios, 2007) and in the social enterprise in particular. Stakeholder theory, first detailed by Freeman (1998), is based on the idea that the final result of a company should give due regard to the interests of all stakeholders, and not just the company's immediate results.

Ashley, Coutinho, and Tomei (2000) pointed out that corporate social responsibility is linked to a 'systems approach, focused on the relationships among stakeholders directly or indirectly related to the core business'. A socially responsible company is one that adopts modern management strategies, aimed at establishing lasting and transformational relationships with its stakeholders, focused on the principles of participation, cooperation, and multi-institutionality. Such a conception of the socially responsible company is confirmed by international perspectives presented by Leal, Filho, and Idowu (2009).

Companies must then rethink the bases on which they establish relationships with their stakeholders, especially those where neighbouring communities are directly or indirectly affected. These should not consist only of a company's unilateral action of informing the public on matters that affect or are affected by the business somehow. Indeed, the relationships comprise the building of a *family* of trust and cooperation between companies and their stakeholders.

To achieve such relationships, companies must migrate from bilateral relations (mainly short-term, ongoing transactional ones) to perennial, multidisciplinary, and transformational relations. There is no room for relationships and welfare dependence that perpetuate community businesses. Louche, Idowu, and Leal Filho (2010) described the new mindset: it is one that prioritizes business values such as citizenship, ethics, autonomy, empowerment, equity, transparency, and sustainability. One action plan created by the United Nations that is intended to bring about such a prioritization is known as Agenda 21.

The concept behind Local Agenda 21 is based on participation, partnership, consensus, knowledge, and social management. Local Agenda 21 creates, in theory, a forum for discussing and implementing this model at a global, national, and local level. For Kohler (2003), Local Agenda 21 is a reference tool to promote change and mobilization of a development model so that more sustainable societies can be created.

This study analyses how relationship management based on the principles of Agenda 21 helps promote sustainable relationships between companies and communities. It identifies strategic factors that foster these relations. The article also highlights the management aspects necessary to adopt Local Agenda 21 as an instrument of relationship between companies and communities. The aim is to study the program's relationship with Petrobras communities located within its area of influence, known as Petrobras Local Agenda 21.

2   Theoretical

This study reviews the literature on the various approaches established by the most cited authors and scholars and their studies on the investigated areas: sustainability and corporate social responsibility, stakeholder theory, relationship management communities, and Agenda 21.

Corporate social responsibility and sustainability

The classical view of social responsibility is characterized by the idea that society should objectively determine its needs, having the market as its main mediator (referee). With the ability to respond to market demands, reward-seeking interest and self-interest result, turning them into effective gains for society. Thus, the market transforms self-interest into social benefit. However, the market cannot ensure that business will always act fairly, ethically, and in a balanced way. For such a context, the legal model emerged in later years; making laws that inhibit inappropriate entrepreneurial behaviour has become a constant. Along with this, social expectations of businesses are no longer strictly economic and have begun to include subjects that, hitherto, have been foreign to such an environment. Emerging from this theme are social models, which have allowed the creation and development of the model stakeholder (Carroll and Buchholtz, 2009).

The classic definition of sustainability comes from the World Commission on Environment and Development (WCED), informally known as the Brundtland Commission, in its well-known report "Our Common Future" (1987). Therein the commission determined sustainable development to be development that 'meets the needs of the present without compromising the ability of future generations to meet their own needs'.

Aledi and Quelhas (2003) hold that sustainability is a concept that bears three dimensions: the environmental, social, and economic-financial. The authors advocate the responsible use of these three resources to better ensure the longevity of organizations' activities.

Companies today are more frequently adopting socially ethical behaviour. They have been driven to do so by global market forces and especially by the notion of stakeholder's performance. Companies may be economically viable, but if they are socially and environmentally irresponsible they appear to be doomed to failure. Félix (2003) pointed out that companies now realize that they are partly accountable for events concerning exclusion and social injustice.

Hence, companies find themselves under pressure to expand their original concept. They should, in their objectification of results, take into account not only shareholders and business owners but also society. Socially responsible management considers three main factors: the planet (environmental concerns), people (social concerns), and profitability (economic concerns). By looking after these dimensions in a balanced way, a company burnishes its reputation, increasing the trust and loyalty among its various stakeholders.

Scholars and practitioners have consolidated, over the past few decades, the concept and practice of corporate social responsibility. It has advanced through different stages of compliance with legislation, philanthropy, and the pursuit of sustainable development. It is noteworthy that the various approaches and definitions are closely linked to social changes and the historical influence of the institutional environment. What stands out, as Ashley, Coutinho, and Tomei (2000) noted, is its nature as 'inherently interdisciplinary, multidimensional and associated with a systemic approach, focused on the relationships among stakeholders directly or indirectly related to the business'.

Ashley (2002) believed that the concept of corporate social responsibility could not be reduced to just instrumental rationality, which requires 'a new business concept and thus a new social, economic and political mental model'.

Based on this new business concept, this paper presents a model of Enderle and Tavis (1998) cited in Ashley (2002). The model analyses the behaviour of companies and their relations with their various stakeholders, according to three levels of proposed ethical challenges (Ashley, 2002):

- Level 1: minimum requisites to enforce the law
- Level 2: obligations considered beyond that of the minimum required ethical level; meet the expectations of the constitutional context in which the company would operate even without being pushed by legal demands
- Level 3: ideal ethical behaviour standards that go beyond community expectations.

Theory of stakeholders

The literature of business management highlights two objective functions: the maximization of shareholder wealth and the balance of stakeholder interests. With the former, business decisions are taken to always give a return to shareholders, thus maximizing the value of the company. The theory of balancing stakeholder interests argues that decisions are taken to balance and meet the expectations of all stakeholders involved with the corporation. Table 19.1 summarizes the main characteristics of these two theories. The first approach, put forward by Friedman (1970), rejects the stakeholder theory. The line of thought advocated by such authors as Jensen (2001), Key (1999) and Sternberg (1996) presupposes the existence of only one valid concern, the shareholder. Freeman (1994)

Table 19.1 Stockholders' and stakeholders' views

	Stockholder's view	*Stakeholder's view*
Line of Thought	Milton Friedman	Edward Freeman
Social Function of the Company	Maximizing profit	To respect the rights of the public and contribute to the promotion of the common good.
Target Community	Shareholders/owners	All the shareholders affect or are affected by the company.
Voluntary Actions	Viewed as expenses and costs in increasing efficiency of the company.	Contribute to the image and reputation of the companies by moving towards democracy via contributing to a stable society, a fundamental characteristic in the contemporary economy.

Table 19.2 Positioning analysis perspectives facing stakeholder theory

Marxist	*Pluralist*	*Unilateralist/Neoliberal*
Rejects stakeholding, for society goes through a conflict between capital and work.	It is possible to conciliate multiple interests, therefore stakeholders theory is viable.	Rejects stakeholding, for there is only one valid interest, which is the shareholder's.

Source: Stoney and Winstanley (2001).

countered that the goal of organizations is to serve the interests of all stakeholders and no interests are more legitimate than others. We can also cite supporting authors such as Carroll (1999), Clarkson (1995), and Donaldson and Preston (1995).

The work of Stoney and Winstanley (2001), it is important to note, analysed the feasibility of the stakeholder theory in the light of the various lines of thought. These are depicted in Table 19.2.

Stakeholders are in an ongoing exchange relationship with the company. They subsidize the organization in some way (financial resources, expertise, legitimacy) and, in response, they expect their interests to be met. A 'stakeholder theory requires not only an understanding of the kind of influence they have, but also how organizations respond to their interventions' (Pinto and Oliveira, 2004). Therefore, it is important to identify who comprises these communities, what their interests and perceptions are, and how they act. It is important to also identify the stakeholders most critical to business strategies and to define the relationships between companies as well as those whose relations transcend that of legal obligations. Doing all this is paramount to forging a perennial transformational relationship, one that is based on a model of collaboration, cooperation, and mutual trust.

The relationship between companies and their stakeholders should be considered a two-way street, where firms influence and are influenced by various segments of the public. For Wilson (2003), the stronger those relationships are, the easier it is for the companies to achieve their corporate objectives.

Relationship management with communities

As the movement towards sustainability and corporate social responsibility gathers momentum, a growing concern has emerged about sustainable institutional relations. These relations are part of a continuous pursuit of business practices that allow for a dialogue between companies and people (Resende and Kamel, 2007). It is understood, however, that this dialogue fails to hold, as pointed out by Resende and Kamel (2007), in models of economic power and institutional hierarchy, models in which companies lay out the rules for the public.

Bohm (1989) noted that "dialogue" implies seeking common sense to achieve a collective construction. It does not mean trying to impose one or another presumption considered as absolute truth. The dialogue is not intended to be driven by win–win propositions. Such an attitude would allow for collective opinions to prevail instead of those of individuals. In this chapter, dialogue is an instrument of interaction of individuals and purposes, and it only happens when people are imbued with a spirit of participation, involvement, and sharing.

In a business approach, it is pertinent to implement such notions so as to establish management strategies focused on the legitimacy of sustainable relationships. Bocchat, Grassi, and Soares Filho (2006) argued that companies need to manage their relationships in a systematic and systemic way, following the principles of transparency, mutual trust, and interaction that leads to cooperation.

To promote sustainability, a company must take care of its relations, seeking to systematically balance the establishment and fulfilment of commitments to stakeholders, following the principles of dialogue and transparency. A continued connection with market response, democratic societies, and environmental preservation can be achieved only by constantly adapting to changes, brought about by the internalization of issues arising from balanced relationships with all stakeholders (Boechat, Grassi, and Soares Filho, 2006).

Relationship management based on a systemic view

In contextualizing reflections on the interdependence of relationships, it is important to cite the work of Svedsen (1998). Svedsen (1998) presented the evolution of stakeholder theory regarding the systemic approach. He pointed out the basic differences between a stakeholder-focused model, with its reactive style of management, and a system-focused model, with its collaborative style of management.

We can say that in the system-focused model the responsibilities are shared with stakeholders seeking opportunities and solutions. Their approach is focused on building relations and creating mutually beneficial opportunities. The former model is focused on the management of relationships to respond to changes in the institutional environment. Table 19.3 summarizes the characteristics, as they concern relations with stakeholders, of the old and new approaches.

Table 19.3 Characteristics of the old and new approach to relations with stakeholders

Stakeholder's Management View	*View System with a Focus on Collaboration with Stakeholders*
Fragmented	Integrated
Focus on relationships	Focus on building relationships
Emphasis on defence of organization	Emphasis on creating opportunities for mutual benefits
Related to short-term goals of the business	Related to long-term goals of the business
Particular implementation dependent on the department interests and personal style of leadership	Coherent approach driven by mission, objective, values, and corporate strategies

Source: Svedsen (1998).

The system-focused model reinforces the idea that companies operate amidst other entities. Considered as organic systems, companies are inserted in a context of interdependence, interacting with various parts of the institutional environment. It would seem, then, that the only sustainable way for a company to survive and prosper in the twenty-first century is to build a management relationship with its stakeholders and to thus contribute to a sustainability-seeking society.

Agenda 21

The Global Agenda 21 is one of the main documents to come out of the United Nations Conference on Environment and Development (Rio 92). It stands out as the most important commitment of international cooperation to implement sustainable development. The importance of its implementation was reaffirmed in 2002 at the Johannesburg Summit, or Rio + 10. Its central theme is 'the search for a new globalization to ensure equitable and inclusive development' (Vargas, 2002, cited in Kohler, 2003).

Agenda 21 can be defined as a participatory planning process at the global, national, and local levels, targeting a new economic paradigm and civilization. 'Agenda 21 is a document containing commitments to change the pattern of development in the next century' . . . The term *Agenda* is used in the sense of intent and design. It represents the desire for changes to the current model of civilization (Ministry of Environment, 2012).

History suggests that building a new model for sustainability is possible only through debate among all sectors of society (governments, businesses, and civil society organizations) and an articulated interaction of these actors for the common good. In this process, Agenda 21 has emerged as an important instrument of social inclusion and citizenship, allowing the involvement and commitment of people in decisions that affect the development of the community, the city, the state, and the country, as pointed out by UNESCO (2005).

Born (2002) characterized Global Agenda 21 as having 'incorporated some features that allowed it to be interpreted as a product of a participatory process of actions and policies to transform the pattern of development and governance interests and human conflicts, backed dialogue and agreement among the social actors'. In establishing more sustainable societies, Agenda 21 has become a reference tool for change and mobilization of the development model.

3   Methodology

This qualitative, exploratory study generates knowledge that contributes to the solving of specific, everyday problems. Like Gil (1991), we view research as 'a systematic and rational procedure that aims to provide answers to problems that are proposed'.

As for its means, the research is bibliographic and is a documentary and field case study. This method is widely applied in the social sciences, engineering, and particularly in the field of management. Here, the researcher has little or no control over the study's events. Yin (2005) noted that the method is useful when it comes to 'a phenomenon within its real-life context, especially when the boundaries between phenomenon and context are not clearly defined'.

The subject of this study is Petrobras Agenda 21, the community relations program developed by Petrobras. This study aims to analyse how Agenda 21 can contribute to the promotion of sustainable relationships between companies and communities. Thus, it should be noted that the study addresses Agenda 21's construction process within the context of institutional relationship management. The study focuses on the analysis of Agenda 21 as a planning tool aimed at sustainable development on the community action plans created under this program.

Due to the scale of the program, by virtue of the performance of the company studied and its presence throughout Brazil, the study has geographical and temporal limitations.

Considering the geographical scope, this study is limited to analysing a unit of operations and a community crafted by the program in each region, given the complexity of the social, environmental, economic, and cultural contexts of the various regions. We interviewed managers from Petrobras and some representatives of the communities related to the object of this study.

4   Description of program: local agenda Petrobras 21

In 2004 Petrobras started the process of building a new type of institutional relationship with neighbouring communities and their facilities through the implementation of Local Agenda 21 Petrobras. The Brazilian energy company's move was in line with its evolving conception of social responsibility as well as its corporate strategy, as pointed out in its Strategic Plan 2020. This plan commits Petrobras to sustainable development through integrated growth, profitability, and social and environmental responsibility.

Created in 2004 under the name the Environment Watch, the first actions of the program relied on space for dialogue, aiming to foster a dialogue between Petrobras and communities around the theme of Local Agenda 21 and sustainability. Building on the initial results of this process, Petrobras developed a methodology, in a joint venture with the Ministry of Environment, for the construction of Agenda 21.The methodology is rooted in the Footsteps of Local Agenda 21 and aims to build a new type of institutional relationship with the municipalities and communities in the company's areas of influence. The relationships were constructed through an ethical, transparent, and systematic process of dialogue among multiple social actors.

Petrobras, aware of the impacts of its business in the economic, social, spatial, political, cultural, and environmental areas, recognizes its leading role regarding sustainable practices and solutions. In this sense, the Petrobras Local Agenda 21 appears to be a mechanism that induces dialogue and consensus solutions. Besides promoting the exercise of citizenship, Petrobras Local Agenda 21 contributes to sustainable relationships with communities in the company's areas of influence. By adopting the principles and assumptions of Agenda 21 in their management of community relations, Petrobras seeks to promote changes in values and attitudes at both the organizational and community levels. The company's move breaks away from the bilateral logic and short-term transactional values, investing in long-lasting transformational and institutional relationships instead.

5   Analysis of results and discussion

The theoretical basis established the process of collecting data through documentary and field research. The primary data were collected through specific-target interviews, organized into categories of social groups representing the company and communities.

This research, although a single case study, has some important limitations that should be noted. One methodological constraint is its lack of generalizability. Indeed, the sample uses the criteria of typicality and accessibility; it is not a random sample, collected through statistical procedures. The study's aim, however, is not to draw statistical inferences from the sample result, but to gather in-depth knowledge of the variables that may relate to the problem at hand. That is, to examine how relationship management based on Agenda 21 can help establish sustainable relationships between companies and communities, generating benefits for both parties. Consequently, the sample size was not determined statistically, but rather by a representation of the subjects. As Gil (2007) noted, '[T]he purpose of the case study is not to provide accurate knowledge of the characteristics of a population, but rather to provide an overview of the problem and to identify possible factors that influence or are influenced by it'.

Still, concerning the selected sample, another limitation is the choice of research subjects. The program involves many social actors, both internal and external to Petrobras. However, it is not feasible, due to time and financial resources, to interview all managers and community leaders involved with the program. Those who were interviewed, however, were selected for their deep knowledge and mastery of the subject. Thus, despite the limitations, the selection of subjects proved adequate for the purposes of the investigation.

This study was based, it should be emphasized, on field research conducted in the dissertation, on qualitative data relating to the factors identified in this article, and on the methodology of the program to tackle the following: Local Agenda 21 helps to promote sustainable relationships between companies and communities and poses the question: What are the necessary management aspects for the adoption of such an instrument in institutional relationships?

6 Strategic factors for the promotion of relations between businesses

First, it is necessary to contextualize sustainable relationships in this study's theoretical framework and then to identify the strategic factors that promote them. Companies establish their institutional relations by adopting a systemic approach and pragmatic management of relationships with their stakeholders. A company's emphasis is on creating mutually beneficial opportunities. Stakeholders, however, must be mapped and ranked. It is then possible, according to Boechat, Grassi, and Soares Filho (2006), to determine those who should have priority in receiving benefits and how the interests of each stakeholder might best be met.

To enable transformational and perennial relations, it is imperative that companies create mechanisms for dialogue with the targeted communities, engendering cooperation and mutual trust. It is in such fashion that all parties might have their interests met. Earlier one-way communication protocols, from the company to the community, would here be insufficient. These perpetuate dependence and short-term transactional relationships.

These considerations demonstrate the need to rethink, with a view of corporate social responsibility, how companies manage their relations with the surrounding community. According to Ashley (2002), social responsibility is ethical behaviour in business that reflects a company's commitment to its relations with stakeholders. We can thus say that corporate social responsibility is the process of building good relations with stakeholders. At its essence, it enhances interaction, participation, involvement, and sharing so that dialogue happens effectively.

In this sense, the identified strategic factors are listed in Table 19.4. These factors indicate the connections between the themes examined in this study. Table 19.4 is not intended to be prescriptive regarding the classification of institutional sustainability. However, it

Table 19.4 Description of factors of reference authors – prevailing factors promoting sustainable relationships

Factors	Description
Trust	Forms of reciprocity that make cooperation effective. What must prevail in the actual dialogue process is a spirit of mutuality, sharing, and exchange.
Cooperation	Refers to ways of working together in view of the common good. Relations based on cooperation and collaboration reflect concern in the pursuit of common objectives and interests.
Responsibility	Awareness regarding the fact that the actions and attitudes do have positive and negative consequences for the environment. In sustainable relationships, it is important that the sharing of responsibilities moves toward joint solutions.
Social Engagement	Multidisciplinary engagement of society as a whole, including the various representatives of social sectors. In a systematic process of institutional relationship management, to promote the stimulus to the partnership of social actors: governments, businesses, and civil society.
Empowerment	People develop the capacity, power, and autonomy of persons acting as agents of change and transformation, respecting the aspects of culture and local knowledge, thus contributing to building an active citizenship. They should be considered as "subjects" and not "objects" of the building process towards sustainability.

presents factors that might constitute a guide to building sustainable relationships in light of the approaches adopted in this article and from references.

Briefly, these factors consistently lead to the meeting of business objectives and institutional missions and the fulfilling of corporate strategies. The factors set up expectations that lead to cooperative behaviour, behaviour that produces mutual benefits that uphold, in business deals, the principles of ethics and transparency. Thus, we might define sustainable relationships as those relationships that are established systematically and systemically; that follow the principles of trust, cooperation, and partnership; and that reflect the responsibilities of parties in the pursuit of common objectives and interests so as to contribute to the formation of a society moving towards sustainability.

7   The contribution of local Agenda 21 in promoting sustainable relationships between companies and communities

The data analysis confirms that the management based on Agenda 21 helps to spread the five factors identified in this study (shown in Table 19.4). It also confirms that these factors emphasize a culture that values ethics, transparency, respect, sense of belonging, and autonomy. This environment is conducive to establishing cooperative relationships and mutual trust between companies and communities, thus contributing to the promotion of sustainable relations. The quantitative and qualitative data demonstrate, in the relationship process, the importance and established synergy of factors identified in this study. The data also point out a very frequent occurrence of such factors regarding the relationship between Petrobras and the communities. It was found that 100 per cent of respondents, responsible for strategic and operational management of the program, understood that there ought to be effective collaboration of the program in order to disseminate trust, cooperation, responsibility, multidisciplinary involvement (considering the myriad sectors involved in the process), and empowerment of people. According to one respondent, '[T]he methodology of the program is based on these factors. Henceforth, it is only effective when relationships of trust are built, bringing forth collective cooperation among stakeholders'.

The community representatives corroborated this assertion. The assessment identified that 80 per cent believe the program disseminates these factors. The other 20 per cent believed that 'part' of the program helped spread these factors. One of the interviewees justified his response based on discontinuity of the program in his community. It should be noted that, at the time of the study, the program was awaiting approval from the Petrobras Executive Board to continue the next steps. In addition to the previous question, community representatives were asked to identify whether these factors were present in Petrobras relationships with the communities. The results showed that 80 per cent affirmed the presence of such factors.

The program, in terms of spreading these factors, appears to be effective. For all factors, except for engagement, more than 70 per cent of the responses were 'always and often'. In the case of engagement, 'sometimes' was the most prevalent level according to the dependence of involvement and action by other social actors, as it calls for Agenda 21.

Evidently, the views of communities are aligned with that of Petrobras. Such views reveal that these factors are being internalized, manifested in an effective change in relationship style, a change from a perspective of dependency to a more democratic, participatory one that emphasizes autonomy and empowerment.

We then evaluated the degree of importance of these factors and their contribution to promoting sustainable relationships. According to the respondents from both groups, these factors generally have similar weights in their contribution to sustainable relationships, with levels ranging from 'very important' to 'important'.

As highlighted by UNESCO (2005), Local Agenda 21 has proven to be an important tool to bring the company together in order to understand and apply the concepts of citizenship. Indeed, citizenship has become a point of reference in sustainable construction development.

8 Aspects of management required for adoption of local Agenda 21 as a tool of the relationship between the company and communities

By analysing the positive and negative aspects mentioned by participants of Petrobras Agenda 21, we were able to identify management aspects necessary in the adoption of Local Agenda 21. In doing so, we made a correlation between the literature and practice.

One advantage indicated is the capacity to systematize the practice of relationship, standardizing the actions and discourse across the enterprise. This encourages the involvement of other partners, highlighting the role of each social actor. Alongside the development of the program, the company becomes demystified. It ceases to be solely responsible for the problems and solutions of communities and becomes simply a link in a network. It is important, according to Ramos (1981), who postulated the theory of social systems delimitation, to ensure complementarity and balanced coexistence of social organizations towards a common goal. This approach to participation, cooperation, and sharing, a typical process of Agenda 21, is responsible for the maturation of the relationship between Petrobras and surrounding communities.

Another advantage is evidenced by the degree of existing social capital in communities. The social relations of each community can sometimes present a problem; the lack of mobilization and unity among the residents can compromise the success of the implemented actions. Therefore, it is necessary to work intensively at sensitizing and mobilizing people. In fact, Brazil seems to have a long historical tradition regarding the establishment of autocratic relations. As one respondent pointed out, '[T]he democratic process is still recent and most people still wait to be told what to do instead of setting their own courses in life'. Jacobi (1999) stressed the need to create conditions that would encourage more active participation of society in discussions concerning its actions and fate. In this sense, the program contributes to the exercise of active citizenship, empowering people to act as agents of change and transformation in the march towards sustainability. The main advantages and difficulties of Petrobras Agenda 21 in the view of the company's representatives are gathered in Table 19.5.

Within communities, the advantages and difficulties cited by the leaders interviewed align with those listed in Table 19.5. The basic difference between them is the focus of the approach. While Table 19.5 focuses on management aspects and effects on the business, Table 19.6 concerns those related to pragmatic results in the communities.

Table 19.5 Advantages and second vision hampered diagnostic company

Diagnosed advantages	Diagnosed difficulties
systematizes practices of community relations at the company	differences in the degree of understanding and ownership among the operation units of the Petrobras system
establishes definition of the role of each actor in the social relations established	differences regarding the level of commitment of the professionals involved in community relations management
fosters partnerships in the search for joint solutions to shared problems to the communities	lack of engagement of the other stakeholders regarding the strategic program
promotes greater engagement and sharing among the actors involved	different level of mobilization and awareness on the part of communities
collaborates on building social capital, citizenship, and increased capacity to respond to crisis	conflict of interests among the actors involved
encourages greater partnership in the search for joint solutions to shared problems and interests	lack of engagement of other stakeholders regarding the strategic program
provides a better understanding of local diversity	medium and long-term results
formalizes collective dialogue spaces through forums established in the process of appropriation and construction of knowledge	social and environmental relationship complexities at each site or region
promotes the full exercise of citizenship, both within and outside the company	lack of credibility among stakeholders
contributes to the image of the company	economic and social vulnerability of the communities
collaborates with the continuity of the business as it stimulates formation of a sustainable society	high expectation from the community concerning the solving of all the programs elaborated

Source: qualitative data from field research (2010).

Table 19.6 Advantages and hampered diagnostic from the community perspective

Diagnosed advantages	Diagnosed difficulties
create more expressive presence in the communities	work with the issues of cultural communities (culture characterized by passivity, welfare, and immediacy)
understand qualitatively how the communities work	keep the involvement and commitment of residents throughout the process
manage conflicts and seek consensus	work for the collective culture of the common good
foster a culture for the common good	meet expectations and desires of residents
involve other social actors	deal with people's discretion
encourage networking	Medium- and long-term scope of the results
establish a single channel of communication with the company's permanent communities	continue Petrobras Agenda 21, without any interruption
ensure transparency and credibility in the process of social investment by the company, without privileges to specific groups	

Source: qualitative data from field research (2010).

Synthesized by means of diagnosis in Tables 19.5 and 19.6, we listed aspects of management required for the adoption of Local Agenda 21 by the companies in order to contribute to the effectiveness of this instrument in ongoing community relations. They are:

1   Link clearly the values, principles, and actions of the company to the assumptions of Agenda 21.
2   Adopt a mechanism as part of corporate governance to ensure alignment and institutional presence of the theme in business strategies and objectives.
3   Seek out the commitment of top leadership, who should act as sponsors of the process.
4   Mobilize and engage the company managers in implementing the principles and actions of Agenda 21 in the management of community relations.
5   Promote continued education of the workforce that is directly involved in this process.
6   Educate the workforce, particularly managers about community relations as a value to the company; they have a direct impact on the business and corporate image.
7   Disseminate the principles and actions of Agenda 21 to internal and external stakeholders alike.
8   Define the social actors involved and encourage inter-institutional partnerships.
9   Monitor and promote assessment processes to ensure expected results.
10 Disclose to stakeholders the actions and outcomes that this tool produces.
11 Systematically monitor the implementation process of Agenda 21 in relationship management to ensure the application of the methodology at its core.
12 Respect the local cultures and values.
13 Maintain the active participation of citizens by performing mobilization activities and creating awareness in the community.
14 Operate in synergy with public policies and other actors in order to optimize resources and maximize results.

In adopting Local Agenda 21, these aspects are fundamental to success. This instrument allows the existence of a collaborative management, rather than a reactive one, adopting a systemic vision where responsibilities are shared opportunities and seeking joint solutions.

9   Conclusion

In establishing sustainable relationships with the communities that surround their facilities, many companies are making contributions to generate mutual benefits. By interacting with other social actors, companies build social capital in these communities. There are direct results to improve business performance. It is evident that companies that promote the making of a cooperative, democratic, and sustainable system are creating a favourable environment for business sustainability. It may be concluded that businesses thrive if they understand and manage their relationships in a structured and systemic way.

This article has highlighted the importance of companies' establishing sustainable relationships with communities. It has also demonstrated the potential of Local Agenda 21 to be used as a tool for managing these relationships. If companies are to promote a promising and sustainable environment for their activities, they need to build, based on the principles of dialogue and transparency, long-lasting and transformational relationships with the surrounding communities.

By examining Local Agenda 21 from the perspective of responsible management, we can observe that this instrument bears characteristics that suit the main factor in the promotion of sustainable relationships identified in this study. Table 19.7 mentions some of the characteristics and shows the correlation.

Table 19.7 Correlation between the characteristics of Agenda 21 and the most important factors for sustainable relationships

Important factors	Characteristics of Agenda 21
Confidence	• mechanism inducing dialogue and consensus • ability to deal with conflict • enhancing the feeling of belonging and ownership
Cooperation	• focus on sustainable development based on democratic participation and the convergence of interests • fostering the "common good" culture • integrating and synergy instrument regarding the various existing efforts, optimizing resources, and enhancing results
Responsibility	• process inducer that challenges people to create their own vision of a sustainable future and discover the role of each in pursuit of sustainability • encouraging the involvement of every citizen • vision for long-term process connecting the practicalities
Multidisciplinary engagement	• participatory and inclusive approach, which requires the participation of all sectors • promotion of partnerships
Empowerment	• strengthens citizenship and social capital formation • fosters effective conditions for participation and decision • focuses on local action and involvement of people in solving their problems • promotes changes in attitudes and values at individual and collective levels

The community relationship management tool that is based on Agenda 21 spreads the predominant factors considered to promote sustainable relationships; it has the strong potential to generate results and mutual benefits. It is emphasized that the main expected outcome of this process is a consensual participation able to establish win-win relationships for communities. Communities can draw on the results of Agenda 21 to improve their life quality, as can the company. The company may rely on the capital and largest community resilience to achieve their goals.

References

Aledi, C. and Quelhas, O.L.G. (2003). *The Sustainability of Organizations and Management of Ethics, Transparency, and Corporate Social Responsibility*. Rio de Janeiro: LATEC. Available at: http://www.buscalegis.ufsc.br/arquivos/pf_311007_269.pdf, accessed 12 March 2010.

Almeida, F.A. (2002). *The Good Business of Sustainability*, 1st edn. Rio de Janeiro: Nova Fronteira.

Ashley, P.A. (2002). *Ethics and Social Responsibility in Business*, 2nd edn. São Paulo: Saraiva.

Ashley, P.A., Coutinho, R.B.G. and Tomei, P.A. (2000). Corporate Social Responsibility and Corporate Citizenship: A Comparative Analysis, in *EnANPAD 2000: Annual Meeting*, Florianópolis, Brazil.

Boechat, C., Grassi, M.R. and Soares Filho, R. (2006). Brazilian business strategies in light of sustainability. *Book of Ideas*, 6(2), 5–17.

Bohm, D. (1989). *Dialogue: Communication Networks and Coexistence*. London: Pallas Athena.

Born, R.H. (2002). Agenda 21 Brasileira: Instrumentos e desafios para a sustentabilidade, in A. Camargo, J.P.R. Capobianco and J.A. Oliveira (eds.), *Meio Ambiente Brasil: Avanços e obstáculos pós Rio 92*. São Paulo: Estação Liberdade, 79–80.

Buchholtz, A.K. and Carroll, A.B. (2008). *Business and Society: Ethics and Stakeholder Management*, 7th edn. Mason, OH: Cengage Learning.

Carroll, A.B. (1999). Corporate social responsibility: Evolution of a definitional construct. *Business and Society*, 38(3), 268–95.

Carroll, A. B., & Buchholtz, A. K. (2011). *Business and society: Ethics and stakeholder management* (8 ed.). Australia: Thomson South-Western.

Clarkson, M.B.E. (1995). A stakeholder framework for analyzing and evaluating corporate social performance. *Academy of Management Review*, 20(1), 92–117.

Donaldson, T. and Preston, L.E. (1995). The stakeholder theory of the corporation: Concepts, evidence and implications. *Academy of Management Review*, 20(1), 65–91.

Félix, L.F.F. (2003). O ciclo virtuoso do desenvolvimento responsável, in *Instituto Ethos (2003). Responsabilidade Social das Empresas: A contribuição das universidades, 2*. São Paulo: Peirópolis, 13–42.

Freeman, E. (1994). Stakeholder theory of the modern corporation, in Dienhart, J.W. (ed.) (2000), *Business, Institutions and Ethics*. New York: Oxford University Press, 246–57.

Freeman, E. (1998). Stakeholder theory of the modern corporation, in L.P. Hartman (ed.), *Perspectives in Business Ethics*. New York: McGraw-Hill, 171–81.

Friedman, M. (1970). The social responsibility of business is increase its profits. *New York Times Magazine*, September 13, 1970.

Gil, A.C. (2007). *Como elaborar projetos de pesquisa*, 4th edn. São Paulo: Atlas.

Gil, Antonio Carlos. *Como elaborar projetos de pesquisa*. São Paulo: Atlas, 1991.

Hawkins, D.P.B. and Costa, S.P.B. (2002). Responsabilidade social e cidadania empresarial: Uma pesquisa exploratória no setor supermercadista de médio porte de Fortaleza, in EnANPAD 2002: National Association of Graduate Programme in Administration, Salvador, Brazil.

Jacobi, P. (1999). Meio ambiente e sustentabilidade, in CEPAM (eds.), *O município no século XXI: Cenários e Perspectivas*. São Paulo: Especial, 175–83.

Jensen, M. (2001). Value maximization, stakeholder theory and the corporate objective function. *Journal of Applied Corporate Finance*, 14(3), 8–21.

Key, S. (1999). Towards a new theory of the firm: A critique of stakeholder theory. *Management Decision*, 37(4), 317–28.

Kohler, M.C.M. (2003). Local Agenda 21: Challenges of its implementation. Unpublished MSc thesis, University of São Paulo, Brazil.

Leal Filho, W. and Idowu, S. (eds.). (2009). *Global Practices of Corporate Social Responsibility*. Berlin: Springer-Verlag.

Leal Filho, W. and Rios, A.R. (2007). *Accountability Issues in International Development Projects*, 1st edn. Frankfurt: Peter Lang Scientific Publishers.

Louche, C., Idowu, S.O. and Leal Filho, W. (eds.). (2010). *Innovative CSR: From Risk Management to Value Creation*. Sheffield: Greenleaf Publishing.

Machado Filho, C.P. (2006). *Social Responsibility and Governance: The Debate and the Implications*. São Paulo: Cengage Learning.

Ministry of Environment. (2012). Secretary of Institutional Articulation and Environmental Citizenship. Available at: http://www.mma.gov.br/sitio/index.php?ido=conteudo.monta&idEstrutura=18 [Accessed 25 May 2012].

Novaes, R.C. (2002). Sustainable development at the local scale: Local Agenda 21 as a strategy for the construction of sustainability, in *ANPPAS: 1st Meeting of the National Association of Post Graduate Studies and Research in Environment and Society*. Indaiatuba, Brazil, 15.

Pinto, M.C.S. and Oliveira, R.R. (2004). Estratégias competitivas no setor elétrico brasileiro: Uma análise dos interesses e expectativas dos atores da Chesf. *Revista de administração contemporânea*, 8, 131–55.

Ramos, A.G. (1981). *A nova ciência das organizações: uma reconceituação da riqueza das nações*, 1st edn. Rio de Janeiro: Fundação Getúlio Vargas.

Report of the World Commission on Environment and Development: Our Common Future, http://www.un-documents.net/our-common-future.pdf (Retrieved on Oct 15, 2015).

Resende, M.S.R. and Kamel, J.A.N. (2007). Dialogue with stakeholders, ideas and experiences to its viability. *Industrial Management Magazine*, 3(1), 111–22.

Sternberg, E. (1996). Stakeholder theory exposed. *The Corporate Governance Quarterly*, 2(1), 4–18.

Stoney, C. and Winstanley, D. (2001). Stakeholding: Confusion or utopia? Mapping the conceptual terrain. *Journal of Management Studies*, 38(5), 603–25.

Svedsen, A. (1998). *The Stakeholder Strategy*, 1st edn. San Francisco, CA: Berrett-Koeler.

UNESCO. (2005). United Nations Decade of Education for Sustainable Development. Paris. Available at: http://unesdoc.unesco.org/images/0014/001486/148654e.pdf [Accessed 25 May 2012].

Wilson, M. (2003). Corporate sustainability: What is it and where does it come from? *Ivey Business Journal*, March/April, 1–5. Available at http://wwwold.iveybusinessjournal.com/view_article.asp?intArticle_ID=405.

Yin, R.K. (2005). *Estudo de caso: planejamento e métodos*, 3rd edn. Porto Alegre: Bookman.

20 Sustainable supply chain management

The good, the bad, and the ugly

Arpit Raswant and Catherine Sutton-Brady

1 Introduction

"Sustainability" is no longer just the new buzzword of the business world; it is something that many companies in various industries have begun to take very seriously. In this chapter we begin by explaining the role of sustainability in supply chains and show the benefits that companies can achieve through sustainable practices. The chapter presents real-life examples showing how some companies approach sustainability effectively to achieve advantage in their industry, while others fail to see the advantage in good practice and suffer the consequences.

2 The concept of sustainability

For the purposes of this chapter we use the common definition of sustainability as being that which 'meets the needs of the present without compromising the ability of future generations to meet their own needs' (Brundtland et al., 1987). This definition from the United Nations is built on two key concepts, the essential needs of the world's poor and the limitations on the environment's ability to meet present and future needs. The report by Brundtland et al. (1987) is specifically concerned with sustainable development, but aspects of this are especially relevant to sustainable supply chain management (SSCM). The report highlights the importance of development that pays attention to access to resources and the distribution of costs and benefits. In essence, the idea is that to be sustainable, a company's actions must be equitable to all and not exploit some for the good of others. Brundtland et al. state that 'even the narrow notion of physical sustainability implies a concern for social equity between generations, a concern that must logically be extended to equity within each generation (Brundtland et al., 1987).

SSCM is itself defined as 'the management of supply chain operations, resources information, and funds in order to maximise the supply chain profitability while at the same time minimizing the environmental impacts and maximizing the social well-being' (Hassini, Surti and Searcy, 2012). SSCM is therefore concerned with the integration of environmental and/or social issues (Brandenburgh, Govindan, Sarkis and Seuring, 2014).

With this definition and view of sustainability and SSCM in mind we look to the literature on supply chain management (SCM) to outline the reasons companies seek sustainable supply chains by investigating the benefits of sustainability. We will also seek to identify the parameters at play that allow companies to achieve sustainability.

3   Why pursue sustainable supply chains?

The reasons for implementing sustainable supply chains can be both internal and external to the organization (Morali and Searcy, 2013). External pressure on companies to be seen as embracing the concept of sustainability has grown considerably over the since the turn of the millennium (Ageron, Gunaserkaran and Spalanzani, 2012). There is growing pressure from governments, consumers, and other stakeholders for companies to be corporately, socially, and environmentally responsible (Morali and Searcy, 2013). Essentially, companies are mindful of market forces where customers and consumers are demanding products that have been produced sustainably. Also, financial stakeholders such as mutual and superannuation funds are investing in companies seen as being ethical and environmentally friendly (Hassini et al., 2012, Reefke and Trocchi, 2013). On the other hand, regulations are changing and companies are being required to be environmentally friendly (Okongwu, Morimoto and Lauras, 2013). Social issues, such as treating labour forces well, are also a driving force behind SSCM (Hassini et al., 2012).

Corporate social responsibility (CSR), which is seen as leading to good corporate citizenship, can be defined as 'treating the stakeholders of the firm ethically or in a responsible manner' by implementing ethical sustainable practices (Wan-Jan, 2006). Indeed, companies that implement sustainable practices do so not only to satisfy stakeholders but also to increase profitability by creating a better image for the company. Internally, many companies see the opportunities created by adopting SSCM especially when dealing with environmental issues. Companies often gain new customers and overall competitive advantage in their industry as a result (Ageron et al., 2012).

4   Sustainability parameters

As previously discussed, environmental and social issues are seen as key in sustainability (Morali and Searcy, 2013). Within the areas of environment and society, various parameters have been identified in previous research as being important to achieving sustainability in supply chains. These include air emissions, water discharge quality, energy consumption, water use, waste management and land disturbance, jobs, knowledge transfer, health and safety of employees, equal opportunities, and negative side effects on workers (Matos and Hall, 2007). For the purposes of this chapter we will explore three parameters of sustainability: labour, resources, and waste management.

Ideally, a business should consider the well-being of all the stakeholders in the supply chain. This would enhance profitability for all parties whilst bringing experiential process efficiencies, and also foster interpersonal relationships. However, more often than not, depending on the consequences involved, the various difficult and unpleasant accountabilities are shifted in the supply chain. By looking at these three parameters, we hope to understand the idea of accountability for sustainability in the supply chain and show how the companies that collaborate with suppliers tend to achieve better outcome – essentially, when accountability is not shifted but where the company takes control.

5   SSCM triangular approach

We will now draw from case studies, best practices, and market knowledge to develop an understanding of SSCM in action and illustrate the related definitions under the categories of good, bad, and ugly.

6 Labour

An emphasis on SSCM should acknowledge and identify the importance of labour in the production process. Fair treatment of all employees irrespective of their position and location should be a basic requirement. This is in line with the Brundtland Report (Brundtland et al., 1987), which states that 'sustainability requires the enforcement of wider responsibilities for the impacts of decisions . . . [and] that an environment adequate for health and well-being is essential for all human beings including future generations'.

The good: Starbucks Corporation (Seattle, Washington, USA)

Starbucks is an American company that maintains a global chain of coffee shops. It is the single largest player in the coffee industry with a presence in 62 countries and more than 19,000 stores (Starbucks FY13 Annual Report, 2014). With burgeoning revenue of nearly USD$15 billion, Starbucks comes second to none (Starbucks Corp. Annual Financials, 2014). In an era of fair trade, Starbucks in collaboration with Conservation International (CI) developed Coffee and Farmer Equity (C.A.F.E.) Practices and Cocoa Practices to ensure ethically sourced coffee and cocoa (Starbucks Coffee, 2014). These practices focus on product quality, economic accountability, social responsibility, and environmental leadership. While seemingly broad and ambiguous, the implementation of a scorecard system and third-party verification make C.A.F.E. viable. Starbucks' internal ethical sourcing programme is targeted and set to ensure long-term supply of high-quality coffee beans, thus ensuring requisite resources for their business. This programme is dynamic and based on continuous improvements. Coffee "renovation" or replanting, monitoring climate change impacts, and adapting existing processes are encouraged to mitigate any negative environmental effects (Starbucks Ethical Sourcing, 2014). Starbucks has also established Farmer Support Centers in various communities, assisting farmers to achieve their goals through intelligent farm management. Starbucks claims that its ethical practices have positively affected more than a million workers employed by thousands of participating farms (Starbucks Coffee, 2014).

The bad: Apple Inc. (Cupertino, California, USA) and Hon Hai Precision Industry Co. Ltd. (New Taipei, Taiwan)

With approximately USD$159 billion in cash reserves, Apple is certainly one of the richest and most powerful companies in the world (Ro, 2014), though it has existed for only 30 years. Hon Hai Precision Industry's Foxconn is the Taiwanese information technology giant that serves as an original equipment manufacturer for such notable products as iPhone (Apple Inc.), Kindle (Amazon), PlayStation (Sony), and others. (Kan, 2012; Yarow, 2012). Foxconn is China's largest exporter and one of the world's largest employers (Leach, 2012). Some argue that Apple and Foxconn are the best thing that's happened to the Chinese labour market, with increasing wages and increased local employment (Worstall, 2012). However, some inside reports and direct consultation with Foxconn labour in China indicate otherwise (Duhigg and Barboza, 2012). Long working hours, overcrowded employee dorms, harsh working conditions, and other such issues are noted. Internal pressure to lower production costs and deliver products faster has resulted in these labour conditions (Duhigg and Barboza, 2012; Gugliemo, 2013). Apple recognizes this as an issue but seems to do little to resolve it. One may ponder on why it should take activist groups, reported suicides, and horrifying labour stories going viral to encourage Apple to take steps to ensure better work conditions. Isn't Apple's responsibility to verify appropriate working conditions prior to contracting with a company to manufacture their products? Or, is it fair to push the legal accountability to Foxconn? Are Apple and Foxconn both guilty in the issue of labour exploitation? More importantly, is there a mechanism that can mitigate the possibility of such corporate exploitation of the labour in internationalized production and manufacturing operations?

The ugly: Textile and garment industry (Dhaka, Bangladesh)

On 24 April 2013, Dhaka, Bangladesh, witnessed the collapse of the Rana Plaza building, which housed several factories producing clothing for major American and European brands (Al-Mahmood, 2013; Manik and Yardley, 2013). More than 1,130 workers died and more than 2,500 were rescued, but some suffered terrible injuries (Parveen, 2014). Reports suggest that workers found cracks in the building the day before the collapse but authorities were indifferent. Allegedly, workers were threatened and forced to labor in factories in Rana Plaza (Gomes, 2013).

The strength of Bangladesh's USD$20 billion garment industry is the fact that it has around 5,000 factories. However, there are fewer than 200 qualified inspectors, and it can take more than five years to inspect working conditions in all the factories. There have been a couple of initiatives since the Rana Plaza collapse: Bangladesh Accord for Fire and Building Safety is a legal approach that mandates signatory companies to undertake garment factory inspections and worker training, and the industry-sponsored voluntary Alliance for Bangladesh Worker Safety, which undertakes factory inspections, develops corrective action plans and helps with remediation. It also provides training to managers and security personnel (Khullar, 2014). However, there is a long road ahead for the victims. Shortly after the fire a trust fund was set up to support the victims and their families. Although some 18 retailers and organizations donated money to the trust fund, many brands that made clothes in Rana Plaza factories have not provided any compensation to affected parties (Hildebrandt, 2014). Logic dictates that incidents of this nature should be avoidable by taking basic precautionary measures in the workplace. Cutting production costs to maximize profit is a preferred strategy especially for labour-intensive industries; however, a company should evaluate production as a part of its whole supply chain. Instead of stirring up CSR initiatives as reactive approach, corporate social responsibility should be proactive. In the case of Rana Plaza, workers' lives could have been saved if companies that outsourced their production to factories based in Rana Plaza had shown a proactive attitude towards suppliers' conduct and labour conditions. All companies that outsourced their production to contractors and subcontractors based in Rana Plaza are at fault. These companies failed to be responsible and act when needed. To be truly sustainable, we need a mechanism to increase the accountability of all the parties in supply chain management.

7   Sustainability parameter: Resource maximization

The presumption that resources are limited raises the importance of maximizing their usage. An ideal SSCM should have a clear focus on conserving and efficiently using resources. It should attempt to achieve the best possible operation that improves the company's profitability whilst respecting the labour involved and the shared environment.

The good: Carbon Recycling International (Reykjavík, Iceland)

Carbon Recycling International (CRI), founded in 2006, is a venture-based Icelandic-American company with its headquarters in Iceland and an office in La Jolla, California (CRI, 2014). CRI converts carbon dioxide from industrial emissions to methanol. Renewable methanol (RM), a liquid fuel, can be blended with gasoline for automobiles and can also be used in biodiesel production. RM is thus considered a "cleaner" fuel, as it requires limited resources and can be produced with renewable energy, unlike other renewable fuels such as ethanol and biodiesel, which are produced using fossil fuels and scarce agricultural resources. CRI expects to increase production by a factor of 100 before 2018 to supply the European market (Valdimarsson, 2013). CRI is exemplary in maximizing its resources as its technology uses Iceland's green energy to process carbon dioxide and produce renewable fuel. CRI provides the energy industry with a real and sustainable alternative to fossil fuels.

The bad: Water bottle industry (worldwide)

It is quite common for pretty much all of us to grab a bottle of water on our commute to work or the gym, for a quick run, or just to store them at home for weekend get-togethers. For the consumer this is both easy and cost-effective – or is it? Maybe it is *too* easy. One could argue that the community cost of this phenomenon is far greater than people consider. With the global market for packaged water exceeding USD$100 billion, we as a global community use around 50 billion plastic bottles a year (Newcomer, 2014). These seemingly benign bottles release toxic chemicals, and around 80 per cent of them go straight to landfill after one use. Furthermore, decomposition can take 450 years on average. Should the companies that produce and sell packaged water be held responsible? Should we blame the consumer? The government? In addition, to make the matter more interesting, there is no guarantee that bottled water is safer or cleaner than water from the tap (Newcomer, 2014). As consumers, what can we do? We can resort to reusable bottles (Baume, 2014). As institutions, how should we act to save the environment? Companies like Apple distribute branded reusable bottles to their employees (Hall, 2014), and some educational institutions, such as Vanier College (Montreal, Canada), have banned the sale of bottled water on campus (CTV News, 2014). As governments, what immediate measure can we introduce? We can promote initiatives such as Beijing's attempt to popularize "recycle-to-ride" devices, which award subway fare credit to people who insert polyethylene terephthalate (PET) bottles into the device, which then processes the bottle for recycling (Watts, 2012).

The ugly: Chonghaejin Marine (Jeju Island, South Korea)

The ferry *Sewol*, carrying 476 people, was sailing from Incheon to Jeju Island when it sank on 16 April 2014, leaving 284 people dead. Some 172 were rescued and 20 were missing, according to a contemporary report (Park, 2014). Most of the victims were students from a high school near Seoul who were on a trip to Jeju Island (BBC News, 2014a). Investigators believe that *Sewol* was carrying 3,608 tonnes of cargo (though it had a recommended maximum of 987 tonnes) with 580 tonnes of ballast water (though at least 2,000 tonnes of water were recommended to keep the ship balanced) (Associated Press, 2014; BBC News 2014b). Prosecutors were able to apprehend all 15 of the *Sewol*'s core crew members and

Chonghaejin's CEO, Han Shik Kim (Kim, 2014). Several crew members, including the captain, were charged with homicide through abandonment as they made no attempt to help the passengers, instead getting themselves to safety, and homicide through occupational negligence.

Supply chain managers often deal with pressure to reduce logistics costs and thereby increase profitability. However, there is a limit to resources utilization. Chonghaejin Marine began the Incheon-to-Jeju-Island route in March 2013, and 57 per cent of trips, or 139 out of 241, carried excess cargo (Park, 2014). In an economic sense, Chonghaejin Marine was maximizing its resources: most trips with excess cargo that the company chose to make didn't result in disaster, but they certainly had the potential to. Sadly, disaster was realized with 476 people on board. Between March 2013 and the disaster, the company profited an additional USD$2.3 million from overloading the ferry. Prosecution of offenders will not bring peace to families of those who never returned home. No amount of money can ease their loss. SSCM should focus on the potential use of resources whilst respecting all direct and indirect stakeholders, but human life must be valued above all else. The *Sewol* ferry disaster could have been avoided if people involved in Chonghaejin's supply chain and the related government agencies and port authorities had abided by the rules.

8   Sustainability parameter: waste management

Most modern production processes involve waste as a by-product. Waste is defined as an unusable incidental or secondary product made in producing the primary good(s). The perfect SSCM should result in close to zero waste, which can be achieved through cleaner processes (Linton, Klassen and Jayaraman, 2007).

The good: Honda (Tokyo, Japan)

Honda is a Japanese public multinational corporation primarily known as a manufacturer of automobiles and motorcycles. On 14 July 2011 Honda announced that 10 of its 14 manufacturing facilities in North America achieved zero waste to landfill, while the remaining four plants were functioning with 'virtually zero' waste to landfill (Honda, 2011). Honda led the industry in a trend which is pushing others to follow. On 27 February 2013 Ford declared that it would increase its environmental strategy with a five-year plan. Ford aimed to decrease the waste that was sent to landfill by 40 per cent per vehicle from 2011 levels. Furthermore, GM invited industry participants on 19 February 2013 to discuss and collaborate on waste reduction and materials utilization (Motavalli, 2013). It was a positive move by the company to proactively approach environmental and sustainability issues. However, such actions can be expedited and structured by government agencies regulating and reinforcing environmental laws in the market space.

The bad: Walmart (Bentonville, Arkansas, USA)

Walmart is an American multinational retail corporation based in Bentonville, Arkansas. With more than 11,000 retail units in 27 countries and e-commerce websites in 10 countries as of 2014, Walmart is a global retail mammoth (Walmart, 2014). On 28 May 2013 Walmart was fined USD$82 million over mishandling of hazardous wastes (Clifford,

2013).Walmart pleaded guilty, bringing to an end an investigation that lasted nearly a decade. Walmart workers reportedly were throwing hazardous products such as bleach and fertilizer in the trash and into sewage systems (Harris, 2013). It is very difficult to calculate the real environmental and health costs to the community in cases of this nature. Companies should adhere to strict checks on internal processes, especially if they deal with dangerous materials, and, compliance failure should be taken very seriously in a timely manner. Personnel found guilty should be made accountable. Monetary fines are welcomed; however, other ways to serve the community should be encouraged, such as forced community service by personnel who were involved in such incidents. The USD$82 million fine might not have made much of a dent in Walmart's balance sheet; however, if personnel are held accountable for their actions, then it can greatly encourage others to be extra careful of their actions.

The ugly: Trafigura (Amsterdam, Netherlands)

Trafigura is a Dutch multinational commodity trading company with an annual turnover of more than USD$133 billion (Trafigura, 2014). In 2010 a Dutch court found Trafigura guilty of illegally exporting toxic waste from Amsterdam to Ivory Coast and hiding the nature of the cargo in its ship the *Probo Koala*. Trafigura was fined €1 million, the employee who coordinated the ship's operations in the port of Amsterdam was fined €25,000 euros, and the ship's captain was fined and given a five-year suspended jail term (BBC News, 2010). In 2006 Trafigura's ship had tried to unload its toxic cargo in Amsterdam, but the port service would not accept the waste without an additional service fee because it was toxic. The company then decided to discharge the cargo in Abidjan, Ivory Coast. People living in the area suffered a range of illnesses and conditions such as nausea, breathlessness, and swollen stomachs, among others (Business and Human Rights Resource Centre, 2014). Trafigura repeatedly denied any wrongdoing and continued to assert that the waste was not toxic. It even entered an agreement with the Ivory Coast government to pay nearly USD$200 million in return for immunity from prosecution, and a Dutch court decided that many allegations were beyond its jurisdiction so prosecution wasn't possible. With the complex structure of legalities across countries, it seems to be easier for firms to get away with harmful actions by paying the various agencies and not getting prosecuted (Harvey, 2012). One may argue that UN could play a stronger and more assertive role to prosecute companies that are involved in toxic waste dumping. However, it will need governments to act together in the interest of the global community. Many environmental disasters cannot be fixed by money, and it can take many years for the environment to return to the natural balance (Business Pundit, 2010).

9   Conclusion

This chapter has explored the idea of SSCM through real-life examples and case studies. It has clearly shown how some companies have mastered the concept while others need to reconsider their operations if they are ever to succeed or be competitive in the marketplace.

There are a number of issues that we can draw attention to, and these revolve around good practice versus bad and their impacts on the business. In fact, while many consumers note a desire to support sustainable companies, the reality is often different. The reality is many will continue to buy from companies even after it becomes clear that their practices are not sustainable. Evidence of this can be found in both the Apple/Foxconn and Rana Plaza examples, where even though these cases attracted worldwide attention it did not directly affect the sale of Apple products or the sales of many of the world's leading clothing brands. Only consumers with very high ethical standards will boycott the product or choose to pay more for the more sustainable one. This leaves many companies in a vicious circle where they are trying to balance external factors of demand with internal concerns about the feasibility and impact on profit of sustainable practice.

We also see that many companies can have truly sustainable supply chains only through collaboration with suppliers. This is nothing new. Gimenez and Sierra (2013) found that collaboration with suppliers allowed for improvement in training and overall better practice throughout the supply chain. We see in the cases cited that the importance of knowing exactly who is part of your supply chain and having good relationships with them is crucial to achieving SSCM. Looking at the Rana Plaza example, we find that had these leading brands taken more care in assessing their suppliers, they would have found that subcontracting to these other factories was taking place. Arguing that they did not know does not wash well with consumers and puts into question their sustainable practices and ethical responsibilities. Apple after the Foxconn incident moved to make changes and ensure they were implemented, but a lot of bad publicity can be avoided if measures are put in place through better collaboration up front.

While we tend to concentrate on the bad examples, the good examples outlined here show how companies can benefit from sustainable practices while also ensuring the future of communities worldwide, as in the Starbucks example or ensuring sustainable resource maximization, as in the case of CRI. Likewise, the example of Honda and the car industry shows that if one company takes the lead, others will follow suit, leaving us with hope for a sustainable future.

Unfortunately, there will always be companies trying to increase their profitability no matter what the cost. The Trafigura and Chonghaejin Marine examples show us that often companies have a total disregard for both the environment and people. In these cases, the only solution is legislation to ensure that they comply or face very large penalties or prosecution – in a sense, forcing such companies to implement sustainable supply chains.

The overriding conclusion is that companies' supply chains must take care not to exploit resources and human capital; must be conscious of waste management in the present and preserve the environment for the future of all. Only then we will truly see sustainability in action.

References

Ageron, B., Gunaserkaran, A. and Spalanzani, A. (2012). Sustainable supply management: An empirical study. *International Journal Production Economics*, 140, 168–182.

Al-Mahmood, S.Z. (2013). Deadly Collapse in Bangladesh. *The Wall St. Journal*, April 24th 2013. http://online.wsj.com/news/articles/SB10001424127887324874204578441912031665482 (Accessed May 10, 2014).

Apple. (2014). http://www.apple.com/30-years/ (Accessed May 9, 2014).

Associated Press. (2014). Tragic Ferry Sewol Repeatedly Overloaded. AP, May 4th 2014. http://www.nydailynews.com/news/world/tragic-ferry-sewol-repeatedly-overloaded-report-article-1.1779217 (Accessed May 12, 2014).

Baume, M. (2014). Ditching the Single-Use Water Bottle. *Marketplace*, May 7th 2014. http://www.marketplace.org/topics/sustainability/ditching-single-use-water-bottle (Accessed May 9, 2014).

BBC News. (2010). Trafigura Found Guilty of Exporting Toxic Waste. *BBC News*, July 23rd 2010. http://www.bbc.com/news/world-africa-10735255 (Accessed Retrieved May 12, 2014).

BBC News. (2014a). South Korea Ferry Company Chief Detained. *BBC News*, May 8th 2014. http://www.bbc.com/news/world-asia-27321257 (Accessed May 12, 2014).

BBC News. (2014b). South Korea Sewol Ferry: What We Know. *BBC News*, May 15th 2014. http://www.bbc.com/news/world-asia-27342967 (Accessed May 17, 2014).

Brandenburgh, M., Govindan, K., Sarkis, J. and Seuring, S. (2014). Quantitative models for sustainable supply chain management: Developments and directions. *European Journal of Operational Research*, 233, 299–312.

Brundtland, G.H., Khalid, M., Agnelli, S., Al-Athol, S.A. and Chidzero, B. (1987). Report of the world commission on environment and development: Our common future, UN General Assembly, available at: www.un-documents.net/our-common-future.pdf (Accessed 1 May 2014).

Business & Human Rights Resource Centre. (2014). Trafigura Lawsuits. Business & Human Rights Resource Centre 2014. http://www.business-humanrights.org/Categories/Lawlawsuits/Lawsuitsregulatoryaction/LawsuitsSelectedcases/TrafiguralawsuitsreCtedIvoire (Accessed May 12, 2014).

Business Pundit. (2010). The World's Worst Environmental Disasters Caused by Companies. http://www.businesspundit.com/the-worlds-worst-environmental-disasters-caused-by-companies/ (Accessed May 4, 2014).

Clifford, S. (2013). Wal-Mart Is Fined $82 Million over Mishandling of Hazardous Wastes. *The New York Times*, May 28th 2013. http://www.nytimes.com/2013/05/29/business/wal-mart-is-fined-82-million-over-mishandling-of-hazardous-wastes.html (Accessed May 6, 2014).

CRI. (2014). Driving Towards a Cleaner World. http://www.carbonrecycling.is/ (Accessed May 11, 2014).

CTV News. (2014). Vanier Takes Aim at Disposable Plastic Water Bottles. *CTV News*, April 26th 2014. http://montreal.ctvnews.ca/vanier-takes-aim-at-disposable-plastic-water-bottles-1.1794161 (Accessed May 8, 2014).

Duhigg, C. and Barboza, D. (2012). In China, Human Costs Are Built into an iPad. *The New York Times*, January 25th 2012. http://www.nytimes.com/2012/01/26/business/ieconomy-apples-ipad-and-the-human-costs-for-workers-in-china.html?pagewanted=all&_r=0 (Accessed May 9, 2014).

Frizell, S. (2014). South Korea Pauses Search for Missing Ferry Passengers. *Time*, May 10th 2014. http://time.com/95043/south-korea-ferry-search/ (Accessed May 12, 2014).

Gimenez, C. and Sierra, V. (2013). Sustainable supply chains: Governance mechanisms to greening suppliers. *Journal of Business Ethics*, 116, 189–203.

Gomes, W. (2013). Reason and Responsibility: The Rana Plaza Collapse. *Open Democracy*, May 9th 2013. http://www.opendemocracy.net/opensecurity/william-gomes/reason-and-responsibility-rana-plaza-collapse (Accessed May 10, 2014).

Gugliemo, C. (2013). Apple's Supplier Labor Practices in China Scrutinized after Foxconn. *Forbes*, December 12th 2013. http://www.forbes.com/sites/connieguglielmo/2013/12/12/apples-labor-practices-in-china-scrutinized-after-foxconn-pegatron-reviewed/ (Accessed May 9, 2014).

Hall, Z. (2014). Apple Giving Employees Company-Branded, Reusable Water Bottles for Earth Day. *9TO5Mac*, April 23rd 2014. http://9to5mac.com/2014/04/23/apple-giving-employees-company-branded-reusable-water-bottles-for-earth-day/ (Accessed May 8, 2014).

Harris, P. (2013). Walmart Pleads Guilty to Dumping Hazardous Waste in California. *The Guardian*, May 29th 2013. http://www.theguardian.com/business/2013/may/28/walmart-pleads-guilty--hazardous-waste (Accessed May 6, 2014).

Harvey, F. (2012). Trafigura Lessons Have Not Been Learned. *The Guardian*, September 25th 2012. http://www.theguardian.com/environment/2012/sep/25/trafigura-lessons-toxic-waste-dumping (Accessed May 12, 2014).

Hassini, E., Surti, C. and Searcy, C. (2012). A literature review and a case study of sustainable supply chains with a focus on metrics. *International Journal Production Economics*, 140, 69–82.

Hildebrandt, A. (2014). Bangladesh's Rana Plaza Factory Collapse Spurs Change, Finger-Pointing. *CBC News*, April 24th 2014. http://www.cbc.ca/news/canada/bangladesh-s-rana-plaza-factory-collapse-spurs-change-finger-pointing-1.2619524 (Accessed May 10, 2014).

Honda. (2011). Ten Honda Manufacturing Facilities in North America Achieve Zero Waste Sent to Landfill. http://www.honda.com/newsandviews/article.aspx?id=6126-en (Accessed May 7, 2014).

Kan, M. (2012). Foxconn Builds Products for Many Vendors, But Its Mud Sticks to Apple. October 24th 2012. http://www.macworld.com/article/2012972/foxconn-builds-products-for-many-vendors-but-its-mud-sticks-to-apple.html (Accessed May 9, 2014).

Khullar, A. (2014). One Year after Bangladesh's Rana Plaza Tragedy, Has Anything Changed? *CNN*, April 24th 2014. http://edition.cnn.com/2014/04/24/world/asia/bangladesh-rana-plaza-anniversary/ (Accessed May 10, 2014).

Kim, C. (2014). South Korean Ferry Operator CEO Is Arrested Over Sinking. *Bloomberg*, May 8th 2014. http://www.bloomberg.com/news/2014-05-08/s-korean-prosecutors-arrest-ferry-operator-ceo-kim-over-sinking.html (Accessed May 12, 2014).

Leach, A. (2012). Foxconn is World's 10th Biggest Employer: 1.2 Million on Payroll. *The Register*, March 20th 2012.http://www.theregister.co.uk/2012/03/20/foxconn_tenth_biggest_employer/ (Accessed May 12, 2014).

Linton, J.D., Klassen, R. and Jayaraman, V. (2007). Sustainable supply chains: An introduction. *Journal of Operations Management*, 25, 1075–1082.

Manik, J.A. and Yardley, J. (2013). Building Collapse in Bangladesh Leaves Scores Dead. *The New York Times*, April 24th 2013. http://www.nytimes.com/2013/04/25/world/asia/bangladesh-building-collapse.html?pagewanted=all (Accessed May 10, 2014).

Matos, S. and Hall, J. (2007). Integrating sustainable development in the supply chain: The case of life cycle assessment in oil and gas and agricultural biotechnology. *Journal of Operations Management*, 25, 1083–1102.

Morali and Searcy (2013). A Review of Sustainable Supply Chain Management Practices in Canada. *Journal of Business Ethics* 117 (3):635–658.

Motavalli, J. (2013). Automakers Work to Achieve Zero-Waste Goals. *Wheels*, March 1st 2013. http://wheels.blogs.nytimes.com/2013/03/01/automakers-work-to-achieve-zero-waste-goals/ (Accessed May 7, 2014).

Newcomer, L. (2014). Why You Should Never Buy Disposable Water Bottles Again. January 14th 2014. http://greatist.com/health/why-you-should-never-buy-disposable-water-bottles-again (Accessed May 8, 2014).

Okongwu, U., Morimoto, R. and Lauras, M. (2013). The maturity of supply chain sustainability disclosure from a continuous improvement perspective. *International Journal of Productivity and Performance Management*, 62(8), 827–855.

Park, M. (2014). What Went Wrong on Sewol. *CNN*, May 16th 2014. http://edition.cnn.com/2014/05/15/world/asia/sewol-problems/ (Accessed May 18, 2014).

Parveen, S. (2014). Rana Plaza Factory Collapse Survivors Struggle One Year On. *BBC News Asia*, April 23rd 2014. http://www.bbc.com/news/world-asia-27107860 (Accessed May 10, 2014).

Reefke, H. and Trocchi, M. (2013). Balanced scorecard for sustainable supply chains: Design and development guidelines. *International Journal of Productivity and Performance Management*, 62(8), 805–826.

Ro, S. (2014). Apple Has More Cash on Hand Than All These Different Countries. *Business Insider Australia*, April 8th 2014. http://www.businessinsider.com.au/global-cash-reserves-companies-nations-2014-4 (Accessed May 9, 2014).

Starbucks Coffee. http://www.starbucks.com/responsibility/sourcing/coffee (Accessed May 12, 2014).

Starbucks Corp. Annual Financials. (2014). http://www.marketwatch.com/investing/stock/sbux/financials (Accessed May 12, 2014).

Starbucks Ethical Sourcing. http://www.scsglobalservices.com/starbucks-cafe-practices (Accessed May 12, 2014).

Starbucks FY13 Annual Report. (2014). http://investor.starbucks.com/phoenix.zhtml?c=99518&p=irol-irhome (Accessed May 12, 2014).

Trafigura. (2014). About Us. http://www.trafigura.com/about-us/ (Accessed May 4, 2014).

Valdimarsson, O.R. (2013). Iceland's Carbon Recycling Sees Rising Demand for Renewable Fuel. *Bloomberg*, February 12th 2013. http://www.bloomberg.com/news/2013-02-12/iceland-s-carbon-recycling-sees-rising-demand-for-renewable-fuel.html (Accessed May 11, 2014).

Walmart. (2014). Our Business. http://corporate.walmart.com/our-story/our-business/ (Accessed May 6, 2014).

Wan-Jan (2006). Defining corporate social responsibility. *Journal of Public Affairs*. 6: 176–184.

Wan-Jan, W.S. (2006). Defining corporate social responsibility. *Journal of Public Affairs*, 6, 176–184.

Watts, J. (2012). Beijing Introduces Recycling Banks That Pay Subway Credits for Bottles. *The Guardian*, July 4th 2012. http://www.theguardian.com/environment/2012/jul/04/beijing-recycling-banks-subway-bottles (Accessed May 8, 2014).

Worstall, T. (2012). Apple and Foxconn Are the Best Thing That's Ever Happened to Chinese L Forbes, November 30th 2012. http://www.forbes.com/sites/timworstall/2012/11/30/appl-foxconn-are-the-best-thing-thats-ever-happened-to-chinese-labour/ (Accessed on May 9, 2014).

Yarow, J. (2012). A Tour of the Foxconn Factory Where Teenagers Are Making Your iPhone for $1.78 an Hour. *Business Insider Australia*, February 23rd 2012. http://www.businessinsider.com.au/foxconn-factory-tour-2012–2?op=1#now-watch-the-full-report – 28 (Accessed May 9, 2014).

21 Re-visiting sustainability

An overview of sustainability and collective actions

Ülkü Yüksel and Kıymet Çalıyurt

1 The past and future of sustainability research

Research starting as early as 1999 has looked at sustainability from five different angles: consumer sustainability, firm sustainability, societal sustainability, laws and regulations defining sustainability and finally sustainability from a scholarly stance (McDonagh and Prothero 2014). Sustainability in the first category has been examined with regard to individual consumer issues and concerns, consumer behavior and consumer practices. Consumer sustainability comprises such topics as (a) consumer attitudes, perspectives and behaviors, and (b) consumer values and preferences in which sustainable consumption, anti-consumption and simple living has been considered.

The second big category delves into organizational sustainability and organizational strategies with regard to sustainability practices within firms and sustainability of markets. How organizations conduct their marketing communications, how they manage their market orientation and promotional activities such as branding, and also product-related decisions, fall into this big and important category, such as new product development and product design. Many case studies about firms' practices, or practices on a macro level, such as within a country, have been examined. The chapters in this book are about corporate sustainability practices in different countries and regions of the world.

The third category in sustainability research delves into the conceptualization and reframing of sustainability. Here the authors explore the sustainability paradigm from different angles, considering the institutional, social, and systems perceptions and delving into a dominant societal ideology and theory of sustainability.

The fourth category of sustainability research explores legislation about sustainability within a society – specifically, environmental laws, legislations, regulations and public policies which involve social marketing in general and environmental labelling policies in particular. Finally, some sustainability research provides a broad literature review and evaluation of sustainability in general (McDonagh and Prothero 2014).

2 Sustainability practices of businesses

Gone is the time when firms were merely responsible for increasing profit for their shareholders. Around the globe, some firms are thoroughly inspected in all facets of their operation, especially when it comes to their social, sustainability and environmental practices (Sen and Bhattacharya 2001). This is because sustainability and corporate social responsibility (CSR) have rapidly gained the public's interest and awareness in the past two decades. Governments, not-for-profit organizations and also individuals, as citizens or consumers (Webster 1975) particularly, hold firms accountable for their unethical, unsocial, unjust or unfair actions (Feldman and Vasquez-Parraga 2013).

3   Perceived firm sustainability and collective actions

Injustice or inappropriate corporate actions, such as practices neglecting sustainability, may prompt negative attention from consumers (Miller and Sturdivant 1977) and movements against these irresponsible firms. As a demonstration of dissatisfaction with undesirable corporate practices, consumer movements began to gain power in the 1960s and have since advanced into organized and collaborative campaigns. These campaigns have fundamentally influenced the way firms perceive and engage in CSR (Carrigan and Attalla 2001; Denegri-Knott, Zwick and Schroeder 2006), especially from the perspective of sustainability. For example, people dynamically declare their dissatisfaction with big firms' unwarranted actions. As such, there are collective movements, for example, against Greenpeace's ongoing campaigns targeting unsustainable environmental practices (Carrigan and Attalla 2001).

Previous studies assert that a firm's involvement in sustainable practices is positively correlated with the image of the firm (Dawar and Pillutla 2000) and its products or brands (Ellen, Mohr and Webb 2006). Consumers engage in boycotts and buy only from firms which follow sustainable practices in order to reward those firms (Friedman 1996). Societal disapproval sometimes takes the form of public interest advocacy and actions such as boycotts (Yuksel 2013) to penalize firms for undesirable actions (Neilson 2010). "Boycotts are defined as temporary acts of exiting a relationship with an organization owing to some form of dissatisfaction, accompanied by a promise to re-enter the relationship once certain conditions have been met" (Yuksel 2009, p. 206). Thus, in boycotts, people "refuse to purchase and/or use a brand that they had been using, and, were it not for the circumstances precipitating the boycott, would continue to use" (Yuksel 2009, p. 206). Characteristically, such consumer reactions are undertaken for political, ethical, social or environmental reasons, mostly relating to sustainability concerns and affecting the 'general good' (Dolan 2002; Shaw 2007; Yuksel and Myrteza 2009; Zack 1991).

In addition, many consumers share their ideas with others on personal blogs or social media and punish firms which they perceive as not paying enough attention to sustainable practices (Kerr, Mortimer, Dickinson and Waller 2012). These collective actions as well as social actions do influence firms' response strategies (Yuksel and Myrteza 2009). Accordingly, firms change their ill-received corporate practices in response to public interest advocacy and actions which are a sign of customer disapproval (Smith 2002).

4   Understanding sustainability

The chapters in this book discuss and agree with the fact that consumers' and societies' reactions to unfavourable corporate practices made it vital for businesses to pursue sustainability. Given that sustainability in management can be perceived from several viewpoints, it is important to understand the aim of these strategies. The principal goal of sustainable management is to engage in superior business practices by combining all resources that are needed more effectively, efficiently and ethically. Thus sustainability involves a holistic process of continuity, competence, efficiency, resourcefulness, economies of resources and responsibility, which simultaneously provides benefits for all stakeholders. Stakeholders in this context represent all people involved in the firm's practices, the public that may be affected by the business practices and the environment and the business itself. By following sustainable practices, businesses may engage in reducing their energy expenses, waste costs and material and water expenses. In addition, businesses should attempt to decrease detrimental elements of their operation, such as employee turnover, by improving employee productivity as well as financial risks and expenses. Sustainability programs should be embedded into all levels of the organizations and audited systemically. Sustainable strategies should be all-encompassing and be aligned with all other plans within the organization.

5   Sustainability from various perspectives

Our commitment to develop this book originated from our belief that sustainability research often challenges companies, employees, employers, citizens, consumers and society in general to question their particular actions. By doing so, it plays an imperative role in explaining how stakeholders can develop sustainable and collectively progressive societies. This book comprises four part including 15 blind peer reviewed articles and invited commentaries.

6   Sustainability and management

In general, the chapters in this book agree that competition for resources in future will not only be an economic one. For example, in Part I, about sustainability and management practices in Europe, Crowther and Seifi criticize the narrow view of sustainability as a matter of limited resources. The authors state that considering competition for the world's restricted resources as an economic competition only is limiting because, due to geopolitical concerns, it may take the form of pressure on certain countries. In their chapter the authors discuss various factors that have brought sustainability to prominence. These are a combination of concern for the overuse of raw materials as well as energy consumption and preservation. The authors conclude their research stating that the discourse in the developed world is towards the conservation of resources and towards energy efficiency as reflected in both manufacturing resources and consumer buying decisions. They state that although the effects of resource depletion on the economic environment have been accepted in general, it is still not fully recognized that development in other parts of the world will exacerbate the pressure on the economic environment, resulting in a greater need to compete for the available resources. It is yet to be recognized that this competition will not only be an economic completion but also a physical one as the world adjusts to a new geopolitical environment. They suggest that sustainability should reflect the view that no society should use any resources that cannot be regenerated, which reflects the notion of the 'carrying capacity of the ecosystem' (Hawken 1993) and should be explained via input–output systems for resource consumption. The author asserts that unsustainable practices of the developing world negatively affects not only these countries but also Western societies, and calls on all countries to act more responsibly toward the world's resources.

Overall, the authors reach a consensus on the idea that value should not be considered as the only economic performance indicator. For example, in their article about the representation of produced value for health care institutions in Italy, Gulluscio and Torrecchia propose "socially responsible reporting" through "non-social" reporting tools for the Italian health care industry. They criticise the fact that in public administration of health care, performance assessment has been mainly based on economic indicators, such as financial and balance sheets in financial statements. They conclude that the overall capacity of public health agencies to "create value" cannot be confined simply to achieving conditions of economic equilibrium or to some other financial and capital-related measure – it should also encapsulate the ability to meet health related needs to be considered as effective and efficient. This is because conventional documents, such as financial statements, omit a number of factors that are important in the production process and payment of benefits, which play a crucial role in creating value.

A similar suggestion has been put forward by Maria Aluchna in her chapter about sustainability in Polish companies, from the perspective of WIG20 firms. She concludes that a sustainability approach should not only focus on financial measures and shareholder value but must also take into account the dimensions of social and environmental performance. As such, companies as well as societies and communities need to transform their traditional business models to incorporate environmental constraints and the expectations of global stakeholders. The author concludes that, despite the fact that some companies in the socially and environmentally controversial sectors of energy generation, coal mining and oil and gas extraction incorporate notions of sustainability into their mission, strategies and reporting, real implementation of the sustainability principles behind the declarations still remains an open question requiring further research and studies.

Companies that focus on sustainability issues are valued by consumers and the public and improve their financial performance; it is important to develop corporate strategies building on consumer perspectives of sustainability. As such, Wagner and Stich propose a conceptual framework in which they display a classification of consumer sustainability and state that, in addition to a firm level classification, it is also important to find out how consumers classify the concept of sustainability. The authors conclude that, like other firm level classifications, consumer classifications of sustainability also involves ecological, social, and individual phases of sustainability. However, the importance of these phases depends on the perceived closeness versus distance of the particular subject matter for the consumer.

The importance of supporting, reporting, and auditing to manage sustainability practices is highlighted by many authors in this book. Some authors declare the need to prefer sustainability reporting over traditional reporting. For example, Akarçay and Öğüz declare that traditional financial reporting has become inadequate to meet the needs of enterprises and their stakeholders, given social and environmental issues have also become the responsibility of the enterprises. Thus they advocate a sustainability reporting system as a mechanism in which the economic, environmental, and social implications of the corporation activities should be listed. Not only the reporting system but also an auditing system should be incorporated into sustainability practices. For example, Erkan, Okutmuş and Ergül propose the development and implementation of systematic internal control systems as a solution to prevent mistakes and frauds in the context of the hospitality industry. Not limited with the tourism and hospitality industries, financial sectors also support sustainable projects. For example, in her article on approaches to sustainability in the banking system, Bian advocates the 'green credit' and its implementation in China in which banks support those projects developed by enterprises that are supporting environmentally or socially responsible development. The author highlights the needs for some further reforms and suggests that insurance against environmental pollution liability to be promoted and pilot programs for compulsory environmental pollution liability insurance to be launched. Authors also highlight the impact of ethics on the society. For example, Abutalibov, Mammadov, and Guliyev declare the importance of ethical concerns in management and business administration and their combined effects on social and the economic development.

Ethics is also considered in its many effects on decision-makers and auditors. Examining the influence of moral intensity components of the auditors' ethical decision-making process – that is, ethical sensitivity, ethical judgment and ethical intentions – Johari, Sanusi, Rahman and Omar report a relationship between human capital, governance and a firm's performance. Exploring effort, ethical orientation and audit judgment performance in Malaysia, they conclude that auditors' ethical decision-making is a result of differences in environmental and cultural factors.

Clearly, in order to embed sustainability into the daily practices of consumers, companies and countries, sustainability should be integrated into the educational system. Lai-ling Ling and Cook share their thoughts on sustainability in education and in marketing by reflecting on what communication skills are cultivated when information about sustainability is transmitted. They discuss the issues of multigenerational and cross-cultural equity, and corporate sustainability in marketing education. They conclude that marketing educators should understand how to sustain students by acknowledging how to build on the best of the past, adapting and melding it with the present and sustaining it for the future.

Employing a consumer stance in investigating sustainability, Francis and Davis indicate how "Consumption Consciousness" relates to sustainability. They explore the consumer-citizen's Consumption Consciousness by developing the Consumption Consciousness measurement scale. They consider the components of Self, Environmental and Social as formative indicators. Their model works towards identifying consumer typologies from the various combinations of component scores. Measuring Consumption Consciousness this way allows the researcher to perform profile analysis and benchmark consumer attitudes. For example, the gap between sustainable attitudes and unsustainable behaviour and the factors that contribute to this gap can be examined. For marketers, survey findings could inform segmentation, targeting and positioning, as well as create a checklist for assessing the sustainability rating of their brand or product offering. Meanwhile, policy-makers can use such survey results to identify the sustainability issues for which awareness and education initiatives are required, and monitor the effectiveness of such initiatives.

Considering the past, present and future of sustainability, Parameswaran, Parameswaran, Kooy and Kuzee delve into the role marketing plays in understanding sustainability from a North American perspective to provide a rigorous theoretical foundation, delineation and connection to strategic marketing thought. They assert that for the past decade and a half, the focus has been on improving a product's or firm's sustainability attributes. They suggest that in the future, sustainability marketing and communication should expand beyond the characteristic or activity-based marketing into the "root use" of the product or services offered by probing questions such as, "Why is it needed?". They conclude that a challenge in addressing sustainability arises because of the disparity in incomes and consumption between industrialized nations and the developing world.

Authors agree on the importance of the corporate role in building sustainable relationships with communities. A tool for managing such relationships, called Local Agenda 21, has been established in Brazil. Figueiredo, Quelhas, França, Meiriño, and Leal explain the importance of privileging autonomy, empowerment and interaction among social actors in such company-community relationships. In their model they offer some important factors for sustainability and define them within the framework of Agenda 21: (1) Confidence includes a mechanism inducing dialogue and consensus, an ability to deal with conflict situations, and enhancing the feeling of belonging and ownership; (2) Cooperation is about focus on sustainable development based on democratic participation and the convergence of interests, fostering the common good culture, and integrating and synergy instrument regarding the various existing efforts, optimizing resources and enhancing results; (3) Responsibility comprises the process inducer that challenges people to create their own vision of a sustainable future and discover the role of each in pursuit of sustainability, encouraging the involvement of every citizen, and long-term process vision connecting the practicalities; (4) Multidisciplinary engagement is about a participatory and inclusive approach, which requires the participation of all sectors and promotion of partnerships; (5) Empowerment dealing with strengthening citizenship and social capital formation, promoting effective conditions for participation and decision, focus on local action and involvement of people in solving their problems, and promoting changes in attitudes and values at individual and collective levels. In this framework the authors propose their strategy for community relationship management, Agenda 21, as a tool for managing the relationship between firms and their communities, via a case study on Petrobras. They highlight the importance of privileging autonomy, empowerment and interaction among social actors. They conclude that if companies are to promote a promising and sustainable environment, they need to build long-lasting and transformational relationships with the surrounding communities, based on the principles of dialogue and transparency.

Studying these various cases assists us in understanding the sustainability practices of firms and countries or the lack thereof. For example, the chapter on the good, bad and ugly cases by Raswant and Sutton-Brady lists some positive and negative examples of company practices with regard to their sustainable strategies (or lack thereof) in managing their supply chain. The companies are from the US, Taiwan, Bangladesh, Iceland, South Korea, Japan and the Netherlands. The authors conclude that sustainability is vital for companies to boost their firm value in the long run. Both for-profit and not-for-profit organizations should make use of sustainability strategies as a crisis management tool if they face a disaster. However, in order to manage sustainability effectively, those practices need to be aligned with company policies and audited frequently and systematically as a method of control.

7   Conclusion

Injustice or inappropriate and unacceptable corporate actions such as those relating to sustainability may attract consumers' attention (Miller and Sturdivant 1977) and provoke movements against these firms that are perceived as irresponsible by consumers, governments and non-profit organizations. The chapters in this book all agree that sustainability is vital for companies to increase their long-term value for countries and societies to improve their standard of living now and in the future.

Sustainable development should not be considered as an economic issue or burden with regard to resource depletion or energy consumption. Sustainability will even affect nationalborders; thus, addressing some geopolitical concerns in sustainability will become important.

From a corporate perspective, sustainability should not only be considered for its contribution to financial performance measures. Rather it must be considered as a value-added activity beyond financial benefits. Sustainability may be considered not only from a firm perspective but also from a customer perspective. Consumer sustainability measures should list some consumer classifications to address them appropriately. in much the same way as social responsibility and environmental disclosures should be highlighted. Accordingly, Kaya and Bayraktar as well as Taskinsoy and Uyar suggest an environmental reporting and auditing system be implemented to enable internal control. Ethics and particularly business ethics play an important role in understanding the importance of sustainability. Thus an ethical mind-set should be embedded into citizens' mind-sets which may enhance sustainable practices.

References

Carrigan, Marylyn and Ahmad Attalla. "The Myth of the Ethical Consumer: Do Ethics Matter in Purchase Behaviour?" *Journal of Consumer Marketing* 18, no. 7 (2001): 560–78.

Dawar, Niraj and Madan M. Pillutla. "Impact of Product-Harm Crises on Brand Equity: The Moderating Role of Consumer Expectations." *Journal of Marketing Research* 37, no. 2 (2000): 215–26.

Denegri-Knott, Janice, Detlev Zwick, and Jonathan E. Schroeder. "Mapping Consumer Power: An Integrative Framework for Marketing and Consumer Research." *European Journal of Marketing* 40, nos. 9–10 (2006): 950–71.

Dolan, Paddy. "The Sustainability of 'Sustainable Consumption'." *Journal of Macromarketing* 22 (December 2002): 170–81.

Ellen, Pam Scholder, Deborah J. Webb, and Lois A. Mohr. "Building Corporate Associations: Consumer Attributions for Corporate Socially Responsible Programs." *Journal of the Academy of Marketing Science* 34, no. 2 (2006): 147–57.

Feldman, Percy Marquina and Arturo Z. Vasquez-Parraga. "Consumer Social Responses to CSR Initiatives Versus Corporate Abilities." *Journal of Consumer Marketing* 30, no. 2 (2013): 100–11.

Friedman, Monroe. "A Positive Approach to Organized Consumer Action: The 'Buycott' as an Alternative to the Boycott." *Journal of Consumer Policy* 19, no. 4 (1996): 439–51.

Hawken, P., (1993), *The Ecology of Commerce A Declaration of Sustainability*, Harper Collins.

Kerr, Gayle, Kathleen Mortimer, Sonia Dickinson, and David S. Waller. "Buy, Boycott or Blog: Exploring Online Consumer Power to Share, Discuss and Distribute Controversial Advertising Messages." *European Journal of Marketing* 46, nos. 3–4 (2012): 387–405.

McDonagh, Pierre and Andrea Prothero. "Sustainability Marketing Research: Past, Present and Future." *Journal of Marketing Management* 30, nos. 11–12 (2014): 1186–219.

Miller, Kenneth E. and Frederick D. Sturdivant. "Consumer Responses to Socially Questionable Corporate Behavior: An Empirical Test." *Journal of Consumer Research* 4, no. 1 (1977): 1–7.

Neilson, Lisa A. "Boycott or Buycott? Understanding Political Consumerism." *Journal of Consumer Behaviour* 9, no. 3 (2010): 214–27.

Sen, Sankar and Chitra Bhanu Bhattacharya. "Does Doing Good Always Lead to Doing Better? Consumer Reactions to Corporate Social Responsibility." *Journal of Marketing Research* 38, no. 2 (2001): 225–43.

Shaw, Deirdre. "Consumer Voters in Imagined Communities." *International Journal of Sociology and Social Policy* 27, nos. 3–4 (2007): 135–50.

Smith, N. Craig. "Changes in Corporate Practices in Response to Public Interest Advocacy and Actions", Centre for Marketing Working Paper No. 00–704 January 2000 http://facultyresearch.london.edu/docs/00-704.pdf (Retrieved on April 15, 2015).

Webster Jr., Frederick E. "Determining the Characteristics of the Socially Conscious Consumer." *Journal of Consumer Research* 2, no. 3 (1975): 188–96.

Yuksel, Ulku. "Non-Participation in Anti-Consumption Consumer Reluctance to Boycott." *Journal of Macromarketing* 33, no. 3 (2013): 204–16.

Yuksel, Ulku and Victoria Myrteza. "An Evaluation of Strategic Responses to Consumer Boycotts." *Journal of Business Research* 62, no. 2 (2009): 248–59.

Zack, Jeffrey. "The Hullabaloo Over Boycott Ballyhoo." *Business and Social Review* 78 (Summer 1991): 9–15.

Index

 Taylor & Francis eBooks

Helping you to choose the right eBooks for your Library

Add Routledge titles to your library's digital collection today. Taylor and Francis ebooks contains over 50,000 titles in the Humanities, Social Sciences, Behavioural Sciences, Built Environment and Law.

Choose from a range of subject packages or create your own!

Benefits for you

» Free MARC records
» COUNTER-compliant usage statistics
» Flexible purchase and pricing options
» All titles DRM-free.

 REQUEST YOUR **FREE** INSTITUTIONAL TRIAL TODAY

Free Trials Available
We offer free trials to qualifying academic, corporate and government customers.

Benefits for your user

» Off-site, anytime access via Athens or referring URL
» Print or copy pages or chapters
» Full content search
» Bookmark, highlight and annotate text
» Access to thousands of pages of quality research at the click of a button.

eCollections – Choose from over 30 subject eCollections, including:

Archaeology	Language Learning
Architecture	Law
Asian Studies	Literature
Business & Management	Media & Communication
Classical Studies	Middle East Studies
Construction	Music
Creative & Media Arts	Philosophy
Criminology & Criminal Justice	Planning
Economics	Politics
Education	Psychology & Mental Health
Energy	Religion
Engineering	Security
English Language & Linguistics	Social Work
Environment & Sustainability	Sociology
Geography	Sport
Health Studies	Theatre & Performance
History	Tourism, Hospitality & Events

For more information, pricing enquiries or to order a free trial, please contact your local sales team:
www.tandfebooks.com/page/sales

 **Routledge**
Taylor & Francis Group

The home of
Routledge books

www.tandfebooks.com

For Product Safety Concerns and Information please contact our EU
representative GPSR@taylorandfrancis.com Taylor & Francis Verlag GmbH,
Kaufingerstraße 24, 80331 München, Germany

Printed and bound by CPI Group (UK) Ltd, Croydon, CR0 4YY
01/05/2025
01858383-0003